The Last Days
Are Here Again

Other books by Richard Kyle

From Sect to Denomination: Church Types and Their Implications for
Mennonite Brethren History
The Mind of John Knox
The New Age Movement in American Culture
The Religious Fringe: A History of Alternative Religions in America

The Last Days Are Here Again

A History of the End Times

Richard Kyle

Baker Books

A Division of Baker Book House Co
Grand Rapids, Michigan 49516

Published by Baker Books
a division of Baker Book House Company
P.O. Box 6287, Grand Rapids, MI 49516-6287

Second printing, October 1998

Printed in the United States of America

Library of Congress Cataloging-in-Publication Data

Kyle, Richard G.
    The last days are here again : a history of the end times / Richard Kyle.
        p.   cm.
    Includes bibliographical references and index.
    ISBN 0-8010-5809-0 (pbk.)
    1. End of the world—History of doctrines. I. Title.
BT876.K95   1998
236'.9'09—dc21   98-13574

For information about academic books, resources for Christian leaders, and all new releases available from Baker Book House, visit our web site:
http://www.bakerbooks.com

To my secretary of many years, Marcella Mohn

Contents

Preface

It was October 1956. Israeli forces struck swiftly, rolling the Egyptian army back across the Sinai Peninsula. British and French troops seized the Suez Canal. The Soviet Union threatened to intervene on behalf of Egypt. Were these the opening shots of Armageddon? I thought so. At that time I was a teenager who had been raised in a Plymouth Brethren church. Coming from such a background, I had drunk deeply at the fountains of dispensational premillennialism. I had been reared on the Scofield Reference Bible. Thus I firmly embraced the premillennial beliefs regarding the Antichrist, rapture, tribulation, Armageddon, and millennium.

With great anxiety I went to the house of a leading elder. (Plymouth Brethren do not have paid pastors.) He assured me that believers would be raptured before Armageddon. This helped to assuage my anxieties. So did President Eisenhower. The American presidential elections loomed on the horizon, and he was not about to allow Armageddon to complicate his reelection. So he pulled the rug out from under the Israelis, British, and French. Thus the crisis passed, and Armageddon would have to wait for another day.

But my interest in end-time ideas did not pass. At that young age my eschatology was quite limited. I knew of only one view—dispensational premillennialism. Since then I have learned about the many ways people see the end of the world. Some of these perceptions grow out of the Christian faith; others have occult or secular sources. My studies in

Christian history introduced me to the considerable diversity in the way God's people have viewed the last days. While the belief in Christ's return has persisted through two thousand years of Christian history, it has taken many shapes, largely because apocalyptic thinking is often conditioned by contemporary events. In writing two earlier books, *The Religious Fringe* and *The New Age Movement in American Culture,* I encountered the doomsday ideas of many alternative religions. Then I widened my search to include the way scientists, filmmakers, and fiction writers have viewed the last days.

The approach of the year 2000 has prompted an avalanche of publications regarding the end of the world. Why write another one? Most of these publications have been penned by popularizers who have pushed a particular view; some have even made their own predictions regarding the end. By contrast, other authors have written sober histories and theological works assessing millennialism and eschatology. But these works often focus on a particular doctrine or time period. This volume attempts to survey the way Christians over nearly two millennia have viewed end-time events. I make no claim to comprehensiveness. Instead, I have focused on the major doomsday themes and the way apocalyptic thinking has shifted over the centuries. I have also added a few wrinkles to a study of the last days. Included are substantial portions on how fringe religions see the end of the world, for mainstream Christianity does not have a corner on this subject. Neither does religion for that matter. Thus I have also described the secular apocalypse—how scientists and literary figures view doomsday.

This survey of Western end-time thinking is intended to demonstrate two themes—doomsday ideas have been both persistent and adaptable. To be sure, as they ran the course of Western history, they had their ups and downs, often peaking during times of stress and turmoil and abating during good times. But a fascination with the apocalypse has been persistent in Western thinking. In part, this is because doomsday ideas have been so adaptable. As historical situations have changed, so have apocalyptic ideas, at times demonstrating a chameleon-like quality.

But I do not want to exaggerate the notion of persistence. Apocalyptic ideas have not consistently pervaded the mainstream of Western culture. Rather, end-time visions can be seen as, to use Peter Stearns's analogy, a dormant virus. They remain quiescent until activated by cultural conditions; then they break out, often in smaller sectarian groups. But sometimes apocalypticism can infect the wider culture.

Essentially, this book is an intellectual history. It is the history of an idea, the idea of how the world will end. It focuses on one aspect of what people believe about future events, namely, the last days. Such an approach avoids two pitfalls. First, it makes no pronouncements regarding the future. Doomsday has not yet arrived, and history must concern itself with the past, not the future. In this case, it measures what people in the past have believed about the future. Second, the approach of intellectual history helps to minimize value judgments. This study is largely about what others believe about the end of time, not what I believe. While no historian is free of personal biases, I trust I have not pushed my perspective on other people.

Through two thousand years of Western history millions of people have believed that they were living in the last days. Adopting a historical perspective toward future events helps one to remain judicious and open to whatever lies in store. Many sincere, devout, and knowledgeable people have seen the end as imminent; they have even been people of the Bible, anchoring their beliefs in Scripture. But they have all been wrong. The failure of such prognostications should not dull one's sensitivities to end-time events. Rather, one should view developments historically. Someday the world will end. But sensible people will not jump irrationally at every prediction. Apocalyptic ideas, even those grounded in Scripture, have been shaped by their historical context. None are infallible. Thus Christians must be prepared for Christ's return, but they need to realize that signs indicating the last days are not new—they have been visible for two millennia!

To promote a sensible perspective of the end times, I have attempted to write a descriptive history. This study is neither a devotional nor an attack on various eschatological positions. Some readers might be disappointed at not finding a chapter critiquing the various end-time views. But this is not the job of the historian. By its very nature, of course, the discipline of history leads to a critical analysis. Such an examination should not, however, turn into a polemic.

This study of end-time thought follows a pattern. There are ten chapters, eight of which trace apocalyptic ideas from antiquity to the present. Chapter 1, "The End Is upon Us," describes the current fascination with doomsday and tells why this mind-set has persisted through Western history. The next chapter, "Apocalypse Postponed," begins our journey through Western history. It establishes the biblical basis for apocalyptic thinking and describes the rise and fall of millenarian ideas. The early church largely embraced an intense expectancy regarding Christ's return. But with the legalization of Christianity and the institutionalization of the church, this anticipation waned.

Chapter 3, "The Slumbering Apocalypse," describes the paradox of medieval apocalyptic thought. Officially, the church embraced Augustine's nonmillenarian view of the end. But unofficially, apocalyptic ideas penetrated most levels of medieval society, at times bursting forth into full view. This intense expectancy regarding end-time events did not abate with the Middle Ages, but continued until the late seventeenth century. The next chapter, "The On-Again, Off-Again Apocalypse," describes the apocalyptic mood of the Reformation Era and seventeenth-century England. But after 1700, end-time excitement declined, and for the next three centuries in Europe apocalyptic ideas were largely confined to pockets in society.

Chapter 5 brings the story of doomsday speculations across the Atlantic Ocean. In America millennial thought has been more pronounced than in Europe. "America and the Great Millennial Hope" describes the end-time ideas found in the mainstream of American society. But it does not stop there. This chapter also expands upon the millennialism of alternative religions such as the Millerites, Shakers, Mormons, Seventh-day Adventists, and Jehovah's Witnesses.

The next four chapters focus largely on end-time thinking in twentieth-century America. During this time frame the most influential force driving apocalyptic ideas has been dispensational premillennialism. Dispensational premillennialism has so propelled eschatology on the popular level that two chapters are devoted to this subject. Chapter 6, "Rapture Fever: The Early Years," describes dispensational eschatology until World War II. Chapter 7, "Rapture Fever: The Doom Boom Has Arrived," tells the story of the apocalyptic mania brought on by the premillennial popularizers after 1945.

But the story of doomsday speculation in modern America is not confined to the premillennial popularizers, as we shall see in chapter 8, "Eager for the End: Messiahs and Prophets." Numerous messiahs, prophets, and fringe religions have told us that the end is right around the corner. Moreover, it will not come gently; great catastrophes and upheavals are looming on the horizon.

Such predictions go beyond the lunatic fringe of American society. Sober scientists are warning us that both human-caused and natural disasters could destroy us. Chapter 9, "The End without God," describes the secular apocalypse. Some hardheaded scientists paint a dire picture of the future. Filmmakers and fiction writers have capitalized on such themes and have fed the appetite of millions by producing an avalanche of doomsday novels and movies.

The last chapter, "2000 and a Few Afterthoughts," ties things together. It puts the spotlight on this book's two major themes—the persistency and elasticity of the apocalypse. It also takes a look at the year 2000. Surprisingly, there are fewer predictions for this year than one would think. In the last few pages I shed my historian's garb and make a few personal comments regarding how Christians should relate to end-time thinking.

No one writes a book alone. In the time that this book has been in gestation, I have accumulated debts to several individuals and institutions. I hope that my memory is not short in this regard and that I do not inadvertently omit any thanks that are due. Appreciation must go to the library staff of Tabor College for arranging for the acquisition of many books and articles through interlibrary loan. Without these sources my work would not have been possible. Thanks must go to Robert Clouse of Indiana State University for reading an earlier version of the manuscript. Although he would not agree with all of my interpretations regarding end-time thinking, his comments on my manuscript have been appreciated, and many of them have been incorporated in the final version.

Many debts also have been incurred in the production of this book. I especially thank Marcella Mohn for typing various drafts. Without her efforts this book would have been difficult to produce. Appreciation must be offered to Beth Impson and Deborah Penner for their timely comments regarding matters of writing style. Academic publishing entails its own problems. Therefore, much appreciation must go to the staff of Baker Book House for publishing this volume—especially to its academic editor, Jim Weaver.

Finally, my gratitude goes to some who were involved only indirectly with the writing and publishing process. In particular, I am grateful to my wife, Joyce, and two sons, Bryan and Brent, for sharing me with this project. Without their support and patience this book would not have been possible.

1

The End Is upon Us

"Rape, murder, earthquakes and floods, single-parent families, war, AIDS. They're all part of God's plan to destroy Earth within the next 10 years, according to Rev. Carl Holland of York Assembly of God in York County, Va."[1] While Rev. Holland's words are a bit strident, TV preachers, popular authors, and flamboyant clergy are bringing a similar message to millions of Americans.

On a gentler note, there is the old fairy tale about Chicken Little, who, having been hit on the head by something, was convinced that the sky was falling. Chicken Little ran off to tell the king and along the way picked up several followers who also were convinced that the sky was falling.

Through much of human history there have been the Chicken Littles who have dashed about proclaiming that the sky was falling or that some other catastrophe would soon happen. There have also been many people willing to follow these prophets of doom.[2] This book is about the Chicken Littles of history and those who have followed them.

Apocalyptic thinking, both strident and temperate, is in the air. A sense of ending looms over the land. For only the second time since Christ, history is in a 90s decade that precedes a new millennium. Interest in the end of the world is probably greater now than at any time since the Millerite movement of the nineteenth century.

The year 2000 is an arbitrary date on the calendar. Still, the concept of a new millennium is loaded with immense historical symbolism and psychological power. As a result, eccentrics of many sorts have set their

15

alarm clocks for the year 2000. But they are not alone in approaching the end of a millennium with foreboding. Individuals from all ranks of society are apprehensive. Public opinion polls in the 1990s say that from 40 to 60 percent of Americans pay some attention to prophecies.[3] While they may not embrace specific apocalyptic ideas, they have a sense that something big is about to happen.

Since the 1970s there has been a flood of end-of-the-world predictions. In fact, books on prophecy—whether Christian, occultic, or secular—have been a growth industry. They have become big sellers.[4] Christian fundamentalists insist that the second coming of Christ is imminent. They claim to hear louder than ever "the Four Horsemen of the Apocalypse—War, Plague, Famine, and Death—galloping toward Armageddon." Occultists tell of great calamities to come at the end of this millennium. "New Age astrologers foresee psychic anguish, earthquakes, and economic collapse" before the dawn of the Age of Aquarius. Even down-to-earth scientists have joined in, warning us of impending human-caused disasters.[5]

The End Is Near!

The year 2000 should not evoke such emotion. It is a subjective date. We do not know when Christ was born. Even if we did, arithmetically the twenty-first century begins on January 1, 2001. Also, most of the end-of-the-millennium doomsday predictions do not concentrate on the year 2000, but on dates before and after. Still, 2000 is a round number with a magical appeal. Because nearly all nations have adopted the same secular calendar, the end of this millennium will be celebrated globally and simultaneously within the various time zones. One can assume that if the world is still intact by New Year's Eve 1999, there will be some parties whose likes have never been seen before.[6]

Of all the groups that have been infected by this apocalyptic mood, the Christian dispensational premillennialists have operated at a fever pitch. They point to a series of events as confirmation of biblical prophecy. The return of the Jews to Israel in 1948 began the countdown to Armageddon. Following on its heels came other developments—the threat of nuclear destruction, the European Common Market, Israel's seizure of Jerusalem in 1967, the perception of the Soviet Union as the great northern power, and the Persian Gulf War. Within dispensational circles the popularizers have aroused far more attention than have the more scholarly elements. (For a study of dispensationalism see chs. 6–7.)

During the 1980s the fixation on doomsday even reached the highest levels of American political power. James Watt, the secretary of the interior, declared that this generation might be the last. Secretary of Defense Caspar Weinberger made similar statements.[7] In an interview President Ronald Reagan indicated that recent events had caused him to think of Armageddon: "You know, I turn back to your ancient prophets in the Old Testament and the signs foretelling Armageddon and I find myself wondering if we're the generation that is going to see that come about . . . believe me, they certainly describe the times we're going through." Of course, it is the Book of Revelation, not the Old Testament, that speaks of Armageddon. But otherwise the president's ideas came close to the public pulse.[8] And spurred on by Hal Lindsey's best-selling *Late Great Planet Earth*, a host of fundamentalist preachers, authors, and TV personalities have continued to bring an apocalyptic message to millions of Americans. Jack Van Impe, Salem Kirban, Pat Robertson, Jerry Falwell, to name only a few, warn that floods, famines, earthquakes, diseases, and wars will precede the second coming of Christ.

But the Christian fundamentalists are not the only ones caught up with this millennial madness. The same apocalyptic impulse has driven a number of individuals and groups on the fringes of American religion. During the lifetime of its founder, Herbert Armstrong, the Worldwide Church of God believed that the tribulation would begin in the 1970s. Not to be outdone, the Jehovah's Witnesses have made numerous end-of-the-world predictions—the last ones pointing to 1975 and 1984. An "ascended Master" supposedly told Elizabeth Clare Prophet of a nuclear catastrophe to befall the world in the 1990s, so she urged her followers to build large bomb shelters. The Children of God (now called the Love Family), a radical millennial group, had an end-time countdown culminating in the rapture in the early 1990s. Before their fiery end at Waco, the Branch Davidians evinced an intense apocalyptic outlook. While most New Agers view the future through rose-colored spectacles, some foresee future disasters.[9]

Several famous prophets have had bad vibrations about the next few years. The sixteenth-century French seer Nostradamus foresaw the years 1999–2000 as a time of wars, tremendous upheavals, and possible global destruction. Edgar Cayce, the "sleeping prophet," also saw catastrophic events coming in the 1990s. Jeane Dixon believed that the Antichrist is now alive and will assume great power before 2000. Psychic Ruth Montgomery predicts a cosmic disaster in which the North and South Poles suddenly reverse their positions, thus wreaking incredible havoc.[10]

The Christian tradition does not have a corner on end-time predictions, however. Several other religions have predicted that the world will end around 2000. Some Jewish fundamentalists asserted that Armageddon would occur a generation after the reestablishment of the Jewish state. Some Buddhists believe that the world will end about twenty-five hundred years after Buddha's death (ca. 483 B.C.). Aztec, Hindu, and Hopi prophecies suggest that the world is currently teetering on the brink.[11]

Through history most end-time scenarios have had a religious base. But in recent years apocalyptic thought has undergone at least a partial secularization. It extends beyond religious lines and often reaches the public not in the language of divine revelation, but in the profane dress of science, history, and journalism. "Many who claim the end is near get their inspiration as much from science as from Scripture."[12] In fact, the most "significant outbreaks of millenarianism in our time have been secular."[13]

For much of human history, the end of the world could have come only at the hands of God or a natural calamity. But now humankind can accomplish it without God's help. We have developed the means to destroy ourselves. The ultimate weapon, of course, is nuclear annihilation. As a result, in recent decades millions of Americans have experienced anxiety attacks about a nuclear apocalypse.[14]

But in 1991 the Soviet Union unraveled and the Cold War ended. Thus, nuclear apocalypticism has gone out of style. This vacuum, however, is sufficiently filled by the "ecocatastrophists." They tell of disasters to be brought on by overpopulation, global warming, ozone depletion, chemical weapons, world hunger, AIDS, and other diseases.[15]

If one prefers a more mundane catastrophe, there is an economic apocalypse. There is no shortage of predictions regarding the demise of the American economy or, worse yet, a global economic collapse. In recent decades best-seller lists have included *The Crash of '79*, *The Panic of '89*, *The Great Depression of 1990*, *Bankruptcy 1995*, and *The Coming Economic Earthquake*.[16]

Such predictions regarding the end of the world are not new. They are as old as human history itself. But until the world does come to an end, such prognostications are merely an idea, a belief. And that is what this book is about—the idea of how and when the world will end. Many world religions—Islamic, Buddhist, Hindu, Zoroastrian, and Jewish—have legends regarding the end of time. However, we will look at end-time predictions primarily as they relate to the Western tradition.

A Few Definitions

Before we journey through Western history to see how people have viewed doomsday, we must define some terms. This book concerns end-of-the-world predictions, not apocalypticism or millennialism per se. Still, individuals and groups who envision the end of the world often share an apocalyptic or millennial worldview.

As Bernard McGinn notes, apocalypticism "is a highly complex phenomenon." Thus it cannot be reduced to "a clear and distinct idea." Moreover, the meaning of apocalypticism has shifted through time, often acquiring different connotations in different eras. Accordingly, we must see apocalypticism as a tradition embodied in Western culture.[17] To understand its essence, we must come up with a working definition and a list of its characteristics.

The word *apocalypse* means revelation, the uncovering or unveiling of a divine secret. It is eschatological in nature, that is, it is concerned with final things—the end of the present age, the judgment day, and the age to come. Apocalyptic thinking assumes a particular view of history: history is essentially linear. It does not go round and round. Rather, history progresses from event to event, moving toward a final goal at the end of time.[18]

Apocalyptic is a form of literature claiming to reveal hidden things and the future. As a genre popular in Israel from about 200 B.C. to A.D. 100, it closely reflected the persecution that the Jews experienced during this time. The authors of the apocalyptic writings in the biblical canon have been identified by the Christian tradition. However, other apocalyptic literature is often pseudonymous—it bears a fictitious name. Revealed to seers through dreams and visions, it employs a highly symbolic, imaginative language that is subject to a wide interpretation.[19]

Apocalyptic thinking has several characteristics. It is dualistic, viewing human history as a cosmic struggle between absolute good and evil. The apocalyptic outlook is also catastrophic in that it holds that this historical conflict will be settled by battles and disasters in which evil will be defeated. Although the word *apocalypse* is currently used as a synonym for disaster, this is only a half-truth. "Apocalypse" concerns both "cataclysm and millennium, tribulation and triumph." Finally, apocalyptic thinking is deterministic, assuming that the sequence of events in the final conflict is "preset in a heavenly clock."[20]

The great majority of the individuals and groups who envision the end of the world think apocalyptically in one way or another. While some individuals believe that the world will end gradually and on a positive note, most predict a cataclysmic, disastrous end to history. Even the secular apocalyptists share this view. While they may not see the world ending because of some divine intervention, they do predict upheavals and catastrophes. Many secular apocalyptists foresee these future disasters without the hope of a future golden age.

The words *apocalyptic* and *eschatological* are often used interchangeably. This is technically incorrect. Eschatology means "study of the last things." It is a general term referring to all end-time events and ideas. In contrast, "apocalyptic" is a more narrow term, a specific type of eschatological belief characterized by a sense of impending doom.[21]

Prophecy and apocalypticism have a close relationship, but they are not identical. There are apocalyptic prophets, but some prophets do not proclaim an apocalyptic message. A prophet is one "who foretells the future" or "who seeks to correct a present situation." Generally, prophets receive their message from God apart from visions or dreams. This message, which they proclaim in the name of the Lord, is intended to change a current situation. On the other hand, an apocalyptic seer proclaims a message of doom that offers little opportunity for repentance. This message is usually received through a vision and bears a name other than that of the seer.[22]

Millennialism (or millenarianism) and apocalypticism overlap, but they are not the same. "Millennialism," derived from the Latin word for a thousand, refers to a belief in a thousand-year period of blessedness ("chiliasm," drawn from Greek, has the same meaning). Christian millennialism is based on a literal interpretation of Revelation 20:1–10.[23] Many apocalyptists are millenarians, believing that cataclysmic events will either precede or follow a millennium. Still, there are apocalyptists who do not speak of a millennium, and millennialists who do not believe that the world will experience a catastrophic end. Unfortunately, it is easy to muddle the differences between apocalypticism and millennialism. Many books have done so. Indeed, in describing end-time thinking through history, I probably have fallen into the same trap.

Millennialism falls into three main groups—pre-, post-, and amillennialism.[24] These positions differ as to when Christ will return. But their differences go well beyond the timing of Christ's return. They touch upon attitudes toward life, the way in which Scripture is interpreted, the number of resurrections, and the nature of the millennium itself. Pre-, post-, and amillennialism are relatively modern terms. Thus one must be careful not to impose them on earlier ages. Nevertheless, many of the millennial positions expressed through the course of Western history roughly approximate the outlines of pre-, post-, and amillennialism.

Premillennialists believe that Christ will return before the millennium. They tend to be apocalyptists, believing that the new age will be inaugurated in a cataclysmic and supernatural manner. They also interpret Scripture literally and adopt a somewhat pessimistic attitude toward life. That is to say, they often insist that a catastrophe is on the horizon and reject human schemes for building a heaven on earth and improving human nature. Rather, they believe that God will intervene, probably in a cataclysmic way, to usher in the millennium. They are not pessimistic about all aspects of life, however.

Conversely, postmillennialists say that Christ will not come until the end of a golden age. Many of them are not apocalyptists; they insist that the millennium will come in a gradual, less violent way. Moreover, they tend to interpret Scripture spiritually and to view life optimistically, believing that human efforts will help inaugurate the millennium.

For much of Christian history, amillennialism has been the predominate view. Amillennialists do not interpret Revelation 20 literally—in their opinion, it symbolizes certain present realities. Thus they do not believe that Christ will establish a literal earthly rule before the judgment. Rather, the glorious new heaven and earth will immediately follow the present dispensation of the kingdom of God.

Like apocalypticism, millennial thinking is not confined to the Christian tradition. Millennial beliefs can be found in non-Christian and non-Western religions. Millennialism can also be secular; in fact, Nazism and Communism include millennial strands.

Lastly, we must understand what is meant by the end of the world. Prophets of doom have given it several meanings. It can mean the destruction of the earth, the extinction of humanity, or perhaps only a widespread catastrophe. Some prophets have in view merely the end of an era and the coming of a new age—not the actual destruction of the world.

Why the Western Fascination with Doomsday

Through the centuries humanity has had a huge appetite for apocalyptic thought. Why have people been fascinated with doomsday? What has sustained this interest? These are complex questions that defy simple answers. No one theory can account for the fascination, for it has appeared in all periods of history. Certain ideas in Western culture and conditions in Western history have, however, been particularly influential.

Western Ideas

While nearly all cultures have their doomsday theories, fascination with the end time has been most persistent in the Western tradition. In part, this is a result of certain ideas that are readily found in Western culture.

First, the Christian faith teaches that Jesus Christ will return to earth personally and visibly. While Christians may debate the details of Christ's return, they agree on the reality of the second advent, which will bring an end to the world as we know it. The failure of Scripture to spell out the when and how of this event has spawned all kinds of wild speculations. While the second advent is a nonnegotiable truth for the sober Christian community, it has also become fodder for fanatics.

Another biblical teaching—that the world was destroyed by a flood—has encouraged apocalyptic thinking. Christians believe that God judged and destroyed the first world by water because of its evil and wickedness. They are convinced that this world's sin and violence will bring a second divine judgment.[25] Christians are not alone in believing that a deluge destroyed the first world. Many religions and primitive cultures have similar stories about a catastrophic flood.

Also worth mentioning are the ancient legends of the sinking of the continent of Atlantis. True, many people in the ancient world regarded the Atlantis story as a fable. Still, the story has persisted until the present, and many books have been written about Atlantis. The story of Atlantis is grist for many occultists and their cataclysmic predictions for the modern world.[26] Our point here is not to debate the historicity of the Noahic flood nor even to equate it with the Atlantis story. Rather, the point is that "what we believe is going to happen in the future is profoundly influenced by what we think has already happened in the past." A crucial factor in convincing people that "the world would end catastrophically was their belief that a similar catastrophe had already occurred."[27]

A third factor encouraging speculation about the end of the world is the Western view of history. There are two classic models of history—cyclical and linear. In the perspective of most Eastern religions and ancient cultures, all human events occur in cycles. While the names, dates, and persons involved will change, the same events will happen again. Although the cyclical worldview is not devoid of cataclysmic thinking, it does not encourage predictions about the end of the world. Moreover, those non-Western cultures that do present ideas about the end of the world do so with less anxiety. They usually do not tie their apocalyptic beliefs to particular dates or periods of time—centuries or millenniums. They thus avoid the great fear and hopes so characteristic of Western apocalypticism.[28]

The linear view of history, which began with the Hebrews and their neighbors, gained strength in the Christian tradition. While this model allows for some repetitive patterns, it views history as generally moving in one direction. The present is not a replay of the past. Rather, history moves from one event to the next until it reaches its final goal.[29] The apocalyptic worldview assumes such a model of history: history is moving toward the end of time, the final judgment, and the catastrophes that will accompany those events.[30]

Two other characteristics of the Western view of history encouraged end-time predictions—optimism and determinism. The cyclical model of history is generally pessimistic. The situation may be terrible now. But worse still, events go round and round and there is little hope that they will get better. While Western apocalyptic thinking predicts disasters, there is an optimistic side. Cataclysm will be followed by heaven or a utopia of some sort.

Terminal visions are often deterministic. Most individuals who envision great upheavals or the end of the world see these events as determined by forces beyond their control, usually God. Apocalyptists frequently call individuals to repentance. Yet the die is cast—society is collectively doomed. Evil and wickedness are so great that judgment is inevitable—it will take place according to a divine timetable. Apocalyptic thinkers are not necessarily fatalistic or deterministic on an individual level. But they usually hold to an eschatological determinism, regarding the occurrence of certain end-time events as inevitable.

Also related to the traditional Western concept of history is the notion that the earth is relatively young. On the basis of chronological references in the Old Testament, Archbishop James Ussher of Ireland (1581–1656) calculated that the world had been created in 4004 B.C. This date appeared in the margin of the Book of Genesis in the Authorized Version and was accepted by many Christians as gospel truth. Through the ages many prophets of doom have built their prognostications upon Ussher's date or the belief that the world is young.[31] In fact, even prior to Ussher's calculations many people believed that God had created the world in six days sometime between 6000 and 4000 B.C. According to 2 Peter 3:8, "one day is with the Lord as a thousand years." So for centuries many millennialists based their predictions on the six-day or sabbath theory. They believed that the world would end at the completion of the sixth day or six thousand years. The millennial age or sabbath would then begin.

Conditions in Western History

The persistence of end-time predictions through Western history is due not only to certain ideas that characterize Western culture, but also to specific social, economic, psychological, and political conditions. Apocalyptic and millennial movements are so complex as to defy any simple cause-and-effect explanations. Yet some social theories do help explain why such movements arose in particular periods in history.

Both John Gager and Gerd Theissen regard early Christianity as a millennial movement. They see the early Jesus movement as having grown out of a socially and politically oppressive environment. This movement, they contend, "contained prophetic promises of an imminent salvation and reversal of the present social order." It first centered on a messianic figure and later on other charismatic leaders.[32]

In his classic book *The Pursuit of the Millennium*, British historian Norman Cohn attempts to account for the rise of apocalyptic movements in the Middle Ages. He contends that "revolutionary millenarianism drew its strength from a population living on the margin of society"—peasants, journeymen, and unskilled workers. Such people "lacked the material and emotional support afforded by traditional social groups." Because they were in such a defenseless position, they reacted "sharply to any disruption of the normal, familiar pattern of life." Cohn goes on to point out that the greatest millenarian activities came against the background of natural disasters, namely plagues and famines.[33]

Other scholars have questioned Cohn's ideas. Bernard McGinn and Marjorie Reeves, for example, have demonstrated that apocalyptic speculations were more widespread than once believed. They were embraced not only by the people on the margins of medieval society, but also by its more secure members. Indeed, apocalyptic thinking formed an important component of the medieval mentality.[34]

In *Disaster and the Millennium*, political scientist Michael Barkun argues that disasters are the chief factor in producing apocalyptic millennial movements. These disasters "must be multiple rather than single." They are accompanied by "a body of ideas or doctrines of a millenarian cast" shaped by a charismatic leader. Moreover, millenarian movements originate in a rural-agrarian setting rather than in an urban-industrial context. "Only the disaster-prone, homogeneous countryside seems to call forth the pursuit of the millennium."[35] Barkun's ideas need to be modified somewhat, for some highly industrialized areas experience disasters and thus can fall prey to apocalyptic excitement.[36]

Essentially these theories tell us that apocalyptic movements arise during times of social instability and transition. Such views do not go unchallenged. Yet they do have relevance for explaining apocalyptic movements in Europe and the developing world.

Such theories, however, only partially explain the millennial movements in America. The Millerite premillennial movement in the 1840s did not consist of the socially disinherited. The Millerites lived at a time of profound social change. Yet they were the middling sort, actually slightly better off than the average person.[37] Likewise, the millions of people who buy Hal Lindsey's books or who watch Pat Robertson and Jerry Falwell on television are not powerless. In fact, many of these individuals are part of the religious right, which gained considerable power in the late twentieth century.[38] But while modern Christian fundamentalists are not the downtrodden, their spokespersons sound warnings of doom. They declare that our society is on a collision course with disaster. Disturbed by the sin and violence in our society, they sincerely believe that divine judgment is imminent.

There is another factor at work here. The Christian fundamentalists of our day may not be economically downtrodden, but they are a cognitive minority—that is, their ideas no longer fit comfortably into the mainstream of American society. Fundamentalist thinking assumes a literal reading of ancient writings and a supernaturalist vision—two suppositions that are not at home in the modern world. Moreover, we live in the post-Christian era when Christianity is no longer the definer of cultural values. The Christian faith has been challenged in many quarters. The beliefs and values of the Christian fundamentalists have been ridiculed by many. Intellectually and morally the Christian fundamentalists are a minority, so they long for a divine intervention to rectify the current social order.

The views of the Christian fundamentalists are part of a larger apocalyptic mood that has gripped American society in the late twentieth century. To many Christians, the establishment of the Israeli state in 1948 was confirmation of prophecy. Among the wider public a series of natural and unnatural disasters (Bhopal, Chernobyl, AIDS, earthquakes, global warming, etc.) has heightened an apocalyptic fever. Moreover, the rapid social changes of our day are baffling to many people. They are confused and perplexed. They are uncomfortable with the direction of society, but feel powerless to change it.[39]

We should note here that while sudden change and social chaos create an atmosphere conducive to predictions of the end of the world, this change and chaos must seem to be inexplicable. When disruptions have reasonable explanations, apocalyptic visions do not usually arise. But in the view of the disturbed and disoriented people of the twentieth century, the established systems have failed to explain why such changes have come. Although conditions today are not as cataclysmic as they were in the Middle Ages, they can terrify individuals who do not understand them.

To these considerations a few more must be added. Many people are influenced by a "numerological determinism, a deep-seated conviction that years and historical epochs come in tens and groups of ten." Clearly, the end must be near. Also, "there is a growing appetite for the weird."[40] Many people who don't accept the Christian faith will believe almost anything else. Witness the extreme occultic and fanatical groups that have predicted the end of time—the Branch Davidians, Supreme Truth, Children of God, Church Universal and Triumphant, Christian Identity, some New Agers, and UFO cultists. Given the social and psychological conditions that exist at the close of the twentieth century, it is little wonder that apocalyptic thinking is rampant.

2

Apocalypse Postponed: Early Christianity

"The last times are come upon us," wrote Ignatius of Antioch. A bishop of the church in Antioch during the early second century, he exhorted believers to "weigh carefully the times. Look for Him who is above all time, eternal and invisible."[1] Like many leaders in the early church, Ignatius spoke of an approaching crisis, which he interpreted to be a sign of Christ's imminent return.

In early and medieval Christianity a pattern of end-time thinking emerged. For the first two hundred years or so, Christians intensely expected Christ to return and usher in a golden age. Over the next two hundred years a transition took place. The intense expectancy regarding Christ's return waned, and Christians began to make peace with the world. Official church doctrine declared that the millennium was in progress. Consequently, the breathless anticipation for Christ's return was put on hold for about a thousand years. Yet apocalyptic thinking never died out. In fact, despite being suspect and almost heretical, it penetrated most ranks of medieval society.

Non-Christian End-Time Stories

The Christians were not alone in their belief that the world would soon end. Many people in the ancient world shared a similar conviction. According to the Greeks, for example, the gods at times became angry with humankind and threatened to destroy them by a flood or fire.

From about 300 B.C. to A.D. 200 Stoicism was a popular philosophy with the Greeks and Romans. This philosophy originated with Zeno, who taught that at recurring intervals the world would be destroyed by fire. However, this conflagration would purify the world by eliminating evil. The world would then be reborn, and its future inhabitants would be wiser.[2]

Also on a positive note was the Roman poet Virgil's vision regarding the end of the world. Reflecting the time of Augustus Caesar, the golden age of Rome, Virgil had a millennial vision of a glorious new age in which life would become nearly divine.[3]

Several Eastern religions also predict the end of the world. Hinduism reckons time in terms of cycles consisting of four ages. Each cycle begins with a utopia but ends in disaster—drought, disease, famine, and war. The world is then destroyed by fire, but Vishnu begins the cycle again by re-creating the world. According to a Buddhist story, Buddha, called Maitreya, will one day appear bringing a golden age. Another Buddhist school predicts that the present eon will end when the new Buddha arrives.[4]

Zoroastrianism, the religion of Persia, was popular in the Roman Empire. Its stories regarding the end of the world have a superficial resemblance to Christian ideas. Ahura Mazda, the god of light, is engaged in a 6,000-year struggle with the evil god. This conflict will end when Ahura Mazda takes the good people to heaven and destroys the earth with molten metal. But the earth is then to be restored, and life will then be immortal and sinless. Zoroastrianism apparently influenced Jewish eschatological views after the Babylonian exile (ca. 587–539 B.C.).[5]

Jewish Terminal Visions

Although the Old Testament is not an apocalyptic work, it does contain several apocalyptic books, particularly Ezekiel and Daniel. Apocalypticism grew out of the prophetic movement. The prophets proclaimed Yahweh's requirement of justice and demanded that Israel repent from its moral and spiritual failures.[6] But Israel failed to keep its covenant with Yahweh. Consequently, Israel was constantly besieged and oppressed by its powerful neighbors—Egypt, Assyria, and the Neo-Babylonians—and after 600 B.C. its history turned dark. The nation was dissolved and the people went into captivity in Babylon. When they returned from Babylon, the expected national recovery did not materialize. Instead, the Jewish state became a pawn of larger nations. Pessimism gripped the people. In such an environment Jewish apocalypticism was born. Divine deliverance would not come in the normal course of history. Rather, the seers predicted that God would break into history through some cosmic event—judgment, destruction, and eventually national deliverance.[7]

Ezekiel's Dry Bones

In 587 B.C. Jerusalem fell and the Babylonians exiled many of the Israelites. Nebuchadnezzar wrought terrible vengeance on Israel—sacking Jerusalem, destroying the temple, killing King Zedekiah's children before his eyes, and then blinding him. Such monstrous events are the background to the Book of Ezekiel.

Ezekiel, a priest of the temple, was among the exiles sent to Babylon. He had several spectacular visions, which he recorded in his book. In chapters 37–39 he employs vivid imagery—dry bones, torrents of rain, burning sulfur, and abominable beasts—that set a standard for apocalyptic language.[8] In one vision God carries Ezekiel to a valley full of dry bones. These bones come together and take life. Flesh, skin, and muscles grow on them. God explains that these bones represent the Israelites, who will be resurrected and united in their own land under one king.

Ezekiel next reveals the events of the "latter days," which have been interpreted to be the end of the world. The heathen, including both Israel's neighbors and more distant enemies, are destroyed. The carnage is incredible—wars, plagues, great hailstorms, fire and brimstone. But the vision ends on a positive note. God promises to pour out his spirit on the house of Israel.

Daniel's Dreadful Vision

The Book of Daniel contains stories loved by generations of Sunday school teachers—Nebuchadnezzar's dream; the writing on King Belshazzar's wall; Daniel in the lions' den; and Shadrach, Meshach, and Abednego in the flaming furnace. But Daniel contains much more than riveting Sunday school stories. It is one of the first vivid, coherent accounts of the end of time.[9] We are told that "there shall be a time of trouble, such as never was since there was a nation . . ." (12:1).

Daniel's terrible apocalyptic visions and complex chronologies have been the grist for numerous interpretations. For two thousand years the imagery found in Daniel's revelations has stimulated the imaginations of prophecy interpreters. In general there have been two broad lines of interpretation—futuristic and historical.

Scholars committed to a futuristic method of interpretation believe that the Book of Daniel was penned in the sixth century B.C. by an individual named Daniel. Many evangelical scholars take this approach.

They accept the claims of the book itself—that Daniel wrote it during the exile years. They also insist that the book exhibits a literary unity, presents coherent ideas, and predicts future events. The rise and fall of empires and the terrible calamities that are described were to come in both the near and distant future. Some modern-day popularizers insist that Daniel has in view the Antichrist and a ten-nation confederation that will emerge at the end of time.[10]

The majority of the liberal scholars regard Daniel as basically historical in nature. They date Daniel to the second century B.C., believing that it was predated four centuries to make it seem more reliable. They claim that the book contains historical inaccuracies and a lateness of language that better fits the second century. The author, whose name is unknown, addressed known historical events—the wars of the Hellenistic rulers and Antiochus Epiphanes' persecutions—as if they were in the future. In this way the authority of the prophetic passages was enhanced.[11]

The apocalyptic section begins in chapter 7: "Four great beasts came up from the sea" (v. 3). The first three were later identified as the Medes, Persians, and Greeks. The fourth beast, which was "dreadful and terrible, and strong exceedingly, and . . . had great iron teeth" (v. 7), was fragmented into ten kingdoms. From its ten horns there arose a little horn. This little horn represents a "king of fierce countenance" who will "destroy the mighty and the holy people" (8:23–24). He will "speak great words against the most High, and shall wear out the saints of the most High" (7:25). The little horn has been interpreted two ways. Historically, it is believed to refer to Antiochus Epiphanes, who attacked Jerusalem and desecrated the temple.[12] Those who hold to a futuristic interpretation of Daniel say that the little horn also represents the Antichrist of the last days.

Nearly all authorities regard chapters 11 and 12 as prophecy, not history. Chapter 11 presents a complex prophecy of a king who shall "do according to his will" (v. 3) and have great power. This chapter also foretells alliances and wars involving the king of the south and the king of the north, who is especially blasphemous, speaking "marvellous things against the God of gods" (v. 36). But chapter 11 predicts his doom in a cataclysmic battle at the end of time. As the king of the north goes forth "with great fury to destroy," he shall be defeated and "come to his end" (vv. 44–45). The prophecy continues into chapter 12, where Daniel is commanded to "seal the book, even to the time of the end" (v. 4). Here Daniel's vision presents a glimpse of events after the end of time, including the resurrections of the righteous and the wicked.[13]

Daniel has had an enormous impact on end-time thinking as it developed in the Christian tradition. The themes enunciated in Daniel—the destruction of the wicked, the triumph of righteousness, and the resurrection of the dead—have endured to the present. Of particular importance, Daniel's prophetic timetable has been amazingly flexible. As time has passed and circumstances have changed, Daniel's inter- preters have readjusted the explanation of the book's prophecies to suit the events of their own day.[14]

Apocryphal Apocalypse and More

Between 300 B.C. and A.D. 100 the Jews produced many apocalyptic writings. But none of them joined Daniel as a canonical book in the Jew- ish and Christian Bibles. These other books are called apocryphal, from the Greek word for "hidden."[15]

These years were turbulent for the Jews. The persecution by the Se- leucids, the Maccabean revolt, and the destruction of Jerusalem and the temple by the Romans produced an atmosphere of tension and crisis. Apocalyptic thinking thrives in such an environment.[16]

Some of the better-known apocryphal apocalyptic books include 2 Enoch, 4 Ezra, the Book of Jubilees, the Assumption of Moses, 2 Baruch, and 3 Baruch. These books, of course, are all different, but they include common themes such as the destruction and doom await- ing sinners, the salvation of the righteous, and the coming of a Messiah and the messianic kingdom.[17]

In 1947 a young Bedouin goatherd in search of a stray goat discov- ered a literary gold mine—the so-called Dead Sea Scrolls. These scrolls preserve some of the writings of the Essenes, an ascetic sect which arose in Israel during the second century B.C. The Essenes lived at Qumran and were very critical of the laxness of Jewish religious life.[18] Their writ- ings were among the last of Jewish apocalyptic eschatology. As Israel's troubles increased during the tumultuous century before and after Christ's birth, the Essenes looked for the coming Messiah and the end of the world. They believed the end to be imminent and certain.[19]

Although the end-time themes of the noncanonical books resemble those found in the Bible, they should not be placed on the same level. Christians have differed over eschatological details—especially the chronology of Christ's return. Yet they believe that the major biblical statements about the end will undoubtedly come to pass. No such in- evitability is attributed to the eschatological assertions found in the non- canonical books.

Early Christian Apocalyptic Visions

"Then we which are alive and remain shall be caught up together with them in the clouds to meet the Lord in the air" (1 Thess. 4:17). Jewish apocalypticism rubbed off on the early Christians. Some scholars have debated the extent to which apocalyptic thinking dominated the early church. Nearly all scholars concede, however, that the early Christians expected the end of the world. Indeed, according to one theologian, "apocalypticism . . . was the mother of all Christian theology."[20]

Apocalyptic thinking pervades the earliest canonical Christian epistles. In 1 Thessalonians Paul tells Christians that the Lord will "descend from heaven with a shout, with the voice of the archangel" (4:16). But 2 Thessalonians cautions that this day shall not come until "the man of sin be revealed, the son of perdition" (2:3). In 1 Corinthians Paul declares that Christ will return "in the twinkling of an eye, at the last trump" (15:52). Among the later epistles 2 Peter describes the end of the world by fire: "the heavens shall pass away . . . the earth also . . . shall be burned up . . . and the elements shall melt with fervent heat" (3:10, 12). And it is in 1 and 2 John that we find the only explicit biblical references to the Antichrist.

The Gospels also contain apocalyptic references. Jesus' most detailed eschatological words are in the so-called Little Apocalypse, found in Mark 13 and repeated in different forms in Matthew 24–25 and Luke 21.[21] In these passages Jesus describes the last days and the sequence of events that lead up to the end. A series of disasters—wars, earthquakes, famines, and persecutions—will disrupt the political, religious, and natural orders. And when the gospel is finally preached to all nations, the end will come.[22]

As the end draws closer, the great tribulation will come. Jesus refers to this event as "the abomination of desolation, spoken of by Daniel the prophet" (Mark 13:14). The affliction will be such "as was not from the beginning of creation . . . unto this time. . . . And except that the Lord had shortened those days, no flesh should be saved" (vv. 19–20). But this horrible tribulation will end suddenly in a great cosmic drama—the return of Christ "in the clouds with great power and glory" (v. 26).

In the parable of the fig tree (Mark 13:28–30) Jesus gives another clue as to when the end will come. Christ will return in the generation after the fig tree gets its leaves. This parable along with Daniel's prophecy of seventy weeks (9:24) has tempted countless people to try to calculate the exact time when Christ will return.[23] But what is meant by the fig tree "putting forth leaves"? A contemporary popularizer, Hal Lindsey, claims that the fig tree put forth its leaves when Israel returned to Palestine in 1948. So in one generation from 1948 the end will come.[24] However, in this very parable Christ condemns such speculation: "But of that day and that hour knoweth no man" (Mark 13:32).

The apocalyptic passages found in the Epistles and Gospels present several common themes. On the surface some of these ideas are in tension with each other and are subject to differing interpretations. The

32

central thought of Christ and the apostles is that the end is near. While imminent, it has not yet arrived. Christians are to be prepared for the end and to stop speculating as to when it will come.[25]

The Revelation of John

Through two millennia of Christian history, the Book of Revelation has produced a flood of end-time speculations. Traditionally, it has been ascribed to the pen of John the apostle. The only book in the Bible which focuses primarily on the last days, Revelation is compelling and rich in symbols and images. Consequently, it has gripped the imagination of people from all ranks of society and significantly influenced Western culture.

The tremendous impact of Revelation is due largely to its heavy use of symbols—four horsemen, beasts, the Lamb, a harlot, a dragon, a millennium, and more. These symbols are shrouded in ambiguity and have been interpreted in many ways—sometimes with considerable imagination.[26] Throughout history people have read into the pages of Revelation the events of their own time. In this way nearly every generation has regarded their own age as the last, or has seen this or that person as the Antichrist.

There are basically four ways in which the Book of Revelation has been interpreted, three of which have eschatological implications. (The idealist view sees the book simply as a depiction of the continual struggle between good and evil—there is no prediction of the future.) The preterist view interprets Revelation strictly as a first-century book. John is describing the church's situation in his day. The dreadful symbols are pointing to Nero and the Roman Empire. This interpretation is eschatological in that John sees himself as living in the last days. The end will soon come.[27]

The historicist view sees Revelation as an inspired forecast of human history. Its symbols set forth in broad outline the history of Western Europe from the first church to the second coming of Christ. Some interpreters see the whole book as presaging Western history. For example, they believe that the opening of the little scroll in Revelation 10 depicts the Protestant Reformation. Other interpreters contend that only the letters to the seven churches (chs. 2–3) portray the history of the Christian church.[28] Whatever the approach, the historicist view is used to make end-time predictions.

The futurist view regards all but a few chapters of Revelation as concerned with what will happen at the end of the age. The futurists see the seven seals and all the rest as portraying the events surrounding the second return of Christ and the end of the world.[29] In the modern world the futurist view has led to many doomsday forecasts.

33

Revelation shares much with other apocalyptic writings. But in one respect it breaks new ground. Revelation contains the only biblical reference to an earthly millennium. In some noncanonical apocalyptic writings an earthly Messianic Age is mentioned. However, only Revelation combines a temporary earthly millennium with the prospect of an everlasting kingdom in the New Jerusalem.[30] In fact, this single passage in Revelation 20 has been the mother of most millennial expectations.

The apocalyptic section begins in chapter 4. In typical apocalyptic fashion John tells us of unspeakable disasters, judgment for sin, and ultimate triumph. With a cosmic flair and for fifteen chapters John paints a vivid picture of the coming woes. These horrors are unveiled in series of seven—seven seals, seven trumpets, seven angels, and seven bowls. The last four chapters describe the great victory of the Lamb (Christ), the millennium, judgment, and the New Jerusalem.

The drama takes place mostly in the court of heaven. John is told to "come up hither, and I will shew thee things which must be hereafter" (4:1). The seven seals are broken by the Lamb. These seals tell of coming wars, famine, death, martyrdoms, and earthquakes. Seven angels then sound seven trumpets, each bringing more bad news for humankind (chs. 8–9). Hail and fire destroy one-third of the earth's trees. A third of the sea turns to blood. A falling star poisons the earth's waters. The sun, moon, and stars are darkened. Giant locusts torment those who do not have the seal of God on their foreheads. A supernatural cavalry destroys one-third of humanity.

After a pause the seventh trumpet sounds, triggering a long vision about the dragon called Satan. Satan makes war against heaven and is defeated by God's angels. But on earth Satan gives great authority to the beast, who is the Antichrist. This beast blasphemes God, performs great wonders, and requires everyone "to receive a mark in their right hand, or in their foreheads," in order to buy or sell (13:16–17).

The seven angels proceed to spill the content of the seven bowls one at a time. These bowls contain the wrath of God and bring calamities upon the entire earth. The list of horrors includes plagues, bloody rivers, a scorching sun, darkness, lightning, earthquakes, and the destruction of cities. But victory comes. The evil world system represented by Babylon is destroyed. Christ returns and is crowned King of kings and Lord of lords. Only Satan is left to be defeated. Then an angel chains him for a thousand years in a great pit.

At this point John introduces the only New Testament reference to Christ's thousand-year earthly reign (ch. 20).[31] Many Christians have concluded from this passage that Christ will set up his rule on earth for a limited time. After the thousand years Satan is released and again challenges God. He is defeated and "cast into the lake of fire . . . for ever and

34

ever" (v. 10). John's vision then moves to the resurrection and last judgment. After this judgment the earth and sky are replaced by a new heaven and new earth.

The apocalyptic worldview expressed in various texts of the New Testament has had an important place in the Western intellectual tradition. It has incited revolutions and uprisings; it has inspired poets, artists, sculptors, and composers. The apocalyptic assumption that human activities are being moved by God toward a transcendent goal has also significantly influenced the Western view of history.[32] Until the eighteenth-century Enlightenment the Bible's apocalyptic texts were taken seriously by people in all ranks of society. Since then their influence has waned in scholarly circles. But at the popular level apocalyptic thinking continues to maintain a vital existence, even surging to high levels of interest during times of uncertainty.[33]

Early Millenarian Movements

The New Testament contains several passages suggesting that Christ might not return as soon as expected. Still, most first-century Christians believed that the world would soon end, probably in their lifetime. But as time went on, these early Christians had to confront the delay in Christ's second coming. Some believers still maintained their intense expectation that Christ would soon return and establish his kingdom. Others, however, gradually abandoned their hope for an imminent return.

During the second and third centuries a tension existed in the early church. Some followers of Christ had radical millennial expectations that his earthly kingdom would soon be inaugurated. Other Christians were more oriented to the institutionalization of the church. Apocalyptic movements with their charismatic leaders and end-time expectations are usually anti-institutional. Still, if any movement is to survive, it must establish an adequate organizational structure.[34] The need to institutionalize the early church gradually prevailed over its apocalyptic impulse—but not completely. Inasmuch as Christ's return and the expected end of the world are cardinal Christian beliefs, "the apocalyptic vision was not eclipsed as quickly or as completely in the second and third centuries" as some theologians have claimed.[35]

In fact, millennialism in several forms remained strong in the early church. It came in with Jewish apocalypticism, even thriving at times. Conditions in the second and third centuries provided fertile soil for apocalyptic millennialism. Christians experienced sporadic persecutions that fueled their apocalyptic expectations. Moreover, their struggle against Gnosticism, which argued for a purely spiritual notion of salvation, led to an increased emphasis on an earthly millennium.[36] In addition, early Christianity was essentially a movement among the lower orders, and millennial visions are more at home with the lower social classes.[37] Still, the hope for an early millennium was not shared by all Christians. "In the post-apostolic era millenarianism was regarded as a mark neither of orthodoxy nor of heresy, but as one permissible opinion among others."[38]

Not all early millennial theories fit into neat packages. In fact, some thinkers combined elements of several views. Two basic approaches were, however, particularly prominent. In the area of Ephesus (in modern Turkey) there developed a millennial tradition featuring material blessings. This tradition, which shares some features with modern premillennialism, emphasized the physical aspects accompanying the future rule of Christ over the renewed earth following the resurrection at the end of the present age.[39]

The second basic approach to millenarianism is often called the six-day theory or the "creation day–world age" theory. This notion, based on 2 Peter 3:8 ("one day is with the Lord as a thousand years, and a thousand years as one day"), links the seven days of creation with seven millennia of human history. God created the world in six days and rested on the seventh. Thus God will consummate everything in six thousand years. Arising in the area of Antioch, Syria, this approach prompted Christians to try to calculate the date of Christ's return. A common element here was the belief that the world was about 5,700 to 6,000 years old.[40]

It now remains to give concrete illustrations of early millennialism. Papias (ca. 60–130), bishop of Hierapolis, spoke of a millennium with miraculous material enjoyments: "There will be a certain period of a thousand years after the resurrection from the dead when the kingdom of Christ must be set up in a material order on this earth."[41] The Epistle of Barnabas, written between 96 and 131, is charged with an eschatological expectancy. Following the tradition that the end will come in six thousand years, it maintains a sense of eschatological immediacy. Afterwards, the idea of a week of seven thousand years became common, with the last day signifying the millennium. Another early document, the Didache, also echoes apocalyptic themes and is premillenarian like many of the early Christian writings.[42]

Irenaeus (ca. 140–202), bishop of Lyons, presented perhaps the most complete expression of patristic premillennialism. His end-time chronology included a three-and-a-half-year rule of the Antichrist, an earthly millennium, and the resurrection of the righteous. Irenaeus's millennium was materially oriented, a rerun of the Garden of Eden with miracles, peace, and fruitfulness. Irenaeus even developed a rationale for

36

the millennium—it was a necessary stage preparing the righteous for eternity.[43] And he believed that these events were imminent.

The apologist Justin Martyr (ca. 110–65) combined the six-day theory with the materialist-oriented millennialism of Papias. On one hand, he contended for a millennium in a rebuilt, embellished, and enlarged earthly Jerusalem. On the other, he declined to make eschatology a test of orthodoxy, recognizing that many Christians think otherwise.[44]

The brilliant Tertullian (ca. 160–220) also advocated an apocalyptic eschatology. The prolific writings of this stern and zealous apologist influenced generations of Christians. He believed that the end was imminent. Christ would soon return to earth and set up the New Jerusalem. An advocate of the ascetic life, Tertullian scorned pleasures because he expected Christ to soon arrive in triumph.[45]

While apocalyptic millennialism was strong in the early church, on the whole the early church fathers shied away from specific date-setting. However, Hippolytus (170–236) set an exact date for Christ's return. On the basis of the six-day theory and the belief that about 5,500 years separated Adam from Christ, Hippolytus postulated that the world would expire soon. The six days or six thousand years would be up in about A.D. 500.[46] Similarly, Sextus Julius Africanus (ca. 160–240), on the basis of a supposed date for creation and a tidy pattern drawn from Revelation, first calculated the end to be A.D. 500 and then readjusted it to A.D. 800. Most church fathers, however, spoke of Christ's impending but unpredictable coming.

The most important millenarian movement in the early Eastern church was Montanism. Led by Montanus (ca. 172), who claimed to be a prophet, Montanism was an apocalyptic movement that regarded the gifts of the Spirit as normative. The Montanists expected Christ to return to Phrygia in Asia Minor and there set up New Jerusalem. Because of his intense expectation that Christ would soon return, Montanus demanded that his followers live a strict ascetic life. A synod of bishops condemned Montanism, not for its eschatological views, but for other excesses.[47]

Rejecting Millennialism

Not everyone in the early church espoused this exciting brand of apocalyptic millennialism. And as time went on, it became even less fashionable. The decline of millennialism can be attributed to several factors:

1. The anticipated events of the final days did not develop. No Antichrist came on the scene. Christ did not return in triumphant glory.[48]

2. The political scene changed dramatically. By the fourth century, Christianity had moved from being a persecuted sect to the official religion of the empire. No longer did Christians yearn for a glorious earthly millennium—they were now a privileged religion.
3. Christianity became institutionalized both organizationally and doctrinally. The church developed an ecclesiastical hierarchy and doctrinal norms that tended to restrain the excesses of apocalyptic millennialism.[49]
4. The allegorical approach to interpreting Scripture now became dominant. Premillennialism assumes a literal interpretation of Revelation 20. Scholars in the Ephesus and Antioch circles took a literal approach to the Bible and were generally millennialists. By contrast the theology of Alexandria and Rome favored a more allegorical interpretation of Scripture. This approach tended to spiritualize certain biblical passages, especially Daniel and Revelation. A natural consequence of this development was the demise of millennial expectancy.[50]

Origen (ca. 185–254), an Alexandrian theologian, attacked the notion that the millennium would be an earthly paradise. He rejected the chiliast's literal interpretation of Scripture, opting instead for an allegorical approach to the apocalyptic texts. As a result, Origen substituted a spiritual kingdom for the millennialists' material paradise. In part, his rejection of apocalyptic literalism may have been influenced by an earlier experience. In Matthew 19:12 Jesus speaks of those "which have made themselves eunuchs for the kingdom of heaven's sake." As a young man, Origen had interpreted this passage literally—he castrated himself![51]

Like Origen, Eusebius (ca. 265–339) flatly rejected chiliasm. Famous for his *Ecclesiastical History*, this bishop of Caesarea argued against the literal interpretation of John's Apocalypse, favoring instead an allegorical reading. Eusebius in effect denied that Christ would come to establish an earthly kingdom. Eusebius's opposition to millenarianism left an indelible mark on church history.[52]

The rejection of apocalyptic millennialism must be seen in its proper context. Constantine had been converted to Christianity in 312, thus ending the persecution of Christians. The hope for the imminent return of Christ remained strong as long as Christians were a persecuted minority. But when Christianity became the official religion in the Roman Empire during the fourth century, these millennial aspirations either declined or took new forms.[53]

In the post-Constantinian era, the greatest blow against millennialism came from Augustine (354–430), the bishop of Hippo. This preeminent theologian of the late patristic era rejected the millennialism of his day because of its crass materialism. Some millenarians envisioned an earthly paradise in which Christians enjoyed immoderate leisure and much carnal pleasure.[54]

In his condemnation of millennialism, Augustine was not original. He borrowed heavily from the Donatist thinker Tyconius in interpreting the apocalyptic books of the Bible allegorically. In *The City of God* Augustine saw the Book of Revelation as a description of the history of the church, not as a prophecy of the end of time. The millennium in his view was the present church age.[55]

Actually, Augustine arrived at a position that did not reject outright the concept of a millennium. Rather, he accommodated the millennial idea to suit the current situation of the church. The millennium began with Christ's first coming and is now in progress. "The church now on earth is both the kingdom of Christ and the kingdom of heaven," explained Augustine.[56] In later years such a view became known as amillennialism.

Catholic doctrine had come to regard the church as the vehicle for salvation. Accordingly, Augustine explained the millennium as a spiritual outworking of this the church's preeminent mission. Next on God's schedule was not Christ's return to set up an earthly paradise. Rather, the church would accomplish its mission, Christ would return, and then the judgment.

For the chiliasts the decisive culmination of history was to be Christ's second coming and his millennial rule—both future events. For Augustine the "decisive moment in the history of salvation had already occurred with Christ's First Coming."[57] The chiliasts saw the millennium standing outside of history—a future event. Augustine placed the millennium within history—a present event.

Augustine spiritualized the millennial concept in Revelation 20. Although his ideas on the subject were not without some ambiguity, he would have been aghast at how future generations used them. Indeed, some people used his ideas to interpret the millennium literally and came to the belief that Christ would return one thousand years after either his birth or death—that is, in the year 1000 or 1033.[58]

But on the whole, Augustine's nonmillenarian theology prevailed well into the Middle Ages. In 431 the Council of Ephesus condemned as superstition the belief in a literal millennium. Steadily, official Catholic doctrine distanced itself from end-time speculations.[59]

Persecution, anxiety, stress, and poverty often promote apocalyptic thinking. And there was plenty of such troubles to go around in the first few centuries of the Christian Era. The Jews struggled to retain their religious identity against Roman oppression and the Hellenistic religions.

This atmosphere seeped into the early Christian church, which can be seen as an apocalyptic sect within Judaism. The early Christians fervently believed that the crucified Jesus would soon return. But the present world order did not end as expected. So the early Christians had to come to grips with this delay in Christ's return—a development that caused considerable anxiety in the early church.

Institutionalization usually stifles the apocalyptic mind-set. As long as Christianity remained a persecuted sect, the apocalyptic fires burned brightly. But any movement must institutionalize if it is to survive. Gradually apocalypticism moderated and the church developed a hierarchy. Christianity moved from a minor Jewish sect to a world religion. When this happened, its apocalyptic fever declined. With their millennial expectations dampened, some Christians found other outlets for their zeal—monasticism, mystical visions, ascetic practices, and more.

3

The Slumbering Apocalypse: Medieval Christianity

"The Apocalypse and the attitude toward history which it represented slumbered as a force in Western culture—except for some uneasy tossings—for more than a thousand years," wrote Ernest Lee Tuveson in 1964.[1] More-recent scholarship has certainly modified Tuveson's judgment. Still, the Augustinian view that linked the institutional church to the kingdom of God remained the official and dominant eschatology throughout the Middle Ages.

Taking its cue from Augustine, the medieval church assumed the scheme of six days of history, and then a seventh, which was the eternal sabbath—not the millennium as the chiliasts believed. History was moving in one direction. For six ages God and Satan would engage in a great struggle that would end in divine judgment. However, Augustine and most medieval theologians refused to give any literal significance to such concepts as the millennium, the Antichrist, and Gog and Magog.[2]

Despite the official position there was a continuous flow of interest in apocalyptic eschatology throughout the Middle Ages. While apocalyptic expectations may have been greater among the oppressed of the lower classes, they were widespread. An apocalyptic worldview penetrated the medieval mentality and intrigued people of all social ranks. Though relatively subdued between 400 and 1100, apocalyptic visions soared to greater heights after 1100. Two streams of interpretation of apocalyptic texts flowed through the entire medieval period. The literal-historical interpretation, drawn from the early church, produced most of the end-time predictions. But the symbolic interpretation coming from Tyconius and Augustine was not without its apocalyptic imaginations.[3]

Islam, the Vikings, and the End Time

Christian end-time views were not the only ones known to Europeans in the Middle Ages. In the seventh century after Christ a new religion emerged in Arabia. Led by the prophet Muhammad, this new religion blazed through the Mediterranean area like a wildfire. Within one hundred years Islam dominated the world from the Atlantic Ocean, including parts of Europe, to central Asia. Islam has provided the grist for many end-time predictions. During the Middle Ages and the Reformation Era, many Christians in fact viewed the forces of Islam as the Antichrist.

On the other hand, the Koran, Islam's holy book, has its own predictions about the end of the world. The Koran sets no specific date for the end, but says that the time is near. While Muhammad was vague in predicting when the end would come, he described the final judgment in graphic terms. The sun will darken; seas will dry up; mountains will crumble. The righteous and believers will go to heaven; the sinful and disbelievers will roast in hell.[4]

Warm climates have no corner on predictions of the end of the world. In the cold of northern Europe the early Vikings spawned several end-time stories, the most famous of which is that of *Ragnarok*. These legends may go way back, but the records date to only A.D. 800. These end-time predictions are found in the Norse poems, the Eddas. Of all the end-of-the-world scenarios, that of the Norseman may be the most violent and complete. Even the gods are not spared. "The gods are doomed, and the end is death," say the Eddas. A dramatic, crushing climax takes place in which the world is destroyed.[5]

Stirrings in the Early Middle Ages

Tuveson's contention that apocalyptic ideas slumbered during the Middle Ages best applies to the early years—400 to 1100. During this period no forceful apocalyptic movement arose. Rather, there were pockets of apocalyptic voices.

Apocalyptic visions often arise during times of crisis, and there were crises during the early Middle Ages. But the official nonmillenarian view of the Western Catholic Church often muted the voices of doom and prevented the rise of a major apocalyptic movement. Some individuals did, however, see the collapse of the Roman Empire in the West as a sign of the end. They regarded Rome as the force in 2 Thessalonians 2:7 that restrained evil. Now that Rome was gone, the Antichrist would emerge on the scene. The collapse of Rome also approximated the year 500, the time Hippolytus had predicted for the end of the world.[6]

In the early Middle Ages, people saw the Antichrist several ways—as evil within, an individual, or a collective entity. Thus invasions or threat of invasions from the Huns, Muslims, Magyars, and after 1100 from the Mongols and Turks prompted visions of the Antichrist and his hordes— the peoples of Gog and Magog. A strong ruler could be viewed two ways. If he was tyrannical, he stirred up images of the Antichrist. If seen as a force for good, he might be viewed as the last world emperor—the one who would do battle with the Antichrist.[7]

Sibyl's Crystal Ball

The literature of Hellenistic Judaism included some prophetic books known as the Sibylline Oracles. As early as the eighth century B.C., the Greeks had a prophetess called Sibyl. The surviving prophetic books are, however, part of Hellenistic Judaism and belong primarily to the period from 200 B.C. to A.D. 200.[8] Their influence extends well into the Middle Ages, so much so that when printing was invented, they were one of the first books to be published. In fact, the Sibylline Oracles' influence on prophecy in the Middle Ages is second only to that of the Bible.[9]

The Sibylline Oracles were preoccupied with the end. Their pages echo with end-time themes—attacks on Jews (and later Christians), war, divine judgment, destruction, the coming of a Messiah, and a glorious future. To the delight of apocalyptists, the Sibylline books were extremely flexible. They could be interpreted to suit the times. In fact, they have been described as "religion's lowest common denominator," meaning that they were interpreted and even rewritten as circumstances dictated.[10]

As the years progressed, the oracles became more specific, often spelling out the details of impending annihilation or the end of the world. However, it was their legend of the emperor of the last days that had the greatest impact. When Christianity became legalized, the oracles acclaimed Constantine to be the messianic king. His son Constans I was a staunch supporter of the church. But he was murdered. The oracles predicted that he would return from the dead and usher in the golden age. Constans would reign as the emperor of the last days and eventually turn his power over to God. But before this could take place, the

Antichrist had to be defeated in a terrible final battle. At that point Christ would return.[11]

As time passed, people grew tired of the Constans story. So they updated the Sibylline Oracles and designated other kings as the emperor of the last days. Such adaptability was a key factor in the staying power and popularity of the oracles. For over a thousand years the legend of the last world emperor fascinated the people of Europe.[12]

One Sibylline oracle—the "Pseudo-Methodius"—is perhaps the most important end-time writing of the early Middle Ages. In fact, it is "arguably the most important Christian apocalyptic text after the Apocalypse of John."[13] Written in the seventh century in the Byzantine Empire, this document portrays the tensions caused by the Islamic conquests. Among several new wrinkles it introduces into Western apocalyptic thinking, the "Pseudo-Methodius" identifies the Muslims as one of Christ's end-time opponents—a theme that continued into the seventeenth century. The "Pseudo-Methodius" also contains the first detailed account of the struggle between the last emperor and the Antichrist.[14] Humanity now had two redeemers to fight the Antichrist: a mortal emperor who returns from the dead and Christ himself. Throughout the Middle Ages deceased kings keep resurfacing as the last emperor. Camelot's King Arthur, Frederick Barbarossa, Portugal's King Sebastian, and others were each at one time expected to hear the summons and return to rescue humankind. The story of the last emperor, of course, cannot be found in the Bible, yet the "Pseudo-Methodius" argues that the last emperor is the restraining force of 2 Thessalonians.[15]

Who Is the Antichrist?

The Antichrist is first mentioned in 1 and 2 John. Hippolytus (170–236) interpreted the Antichrist allegorically as being one of the Roman emperors—Nero or Domitian—or any of a number of heretics. Tyconius identified the Antichrist as any of the church's members who performed evil works. (Centuries later this view culminated in the identification of the pope as Antichrist.)[16] But about 950 a monk named Adso gave the most complete description of the Antichrist to date. The Antichrist will be the opposite of Christ in every respect: wicked, proud, deceitful, blasphemous, exalting vices. The Antichrist will be born in Babylon of the Jewish tribe of Dan. He will be instructed in the black arts and perform great miracles. Calling himself God, the Antichrist will reign for three-and-one-half years, persecuting and killing Christians before God comes to judge the world.[17]

What Happened in A.D. 1000?

"In the last night of the year 999 crowds of people singing and praying, waving torches and palm branches, filled the streets and squares of Rome. . . . When the fatal hour struck, the crowd remained transfixed, barely daring to breathe."[18] Such an account captures the imagination and even seems plausible. Unfortunately, it does not jibe with historical evidence. Such pictures are usually drawn from the *Histories* of Raoul Glaber, a Burgundian monk who lived at the turn of the millennium, but generations of medieval historians have examined a broader range of evidence and have argued otherwise.[19] They concede that for decades before and after the year 1000, ordinary believers and some clergy feared the rise of the Antichrist. Still, "there is no evidence that concerns about Antichrist and the end time greatly increased at this time."[20] Moreover, most Christians lacked a precise calendar for even noting the arrival of a new millennium.[21] Not until after 1200 did Western intellectuals begin to develop an exact sense of chronology. And when they did, end-time predictions became more exact. From the thirteenth century to the seventeenth century, Christians moved from a vague sense of the end to more-precise apocalyptic predictions.

End-Time Panic in the Late Middle Ages

Apocalyptic millennialism smoldered on the fringes of early medieval society, only to burst forth after 1100. Previously it existed in popular religion and in many sects. Now apocalyptic millennialism found a home in several of the acknowledged orders of the church. The presence of millenarian ideas in institutionalized Catholicism presented a serious challenge to the church.[22]

Why the Panic?

Why did apocalyptic expectations explode in the late Middle Ages? Apocalyptic thinking emerges during times of change, stress, anxiety, and disasters. The years from 1100 to 1500 experienced all of these and more. This was an era of complex political, social, and intellectual changes that eventually led to the Protestant Reformation. The gradual breakup of the religious and political unity of Western Europe produced an atmosphere charged with apocalyptic expectations. As the church's grip on religious beliefs began to loosen, there was an upsurge of radical millenarian movements.[23]

The Crusades, beginning in 1095, were not a result of apocalypticism. Instead, they stimulated apocalyptic thinking. The rise of Muslim power after 1000 terrified many Europeans and contributed to Islam's image as the Antichrist. The fact that the holy city of Jerusalem was in Muslim hands conjured up apocalyptic visions of the last battle. Many medieval Christians believed that heresy—including Islam and Judaism—had to be stamped out before the end. Also, the Crusades dovetailed with the myth of the last emperor. The public identified him with several rulers—Charlemagne, Louis VII, Frederick II—who were expected to rescue Jerusalem.[24]

Several natural disasters also fostered end-time anxieties. Christians in the Middle Ages—as they do today—felt that any widespread disaster could be a precursor of Christ's second coming. The Black Death reached Europe in 1347. Its impact on apocalyptic thought has been exaggerated. Nevertheless, "many in Western Europe took the plague to be an eschatological sign." Believing that certain events—such as the reign of the Antichrist—must precede the end of the world, "many thought that the Black Death signalled God's displeasure" and in some way pointed to the end.[25] Other natural disasters such as earthquakes and famines also contributed to apocalyptic fears.

Perhaps the greatest impulse for the rise of millenarianism was the various reform movements. A partial list would include the Great Reform inaugurated by Pope Gregory VII, which settled the issue of leadership in Christian society, and the monastic reform movements—Cluniac, Cistercian, Carthusian, Franciscan, and Dominican. These movements gained a momentum beyond the intentions of their originators. They responded to the spiritual hunger of the masses and in doing so stimulated an interest in eschatology and apocalypticism.[26]

The Millennium and Antichrist

In fact, these reform movements contributed some new wrinkles to millennial thought. On one hand, the medieval millennialists were not premillennialists as were the chiliasts of the early church, who believed that Christ would return before the golden age. Instead, the millennialists of the Middle Ages usually held that Christ would return after the millennium—a view that resembled the postmillennialism of a later era.[27] On the other hand, the medieval people normally did not spiritualize the end-time events as did Augustine. There were to be a literal Antichrist and a golden age (variously believed to be 500, 890, 1,000, or 1,400 years). The medieval millennialists also adopted another feature common to modern premillennialists. The Antichrist was usually seen as a single human being—not a collective evil. Further, they expected the Antichrist to appear before the millennium. But unlike modern premillennialism the medieval reformers equated the Antichrist with someone who opposed needed religious changes. Modern premillennialism tends to see him more as a political or military figure.[28]

The sense of an impending end gripped the Middle Ages. Yet this imminent doom was not usually associated with the second advent. As death stared every medieval person in the face, the end-time event expected by most people was the unveiling of the Antichrist. People in the Middle Ages set dates for the coming of the Antichrist, not Jesus Christ. Based on a variety of calculations, the years 1184, 1229, 1260, 1300, 1325, 1335, 1346, 1365, 1387, 1396, and 1400 were proposed. The passing of the proposed date for the cataclysmic event obviously did not discourage future date-setting.[29]

Merlin the Seer

If there were a hall of fame for medieval prophets, three names would certainly make the list—the Sibyl, Merlin, and Joachim. Geoffrey of Monmouth's (1100–1155) masterful *History of the Kings of Britain* made the legendary sixth-century seer Merlin famous. It wove together a mass of legendary material about the British kings and made some sense of the stories about Merlin. Basic to Geoffrey's glorification of the British kings was his account of the rule of King Arthur.[30]

Woven into the Arthur narrative is the story of Merlin Ambrosius. The child of a princess and a demon incubus (an evil spirit who has sex with a sleeping woman), Merlin was a prophet and magician who allegedly brought Stonehenge from Ireland to England.[31] A shadowy figure who traveled throughout Europe, he made many predictions about numerous subjects. Eventually he began to make prophecies regarding eschatological subjects, including the last world emperor. This good champion, as Merlin called him, was to take the Holy Land from the Muslims and then conquer Rome and Italy. In the twelfth and thirteenth centuries Merlin's fame spread rapidly.[32]

Joachim of Fiore and the New Age

Joachim of Fiore (ca. 1135–1202) burst upon the medieval scene and dramatically changed how Western Europeans viewed the end of time. A biblical scholar and Cistercian abbot from Sicily, he was the most original apocalyptic thinker of the Middle Ages. Joachim invented a new prophetic system that proved to be the most influential in Europe until Marxism. He developed one of the most unique theories of history in the Western tradition.[33] The fountainhead for most late medieval eschatological speculations, he also indirectly influenced such ideas right down to the present day.[34] Abbot Joachim's theory of three ages of historical evolution impacted many future philosophies, including those of Gotthold Lessing, Friedrich Schelling, Johann Fichte, Georg Hegel, Auguste Comte, and Karl Marx. Even the modern New Age movement claims Joachim as their predecessor. New Agers believe that the coming new age will share characteristics with Joachim's third stage.[35]

Joachim's prophecies grew out of his historical context and reflected two of its tendencies. First, the late twelfth century was a time of reform and innovation. Joachim was himself a reformer who desired change in the church. His creative prophetic speculations encompassed a new vision and a new direction for the church. Second, the late twelfth century was largely optimistic about the future. Joachim sensed an imminent crisis in history: something big was about to happen. But he was optimistic—he saw history evolving toward an age of peace and spiritual attainment.[36]

Joachim had a complex sense of history, the world, and the end of time—all interpreted through his view of the Trinity. He saw the Trinity as built into the very fabric of time. Thus he divided history into three overlapping ages or *status*—the ages of the Father, the Son, and the Holy Spirit.[37] These three ages roughly corresponded with the Old Testament, the Christian Era until Joachim's day, and the new age to come. But Joachim's scheme was much more complex than this. Not only did these *status* overlap, but they also had long periods of incubation. For example, the incubation period for the third stage began with Benedict of Nursia (ca. 480–547).[38] Now, some seven hundred years later, this incubation stage between the ages of the Son and Holy Spirit was nearing a close. Joachim interpreted the political and religious events of his day as the last gasp of the second stage. The struggle between the church and the empire and the resurgence of Islam convinced him.[39]

Noting that the Gospel of Matthew recorded forty-two generations from Adam to Christ, Joachim believed that this figure held true for each age. Allowing thirty years for each generation, he placed the end of the second stage between 1200 and 1260. But before the third age would come in, the Antichrist had to reign for three-and-one-half years. In an interview with Richard the Lion-Hearted in 1191, Joachim said that the Antichrist had already been born.[40] After the defeat of the Antichrist, the age of the Holy Spirit would be ushered in. This third age would be far less rational and institutional and more spiritual. A purified church would rule over a peaceful, contemplative, monastic world. The Holy Spirit would speak to people mystically, and humankind would experience God directly and become like him.[41]

Joachim was neither a revolutionary nor a millennialist in any strict sense. He did not desire the downfall of the Catholic Church. Rather, his thinking was evolutionary. Joachim desired to purify and transform the church from a life of activity to one of contemplation. He envisioned a reformed and purified Christendom as the goal of this evolutionary process.[42] Yet, in respect to end-time thinking, Joachim turned Europe upside down. While he may not have been a radical, he set some revolutionary ideas in motion. Most important, "Joachim broke decisively with the Tyconian-Augustinian tradition of interpreting the Apocalypse allegorically and instead interpreted it historically."[43] In many circles the apocalyptic images of Daniel, Ezekiel, and Revelation—Antichrist, millennium, Gog and Magog—were no longer spiritualized, but were regarded as real people and events.

The Franciscan Spirituals

The Lateran Council of 1215 condemned aspects of Joachim's theology. Yet in the next three hundred years few eschatological writings escaped the imprint of his ideas. More often than not, the Joachites, as they were called, espoused ideas more radical than those of Joachim. Some Franciscans and Dominicans saw themselves as the barefoot spiritual men predicted by Joachim. Other apocalyptic writers identified Emperor Frederick II with the Antichrist.[44]

Of the two great mendicant orders, the radical aspects of Joachim's ideas infected the Franciscans more than the Dominicans. Between 1220 and 1260 the Franciscans divided into two parties—the Conventionals and the Spirituals. The Spirituals, who were more drawn to apocalyptic ideas, began reading Joachim's writings, and Franciscan Joachitism began.[45]

While the Spirituals accepted most of Joachim's ideas, they believed him to be wrong on one count: the third age did not begin with Benedict of Nursia, but with Francis of Assisi in the thirteenth century. They regarded Francis as so unique that he represented a turning point in history. Adopting Joachim's formula of forty-two generations and thirty years per generation, the Spirituals viewed the year 1260 as the beginning of the end. Of course, at that time they would take on the role of the Catholic Church and become the spiritual leaders of the new age.[46]

The year 1260 came and went. The moderate Franciscans tended to back off from eschatological speculations. But the Spiritualists or Zealots turned to a passionate mysticism and became more fanatical in their apocalyptic outlook. Believing themselves to be involved in a cosmic conflict, they vividly described the wonders of the new age and their conflicts with the Antichrist. They even went as far as to identify as the Antichrist the various popes who opposed them.[47]

49

The Franciscan Peter Olivi (ca. 1248–98) built on Joachim's three ages and divided the church's history into seven periods. He also believed in a "double Antichrist—the Mythical Antichrist, a coming false pope who would attack the Franciscan Rule, and the Great, or Open Antichrist, whose defeat would usher in the final period of history."[48]

The papacy attempted to repress the Spirituals. But they survived in various forms—the Beguines, Beghards, and the Fraticelli. The Fraticelli in Italy carried Joachim's ideas to their greatest extreme, declaring heretical those religious orders that did not practice a life of absolute poverty. One of the most fervently millenarian groups in medieval Europe, they declared Pope John XXII the Antichrist.[49]

Frederick II: Messiah or Antichrist?

Emperor Frederick II Hohenstaufen (1194–1250) strode across the medieval scene and became bigger than life. To some, especially the Germans, he was a savior—the last world emperor. To others, particularly the Italians, he was the Antichrist. Frederick's personality encouraged such speculations—at once brilliant, capable, proud, and cruel. Several generations of apocalypticism and social unrest linked with a bitter territorial and political struggle between the papacy and German rulers produced the myth of Frederick II.[50]

The story of the last emperor had been around for centuries. With Frederick II it became attached to an actual ruler who controlled considerable territory, embracing much of Germany, Burgundy, and Italy. The myth took off when Frederick went on a crusade and recaptured Jerusalem in 1229, crowning himself king of that city.[51]

The pseudo-Joachim writings that pointed to 1260 as the end of the age now focused on Frederick. But he died in 1250, and the legend took a new form: Frederick would return at the end of time and establish a rule of righteousness. Thus Frederick's death was a beginning, not an end. This legend spread like wildfire across the German states and elsewhere in the fourteenth century.[52]

But this is only one side of the myth. Embroiled in a bitter conflict with the emperor, the papacy excommunicated Frederick several times as a blasphemer, perjurer, and heretic. In turn, he threatened to remove from the church the wealth that, as he claimed, caused its corruption. The Franciscan Spirituals saw Frederick as the necessary chastiser of the clergy. Though an indispensable step for the inauguration of the third age, this role of Frederick's was viewed as the devil's work. Thus, both the papacy and its critics, especially the Spiritualists, declared Frederick II to be Antichrist.[53]

The Suffering Flagellants

The spectacle of people beating themselves until they bleed boggles the modern Western mind. But it happened in the Middle Ages. In order to win divine forgiveness, people engaged in self-flagellation—the practice of scourging oneself in imitation of the sufferings of Christ.

After a famine in 1258 and a plague in 1259, bands of men and boys roamed around Italy wailing and beating themselves with iron-spiked leather whips. Many of them were Joachites who expected the end to come in 1260. When this failed to materialize, the flagellant movement declined in Italy. But it crossed the Alps into northern Europe. In the fourteenth century the Black Death and serious food shortages again whipped many Europeans into an apocalyptic frenzy. The flagellants were perhaps the most bizarre expression of this hysteria.[54]

How many of the flagellants were millenarians is a matter of debate.[55] Undoubtedly, some did penance in hope of simply warding off the plague, not ushering in a millennium. Nonetheless, they were apocalyptists in their belief that they were in a holy war. In fact, they slaughtered Jews who they were convinced had caused the plague by poisoning the water. Many flagellants interpreted the horrible calamities of their age as miseries that were to precede the end, whatever form it might take.[56]

The Apocalyptic Taborites

In the early fifteenth century, Bohemia exploded in revolution. A mixture of Czech nationalism, economic deprivations, and social inequalities combined to produce a violent apocalyptic movement—the Taborites, who, according to Bernard McGinn, were the only "textbook case . . . of radical millenarianism" in the Middle Ages.[57] Fomenting the revolution was the fact that while the population was Slavic, the higher clergy in Bohemia were largely German, enormously wealthy, and corrupt. Against this situation Czech preachers began to stir up the people. The most prominent of these preachers was Jan Hus (1371–1415). A professor at the University of Prague, Hus was fiercely antipapal, even labeling the pope as Antichrist. As a result of this and other doctrinal challenges to the church, he was burned as a heretic.[58]

Hus was more dangerous dead than alive. A widespread movement named after him developed. These Hussites were far more extreme than Hus himself. The Hussite movement eventually divided into two wings. The Utraquists were more conservative. While they challenged the Catholic Church on religious issues, they did not break from the church and drew back from social and economic change. But the radical wing, the Taborites, ventured down the path of extremism and revolution.[59]

The Taborites took their name from Mount Tabor, the mountain where they believed Christ foretold his second coming. They introduced a revolutionary doctrine—nothing in religion could be true unless it was found in the Bible. Supposedly, this belief freed their minds from all theological speculation. They also rejected priestly ordination, assuming that clergy and laity were equal.[60]

From the beginning the Taborites were a millennial group. They passively waited for the end in February 1420. When this expectation proved false, they became a revolutionary millenarian movement—seeing themselves as the warriors of God. They formed armies to fight what they believed was God's battle. The religious revolution now became a holy war, with some radicals even urging that evildoers be exterminated.[61]

In the conviction that the end was near, the Taborites' millennialism became more radical. They organized themselves into communal groups patterned after the early church. Under the influence of end-time messages, many Bohemians sold their possessions and fled to the Taborite towns, which they believed would be spared from the judgment. Some even attempted to hasten the end by launching armed attacks on their opponents. The Taborite forces did reasonably well until their crushing defeat in 1434.[62]

Actually, the Taborites were not the most radical Hussite group. The Pikarts, better known as Adamites, were a heresy within Taborism. The Pikarts vaguely embraced a pantheistic concept of God. Denying original sin and the existence of Satan, they believed that they were fully redeemed and good.[63] The Adamites lived as if all prophecies had been fulfilled and the millennium had already begun. In the belief that they were like Christ and as innocent as Adam and Eve in Paradise, they wore no clothes, even in cold weather. They engaged in sexual promiscuity, prohibiting marriage and holding that all men possessed all women in common. Owning no property themselves, they believed that they had the right to seize other people's possessions. Thus they attacked neighboring villages, taking whatever they wanted and ruthlessly killing the inhabitants. The Adamites' savage and lewd behavior proved so shocking that a Hussite army exterminated them.[64]

The Fiery Savonarola

Fifteenth-century Italy experienced a powerful surge of apocalypticism. Wandering prophets preached imminent destruction. The best-known of these prophets, Girolamo Savonarola (1452–98), was a millenarian in the sense of expecting an imminent improvement on earth before the last judgment. Savonarola was also a good example of linking prophecy and politics, for he fashioned apocalypticism into a political ideology.[65]

Social and political turmoil in Italy prompted Savonarola to view the world as a battleground between good and evil. He saw the last days approaching and predicted a disaster for Florence and Italy. But if the Florentines would repent, the catastrophe could be headed off. The Antichrist was about to appear, but he would be defeated, and the Turks and pagans would be converted. In all of this, Florence and Savonarola had a special role. Florence would be Zion, the city of God; and, of course, Savonarola would be its prophet.[66]

In 1494 Savonarola succeeded in establishing a theocratic government in Florence. But this dream came to an abrupt end. Savonarola thought that Charles VIII of France might be the last world emperor. Military defeats dashed this hope, however, and the papacy opposed Savonarola's apocalyptic views. In addition, political and economic problems eroded his power base among the Florentine masses. The ruling Medicis regained control, and the secular authorities executed Savonarola in 1498.[67]

In general, during the Middle Ages there were three approaches to the end. The official church position spiritualized the millennium and identified it with the church. The end would come in the form of the last judgment and then the eternal state. The church thus maintained a non-millennial position. Still, this did not mean that the end of the world was not imminent. Many who upheld the official church doctrine believed that the world would end soon. Modern observers have described this official church position as amillennialism.[68]

Unofficially, a strong current of apocalyptic millennialism erupted in the late Middle Ages. In general, the chiliasts believed that the Antichrist would appear and be defeated. After his defeat and the turmoil associated with it, there would be a golden age of an indefinite length, followed by the return of Christ.

A third strand—the secular apocalyptic—becomes barely discernible during the Middle Ages. The vast majority of the Europeans attributed the Black Death to divine judgment. But as time went on, there were repeated outbreaks of the plague, striking both the righteous and evildoers alike. Some people began to wonder: Did God do all of this? Very gradually some educated individuals began to seek natural causes for such disasters. To be sure, the exact cause of the Black Death was not determined until the twentieth century. But a new factor emerged in endtime thinking—natural causes.

To a large degree, historical forces determined the shape millennialism took in the Middle Ages. The early Middle Ages were not without chaos. But as long as Christendom remained a unity and the Catholic Church maintained a strong grip on society, the nonmillennial orthodoxy held sway. Fringe groups with their wild-eyed apocalyptic ideas were kept in check.

Augustine's nonmillennialism remained the official position of the Catholic Church throughout the late Middle Ages. But the apocalyptic groups could no longer be corralled. Apocalypticism erupted with a vengeance. Joachim of Fiore's ideas opened Pandora's box. And millennial thinking has not been the same since. The critical events of the late Middle Ages—persecution, crop failures, the Black Death, social upheavals, and reform movements—all combined to produce a growing sense of apocalypticism in the late Middle Ages.

4

The On-Again, Off-Again Apocalypse: The Reformation and Beyond

"We have reached the time of the white (pale) horse of the Apocalypse. This world will not last any more, if God wills it, than another hundred years," wrote Martin Luther.[1] Luther believed that he was living in the last days. During the sixteenth century and for much of the seventeenth, many Europeans shared this expectancy—some more fervently than Luther. Modified versions of the two medieval eschatological patterns had carried over into the Reformation and beyond. Luther and some other Reformers largely accepted the official nonmillenarian eschatology of the Catholic Church, but added some apocalyptic dimensions to it. The fervent apocalypticism of the medieval millennialists also spilled over into the sixteenth and seventeenth centuries.

As the seventeenth century wound down, so did the fervent apocalyptic expectancy. To be sure, the eighteenth and nineteenth centuries experienced some lively millennial movements. In addition, many individuals declared that the end was near, and designations of specific individuals as the Antichrist continued to be made. Natural disasters and political upheavals still stirred up apocalyptic imaginations. Terminal visions of a secular sort became more prominent. Nevertheless, when compared to the preceding two hundred years, European society in the years after 1700 experienced fewer end-time anxieties.

Why did apocalyptic eschatology wane in Europe? In part, the supernatural worldview of previous centuries underwent a change. The late seventeenth century saw the rise of deism—the religion of many educated Europeans that called into question the supernatural aspects of Christianity. Also, by the late seventeenth century, phenomena such as witchcraft, magic, omens, prophecies, and astrology were generally on a decline. Many educated Europeans now questioned their validity.[2] The Age of Reason had begun to undercut such beliefs. Because millennial and apocalyptic ideas embrace a supernatural worldview, they too experienced decline. For the apocalyptic mentality to thrive, calamities must appear to be unexplainable. But science could now explain many of the disasters that people encountered.[3]

Among other factors in the decline of apocalypticism, the Industrial Revolution improved the material aspects of life. Famines and disease were less pronounced. The doctrine of progress said that life was getting better, and people believed it. God did not seem interested in destroying the world, and humankind had not yet devised the means to do so. Though millennial movements do exist in such a context, they are usually a variation of postmillennialism, which sees the end of the world only in the distant future.

Consider as well that the secularization of life tends to reduce the sacred apocalyptic. In nineteenth-century Europe, God no longer occupied center stage. People were no longer preoccupied with the world to come—the Antichrist, millennium, and the judgment. To be sure, there is such a phenomenon as a secular apocalyptic, but it had not yet come into full swing.[4]

New Worlds and the End Time

Clearly, there were great diversity and movement of thought in the years from the Reformation to World War I. At the beginning of this era people focused on the fact that Jesus Christ had told his followers that "the gospel must first be published among all nations" (Mark 13:10) before he would return. The prophetic traditions growing out of Revelation and the Sibylline Oracles similarly said that before Christ's kingdom could be established, the entire world must be converted to Christianity. Such a conviction provided impetus for the conversion of Europe.[5]

After the Christianization of Europe, the Catholic Church began to look east. The gospel had already been preached in North Africa. For medieval Christians the rest of the world—as they knew it—was Asia. Thus church leaders suggested that part of God's plan was the conversion of Asia before the end of the world. Such a belief helped fuel the discovery of the New World, which came as a by-product of the quest for Asia.[6]

One individual motivated by the desire to hasten Christ's return was Christopher Columbus (1451–1506). On his fourth voyage (1502) he penned a mystical-apocalyptical *Book of Prophecies*. In this book and in an autobiographical letter intended to be its introduction, Columbus told of two religious motivations for his voyages—the reconquest of Jerusalem from Islam and the conversion of the heathen in the East.[7]

Columbus believed that he and Spain were on a millennial venture. This accorded with a Joachimite prophecy circulating in Franciscan circles: "he who will restore the ark of Zion will come from Spain."[8] In Columbus's view the preconditions for the return of Christ included reconquest of the Holy Land and spreading of the gospel. His voyage west would thus have a twofold effect on his apocalyptic expectations. He would acquire enough gold and wealth to finance Spain's reconquest of Jerusalem, and he would take missionaries to Asia to Christianize the East.[9]

Apocalyptic Visions during the Reformation

Apocalyptic ideas and activities increase during times of stress and upheavals. The sixteenth century was such a time. Beginning with the discoveries of Columbus, the wheels of change spun faster and faster, affecting nearly every area of life—the social, economic, political, and religious. This was a time of great religious experimentation and intense religious activity. Thus many new religious movements were spawned.

As a result, the years from about 1500 to 1650 were charged with apocalyptic expectations. Europeans believed that they were living in the perilous last times. When a summer storm approaches, there are signs in the sky—dark rumbling clouds, lightning flashes, and sudden eerie stillness. People read these signs and take appropriate shelter. The same is true with eschatology. The sixteenth century had many "calendarizers"—people who make end-time calculations. They saw the events of their time in the light of Daniel, Revelation, and even astrological predictions. Many Europeans concluded that they were standing on the extreme edge of time.[10]

Each of the three major religious groups in Europe during the sixteenth century—the mainstream Protestants, the Radicals, and Catholics—had their eschatological distinctive. The Radicals produced some violent millennial movements that shocked all of Europe. Some mainstream Protestant Reformers de-emphasized eschatology, but others articulated nonmillenarian apocalyptic ideas, especially in their scathing attacks on the papacy. In response, Catholic thinkers countered with their own eschatological perspective.

Radical Upheavals

The Radical Reformation had little cohesiveness. It was largely a group of sects that revolted against Rome but did not fit the Protestant patterns. In general, the Radicals felt that the Lutheran and Zwinglian reforms had not gone far enough. Of these diverse groups, the Anabaptists and Spiritualists generated the most notable apocalyptic upheavals.[11]

The Anabaptists took Luther's and Zwingli's teachings a step further. To the mainstream Protestant call for religious reforms, the Anabaptists added social and political changes that challenged the very fabric of society. As a result, they experienced persecution at the hands of both Catholics and Protestants alike. While the Anabaptists shared the general apocalyptic mood of the sixteenth century, this persecution intensified their end-time expectations.

"All Anabaptists were united in their conviction that the return of Christ was near," and that "Christ and Antichrist were locked in the final struggle."[12] Conrad Grebel warned that the Messiah was about to return. The monster persecuting the church would soon be destroyed, said Michael Sattler. Amid intense persecution Jacob Hutter's letters and Menno Simons's writings indicate that they expected the end to come soon. While the Anabaptists increasingly interpreted their sufferings in apocalyptic terms—as the last onslaught of Satan against the saints—the vast majority quietly waited for Christ to return. There were two major exceptions to this peaceful anticipation—Thomas Müntzer and the debacle at Münster.[13]

Thomas Müntzer (ca. 1488–1525) shot across the Reformation sky like a meteor—bright and flashy but short-lived. Müntzer was one of history's pure revolutionaries. Most revolutionaries have some restraints; Müntzer did not. He believed that the Holy Spirit spoke directly to him and that he was God's instrument for purging the ungodly. Technically, Müntzer was neither a Lutheran, a Zwinglian, nor an Anabaptist. Somewhat like Jim Jones and David Koresh of our day, no one would claim him. Only the modern-day Marxists love him and make a hero out of him. George Williams's classification of Müntzer as a revolutionary Spiritualist comes close to the mark.[14]

Müntzer began as a follower of Luther. But Luther was too tame for him. Luther's doctrine of justification by faith alone did not excite Müntzer. On the other hand, Taborite doctrines and bloodthirsty millenarian beliefs that had crept into Germany from Bohemia propelled Müntzer into action.[15] His chance came when peasants, artisans, and miners who had been spurred on by Luther's religious reforms demanded even more changes. They sought the rectification of economic and social grievances associated with the old feudal order. In some localities violence broke out into the so-called Peasants' War of 1525. While he did not incite this rebellion, Müntzer joined the fray and brought an apocalyptic dimension to it.[16]

Müntzer was a well-educated, spellbinding speaker with an apocalyptic vision. He had little real interest in redressing the peasants' grievances. Rather, the end times had become an obsession with him. The last days were at hand, and Müntzer's program was a war of extermination against the ungodly. While he believed in a future millennium, Müntzer's emphasis was on the violent war that would usher in the golden age.[17]

Using apocalyptic language from Daniel and Revelation, Müntzer incited the peasants to new levels of violence. In a fiery speech at the climactic battle of Frankenhausen, Müntzer infused the peasants with confidence. He reputedly told of a vision in which God had promised them victory. Müntzer himself would catch the enemy's cannonballs in his coat sleeves. The appearance of a rainbow was seen as a confirmation that a miracle was to take place. The rebels sang hymns, expecting Christ to return and lead them to triumph. However, the German princes crushed them, and Müntzer was beheaded.[18]

The next episode of violent apocalypticism occurred in the northwestern German city of Münster. But this story begins a little earlier with Melchior Hofmann (ca. 1495–1543), a persistent "calendarizer" who set several dates for Christ's return. Similar to Joachim of Fiore, he divided Christian history into three periods, the third beginning with the Reformation. As time went on, Hofmann's theology drifted toward millenarianism.[19] Considering himself a prophet of the end time, Hofmann preached the imminence of the final judgment. In the process he won many followers, called Melchiorites. However, Hofmann was different from Müntzer—he rejected the use of force. Hofmann predicted that Christ would come in 1533. After the slaughter of unbelievers, Strasbourg would become the New Jerusalem. When this date failed, he readjusted his calendar, and did so several times thereafter. The Strasbourg authorities put Hofmann in prison, where he died. Yet the end-time expectations he had aroused did not die with him.[20]

When Strasbourg did not become the New Jerusalem, the scene shifted to Münster. The link was Jan Matthys (d. 1534), who had been baptized by one of Hofmann's followers. The Melchiorites being strong in the Netherlands and northwest Germany, apocalyptic views had appeared in Münster even before Matthys arrived. However, Matthys did not follow the way of peace advocated by Hofmann. Instead, he soon became a revolutionary and a fanatic.[21] He quickly dominated Münster and transformed his apocalyptic vision into public policy. He concluded that Hofmann's new age had arrived. Münster would be the New Jerusalem, the refuge for the righteous. Of course, he was to be God's prophet, and the wicked were to be destroyed.[22]

The activities in Münster alarmed both the Protestant and Catholic authorities, and they sent an army to besiege the city. Believing a miracle would happen, Matthys attacked this army with a small band of men and was promptly killed. His successor, John of Leiden (also known as Jan Bochelson), was even more radical. He proclaimed himself the Messiah of the last days and imposed his absolute authority on the people. Münster became akin to an Old Testament theocracy, even practicing polygamy.[23]

The end of the world may not have been at hand—but it certainly was for Münster. The Anabaptists there desired the end to come quickly, because the world was so corrupt. Ironically, the besieging army broke through in 1535, massacring this group of extremists.

The horrible episodes associated with Thomas Müntzer and the city of Münster sent shock waves through Europe. They discredited both the Anabaptists and millenarianism. The Anabaptists retreated to their separatist communities and ceased to engage in further eschatological adventures. Both Protestants and Catholics continued to distrust millennialism of any kind and generally shied away from eschatological speculations.[24]

Mainline Protestantism: The Papacy as Antichrist

The excesses of the Peasants' War and the debacle at Münster influenced the eschatological thinking of the Protestant Reformers. While they made great contributions to the Christian faith, their end-time ideas were shaped by the events of their age. They pulled back from millenarianism in stark horror. No major Reformer was a millennialist. Some, such as Calvin and Zwingli, were even antiapocalyptists and said little about end-time events.

Nonetheless, a definite Protestant apocalyptic tradition did develop in the sixteenth century. Several general characteristics of this tradition can be noted:

1. The Protestant Reformers either spiritualized the millennium or believed that it had already occurred.

2. Nearly all Reformers regarded the papacy as Antichrist. The Turks, who threatened Europe at this time, were seen as in league with the Antichrist—perhaps they were to be identified with Gog or Magog.
3. Many Protestants used the historicist method to interpret the Book of Revelation; they matched the symbols of Revelation with various periods in church history.
4. The Reformers usually adopted an apocalyptic view of history, seeing it as a cosmic conflict between the forces of God and Satan.
5. The Protestant apocalyptists insisted that they were living at the end of time. A few were moderate date-setters, vaguely predicting when the world would end. They believed that the world would last six thousand years—and this time was about up.

In the conviction that he was living at the end of time, Luther's theology was thoroughly eschatological. Several themes emerge from Luther's thinking on the last days. In the Middle Ages many people had designated a particular pope or ruler as Antichrist, but they did not regard the institution of the papacy itself as Antichrist. In fact, some medieval reformers looked for the angel pope to set things right. To the contrary, John Wyclif (ca. 1329–84), the English Reformer, linked the papal institution with the Antichrist. Building on Wyclif's thinking, Luther spoke of the papal institution as Antichrist. This view became the norm in Protestant circles.[25] Luther also made nasty remarks about the Turks, regarding them as an instrument of the Antichrist. He even designated them as Gog, but only the papacy could be the Antichrist.[26]

Luther also revived the historicist interpretation of the Book of Revelation. He maintained that the prophecies found in the Apocalypse had historical significance for two periods: the early church before Constantine and Luther's own age. This limited periodization of Revelation led to Luther's identification of the Antichrist with the papacy and to the conclusion that the end of history was imminent.[27]

In many ways Luther built on the reformist tradition of the Middle Ages. But he rejected its millennialism. He did not look forward to a golden age. In other respects Luther was somewhat inconsistent on the subject. At times he spiritualized the millennium; on other occasions he spoke of the millennium as being past—it had begun with the early church and ended with the rise of the Turks or with the papacy's becoming Antichrist.[28] Luther saw himself as living in the interval between the millennium and the end of the age. He even engaged in a little harmless date-setting. The world was about 5,500 years old, so the eternal sabbath would begin in about 500 years. But Luther believed that the

Lord would shorten the time for the elect's sake. Thus there might be only about 100 years to go.[29]

A number of other Protestant Reformers echoed Luther's nonmillenarian apocalypticism. They pushed two themes: the papacy was Antichrist, and Christ would return soon. Germany in particular vibrated with apocalyptic excitement. Luther's successor Philipp Melanchthon (1497–1560) viewed many contemporary events as signs that the end was near. More horrors and afflictions were to come, and by 1600 the advance of the Turks would place Germany in the hands of Gog and Magog.[30]

The Reformed tradition witnessed less apocalyptic activity than did the Lutheran. But such thinking was alive and well. For example, John Knox (1514–72), the leader of the Scottish Reformation, vehemently declared the Antichrist to be the papal church and not an individual pope. Moreover, he viewed all of history through apocalyptic spectacles, that is, as a cosmic struggle between the servants of God and Satan.[31] Heinrich Bullinger (1504–75), Zwingli's successor at Zurich, also denounced the papacy as Antichrist. Like Luther, he saw the millennium as past and believed that he was living in the last days when Satan had been unleashed to harass the godly.[32]

The Catholic Position: The Antichrist Is in the Future

The Catholic Church obviously rejected the Protestant claim that the papacy was Antichrist. Some Catholic writers simply reversed the table and designated Luther as the Antichrist. However, most Catholic theologians favored a more sophisticated approach. They insisted that the Antichrist was an individual—not a collective entity—who would appear in the future.

In the Middle Ages even canonized saints had labeled individual popes as Antichrist. This was not as bad as designating the office of the papacy as Antichrist. The church had to distance itself from such thinking. The Jesuits took the lead in this effort. They argued "that the papacy could not be Antichrist because the Last Enemy was a future figure without ties to current events."[33]

Among the Jesuits who insisted that the Antichrist was still to come, the approach of the Spaniard Franciscus Ribeira had significant implications for future millennial thought. Both Catholics and Protestants who identified the Antichrist as a contemporary pope or leader generally took a historicist interpretation of John's Revelation. Ribeira reintroduced a somewhat literal futuristic approach to the Apocalypse of John. In doing so he concluded that the Antichrist was a future renegade Jew.[34] By means of a similar literal futuristic reading of Revelation, many modern premillennialists have arrived at doomsday conclusions.

Nostradamus: God Won't Do It!

> The young lion will overcome the old one
> On the field of battle in a single combat:
> He will put out his eyes in a cage of gold:
> Two fleets one, then to die a cruel death.

Nostradamus's obscure quatrains have intrigued people from the sixteenth century to the present. In fact, his prophecies are currently enjoying an immense popularity—bookstores cannot keep his writings in stock, for his doomsday predictions point to the end of the twentieth century.

Michel de Notredame (1503–66), better known as Nostradamus, reflects the ideas of the French Renaissance—not the Reformation. His parents were prosperous Jews who converted to Christianity. Nostradamus became a physician and spent much time caring for those afflicted with the plague. In time he developed an interest in astrology and prophecy in general. Given the sixteenth century's intense religious hatreds and the fear of sorcery and witchcraft, Nostradamus's occult studies gained for him suspicion and hostility.[35]

By 1550 Nostradamus had become fully engaged in the prophecy business. He began to write almanacs. But he soon embarked upon a project with far-reaching implications—the *Centuries*. Composing prophetic four-line verses, he arranged them in ten books of one hundred verses each—hence the name *Centuries*. Nostradamus's fame rests upon this volume, which contains prophecies from his time to 3797.[36]

The quatrains are not in chronological order. They jump back and forth through history, allegedly prophesying events at different points in time. Moreover, Nostradamus's predictions are couched in obscure, ambiguous symbols—and can thus be interpreted in many ways. To further complicate matters, he does not date his prophecies. Nostradamus's vagueness can in part be attributed to the threat of persecution; it may also be that he enjoyed being mysterious.[37]

Nostradamus's most intriguing predictions pertain to the end of the twentieth century. However, many of his prophecies appear to relate to earlier events—the death of kings, the line of future French monarchs, the French Revolution, the Great Fire of London, World War I, the rise of Hitler, and more. The nature of his prophecies made him a legend in his own time, and nearly every generation since has found his writings relevant. The accuracy of his prophecies is debated. His supporters claim that he was right on target. But his detractors debunk his vague predictions.[38]

Nostradamus is notable for having furthered a different approach to doomsday. Nearly all previous end-time thinkers had expected God to bring an end to the world. But as the Black Death continued to kill the good and bad alike, people began to question this age-old premise. Nostradamus advanced the notion of a secular end of the world. He saw the apocalypse as a political event; the world would end as a result of secular causes. Accordingly, Nostradamus never spoke of a divine judgment or a future paradise.[39]

Millenarianism in England

For much of the sixteenth and seventeenth centuries, apocalyptic excitement gripped England. End-time expectations gradually grew until they peaked in the 1640s. By then England was drunk on the millennium. Ordinary people, not simply the scholars, made end-time calculations. Talk that doomsday or the millennium would arrive on this day or that became common in England. By the mid-seventeenth century there developed a consensus in England that certain events were imminent: the defeat of the Antichrist, the return of Christ, and the start of the millennium.[40] In fact, the label *Antichrist* became so widespread as to almost lose meaning. Before 1640 nearly everyone—including the Church of England—applied the term to the papacy. After 1640 the Puritans began to designate the hierarchy of the Church of England as the Antichrist. In due time radical elements began to label even the Puritan leaders and the entire political structure as Antichrist.[41] At one time or another, many leaders in English society were tagged as the Antichrist.

Apocalyptic expectations often occur during times of turmoil and upheaval. And the England of the sixteenth and seventeenth centuries was just such a time. These centuries witnessed the break from Catholicism, Queen Mary's persecution of Protestants, the defeat of the Spanish Armada, the English Civil War, the beheading of Charles I, and the Thirty Years War on the Continent. Such events were often interpreted in apocalyptic terms and stimulated a millennial explosion in England.

The Sources of Apocalypticism

The tremendous surge in end-time thinking in both England and on the Continent came from several sources. Most apocalyptic beliefs came from the Bible, especially Daniel and Revelation. But Scripture was not the only source. Many devout Christians, especially the date-setters, merged a range of prophetic writings—the Bible, noncanonical pseudo-Christian sources, astrology, and more.

End-time prognosticators tended to blur the distinctions between biblical and nonbiblical prophecy. Included in the apocalyptic mixture were the prophecies of Merlin, the Sibylline Oracles, Nostradamus, and Joachim of Fiore. Among the other sources were the Prophecy of Elias, a third-century prophecy dividing world history into three ages of two thousand years each; the Arcadian dream of harmonious peace; and the prophecies of Mother Shipton—a seeress who allegedly lived in the early sixteenth century.[42]

Most significant, a number of calendarizers included astrological information in their calculations. Medieval Europeans had believed that "the stars were God's instruments and contained a key to the future"; this "traditional link between astrology and the Apocalypse survived the Reformation little changed."[43] The conjuncture of Jupiter and Saturn in 1583 produced many end-time anxieties. The total eclipse of the sun predicted for March 1652 sent apocalyptic shudders throughout Europe. Even the German theologian Johann Alsted and English scholars such as John Napier and Thomas Brightman drew from astrological data and assorted prophets.[44]

Early Anxieties

Continental apocalyptic ideas easily took root in the fertile English soil. Because the English Church had broken from Catholicism, it became easy to point to the papacy as Antichrist. When the Catholic Queen Mary took the throne, many Protestants fled to the Continent, thus coming into contact with continental apocalyptic ideas. Persecution fueled the apocalyptic expectations of these Marian exiles, and upon their return to England they promoted end-time thinking.

These early Puritans shared a number of apocalyptic ideas with the continental Reformers. In no uncertain terms they designated the Roman papacy as the Antichrist. They interpreted the Book of Revelation historically and thus viewed the millennium as a past event—occurring from about 300 to 1300. These Puritans also expected the world to end soon—probably within a hundred years.[45] Just as Luther and Melanchthon did not believe that the world would last much beyond 1600, the English Reformers John Foxe, John Napier, and Robert Pont believed that the year 1600 would mark the beginning of a series of events preparing the world for the last judgment. Other English apocalyptists such as Hugh Broughton, Thomas Brightman, and Sir Walter Raleigh put the end off for a hundred years or more.[46]

The Millennial Explosion

English millennialism peaked in the late 1640s and 1650s and then declined. Millenarian ideas may have been more widely circulated during the English Civil War than at any time or place in history. Social, political, and religious forces all combined to produce this millennial explosion.[47]

From the Reformation onward, many people had interpreted current events in the light of biblical prophecy. The seals, trumpets, and bowls of Revelation were all seen as unfolding before people's eyes. The Reformation paved the way for Christ's return by exposing the papal Antichrist. The defeat of the Spanish Armada in 1588 convinced many that England was God's instrument—the elect nation. The advance of the Turks into Europe horrified many English, persuading them that the hordes of Gog and Magog were at their doorstep.[48]

Continuing this vein of thinking, most contemporary English people saw the Thirty Years War as a religious conflict. When James I and Charles I refused to aid the Protestant cause, disappointment set in. Charles I's marriage to a Catholic bride compounded this feeling. On the domestic level the policies of James and Charles continued to alienate the nation until the Stuart regime collapsed in the 1640s.[49]

Among ecclesiastical figures Archbishop William Laud promoted the Catholic-leaning wing of the Church of England. Not only did he retain many relics of Catholic worship, but he also repressed the Puritan dissenters. The Puritans thus began to regard the Church of England as anti-Christian and in some cases as Antichrist. In despair some Puritans migrated to America; others stayed to resist the unacceptable policies. Wherever they were, the Puritans attached considerable eschatological significance to these events, regarding them as part of a great cosmic conflict.[50]

Not surprisingly, millennial ideas began to change. Previously, the Protestant Reformers had either spiritualized the millennium or seen it as a past event. In the late sixteenth and early seventeenth century, John Napier, Thomas Brightman, Joseph Mede, John Owen, and others began to speak of a future golden age. But for the most part these men were not clear as to when Christ would come. Thus they cannot be categorized as pre- or postmillennialists.[51]

The 1620s seemed to be the watershed in respect to the millennium. Prior to this time the English Puritans hesitated to advocate what the Reformers had labeled as heresy—the idea of a future millennium. But under the influence of the German theologian Johann Alsted, they embraced the ancient doctrine of a future millennium. Alsted predicted that the millennium would begin in 1694.[52]

By the 1630s a sharp line divided those who believed in a past millennium from those who believed in a future millennium. But within the millennial camp other issues were a bit murky. Premillennialists and postmillennialists both believe in a future golden age, yet they differ as to whether Christ will come before or after the millennium. On this count the Puritans were either ambiguous or failed to draw a sharp line.[53] The millenarians also disagreed on the nature of Christ's millennial rule. Some said that Christ would reign spiritually from heaven through his saints. Others insisted that he would rule literally on earth. Still, in the context of the millennial excitement of the day, these differences were insignificant. For "a millenarian was a millenarian regardless of how he explained the advent."[54]

From 1642 to 1660 England witnessed a civil war, the execution of a king, a commonwealth, and a military dictatorship. These events, especially the defeat of Charles I and his beheading, catapulted some radical groups into an apocalyptic frenzy. Some of these bodies came from the lower ranks of society who saw an egalitarian new order emerging. Groups on the extremist fringe included the Ranters, Muggletonians, Diggers, Quakers, and Fifth Monarchists.[55]

The most radical and best known of these English millenarians were the Fifth Monarchists. They derived their name from Daniel's vision of four beasts (ch. 7). These beasts—the Assyrian, Persian, Greek, and Roman Empires—would at the end of time be destroyed and replaced by a government of God and the saints—the so-called fifth and last monarchy.[56] This reign of God on earth would of course begin in England, and the saints were to be the Fifth Monarchists. The Antichrist was to be destroyed, England purified, and then the kingdom of Christ would spread throughout the world. The English armies led by Oliver Cromwell would sweep through Europe and defeat the pope. The Jews meanwhile would return to the Holy Land and defeat the Turks. These events would come to pass between 1655 and 1657.[57]

The Fifth Monarchists were millenarians along the line of Münster. They believed that it was their duty to establish the kingdom of God by force if necessary. Thus these radicals fused "millenarian theology and political extremism. They saw the millennium in political and social terms rather than in the largely theological and passive terms of earlier English millenarians."[58] When they attempted to trigger the end of the world by armed insurrection, they were defeated and faded away in the 1660s. The accession of Charles II to the English throne in 1660 cooled this inflammatory apocalypticism. Nevertheless, the portentous year of 1666 stirred many imaginations. They connected 1000 (the millennium) with 666 (the mark of the beast) to arrive at the date of 1666. In fact, the Quaker George Fox wrote that in 1666 nearly every thunderstorm aroused end-time expectations.[59]

Apocalypticism in Modern Europe

After the apocalyptic outburst of the sixteenth and seventeenth centuries, end-time thinking continued in Europe. But it was less intense and not as far-flung. Prophecy was still serious business. For the most part, however, the social and political climates were not conducive to widespread popular millennial movements. The radical excesses of earlier years caused conservatives to pull back. Talk of the Antichrist, the New Jerusalem, and the second advent no longer dominated everyday conversations.[60]

Yet there were plenty of exceptions to this general trend. Many individuals, including Isaac Newton, continued to speculate on end-time events. Natural, social, and political disasters—the Lisbon earthquake, the persecution of the Huguenots, the French Revolution—still prompted apocalyptic outbursts. Apocalypticism even burst forth in several mass movements—the Old Believers, Camisards, English Prophets, Southcotts, and Darbyites.

In all of this, several future trends could be detected. The lines between pre- and postmillennialism had tended to be murky. By the eighteenth century the contours of these positions took a more definite shape. The premillennialists saw the world as getting steadily worse. Only the second coming of Christ could rescue humanity from a catastrophic disaster. Postmillennialism viewed the future in more optimistic terms. Christianity would gradually spread throughout the globe, thus making a thousand-year period of peace and harmony a reality. Christ would return only at the end of this golden age.[61] Of these two views, postmillennialism, which was embraced by the more liberal and educated elements of society, tended to dominate until about 1850. Premillennialism was often found in popular circles.

Another future trend—a secular eschatology—began to emerge. Premillennialism foresaw a catastrophic end to the world. But in a world that was becoming secularized, God was losing his monopoly over disasters. Several seventeenth- and eighteenth-century scientists evoked science in defense of prophecy. For example, William Whiston, Newton's successor at Cambridge University, was influenced by Edmund Halley's study on comets. He argued that the close passage of a comet had caused Noah's flood. The earth's destruction by fire, predicted Whiston, would come by the same means.[62]

Scientists like Whiston did not rule God out as a cause of the end. Still, their scenarios contained no second coming or last judgment. A comet would bring a catastrophic end to the world. Modern prophetic writers have a similar dilemma. They speak of a nuclear holocaust or an ecological disaster. What role does God play in a human-caused calamity?[63]

Postmillennialism also has its secular thrust. In this view, the world will not end until sometime in the distant future, after society has become better and better. Some postmillennialists have secularized the millennium into a utopia to be attained through human progress. Thus postmillennialism has become equated with the idea of progress—the advancement of knowledge and the human condition.[64]

The Old Believers

The mass suicide of the People's Temple in Jonestown, Guyana, in 1978 had a precedent—the Old Believers. The Old Believers were a dissident group breaking from the Russian Orthodox Church in the seventeenth century. Their story in faraway Russia has little connection with present-day apocalypticism in Western Europe. Yet rarely has apocalypticism had such dire consequences. Thus their story should be told.

The Russian Orthodox Church regarded itself as the third Rome, the restraining force of 2 Thessalonians 2:7. With the fall of Rome and Constantinople, the task of restraining the Antichrist had fallen to the third Rome—Moscow. If the third Rome were to fall to the Antichrist, the world would end. This type of apocalyptic fever found its way into segments of Russian Orthodoxy.[65]

The troubles began under Tsar Alexis I (1645–76). The patriarch Nikon reformed the traditional Russian liturgy to conform to the practice of Greek Orthodoxy. Because Eastern Orthodoxy holds that true belief cannot be separated from true worship, elements in the Russian Church protested these liturgical changes, regarding any modification of the church service as an obstacle to salvation. The most fervent opposition came from the Old Believers. They believed that they were living in the last days, and that the tsar and patriarch were the beasts of Revelation 13.[66]

According to Russian doctrine, the Moscovite Orthodoxy was the only path to salvation. If Moscow were to fall, there would be no fourth Rome; the world would end. Convinced that they were defending the true Orthodox values, the Old Believers were willing to become martyrs, to fight the political and religious authorities who they thought embodied the Antichrist.[67] Their resistance brought government sieges. Some were slaughtered by the government's forces, but in the last decades of the seventeenth century an additional twenty thousand Old Believers burned themselves to death. On a smaller scale, these suicides continued until the mid-nineteenth century.[68] The mass suicides of Old Believers represent one of the worst apocalyptic disasters in history.

End-Time Excitement in France

On several occasions from about 1670 to 1850, French society experienced some apocalyptic excitement—much of it brought on by either the revocation of the Edict of Nantes or the French Revolution. After a century of religious struggles, the Edict of Nantes (1598) had granted the French Protestants (Huguenots) the right to worship. In 1685 Louis XIV revoked the edict, and persecution set in. The French Revolution (1789–99) represents one of the most turbulent periods in modern Western history. As one would expect, it ignited a round of eschatological speculation.[69]

In general there are two approaches to millennialism—the scholarly type that calculates when the end will come, and the popular movements. In France the popular prophetic type dominated. This form of millenarianism, which drew its inspiration from popular piety and mysticism, focused on the return of Christ and the coming of a new age. The Camisards, the Jansenist Convulsionaries, and the followers of Suzette Labrousse and Catherine Theot are examples of popular millenarianism.[70]

When Louis XIV began to persecute those who had embraced the Protestant faith, the Huguenots in southern France rose in revolt. These rebellious Huguenots of Languedoc were known as the Camisards. They incorporated millenarian and fanatical elements into their faith and saw their sufferings as divine preparation for the coming millennium.[71] Unlike the Anabaptist revolutionaries and the Fifth Monarchists, however, the Camisards did not seek radical social change or a redistribution of wealth. Rather, they simply desired to purify the world in preparation for the impending millennium.[72]

Among the Camisards a number of prophets arose—most claiming to be inspired by the Holy Spirit and uttering end-time predictions. Best known was Pierre Jurieu, who predicted that the judgment day would come in 1689. Other end-time predictions pointed to the years 1705, 1706, and 1708. These prophecies of the Antichrist, persecution, and the triumph of the godly helped lead to rebellion.[73] The French authorities brutally crushed the Camisards, executing more than twelve thousand of them. Fierce resistance continued until 1704, when many Camisards left France for England.[74]

Seventeenth- and eighteenth-century France witnessed several other movements and individuals who said that the end was at hand.

Jansenism, an austere form of French Catholicism, produced the Convulsionaries. Some of them predicted the world would end in the distant future—2000. But most Convulsionaries focused on God's wrath and a more immediate doomsday. A few even declared themselves to be Elijah, the biblical prophet who was to return at the end of time.[75]

Finally, there was the French Revolution, which sparked one of the most fervid outpourings of political apocalypticism in modern times. Many individuals in Europe interpreted the excesses of the revolution in eschatological terms. Moreover, these apocalyptic speculations did not end with the defeat of Napoleon in 1815, but continued until the 1870s when Napoleon III left the political scene.[76]

Contemporaries saw the French Revolution in one of two ways—the beginning of a new age or the work of the Antichrist. In France two women who claimed to be prophets gave the revolution a positive reading. The prophecies of Suzette Labrousse and Catherine Theot saw the revolutionary events as the beginning of a new reign of God. However, apocalyptists outside of France regarded the French Revolution as the work of the Antichrist. Some even believed Napoleon to be the Antichrist.[77]

An Early Coming of the New Age

A different type of end-time thinker paraded across the eighteenth-century scene—Emanuel Swedenborg (1688–1772). The eschatological views of this brilliant Swedish mystic and scientist better relate to the occult-mystical tradition than to the Christian faith. After his death his followers published his writings and established the Church of New Jerusalem.[78]

Swedenborg had a vision which he said had carried him into the spiritual world, where he had been able to see eternal truths. He began to write voluminously, believing that his writings were the dawn of a new age in the history of the world. Most important, Swedenborg declared that the last judgment had occurred in 1757, and that the second coming of Christ was already being fulfilled spiritually. His focus on this invisible new age can be seen as a forerunner of New Age ideas.[79]

Some Strange British Millenarians

The millenarian excesses during the Puritan revolution "served to damn the whole movement," says Ernest Sandeen.[80] As a result, postmillennialism tended to dominate in eighteenth-century England. Since postmillennialism sees Christ returning only at the end of a literal millennium, it serves to cool the flames of end-time thinking.

71

Nevertheless, an apocalyptic eschatology did have its adherents in eighteenth-century Britain. The social dislocations of the early Industrial Revolution and the challenges of the Enlightenment caused an uneasiness that promoted end-time speculations. Some of these calculations were sophisticated and represent a continuation of the scholarly apocalyptic tradition. Others, however, grew out of the lower classes and were more popular and ecstatic.[81]

An even more important factor in the revival of interest in prophecy was the French Revolution. Many English interpreted the French Revolution in apocalyptic terms. As the dramatic events of the 1790s unfolded, people believed that the prophecies of Daniel 7 and Revelation 13 were being fulfilled before their very eyes. Thus nineteenth-century Britain witnessed a strong millenarian movement.[82]

In the late seventeenth century, a number of well-educated English people had speculated about the end of the world. Thomas Beverly, an Anglican rector, predicted that the end would come in 1697. John Mason, another Anglican rector, drew from the writings of Archbishop James Ussher and Johann Alsted and calculated that the millennium would begin in 1694. A similar curiosity about when the world would end prompted Isaac Newton to jump from math to prophecy and write intensively on the books of Daniel and Revelation.[83]

But the scholarly approach to eschatology would give way to the popular. Mason himself began to base his end-time predictions on the voices and visions that came to him. As time went on, he became increasingly bizarre, even insisting that he would not die. When he did die, his followers believed that he would rise on the third day.[84]

In 1706 the Camisard prophets arrived in England, declaring Christ's kingdom to be at hand. Their ideas touched many groups and individuals, adding an ecstatic dimension to the English millenarian tradition. One group within the Church of England, the Philadelphians, incorporated a mixture of mystical and occult ideas. They insisted that Christianity had only so much time to purify itself—and this time was about to expire.[85]

The English Prophets were a group more directly under Camisard influence. Along with the Camisards they traveled throughout England and Scotland preaching an impending doom and destruction. Their efforts tended to be unsuccessful. Unfulfilled prophecies shook confidence; internal disputes and external opposition drained energy. As the end of time seemed less immediate, the members began to drift to other religious groups.[86]

With the coming of the French Revolution, apocalyptic activities were reignited in England—some quite bizarre. Previously the English had pointed to the papacy as Antichrist. But now the English regarded the anarchic activities of the French Revolution as the apocalyptic beast. Some even saw Napoleon as Antichrist. Such eschatological speculations did not cease with the demise of Napoleon. Instead, the nineteenth century experienced the revival of British millenarianism.[87]

One of the strangest prophetic figures at this time was Richard Brothers. Convinced that God was speaking to him, Brothers wrote several prophetic works in the 1790s. He predicted that the millennium would begin in 1795. In the belief that his lineage was divine, Brothers insisted that he would lead the ten lost tribes back to Israel. But in one prophecy he said that God wanted him to wear the crown of England. The government arrested him, and he spent the remainder of his life in a lunatic asylum, where he planned the New Jerusalem.[88]

Equally strange was Joanna Southcott. She made a number of predictions and was right often enough to gain a reputation as a prophet. In the 1790s she won a large following by convincing people that the millennium was at hand.[89] But events took a startling turn in 1814. A spiritual visitor allegedly told Southcott that at age sixty-four she was to give birth to the second Jesus Christ. This virgin birth was to be the second coming and would lead immediately to the last judgment. A number of physicians confirmed Southcott's pregnancy. Suddenly London was alive with end-time excitement. The child was due in the autumn. By November the baby had not arrived. Southcott began to doubt her divine mission, and the pregnancy symptoms receded. In December she died. Her movement, though of lower-class origins, had not inspired a social revolution. Instead, by focusing on the coming millennium, it had barely touched the real world.[90]

Darby and the Great Parenthesis

"In a moment, in the twinkling of an eye, at the last trump . . . we shall be changed" (1 Cor. 15:52). The notion of the sudden secret rapture of the church has captivated millions of Christians. More than any other eschatological doctrine, premillennial dispensationalism has taught the "any moment" second coming of Christ. Dispensationalism also emphasizes that God has dealt differently with humankind through a series of ages or dispensations. Classic dispensationalism divides history into epochs—usually seven. We are currently living in the sixth dispensation—the church age.[91]

Today, dispensationalism far exceeds other belief systems in promoting end-time thinking. Where did it come from? Its exact origins are shrouded in mystery. But there can be no question that John Nelson Darby (1800–1882) became its foremost advocate. Born into an Anglo-Irish family, Darby graduated from Trinity College. Ordained three years later, he served in the Church of Ireland. Uneasy about the established church, however, Darby joined the Plymouth Brethren, a separatist sect with an interest in prophecy. As a member of this group, Darby systemized dispensationalism and spread its major principles throughout the English-speaking world.[92]

Premillennialism had surged in Britain during the nineteenth century. But it was the historicist version, which tied itself to a chronology of events predicted in the Bible, especially Revelation. As a result, the premillennialists became "committed at least implicitly to some kind of schedule of expectations." In the process, they lost considerable prophetic flexibility. With their "millennial arithmetic," they often played the "date-setting game."[93]

Now Darby came along with a new type of premillennialism. Dispensational premillennialism belonged to the futurist school, which held that, except for the first few chapters, Revelation foretells developments taking place in the last days. In taking this position, Darby freed himself from the necessity of tying current events in with Revelation. According to the historicist school, certain events had to happen before Christ would return. But Darby said that no event stood in the way of Christ's return. This teaching of the imminent return of Christ "proved to be one of the greatest attractions of dispensational theology."[94]

Beyond the futuristic approach to prophecy, Darby's eschatology stood on two principles—his doctrine of the church and his method of interpreting the Bible. He sharply separated Israel and the church, insisting that God had a different plan for each. Moreover, Darby interpreted the prophetic passages of the Bible with a rigid literalism.[95] Building on these principles, Darby developed an exact scheme for end-time events. Christians are currently living in the "Great Parenthesis," the period between the crucifixion and the rapture. The next event on God's calendar is the secret rapture. Believers will rise to meet Christ in the air. Then the horrors described in Revelation will take place, including the tribulation, the reign of Antichrist, and Armageddon. At this point Christ will return to set up his thousand-year rule. After the millennium Satan will be defeated and the final judgment will take place.

Darby's system was not original. Futurism began with the sixteenth-century Catholics, and elementary forms of dispensationalism go back at least to Joachim of Fiore. Even the rapture doctrine had earlier precedents, including Increase Mather. Still, Darby combined all of these ideas into a coherent system—one that has significantly influenced modern apocalyptic thought.[96]

Bad News from the Virgin Mary

In eighteenth- and nineteenth-century France, many believed that the return of Christ would be preceded by an age of Mary. This dramatic devotion to the Virgin Mary was reinforced in the 1840s and 1850s by two Marian sightings.[97] In 1846 there had been a major crop failure in southeastern France. The Virgin appeared in that year to two shepherd children on the mountain of La Salette. She criticized humanity's sinful behavior and predicted further calamities if people did not mend their ways.[98]

One of the most famous Marian visitations occurred in 1858 in the small village of Lourdes in southwestern France. Here the Virgin appeared eighteen times to Bernadette Soubirous, a fourteen-year-old illiterate girl. In one of her messages Mary announced to Bernadette: "I am the Immaculate Conception." The immaculate conception of Mary soon became official Catholic doctrine. And with a reputation for the miraculous, Lourdes became a major shrine for pilgrims. Also, the Marian appearances convinced many that the age of Mary and the end times had arrived.[99]

But the Marian appearances with the strangest end-time messages occurred at Fatima in central Portugal. Between May and October 1917 Mary is claimed to have appeared six times to ten-year-old Lucia dos Santos and two of her cousins.[100] Lucia revealed the contents of three special revelations to Catholic authorities, who wrote them down. Ten years later, the church permitted Lucia to disclose the contents of two of these messages. They contained prophecies regarding the end of World War I (which was raging in 1917), the rise and collapse of Russian Communism, and the coming of World War II.[101] But there was the third and presumably more terrifying revelation, which was sealed and kept secret in the archives of the local bishop. Supposedly, Pope John XXIII opened and read the document in 1960. Yet he and the succeeding popes have refused to discuss its contents. What did it say? Few people know for sure. But the most common story says that the message predicts a catastrophic end to the world during the tenure of the fifth pope after the opening of the document. John Paul II is the third pope since 1960. This story explains why the church has kept the contents secret—it fears the masses would become immoral or suicidal if they knew the end was at hand.[102]

Some Limited Endings

Like much of Western history, postmedieval Europe has witnessed peaks and quiet periods of apocalyptic activity. To a large extent, the ebb and flow of end-time thinking has paralleled the stress and changes in Western culture. In particular, the years from 1500 to 1650 were charged with apocalyptic excitement. The social, economic, and political upheavals of the late Middle Ages spilled over into the Reformation Era. Religious reform spanned several centuries. Such conditions produced an apocalyptic atmosphere that may have peaked in seventeenth-century England.

But in Europe the widespread apocalyptic mood declined after 1650. Talk of end-time events no longer provided the grist for everyday conversations. Still, interest in eschatology was not dead. A number of individuals and groups insisted that the end was at hand. Christ would soon return and usher in the millennial state. Religious persecution, natural disasters, political upheavals, and social changes encouraged apocalyptic anxieties.

Yet in modern Europe such apocalyptic feelings usually did not become widespread. They did not grip society as they had from 1500 to 1650. Prophetic individuals had their followers, but only a few mass movements arose. Natural disasters and political upheavals still conjured up end-time predictions—but usually on a more limited basis than in centuries past. The modern world with its rational and secular outlook put a damper on apocalyptic activities.

Instead of being widespread, doomsday often had a local face. To those involved in limited catastrophes, their world had ended. For example, the 1755 Lisbon earthquake set the city ablaze and killed sixty thousand people. Entire villages in the area were swallowed up. Bodies were piled six to seven deep. Indeed, their world had ended.[103]

Such limited endings also had a secular look. The Holocaust ended the world of the Jews involved in Hitler's Final Solution. Hitler slaughtered millions of Christians, Jews, gypsies, and dissidents. Perhaps no savagery in history approaches that of the Nazis. But Stalin certainly tried. There was a second, less publicized holocaust. From 1930 to 1947 Stalin murdered from 10 to 30 million people.[104] Indeed, these natural disasters and secular holocausts were doomsday in microcosm!

Secular doomsdays can also be found in the non-Western world. In 1945 nuclear bombs wreaked destruction and death on Hiroshima and Nagasaki, killing or wounding 150,000 people. The world was abruptly ushered into the nuclear age. Nuclear destruction, of course, conjures up all kinds of end-of-the-world images. The developing world has also had its Hitlers and Stalins who brutally slaughtered millions of people. For starters try Mao Tse-tung of China, Pol Pot of Cambodia, and Idi Amin of Uganda. Like the Nazi and Soviet holocausts, these horrors came not from God or natural sources, but from ourselves.

5

America and the Great Millennial Hope

End-time expectations go right to the heart of American religion. Unlike Europe, where millenarianism usually existed on the fringes of society, in America it has been more central to the religious experience. In various shapes the millennial hope has been an enduring strand in American religion, so much so that Catherine Albanese has described it as the "red thread" in the tapestry of American religion. Similarly, Ernest Sandeen has said that end-time excitement was so strong by the early nineteenth century that America was "drunk on the millennium."[1]

For much of the colonial period and well past the Civil War, post-millennialism dominated the American millennial scene. On the whole, this strand of millennialism lacked apocalyptic qualities. It did not see the world ending anytime soon. Rather, the gospel would penetrate society, and life on earth would gradually improve until Christ's return. Still, there were plenty of exceptions to this general pattern. The early Puritans looked for Christ's imminent return. Even the early postmillennialists used apocalyptic language, insisting that the Antichrist had to be defeated before the millennium could begin. Historicist premillennialism surged in the early nineteenth century, culminating in the Millerite movement. There were also numerous communal and Adventist groups who believed either the millennium or the second advent to be at hand.

The Puritan Divines

Millennial fever literally gripped seventeenth-century England. Not surprisingly, then, apocalyptic frenzy infected the Puritans migrating to America at this time. As part of their cultural baggage, they brought with them an intense eschatological expectation.[2] For the most part they maintained the millennial ideas prevalent in seventeenth-century England, but tailored them for the American environment.

From the beginning the Puritans endowed America with a millennial mission. The Reformation had broken the grip of the papal Antichrist. But the Europeans failed to build on this good start; they proved unequal to the divine call of restoring the true Christian faith. Thus God selected a small remnant to go to the New World and set up a New Jerusalem, a "city upon a hill," the holy Christian commonwealth.[3] In various forms this millennial mission has run the course of American history. It has fueled diverse and even contradictory expressions of American culture—revivalism, civil religion, missions, nationalism, sectarian communalism, and social reform movements. Through the years Americans have tended to see themselves as the chosen nation and their enemies as demonic.

The early Puritans were fervent millennialists, insisting that the millennium was coming. Like the English millennialists, they often blurred the distinctions between pre- and postmillennialism. Most Puritans looked for the apocalyptic events surrounding the defeat of the Antichrist and the inauguration of Christ's kingdom. Whether Christ would come before or after the millennium was disputed and unclear.[4]

Some Puritans, however, can best be seen as chiliasts or premillennialists. Increase and Cotton Mather, for example, held Christ's return to be imminent. Believers would be caught up into the air, and then the disasters and persecutions would begin, followed by the millennium. However, the postmillennial idea envisioning the return of Christ after the millennium was also common at the end of the seventeenth century.[5]

Before 1660, the Puritans often reflected the same millennial themes as did their English counterparts—notably the defeat of the Roman Antichrist and the Turks.[6] But increasingly the Puritans Americanized the apocalyptic tradition, finding prophetic meaning in their own experience. Increase Mather (1639–1723) saw the millennium as in the future and found an apocalyptic meaning in current events. He suggested that the red horse of the Apocalypse foretold the bloodshed of King Philip's War (1675–76), a conflict that pitted the colonialists against the Indians.[7]

Increase's son Cotton (1663–1728) further Americanized the apocalypse. He "inaugurated an era of apocalyptic expectation in America that
did not lose its force until after the American Revolution."[8] He focused
on the many problems that the Puritans encountered in the wilderness,
including Indian massacres. Though he did not go so far as to label the
Native Americans as the Antichrist, he did attribute to them a cosmic
significance, regarding them as in league with the Antichrist.[9]

Cotton Mather was also a date-setter. On the basis of events involving
the Turks and the revocation of the Edict of Nantes, he tentatively calculated the end to come in 1697. When this date passed, he quietly readjusted the time first to 1736 and then back to 1716. Of course he had
no doubt where the New Jerusalem would be located—New England.[10]

The Mathers regarded the millennium as a golden age characterized
by miracles. It was more than a mere improvement of the human condition or the universal preaching of the gospel. We should also note that
Increase Mather's perception of the second advent foreshadowed that
of the dispensationalists—a rapture in which believers are taken into
the air.[11]

Much of the date-setting done by the Puritans rests on the Book of
Revelation's statements that the Antichrist's reign would last 1,260 days
(or 42 months). Many people at this and other times extended the 1,260
days to 1,260 years. By adding 1,260 years to what they believed to be
the date at which the Antichrist's rule began, they could predict the end
of his reign. Some Puritans, believing that the Antichrist's rule began in
the fifth century, calculated the end to be around 1700.[12]

Postmillennialism: The End Is Way Off

Cotton Mather's brew of eschatology and date-setting was not to everyone's liking. As the eighteenth century advanced and rationalism gained
strength, apocalypticism faded. Progressive postmillennialism held sway
until the late nineteenth century.

At first, postmillennialism maintained an evangelical orientation, believing that the gradual improvements would be the fruit of human efforts and the work of the Holy Spirit. In fact, postmillennialism forged
a link with another nineteenth-century movement—perfectionism.
Christian perfectionism places a strong emphasis on holiness, contending that the believer through God's grace can achieve and maintain
a moral perfection in this life.[13] Both postmillennialism and perfectionism promoted evangelism, morality, and a better quality of life.

But as the nineteenth century progressed, this evangelical postmillennialism gave way to more-secular versions—the idea of progress, civil

religion, the social gospel, and the millennial mission of America. In particular, the idea of progress—that humanity is advancing toward a better world—complemented secular postmillennialism. Perfectionism also fueled several humanitarian movements—abolition, suffrage, and temperance—and blended in with secular postmillennialism.[14]

But our concern is with the end of the world. Evangelical postmillennialism addressed this subject. It contained pockets of apocalypticism and even pointed to the end of time, though it be in the distant future. Several eighteenth-century events set off these eschatological speculations—the first being the Great Awakening. The religious revivals of the 1740s ignited end-time expectations. Along with a number of other New England ministers, Jonathan Edwards (1703–58) saw the Great Awakening as a prelude to the millennium.[15] But Edwards's apocalypticism was not that of the Mathers. He was a postmillennialist, mingling human and divine efforts to usher in the golden age. He foresaw the millennium as taking place on earth within history, and as being "achieved through the ordinary processes of propagating the gospel in the power of the Holy Spirit."[16]

Still, Edwards had his apocalyptic moments. He designated the Roman papacy as Antichrist. The Antichrist had risen gradually, but the Reformation dealt him a blow from which he could not recover. Thus his days were numbered. Believing that the Antichrist had achieved power in 606, Edwards calculated that the beast would fall by 1866 (606+1260 years = 1866).[17] He also regarded the Great Awakening as an early sign of the approaching millennium. Edwards saw the emotionalism that accompanied these revivals as an outpouring of God's Spirit upon the land—a necessary step toward the millennium. These revivals would transform America. Religious conditions would gradually improve, allowing the millennium to begin in America by 2000.[18]

But the Great Awakening failed to bring the anticipated results. It came to an end. And to the dismay of Edwards and other revivalists, a new age did not dawn. So the American believers looked for apocalyptic signs in other contemporary events—especially the French and Indian War and the Revolutionary War. Most of the revivalists did not lose their optimism, interpreting these events in the light of the postmillennial eschatology.[19]

Bible expositors in the 1750s and 1760s explained end-time events in both political and religious terms—a trend that would continue. The war with France provided fresh fodder for eschatological expectations. The colonists politicized their view of the millennium—identifying God's prophetic plan with British interests in North America and associating Catholic France with the Antichrist. Thus Britain's military victories over the French Antichrist signaled the beginning of a millennium of religious and civil liberty. By the end of the French and Indian War, Americans began to blur distinctions between the kingdom of God and the emerging American nation.[20]

With the defeat of Catholic France in North America, the colonists looked for the complete destruction of the Antichrist. But this did not happen. So the colonists, as believers have done throughout Christian history, looked for the Antichrist elsewhere. They had only to look for the nearest enemy—the British government.[21]

The Revolutionary War stimulated all kinds of millennial expectations. Apocalyptic thinking certainly did not cause the War of Independence, but on the popular level it did provide some meaning for the struggle. Colonial ministers used apocalyptic language in support of the patriot cause and as an explanation for the sufferings.[22]

With the Stamp Act crisis, Americans began to change their perception of the Antichrist. Previously they had identified the political and religious despotism of Catholicism and the papacy as Antichrist. Now the colonists looked for other forms of tyranny. At first they found it in the British Empire. They then extended this perception to the Church of England and the episcopacy.[23] By 1773 the Americans even portrayed King George III as the Antichrist. While the notion had little impact, someone calculated that in Greek and Hebrew the numerical equivalent of the letters in the words "Royal Supremacy in Great Britain" totaled 666.[24]

Many Americans regarded the Revolutionary War as a holy crusade that would usher in the millennium, and with the American victory millennial optimism soared. The Second Great Awakening in the early nineteenth century also brought another wave of postmillennial hope. This evangelical postmillennialism complemented the revivals and perfectionism of that day. Most religious and academic leaders preached a progressive millennialism. For example, Timothy Dwight, president of Yale, predicted that the millennium would come by 2000.[25]

But a different type of postmillennialism also came to the forefront. Previously the Americans believed that God's people would prepare the world for Christ's kingdom through prayer and preaching. Now they began to equate the kingdom of God with the political and moral destiny of America.[26] Indeed, in the nineteenth century Americans believed that God was smiling on their cause. This new postmillennialism justified American territorial expansion in the West. Religious leaders saw the advances in learning, the arts, science, morality, and religion as signs that the millennium was coming. In pursuit of a Christian commonwealth in America, postmillennialism sparked a number of reform efforts—abolition, temperance, and suffrage. Eventually it developed into a more secular millennialism largely devoid of religious impulses.[27]

Fringe Groups and Millennialism

The millennial idea powerfully affected both mainstream and fringe religions throughout the course of the nineteenth century. Early-nineteenth-century America witnessed an explosion of new religious movements such as had not been seen since the sixteenth century. Many of these bodies combined millennial ideas with beliefs common at that time, especially perfectionism and communalism. In doing so, these fringe groups gave a new twist to end-time thinking.[28]

A wave of communal social orders came about in the early nineteenth century. By their very nature, communal groups separate from society in their quest for the ideal. The perfectionism so prevalent in antebellum (pre–Civil War) America found its way into the communal sects. Even if they did not believe that society could be perfected, they endeavored to build for themselves a perfect way of life in their cloistered communities.[29]

To a large extent, most of these groups were millennialists, though their eschatology cannot be neatly categorized as either pre- or post-millennial. In one form or another, they placed considerable emphasis on the return of Christ or the start of the millennium. Millennialism may not have been the distinctive for which these groups were best known, but it did provide the rationale for some behavior that otherwise would make no sense. Most notably, the belief that the millennium was at hand led some radical sects, including the Society of the Public Universal Friend and the Shakers, to adopt group celibacy.

The Public Universal Friend

The Society of the Public Universal Friend was an early indigenous American communitarian movement with some millenarian characteristics. It flourished in New York, Rhode Island, and Connecticut from 1776 to 1863. Founded by Jemima Wilkinson (1752–1819), the daughter of a prosperous Quaker farmer in Rhode Island, this sect bore resemblance to the Shakers in a number of ways, including its millennial beliefs.[30]

Unusual circumstances surrounded the beginnings of the Society of the Public Universal Friend. At eighteen Wilkinson seemed to have died of the plague. Her body grew cold but then warmed up, and she began to speak. The voice coming from within her claimed that Jemima Wilkinson had "left the world of time," and henceforth her body would function as a vehicle for the Spirit of Life, which came to be known as the Public Universal Friend.[31]

Wilkinson believed that the Spirit of God's descent to earth and inhabitation of her body was the second coming of Christ, who would reign on earth for a thousand years. For over forty years the Friend operated from within her body. Among other teachings she proclaimed a message of millenarianism and perfectionism. It was the eleventh hour, the last call of mercy ever to be made to humankind.[32]

The Shakers

The United Society of Believers in Christ's Second Appearing, better known as the Shakers, was one of America's most successful and enduring communal groups. The Shakers originated in England, where they had connections with the so-called Shaking Quakers. Ann Lee Stanley (1736–84) led the group to America in 1774, where economic problems forced them to organize into a socialistic Christian community.[33]

Developing in the context of the Second Great Awakening, the Shakers maintained doctrines common in revivalistic circles. Still, they articulated some unique teachings. Mother Ann believed that God is a dual personality. The masculine side of that personality had been made visible in Christ. Now in her a second incarnation of the Holy Spirit had appeared—the feminine element of God, which continued the work done by Christ. In admitting Ann Lee to the Godhead, the Shakers taught that God was a Father-Mother deity, a bisexual being. They considered Christ to be a spirit, appearing first in a masculine form and then much later in Mother Ann.[34]

The Shakers were a millennial church. But it was a curious blend of millennialism and communitarianism that defies classification. Shaker millennialism can best be seen as a "mystical and realized eschatology that experienced Christ's second appearing in the present and not at the end of time."[35] For the Shakers, the second coming of Christ had already occurred, being consummated through Ann Lee, who was the feminine incarnation of God. They also believed that the millennium was at hand, and that they were the vanguard whose prayers and example would direct all humankind into a state of sanctity and happiness. Their mission was to gather in the elect, who could achieve perfection and salvation by denying the flesh.[36]

The Shakers were fanatically antisex. Convinced that sin had begun with Adam and Eve's sex act in the Garden of Eden, Ann Lee insisted that sexual relations were the root of all sin. Men and women would achieve salvation only by overcoming this fleshly desire. They could not marry or cohabitate. Married converts were "demarried" in an unusual ceremony. In fact, it was forbidden to watch animals (or even flies) mate.[37]

Taking celibacy to extremes, the Shakers felt that they alone among the world's peoples were carrying out God's will. If this Shaker dogma prevailed, the human race would be eliminated. But such a possibility presented no problem for the Shakers—they believed that since the millennium was at hand, there was no real reason for the continuance of humankind.[38]

The Mormons

"We believe in the literal gathering of Israel, and the restoration of the Ten Tribes; that Zion will be built upon this continent [North America]," said Joseph Smith—the Mormon leader.[39] The Church of Jesus Christ of Latter-day Saints, better known as the Mormons, is one of the most successful millennial religions in American history. Many of the millennial groups encountered in this book have long since ceased to exist. Not so with the Mormons—they are still thriving.

Mormonism began in the 1820s in western New York State, an area known as the Burned-Over District because it had experienced numerous religious revivals. Here Joseph Smith (1805–44) had a revolutionary experience: he was led by the angel Moroni to discover the Golden Plates, which developed into the Book of Mormon.[40] Supplementing the Bible as sacred scripture, the Book of Mormon describes the emigration of the lost tribes of Israel to America before the birth of Jesus. According to the Book of Mormon, Jesus appeared to these people after the resurrection and set up a church among them. Thus the Book of Mormon "established the Hebraic origins of American Indians and supplied America with a biblical past."[41]

Having adorned America with a sacred past, the Mormons naturally Americanized the millennium. This millennial belief held up America as the Promised Land and as the place where the New Jerusalem would be erected. After all, America is where the lost tribes of Israel chose to migrate. This emphasis reflected the nationalism and optimism of American society as well as the postmillennialism so prevalent in nineteenth-century religious circles.[42]

Yet Mormon millennialism was not this simple. It evidenced several tensions involving both pre- and postmillennial characteristics. At first Smith taught an apocalyptic, premillennial eschatology. But this seemed to fade as the Mormons began to concentrate more on the building of Zion as a place than on an imminent beginning of the millennial kingdom. Yet the Mormons expected their cause to triumph through a cataclysmic judgment rather than the gradual conversion of the world. They waited anxiously for the fulfilment of the signs of the times, while they also labored mightily to build the New Jerusalem in Utah.[43]

All in all, the premillennial characteristics of the Mormons' eschatology outweighed its postmillennialism. To be sure, they often urged
human efforts to build the kingdom. Also, they occasionally waned in
their expectation of an imminent millennium. But they maintained an
apocalyptic dualism, dividing the world into opposing factions. The Mormons believed that salvation would come swiftly rather than gradually,
be accomplished with the help of supernatural beings, and completely
transform life on earth.[44]

For the end to come, the Mormons held that three events must tran-
spire. First, "the tribe of Ephraim, the Mormons themselves," must
gather in Zion—which they believed to be Independence, Missouri. (Despite their having been chased out of this Zion, this belief is still maintained.) Next, "the tribe of Judah—the Jews—will gather in Palestine."
Lastly, "the ten lost tribes of Israel will be found" and gather in Zion. "At
this point, Christ will return" to begin the millennium.[45]

Other Unusual Millennial Groups

Nineteenth-century America witnessed the rise and fall of other unusual millennial bodies. A number of these groups combined perfectionism and millennialism with unorthodox sexual practices. The Universal Friend and the Shakers advocated celibacy, the Mormons
polygamy; the Oneida Perfectionists and the Rappites went down similarly diverse paths.

The Oneida Community, founded by John Humphrey Noyes
(1811–86), was a very successful and widely publicized communitarian experiment with evangelical roots. The doctrine of perfectionism,
that human beings could be without sin, propelled Noyes's innovations,
including a new marriage system. Noyes believed that the traditional
family relationship bred injustice, competition, and dissension. So he
proposed a form of communal marriage in which every male was hus-
band to every woman in the community, and every female was wife to
every man.[46]

The basis of Noyes's perfectionism resided in his postulation that
Christ's second coming had occurred in A.D. 70. When the Romans destroyed the temple in Jerusalem, Christ had appeared spiritually to his
apostles. Thus, liberation or redemption from sin was an accomplished
fact for the followers of Jesus, who were potentially perfect beings. But
the relationship of Christ's invisible coming in A.D. 70 to the millennium
presented problems for Noyes. Was the millennium now in progress?
Or had it been delayed? On these questions Noyes was ambivalent and
defensive. He even suggested that Christ would appear a third time in
the not-too-distant future.[47]

The Rappites were also a communal group with imminent end-time expectations. Like the Shakers, George Rapp (1757–1847) insisted on rigid self-discipline, including strict celibacy and the holding of all property in common. Accordingly, the Rappites regarded themselves as a righteous remnant who would be judged holy when Christ returned in the near future. In fact, Rapp believed that the millennium had recently begun.[48]

Some communal movements with a secular orientation also looked for the millennium. For example, the rationalist Robert Owen (1771–1858) regarded communitarianism as a step toward a heaven on earth. Owen was not even a Christian, let alone a biblical millennialist. Yet he announced the arrival of a secular millennium or utopia.[49] By the word *millennium* Owen meant a society free from crime, misery, and poverty—an ideal which he believed to be universally possible. For him, the end was the imminent collapse of the capitalist civilization. In the Owenite movement the line between social and religious millenarianism became blurred. Owen began to use religious language, and after 1835 the movement exhibited some trappings of a religious cult.[50]

The Christadelphians are a nontraditional religious group begun by John Thomas (1805–71) during the first half of the nineteenth century. Unlike other movements originating at this time, the Christadelphians are not communal, nor do they have any unusual views on sexual relationships. Rather, they are an antitrinitarian millennial group with some unusual doctrinal and social characteristics. They still exist in small pockets in America and in larger numbers in Britain.[51]

Thomas insisted that the central message of Scripture was the hope of the kingdom that would come with the second advent of Christ, which he believed to be imminent. The Christadelphians held that the promises of Scripture related to the Jews and those who voluntarily became Jews. Their eschatology thus had a Hebraic focus. They rejected any teaching of a heaven beyond the skies, instead believing that the saved will live on a renewed earth. Therefore, the Christadelphians emphasized the earthly promises made to Israel and expected the returning Christ to reign permanently in Jerusalem.[52]

The Midnight Cry: The Millerites

Nearly every year we hear of some well-publicized prediction regarding the end of the world. Occasionally, a prophet gathers a following, and an end-of-the-world panic results. In the mid-nineteenth century, northeastern and midwestern America experienced such an event.[53]

"I am fully convinced that somewhere between March 21st, 1843, and March 21st, 1844, according to the Jewish mode of computation, Christ will come," declared William Miller (1782–1849).[54] But March 21, 1844, came and went without the return of Christ. Miller confessed his error and acknowledged his disappointment, but still insisted that Jesus would soon return. Under great pressure Miller and his associates set another date—October 22, 1844.

Such were the predictions of William Miller, a simple farmer and Baptist layman from Low Hampton, New York. Ernest Sandeen has called Miller "the most famous millenarian in American history." Without a doubt, his preaching spawned the most popular end-time movement that America has seen.[55]

It is true, of course, that postmillennialism was the dominant end-time perspective until late in the nineteenth century. Increased knowledge, material progress, cultural advances, and the growth of democracy propelled the optimistic vision of America's millennial future. Hopeful Americans even saw the Civil War as but an interlude in which God punished the nation for slavery. Still, premillennialism was not dead in the early nineteenth century. It must be remembered that the line between pre- and postmillennialism was not hard and fast. The distinction in millennial studies between the pessimistic premillennialists who focused on catastrophe and the optimistic postmillennialists who focused on progress did not always hold up. Premillennialists often participated in social reform movements, and some postmillennialists spoke of end-time events as if they were right around the corner. For example, the prominent evangelist Charles Finney had a postmillennial vision of the millennium as beginning in three years.[56]

There were, then, always a number of individuals who taught premillennialism. Some events in the late eighteenth and early nineteenth centuries increased their numbers. In particular, the French Revolution fostered an interest in prophecy. The turbulence of the revolution created an apocalyptic mood, causing many to believe that the end was near. The demolition of papal power in France was of special interest to Bible scholars in both Britain and America who believed that the papacy had to be destroyed before the millennium could come.[57]

Other European premillennial ideas reached American shores, especially from Britain, where historicist premillennialism surged in the nineteenth century. While there is no evidence that Miller encountered these ideas, his teachings bore a striking resemblance to British premillennialism. Even Miller's emphasis on 1843 as the year for Christ's return was not unique, for historicist premillennialists in Britain (and some in America too) believed that something cataclysmic would occur in 1843. Where Miller did disagree with the British premillennialists was over the issue of Israel. In Miller's end-time predictions, there was no place for the conversion of the Jews or their return to Palestine.[58]

Although at this time the revivalism of the Second Great Awakening was producing an optimistic postmillennialism, enough negative events were occurring to encourage premillennialism and its catastrophic view of history. Focusing on Christ's statement that wars and rumors of war would characterize the end times, premillennialists were always on the watch for war between major European powers. The fate of the Ottoman Empire and the advance of Russia into this area—events the Millerites believed were predicted in the Book of Revelation—occupied a special role in their calculations.[59]

On the domestic scene, a number of events generated a premillennial excitement. The influx of Catholic immigrants to America aroused apocalyptic feelings. Premillennialists drew dire inferences from disturbances in the natural world: the early nineteenth century witnessed a solar eclipse, dramatic meteor showers, great storms, fires, earthquakes, and crop failures. Economic problems intensified the end-time anxieties. The prosperity of the Jacksonian years gave way to the Panic of 1837 and the following depression.[60]

The Millerite movement was actually a child of American evangelicalism. In fact, Millerism has been called "evangelicalism with a twist."[61] Except for predicting the exact date of Christ's return, Millerism did not substantially differ from its evangelical neighbors. The major impulses of antebellum evangelicalism—millennialism, perfectionism, voluntarism (emphasis on human choice), and revivalism—all helped shape Millerism. Indeed, even in respect to date-setting, the Millerites were not unique—others did the same.[62]

This popular millennial movement did not originate with some raging fanatic or silver-tongued demagogue. Rather, Miller was a self-educated farmer with few charismatic qualities. For a while he flirted with deism. But in 1816 he was converted and returned to his Baptist roots. Miller began an intensive study of the Bible, which eventually centered on millennial prophecies and biblical chronology. By 1818 his end-time views were settled. Still, he restudied his conclusions for several years and in 1831 began to publicly present his ideas.[63]

Miller set forth a number of principles for understanding biblical prophecy. But his thinking rested on two basic approaches to Scripture. (1) He embraced a historicist interpretation of the Book of Revelation— the prophecies of the Apocalypse relate to various periods in history. This approach to premillennialism tended to lock the interpreter into a specific prophetic timetable. (2) Whenever possible, Miller interpreted Scripture literally. Figures, parables, and numbers were exceptions: they have a symbolic meaning. Employing these two approaches, Miller looked for the fulfilment of prophecy in both historical events and future developments.[64] Enlarging on historicist premillennialism, which said that Jesus would return before the millennium and that the millennium would not be ushered in by the gradual reform of human institutions, but by a catastrophic destruction of the world's kingdoms, Miller specified when all of this would happen.[65]

Miller's prophetic calculations were quite elaborate. But the key to his biblical arithmetic can be found in Daniel 8:14: "And he said to me, Unto two thousand and three hundred days; then shall the sanctuary be cleansed." Miller believed that this sanctuary cleansing referred to the return of Christ, which would purge the world of evil and usher in the millennium.[66] On the assumption that one prophetic day equals one year, Miller theorized that Daniel's 2,300 days meant that 2,300 years must pass before Christ's return and the final cleansing of the earth. Using Archbishop James Ussher's chronology, Miller calculated that the 2,300-year period began in 457 B.C., when Ezra and seventeen hundred Jews returned to Jerusalem. This date in turn reflected Daniel 9:24: "Seventy weeks are determined upon thy people . . . to make an end of sins." Interpreting the "end of sins" to be A.D. 33—the time of Christ's crucifixion—Miller went back 490 years ("seventy weeks") to arrive at 457 B.C. Then, beginning the countdown in 457 B.C., Miller added 2,300 years (which included Daniel's seventy weeks) to arrive at 1843.[67]

Over the next few years, Miller continued to recalculate his figures, bolstering his conclusion that the end would come in 1843. But because so many changes had been made to the calendar over the previous two thousand years, Miller still hesitated to publicly designate an exact year for Christ's return.[68] In fact, Miller said little about his discovery to anybody. But by 1831—when he was almost fifty—his friends persuaded him to go public with his message. Miller took to the preaching circuit throughout New York and Vermont, delivering eight hundred sermons by 1839.[69]

Still, Millerism remained a small rural movement until Miller converted Joshua V. Himes to his biblical chronology. Himes, pastor of Chardon Chapel in Boston, proved to be a gifted publicist and organizer. Himes spread Miller's ideas by the extensive use of newspapers, camp meetings, and evangelistic tours. Millerism's greatest distinctive was the use of the biggest tents America had seen, seating up to four thousand.[70]

Himes made Miller a national figure and greatly expanded his movement through the Northeast and Midwest. Numbers vary, but Millerism is usually estimated to have ranged from thirty to a hundred thousand. Who were the Millerites? David Rowe defines them as people who not only believed in "the imminent apocalypse but acted on behalf of that belief" to specifically support Miller's ideas. While millennial groups usually draw poor people from the lower social orders, this was not so with the Millerites. On the whole, they came from the middle classes and were probably better off than the average person. Moreover, the Millerites were generally sober people unmarked by fanaticism.[71]

Until 1842 Miller often qualified his predictions, looking for the second advent about 1843. Under some pressure to be more specific, at the beginning of 1843 Miller used the Hebrew calendar to calculate that Christ's return would occur between March 21, 1843, and March 21, 1844. This more specific dating generated excitement, and Millerism became more popular.[72]

During 1843 and early 1844 the Millerites stepped up their activities and the crowds increased. Even the secular newspapers took notice of the Millerite doctrines. So did the mainstream clergy, who opposed the Millerites' date-setting. As the year passed, the Millerites were often mercilessly ridiculed and lampooned for insisting that the end was at hand. Stung by such attacks, the Millerites identified both Catholicism and mainstream Protestantism as Babylon and partisans of Antichrist.[73]

March 21, 1844, passed and Christ did not return. The Millerites faced a crisis of faith. Miller made no attempt to excuse his mistaken date, but he did not give up his belief regarding Christ's imminent return: "I confess my error and acknowledge my disappointment; yet I still believe that the day of the Lord is near."[74] Although the movement was at a low ebb in the spring of 1844, many dedicated followers searched the Scriptures for evidence of a new date.

Psychologically, it would seem that the Millerites were not satisfied with the belief that Christ would return shortly. They needed an exact date—"and they got one."[75] As early as February 1844, one of Miller's followers, Samuel S. Snow, advanced the seventh-month scheme. According to Snow, the prophetic chronology fixed the date of the Lord's advent at the tenth day of the seventh month of the Jewish sacred year. The Millerites identified this date with October 22 of the Gregorian calendar.[76] At a Millerite camp meeting in August of 1844, this new date became public. It infused the movement with new vigor. At first Miller hesitated to accept this new date for Christ's return, but events had snowballed beyond his control. Despite lingering doubts he endorsed the new date on October 6—two weeks before the end was supposed to come.[77]

The Millerites had now painted themselves into a corner. There was no setting a new date. From about mid-August to October the Millerites engaged in a frenzy of activities. They flooded the country with their periodicals, books, and pamphlets. Many withdrew from their churches in anticipation of the second advent. They were instructed to get their affairs in order. Many did—selling their property, closing their stores, resigning their jobs, and abandoning their animals and crops. Even in such a frenzy few Millerites engaged in fanatical activities. To the end they were generally sane people.[78]

But the Great Disappointment came. When the Lord did not return as expected, massive confusion and disillusionment set in. All millennial movements are disappointed when their predictions fail to materialize. But because the Millerites were so specific in their date-setting, their disappointment was even more acute.[79]

The Great Disappointment was the last straw. The Millerite movement fragmented and went in several directions. Some went back to their churches. Others were so disillusioned that they abandoned the evangelical faith. A few retreated to the ultimate refuge—they joined some separatist groups such as the Shakers. But most Millerites still believed that the second advent was near. These people formed various Adventist groups, the largest being the Seventh-day Adventists.[80]

Despite its visibility the Millerite movement had little influence on subsequent end-time thinking. It did, however, have three long-term effects: (1) Millerism spawned the Seventh-day Adventist Church; (2) it discredited historicist premillennialism, causing it to fade out almost entirely after 1844; and (3) the Millerite fiasco demonstrated the perils of setting definite dates for Christ's return.[81]

Cleansing the Sanctuary: The Adventists

"Following any apocalyptic failure such as the Millerite disappointment of 1844, there are several options open to the faithful followers." One alternative is to disband the group and return to normal life. Spiritualization is a popular option; this entails "the process of claiming that the prophecy was in error to the extent of its being seen as a visible historical event, and the attempt to reinterpret it as a cosmic, inner, invisible, or heavenly event." A final alternative for the "disappointed apocalyptic is to return to the source of revelation (the Bible, a psychic-prophet, or an analysis of contemporary events) and seek a new date." A less committed form of this option is to set a vague new date, such as in "the near future."[82]

Following the First Disappointment of 1843, some minor recalculations of biblical chronology pointed to October 1844. This readjustment satisfied most Millerites. Even after the Great Disappointment of 1844, some Adventist leaders did more of the same. They set new dates for the second advent—1845, 1846, 1849, and 1851.[83] But after the Great Disappointment this new arithmetic would not suffice. For most Adventists only a change in end-time thinking could soothe the disillusionment of 1844.

The Seventh-day Adventists did an about-face by resorting primarily to the spiritualization option. In doing so, they developed into a large religious organization. "Millenarians cannot last *as millenarians*," notes Jonathan Butler. "The sooner the group can shed its short-term millenarianism, the sooner it can accommodate to the practical business of life in the world." So the Seventh-day Adventists stopped setting dates for Christ's return and spiritualized the Great Disappointment. By shortening their millenarian phase, they became a stable religious denomination.[84]

The Seventh-day Adventist eschatology had many strands. But its end-time thinking focused on two ideas—a spiritualization of the Great Disappointment and Sabbatarianism. After allegedly receiving a vision, Hiram Edson reexamined Daniel 8:14. With help from O. R. L. Crosier, he set forth the idea that only the event of October 22, 1844, not the date, had been misinterpreted. Miller had interpreted the cleansing of the sanctuary in Daniel 8:14 as a prophecy that Christ would return to earth and purge it. The Adventists now believed that on that fateful day in October Christ actually entered into the most holy compartment of the heavenly sanctuary and performed his cleansing work.[85] So the cleansing of the sanctuary referred not to the second advent, but to Christ's "investigation of the sins of God's people in preparation for the end of the world." With this doctrine of investigative judgment the Adventists accomplished two things: they spiritualized the failed prediction of October 1844 and established a framework to order their lives while they waited for the end.[86]

The early Adventists believed Christ had two distinct ministries. He had been forgiving sins since his work on the cross. Yet for the repentant sinner some sin still remained on the heavenly records. So on October 22, 1844, Christ entered the holy compartment of the sanctuary. Here he investigates the lives of those who have been forgiven to see if they merit eternal life. When this investigative judgment has been completed, Christ will leave the heavenly sanctuary, return to earth, and usher in the terrible Day of the Lord. Following this judgment the millennium will begin.[87]

Led by Ellen G. White and others, the Adventists soon began to associate Sabbath observance with the event of October 1844 and their new understanding of Christ's ministry in the heavenly sanctuary. They believed that the message of the third angel in Revelation 14:6–12 forecast their movement. The angel called forth a people from the fallen churches to obey God's commandments, including Sabbath observance.[88] The reason why Christ did not return in 1844 is that Christians had not kept the Sabbath. The second advent will occur only after two events have transpired—Christ has to complete his priestly work in the sanctuary, and God's people must observe the Sabbath. In fact, because the Catholics and Protestants worshiped on Sunday, the Seventh-day Adventists viewed them as the two horned beasts of Revelation 13.[89]

Countdown to Armageddon: The Jehovah's Witnesses

"Ours has been one of the greatest 'Chicken Little' religions in modern history. For over a hundred years the sky had been going to fall shortly. Yet apparently Jehovah hasn't been listening," wrote one disillusioned ex–Jehovah's Witness.[90] The Jehovah's Witnesses may be the most persistent date-setters in history. Most such groups make one or perhaps two failed predictions. But the Jehovah's Witnesses won't quit. Their leaders have earmarked the years 1874, 1878, 1881, 1910, 1914, 1918, 1925, 1975, and 1984 as times of eschatological significance.

Although millenarians supposedly cannot last long as millenarians, the Jehovah's Witnesses seem to have defied this conventional wisdom. Indeed, "they have preached millenarianism longer and more consistently than any major sectarian movement in the modern world."[91] The belief that God is going to bring an end to the world in the present generation propels their thinking. "Millions now living will never die," proclaimed Joseph Rutherford, one of their leaders.[92]

Movements that predict the end of the world in the near future have a short life span. How have the Jehovah's Witnesses explained their prophetic failures? First, they have spiritualized a number of eschatological events, claiming that they occurred invisibly. Second, they recalculate their numbers and insist that their predictions will be fulfilled in the near future. Third, the Jehovah's Witnesses reinterpret their earlier prophecies, downplaying former predictions—even admitting mistakes. Finally, their organization is so autocratic that the rank and file have little choice but to accept the explanations.[93]

But the Jehovah's Witnesses have done more than survive. They are one of the most successful and well publicized of the Adventist bodies. In the 1990s official members and affiliates numbered over 11 million worldwide. Actually, the Jehovah's Witnesses are the most prominent of about a dozen "Russellite" groups, the Adventist offshoots of the Bible studies conducted by Charles Taze Russell (1852–1916).[94]

The Jehovah's Witnesses, also called the Watchtower Society, are set off from the Christian tradition by their unorthodox beliefs. They deny most traditional Christian doctrines, in particular the Trinity and the deity of Christ and the Holy Spirit. Their lifestyle also erects some enormous barriers to any meaningful interaction with society. Since Satan dominates the world, especially the institutional aspects of business, politics, and religion, dedicated Jehovah's Witnesses separate themselves from social institutions.[95] In addition, the eschatology of the Jehovah's Witnesses, which has been a basic theme of Watchtower literature from its early years, is confusing and contradictory.

In the years following the Great Disappointment of 1844, Russell came under the influence of several Adventist preachers, especially Nelson H. Barbour. Surpassing their Millerite predecessors, Barbour and Russell began to set dates for Christ's return.[96] Convinced that Archbishop Ussher's chronology contained errors, Barbour developed his own formula. This new biblical arithmetic concluded that 1873 was the six thousandth year from Adam's creation. Thus the millennial rule of Christ—the seventh day—was about to dawn.[97] When nothing happened in that year, in Adventist style Barbour and Russell spiritualized the return of Christ. Pointing out that *parousia* (the Greek word used to designate Christ's return) actually meant "presence," they concluded that Christ's presence on earth had begun in 1874. However, until right before the battle of Armageddon, Christ's invisible presence will be known only to his faithful followers. At Armageddon Christ will appear physically and reveal his wrath to all humanity. Russell also taught that during the period of Christ's invisible presence the saints will be invisibly raptured—a view resembling the teachings of John Nelson Darby and the Plymouth Brethren.[98]

By 1878 Russell began to differ with Barbour, developing his own distinct views. While his ideas resembled those of the earlier Adventists and millenarians, Russell shaped a twisted form of premillennial eschatology; he drew his ideas from a literal, contrived interpretation of Daniel and Revelation, and one nonbiblical source—the Great Pyramid of Gizeh. Like certain medieval and Renaissance occultists he believed that God had designed the measurements of the Great Pyramid as an indicator of the end times.[99]

Russell also taught that Christ was choosing a church of 144,000 (Rev. 7; 14:1). These spiritual Israelites will rule with Christ as king-priests during the millennium, at which time all of humanity will be raised. They will then learn God's will and have the opportunity to accept or reject it. Those who accept God's teachings will pass through Armageddon and live on the new earth, the new Eden. At the close of the thousand-year period, Satan again will be loosed to deceive the nations. But God will destroy him.[100]

Russell believed that the harvest or gathering of the elect would be complete by 1881. Because Christ obviously did not return in 1881, Russell had to adjust his dates. Reinterpreting Daniel to his needs, he adjusted his biblical math forty years—from 1874 to 1914. Russell also added a new wrinkle to his eschatology. In addition to the 144,000 king-priests, there will be a second class of heavenly servants, referred to as the great company or sheep.[101]

As the Russellite movement grew after 1890, the date 1914 assumed great importance and continues to be a landmark year. On that date "Christ's active rulership began," commencing in his judgment and "his selecting the Watch Tower organization as his official channel" for governing his earthly interests.[102] Russell predicted that 1914 "would see the destruction of the Gentile nations and the time of troubles that would lead to Armageddon." The saints were to be taken "up to heaven with Christ, and the millennial rule of Christ over the earth was to be inaugurated." The booming guns of World War I in 1914 convinced Russell that his millennial calendar was on target. His followers grew excited. The end was right around the corner. When it did not come in 1914, Russell slightly adjusted his timetable to 1918.[103]

But Russell did not live to see his prediction fail. He died in 1916. His followers were not prepared to see their leader die before the end of the world. They were even more disillusioned because Christ had not taken him physically up to heaven.[104]

After Russell's death a power struggle ensued. Out of this dissension Joseph Franklin Rutherford (1869–1942) emerged as the leader of the Jehovah's Witnesses. Rutherford began a campaign to refigure some of Russell's eschatology, developing predictions of his own. Here we see clear evidence that "Biblical chronology is the play dough of millenarians. It can be stretched to fit whatever timetable is needed, or it can be reduced to a meaningless mass of dates and figures so that future predictions can be molded out of the original lump."[105] Rutherford accounted for the failed predictions regarding 1914 and 1918 by repudiating much of Russell's teachings. He then set forth a new chronology based on his interpretation of Daniel and Revelation. Rutherford argued that Christ has been invisibly present since 1914, not 1874, as Russell had said. The time of the end began in 1914. On the whole, the rank-and-file Jehovah's Witnesses accepted this flip-flop with few murmurings.[106]

Rutherford now pointed to 1925 as a new date for the completion of all things. Inasmuch as the millennium was about to begin, he made his claim that "millions now living will never die." Further, because by 1918 the ranks of the 144,000 king-priests had been filled, he gave added attention to the great company, the second class of servants who would live on earth and represent the earthly establishment of the kingdom of God.[107]

That the completion of all things did not come in 1925 became a serious problem for the Witnesses. Many had quit their jobs and sold their homes in the expectation that they would soon be living in an earthly paradise. This was another great disappointment, and thousands left the movement. Fifty years later, the Watchtower Society repudiated the 1925 prediction. The society even reported Rutherford's admitting "that he made an ass of himself over 1925."[108]

But this debacle did not stop the Jehovah's Witnesses from making future predictions. To be sure, they held off for a while, waiting until 1966 to make another major prediction. In that year the Watchtower Society leaders pointed to 1975 as the probable date for the end of the world. Now declaring 4026 B.C. to be the date for creation, they counted forward six thousand years.[109]

But doomsday did not come in 1975. Once again, the disillusioned Jehovah's Witnesses defected in droves. The society's leadership apologized for the misunderstanding over 1975. Still, they picked another date for doomsday—1984. Despite grumblings and defections the movement continues to grow. This growth is driven by the belief that the end of the world is right around the corner. But in the late 1990s the Jehovah's Witnesses appear to be taking a more fluid approach to eschatology. They still insist that the end is near, but are not making any specific predictions. In fact, the society appears to be retreating from its position that 1914 was the beginning of the end.[110]

Native American Millennialists

During the nineteenth century, white Christian Americans did not have a corner on apocalyptic thinking. Two non-Caucasian groups—black Americans and Native Americans—experienced severe social dislocation. Among one group the apocalyptic element was significant; with the other it was minimal. Some Native American groups embraced an apocalyptic outlook—in part because they had a long history of millennial beliefs, in part because they had charismatic leaders to nurture such ideas.

With black Americans chiliastic expectations did not flourish. Why? The slave experience deprived blacks of much of their historical past—including African religious traditions with their millennial dreams. After emancipation the former slaves focused on issues of conversion and sanctification, not apocalyptic aspirations. African-Americans were not without futuristic hopes, but they usually centered on achieving social justice within the current time dimension.[111]

But our concern is with apocalyptic groups. Since early times the world of the Native Americans had seemed endless. The dense forests, rolling plains, and majestic mountains of North America were Indian lands. Hunting, fishing, primitive agriculture, and food gathering sustained the Native Americans. But the coming of the Europeans ended all of this. For centuries white people encroached upon Indian lands, dramatically altering the Native American way of life.

With their world in disarray, the Native Americans experienced a cultural apocalypse. Faced with calamity and abandonment by their gods, they sought explanations. Native Americans longed to change the present order. Some looked for a return to an older, happier world; others looked for saviors to rescue and lead them to an improved future.[112] The shaman had traditionally been the mediator with the supernatural. Prophets and messiahs now came, presenting apocalyptic visions to the Native Americans and promising deliverance from the evil white man.[113]

This cultural apocalypse reached its climax in the last third of the nineteenth century. After 1840 the movement of white Americans into the lands west of the Mississippi accelerated. As Native Americans were forced onto reservations and their tribal culture came unraveled, hostility toward the white Americans exploded. For these American Indians, the cultural, political, and economic situation was desperate.[114] The solution was the ghost dance, a millennial movement that arose in 1870 and then again in 1890, primarily among the Rocky Mountain and midwestern tribes. In both cases, charismatic Indian messiahs received apocalyptic revelations which prompted their followers to recall and expect a return to their history. For example, in 1890 the Paiute Indian "Wovoka taught that the time was coming when the whites would be supernaturally destroyed and dead native Americans would return to earth." On that day game animals would be "restored to their original numbers, and the old way of life would flourish again on a reconstituted earth where sickness and old age would be no more."[115] To hasten this great day, Native American messiahs instructed their followers to perform the ghost dance at regular intervals. The participants in this ceremony went into a trance. Visiting the spirit world and returning to the past, they conversed with dead relatives and caught glimpses of the old Indian way of life.[116]

This new religion spread rapidly, encouraging great hostility toward whites. It set in motion a chain of events that culminated in the massacre at Wounded Knee in 1890. The ghost dance pointed to a new age that would bring the destruction of the oppressive white culture. On the whole, however, it represented more a restoration of a past golden age than the introduction of a radically new age. At its core was a yearning for a transformation of the present.[117]

Apocalypticism American-Style

Apocalypticism has reared its head throughout American history. Millennialism in its various forms has been far more central to the Ameri-

97

can experience than it was in Europe. Still, apocalyptic thinking has not been constant. From the seventeenth through the nineteenth centuries, it had its ups and downs—often in response to social, economic, and political instability.

The interest in apocalyptic matters has frequently been generated by prominent individuals. At times apocalyptic thinking has been stimulated by the pens of theologians such as Cotton Mather and Jonathan Edwards. But more often it has been shaped by prophets or charismatic figures, that is, by individuals whose authority rests on their own rare ability and gifts. Normally, their pronouncements are not recognized by the established ecclesiastical structure. Rather, they often gain their following by oratory, emotional preaching, or a charismatic personality. William Miller's profile does not quite fit this pattern. Still, our generalization does apply to the leaders of most nineteenth-century fringe religions—the Shakers, Mormons, Christadelphians, Seventh-day Adventists, Jehovah's Witnesses, and Native American groups.[118]

From the seventeenth through nineteenth centuries, apocalyptic thinking in America was largely driven by three factors—carryovers from Britain, America's millennial mission, and social change. Seventeenth-century England seethed with apocalyptic ideas that the Puritans brought with them to the New World. Thus early Puritan apocalypticism was largely an adaption of British millennialism adjusted to suit the American scene. This Americanization of apocalyptic thinking continued apace in the eighteenth century, fueled by such events as the Great Awakening and the Revolutionary War. More often than not, optimistic postmillennialism dominated end-time thinking well into the nineteenth century. It furthered the utopian vision of America as God's instrument for ushering in the golden age.

But events would revive premillennialism with its more catastrophic view of the end. The Lisbon earthquake and the French Revolution were thought to signal some ominous apocalyptic events. In addition, much of the first half of the nineteenth century vibrated with social change. The growth of industrialization, urbanization, democracy, and slavery created an atmosphere conducive to apocalypticism. Revivalism, pietism, perfectionism, romanticism, Darwinism, and fundamentalism all combined to drive apocalyptic ideas to their greatest level of excitement since that reached in seventeenth-century England.

6

Rapture Fever: The Early Years

"And as he sat upon the mount of Olives, the disciples came unto him privately, saying, Tell us . . . what shall be the sign of thy coming, and of the end of the world?" (Matt. 24:3). Christ answered this question in general terms—wars, rumors of wars, false teachings, false prophets, and an increase in wickedness. Throughout Christian history apocalyptic thinkers have seen these signs as occurring in their time. In the twentieth century this end-time watching may have reached epic proportions. Prophecy buffs have gone to great lengths to match specific contemporary events with texts from Ezekiel, Daniel, and Revelation. In doing so, they have constructed an elaborate prophetic jigsaw puzzle. But unlike most puzzles this one has a chameleon-like character—it has been regularly adjusted to suit the changes in current events.

Millenarian expectations have erupted at the edges of Christian societies since the Middle Ages. However, the doom boom of the twentieth century has a unique twist. The framework is twentieth-century political, military, and religious developments; but, most important, "the apparatus of modern communications—cable television, video recording, and mass market paperbacks—has brought apocalyptic themes from the theological and social margins . . . into the main stream of American cultural awareness." Not since the years before the Civil War have so many Americans been exposed to so many apocalyptic ideas.[1]

Many Americans have accepted these end-time predictions. According to a 1983 Gallup poll, 62 percent of Americans have "no doubt" that Jesus Christ will return. More recently, a 1994 *U.S. News and World Re-*

port poll found that 60 percent of Americans believe that the world will end; about a third think it will end in the near future. And over 61 percent believe in the second coming of Christ. In addition, public data in the 1990s indicate that 40 to 60 percent of Americans pay some attention to prophetic beliefs.[2] While they may not have formulated specific ideas, they sense that history is at a turning point.

Apocalyptic themes today generally rest on the theology of Protestant fundamentalism, especially the dispensational variety. While fundamentalism and dispensationalism overlap substantially, they are not identical. There are fundamentalists who are not dispensationalists and vice versa. Also, not all fundamentalists are premillennialists.[3]

Fundamentalism is a broader movement than dispensationalism. George Marsden has defined it as "militantly antimodernist evangelical Protestantism."[4] It draws from a variety of religious traditions, including dispensationalism.[5] But while fundamentalism is primarily a religious phenomenon, it can also be seen as a social reaction to the forces of modern urbanized, industrialized America. Fundamentalism's confrontational approach to the modern world has promoted an apocalyptic outlook within its ranks.

Dispensationalism is a theology with its own distinctives. One of these features is premillennialism, which is built into the system. There are about 16 million premillennialists in America, the vast majority being dispensationalists.[6] This dispensational premillennialism has been the primary driving force behind the end-time thinking that has gripped modern America. As the key vehicle in the twentieth century for conveying apocalyptic ideas, it deserves a serious scrutiny. So the next two chapters will deal with premillennialism, especially the dispensational variety. Chapter 6 will note the developments before 1945, chapter 7 will focus on what has happened since 1945.

Classic Dispensational Eschatology in a Nutshell

We have already encountered dispensational theology in chapter 4. It began with John Nelson Darby. Classic dispensationalism divides history into ages, contending that God tests humanity differently in each dispensation. It separates Israel from the church, insisting that we are currently living in the church age. In respect to eschatology, dispensationalism's distinctive is the secret, "any moment" rapture.

Resting on a literal interpretation of the prophetic passages, dispensational eschatology is overwhelmingly premillennial and pretribulational. The specifics (nations and individuals) have changed since Darby.

100

Yet with classic dispensationalism and those who have popularized this tradition, the outline remains essentially the same:

By means of a secret rapture, millions of Christians will suddenly vanish. Snatched up to heaven to meet Christ in the clouds, they will not have to face the trials that are to come upon the earth. This disappearing act ushers in the seven-year tribulation. For the first three-and-one-half years, human conditions gradually deteriorate. Meanwhile, political and military power shifts to a European confederacy led by the Antichrist. This strong man miraculously survives a head wound and gains unprecedented power. At a point of crisis he orchestrates a seven-year peace treaty in the Middle East. However, the Antichrist, who bears Satan's mark—666— then demonstrates his true nature. About midway through the tribulation he and his assistant, the false prophet, terrorize the world and compel everyone to bear the mark 666 on their hands or forehead.

At this point the Antichrist moves to Jerusalem from Rome, where he has been ruling. In the rebuilt temple of Jerusalem he blasphemes God, breaks the peace pact, and persecutes Israel. All chaos breaks out— looting, arson, famines, pollution, plagues, drug abuse, occultism, demon possession, economic dislocations, and lawlessness are rampant. Natural disasters abound: earthquakes destroy the land, the weather becomes bizarre, and stars fall from the sky.

Then, as history draws to a close, a great battle takes place. Armies from the North, the Far East, and Arab nations meet on the mountain of Megiddo in Israel. The bloody battle of Armageddon rages for about a year, killing millions of people. Jesus Christ now appears, destroying what is left of the armies and throwing the Antichrist and the false prophet into the lake of fire. The long-awaited millennium—the thousand-year utopia—now begins. From Jerusalem, Jesus and his saints will rule the world.

But this is not the end. After the thousand years of peace, Satan is released from the bottomless pit. Organizing an army for the final battle, he challenges God for one last time. Fire comes down from heaven, destroying these satanic forces, and the devil is cast into the lake of fire. The dead are now resurrected for the last judgment. The individuals whose names are not found in the book of life are cast into hell forever. God now creates a new heaven and a new earth. Peace and joy will now reign forever.[7]

The Rise of Dispensationalism

The last half of the nineteenth century witnessed two significant shifts in respect to end-time thinking. The dominant postmillennialism gave way to premillennialism. And within premillennialism, futuristic dispensationalism supplanted the old historicist version. These two important changes have largely shaped the apocalyptic outlook of evangelical Protestantism—a subculture which has become the dominant eschatological voice in modern America.

In 1860 the majority of American Protestants embraced postmillennialism, but by the early twentieth century it had largely disappeared. In part, this change occurred because many evangelicals defected to the growing premillennial ranks. To some extent, the rise of premillennialism and the decline of postmillennialism can be seen as the two sides of the same coin. But this is only part of the story. Postmillennialism also gradually receded among the more moderate to liberal Protestants, but they did not embrace premillennialism instead.[8]

Several factors contributed to the erosion of postmillennialism. Evangelical postmillennialism had gradually acquired a secular character. Previously, evangelicals had seen God and humanity as working hand in hand to usher in the thousand-year golden age. Some Protestants now began to equate the kingdom of God with America; others came under the influence of the new biblical criticism associated with theological liberalism. These new biblical studies undercut the supernaturalness of the Christian faith, including the apocalyptic elements of Daniel and Revelation and the second coming of Christ.[9]

Changing conditions in the late nineteenth and early twentieth centuries also tarnished postmillennialism. Postmillennialism rests on the premise that the world will get better and better. The Civil War, the decline of evangelicalism, the influx of Catholicism, and the outbreak of World War I cast a shadow across this optimistic outlook. In the eyes of many, the situation was getting worse and worse. Under these circumstances postmillennialism became less believable.[10]

Historicism versus Dispensationalism

Premillennialism's resurgence after the Civil War surprised most American evangelicals. Postmillennialism was still riding high, and premillennialism had been dealt a staggering blow by the Millerite fiasco. But circumstances would soon change, notably within the ranks of premillennialism itself.[11] The Great Disappointment of 1844 had decimated historicist premillennialism, but a futurist premillennialism called dispensationalism soon arrived on the scene. This new perspective not only revived premillennialism, but became the dominant evangelical eschatology in the twentieth century.

Historicist and futurist premillennialism differ at significant points. The historicist version looks back—contending that Revelation describes various periods in Christian history. It locks the interpreter into millennial arithmetic and makes date-setting an irresistible temptation. Herein lies a potential for disaster. Many historicists set dates—thereby making themselves the laughing stock of the evangelical movement.[12] By contrast the dispensationalists adopt a futurist interpretation of John's Apocalypse. This approach looks forward—insisting that Revelation points to events beyond this current age. Thus no prophecy has to be fulfilled before Christ's return.[13]

Here lies the genius of dispensationalism. It does not lock itself into a specific schedule for the second advent. On one hand, it avoids setting exact dates for Christ's return (though some dispensationalists have fallen into this trap). On the other, it maintains an intense expectancy for the secret rapture.[14] Christ could return at any time. Yet he might delay his return for years. While the historicist premillennialists were wedded to an exact millennial arithmetic, the dispensationalists lived with "maybes." They did not dare quit their jobs or sell their homes. Their understanding of prophecy lacked the precision of the Millerites and "forced them to live in the tension of now/not yet."[15]

Nevertheless, the dispensationalists did maintain a countdown for Christ's return. Drawing from passages in Daniel 9, they reckoned from Artaxerxes' decree to rebuild Jerusalem. But their arithmetic was different from that of the Millerites. The Messiah was to return at the end of Daniel's seventieth week (490 years). But the Roman authorities had crucified Christ 483 years (69 weeks) after Artaxerxes' decree.[16] The dispensationalists extricated themselves from this difficulty by devising a postponement theory. When the Jews rejected Christ as their Messiah, God suspended his prophetic schedule at the end of Daniel's sixty-ninth week. Therefore, Christ did not return, and God turned his attention away from Israel to the Gentiles.[17]

With their postponement theory the dispensationalists strictly separated Israel from the church—thereby significantly impacting their eschatology. Given God's postponement of his prophetic timetable, it was understood that none of the prophecies point directly to the Christian church. Instead, the church stands in a "mysterious, prophetic time warp, a 'great parentheses.'" The dispensationalists believed that God would not deal with the church and Israel at the same time; God would remove the church from earth before proceeding with his final plans for Israel.[18]

The historicists and dispensationalists also differed over the nature of the second advent. The dispensationalists taught that Christ's return would be a secret event evident only to the raptured saints. The historicists had insisted that it would be a dramatic public event. In effect, the dispensationalists contended that the second coming will occur in two stages: the church will be removed in a secret rapture; then, after the tribulation, Christ will return in a public event.[19]

The Arrival of Darbyism in America

Darby's prophetic views spread throughout Britain and Europe. After the Civil War they also caught on in America, where they had their greatest impact. By World War I dispensationalism had won many adherents among American evangelicals. In a modified form Darby's influence on end-time thinking in America has been immense—perhaps more than that of anyone else in the last two centuries.[20]

Between 1859 and 1872 Darby traveled extensively in the United States teaching his distinctive dispensationalism. He won many prominent ministers and laypersons to his teachings, especially in Presbyterian and Baptist circles. A number of evangelicals embraced most of his dispensationalism, including the secret rapture of Christians. Yet few accepted his views regarding strict separation from the "apostate" denominations. To his dismay, evangelicals did not regard the denominational structure of the churches as hopelessly corrupt.[21]

Another English prophecy writer, Sir Robert Anderson (1841–1918)—an investigator for Scotland Yard and a staunch Darbyite—influenced American evangelicalism. His book *The Coming Prince* (1882) gained an immediate American audience, going through eleven editions—one as late as 1986.[22] As an avid prophecy scholar, Anderson added some wrinkles to Darby's system. For example, beginning with the usual assumption that a day equals a year, he argued that Daniel's 69 weeks refers to the period between Artaxerxes' command to restore Jerusalem and the coming of the Messiah Prince. This designation of 483 years (69 x 7 = 483) foretold Christ's triumphant entry into Jerusalem.[23]

Moody's Promotion of Premillennialism

By the 1870s the great evangelist Dwight L. Moody (1837–99) was preaching the premillennial return of Christ. The source of his premillennialism is uncertain. His conversion to this doctrine may have been due to contacts with the Plymouth Brethren on a visit to England. Or Darby may have been persuasive on a trip to Chicago.

Moody's theology can hardly be described as systematic. Thus he made no clear distinction between the nuances within premillennialism, for example, between the pretribulational rapture and the posttribulational coming.[24] He did, however, contribute significantly to the rise of dispensationalism. His followers did not shy away from declaring their allegiance to the tenet that the pretribulational rapture could occur at any moment.

Nearly every evangelist after Moody followed in Darby's train. Included would be Billy Sunday, Reuben A. Torrey, W. J. Erdman, J. Wilbur Chapman, and George Needham. A number of leaders in the evangelical missions movement also embraced Darbyism. Among them were A. B. Simpson, who founded the Christian and Missionary Alliance, and Robert Speer of Presbyterian missions.[25]

Promotion by the Networks

Moody and his successors established networks to promote the new premillennialism. A number of Bible schools sprang up, at least fifty of which spread the dispensational message—the most prominent being Chicago's Moody Bible Institute, the Bible Institute of Los Angeles (Biola), and the Northwestern Bible Training School of Minneapolis. Almost without exception these Bible institutes taught the secret pretribulational rapture. So did a number of evangelical magazines, including Arno Gaebelein's *Our Hope*, James Brookes's *The Truth*, and Charles Trumbull's *Sunday School Times*.[26]

Among the institutions spreading the new premillennialism, the Bible conferences loomed large. At a series of Bible prophecy conferences from about 1875 to 1900 the dispensationalists encountered other conservative evangelicals and won many converts to their cause. The dispensationalists gradually came to dominate the other premillennialists, and especially the posttribulationists. By addressing issues other than eschatology these meetings forged the new premillennialism into a protodenominational movement with larger doctrinal concerns and much energy.[27]

A Closing of the Ranks of Fundamentalists and Dispensationalists

In the last half of the nineteenth century, evangelical Protestantism came under attack from several quarters—liberal theology, Darwinism, and the social gospel.[28] In such a climate the evangelicals circled their wagons. They systematized their beliefs in *The Fundamentals* (1910–15), a series of volumes that set forth what evangelicals believed to be the heart of the Christian faith—the inerrancy of Scripture, the virgin birth of Jesus, the resurrection, and the physical return of Christ.[29]

In this struggle against theological liberalism the evangelicals sought allies. At first the new premillennialists were suspect. Most evangelicals did not embrace their teaching of a secret rapture at any moment. But the dispensationalists did staunchly uphold the basic Christian beliefs.

105

So the evangelical mainstream gradually welcomed the new premillennialists into their ranks—a step that did much to legitimize their eschatology. And eventually the dispensationalists won over many evangelicals to their belief in a secret rapture.[30]

Scofield and His Bible

By the early twentieth century, dispensationalism had caught on in a big way among American evangelicals. Cyrus Ingerson Scofield (1843–1921) had a lot to do with this development. Although dispensationalism has no classic statement equivalent to Communism's *Das Kapital, The Scofield Reference Bible* has done much to shape the movement. James Barr has described it as "perhaps the most important single document in all fundamentalist literature."[31]

In some ways Scofield lived two lives—before and after conversion. He fought for the Confederacy during the Civil War. After the war he married, studied law, and began a practice in Kansas. Scofield then abandoned his wife, who later divorced him. Jailed in 1879 in St. Louis for forgery, he experienced a conversion while in prison. He then fell under the influence of the Darbyite pastor James Brookes and also met Dwight Moody.[32]

In 1882 Scofield became the pastor of a Congregational church in Dallas. Here he wrote *Rightly Dividing the Word of Truth* (1888), a classic which is still in print, and began a monthly publication, *The Believer.* In 1895 he left Dallas to engage in a number of activities, including teaching at Moody's school and participating in Bible conferences. By 1902 he devoted himself full-time to writing and speaking tours.[33]

Scofield's enduring legacy rests on his *Reference Bible*—published in 1909, expanded in 1917, and revised in 1967. Sales of this Bible total about 10 million. The Scofield Bible immediately became the standard of dispensationalism, and for ninety years has been the major vehicle for distributing dispensational ideas.[34]

Scofield's *Reference Bible* packages dispensationalism in an attractive format. It provides paragraphing, cross-references, and notes to the King James Bible that reflect Darby's dispensationalism. Unlike most commentators, who put some distance between the biblical text and their notes, Scofield placed his notes and the biblical text on the same page.[35] As a result, his comments often acquired the authority of Scripture. *The Scofield Reference Bible* has been "subtly but powerfully influential in spreading [Darby's] views among hundreds of thousands who have regularly read that Bible and who often have been unaware of the distinction between the ancient text and the Scofield interpretation." Readers often fail to remember where they first encountered a particular idea—in Scofield's notes or the biblical text.[36]

Scofield defines a dispensation as "a period of time during which man is tested in respect of obedience to some specific revelation of the will of God." His seven dispensations refine Darby's basic ages: innocence, conscience, human government, promise, law, grace, and the kingdom. Each age ends in human failure and divine judgment for this short-coming.[37] Thus a sense of apocalypticism pervades Scofield's thinking. Except for the final dispensation, little progress can be seen in his view of history. Like most premillennialists he regarded human nature as contemptible and held little hope for the betterment of society. Humanity was moving down the road to destruction. Like other premillennialists he also predicted that the Jews would return to Palestine in the last days and identified Russia with the Gog of Ezekiel 38. Then will come the final dispensation, which will usher in both destruction and triumph. After Christ raptures the church, the terrible tribulation will begin. Christ will then return and rule for a thousand years.[38]

Standing at Armageddon

During the first fifty years of the twentieth century, the world stood at the brink of Armageddon. The talk of wars and rumors of wars made a particularly deep impression at this time. "All our present peace plans will end in the most awful wars and conflicts this old world ever saw," said Reuben A. Torrey in 1913.[39]

The years after 1914 gave premillennialism a tremendous boost. This era witnessed tragedy after tragedy. But "things were never better for American premillennialism."[40] The basic prophecies of the early dispensationalists in the nineteenth century began to take concrete form in the early twentieth century. In the eyes of the dispensationalists, world war, the return of the Jews to Palestine, the Russian Revolution, the redrawing of the European map, and the rise of totalitarianism were all predicted in Scripture. Indeed, most of the major themes so conspicuous in modern popular dispensationalism had taken shape before World War II, the only exceptions being the threat of nuclear annihilation and control of the masses by the Antichrist through television and computers.[41]

The apparent fulfilment of ancient biblical prophecies enabled dispensationalism to take solid root in the evangelical subculture. Within premillennialism the tenet of rapture at any moment had prevailed over the posttribulationists. In Pentecostalism and early fundamentalism dispensational premillennialism had taken hold. Further, the modernist-fundamentalist conflict of the 1920s fragmented many denominations. What emerged was a separatist fundamentalism with its own churches, schools, mission agencies, and publishing houses. Dispensationalism thus had a subculture and an institutional structure to perpetuate itself.[42]

Armageddon–Almost

The guns of August 1914 glued the attention of prophecy buffs to current events. Prophecy was being fulfilled before their very eyes—so they believed. World War I and related events roused interest to a high level of expectancy. The apparent apocalyptic happenings moved the new premillennialism out of its narrow confines. In fact, the war gave premillennialism its widest audience since the rise of dispensationalism.[43]

The new premillennialism had a script for the last days, and, remarkably enough, current events seemed to be following it. Premillennialists held fast to their established positions. The prophetic clock, which had been stopped since the time of Christ, now began to tick.[44]

Some premillennialists saw World War I literally as the opening shot of the prophetic Armageddon. They believed Scripture spoke of a terrible war, the secret rapture of believers, and then Armageddon. "We are not yet in the Armageddon struggle proper, but at its commencement, and it may be . . . that Christ will come before the present war closes, and before Armageddon," stated *The Weekly Evangel*. Scofield saw World War I as the death struggle of the world system with the kingdom of God to follow.[45]

The Balfour Declaration of 1917 aroused even more end-time expectations. With the exception of the Millerites, most premillennialists had placed great importance on the Jews and events in Palestine. In fact, before the end could come, the Holy Land had to be in Jewish hands. This expectation was in keeping with the dispensationalists' belief that God had two distinct peoples—Israel and the church. The Jews disobeyed God and rejected Christ as Messiah. So God suspended his dealings with them and turned to the church. But God was not through with the Jews. At the end of the church age and after the secret rapture, he would again turn his attention to the Jews. They would have a national state in Palestine and endure intense suffering, after which Christ would return and set up his kingdom. The Jews would have a special place in this kingdom and once again enjoy the blessings of God.[46] Clearly, without the return of the Jews to Palestine God's cosmic plan as perceived by the dispensationalists would fail. A key piece in the dispensational eschatological puzzle would be missing.[47]

Accordingly, events in the Middle East captivated the dispensationalists. Here secular forces began to give life to premillennial theology. In the late nineteenth century Theodor Herzl (1860–1904) founded Zionism, a philosophy and movement promoting the return of Jews to Palestine. Most dispensationalists supported this secular Zionism because it embraced a central plank of their eschatology—the return of the Jews to the Holy Land. Most prominent among these Christian Zionists were William E. Blackstone and Arno C. Gaebelein.[48]

With anti-Semitism reigning strong in nineteenth-century Europe, especially in Russia, Jews began to move back to Palestine. But the big events were yet to come. In November 1917, Arthur Balfour, the British foreign secretary, established the legal framework for the Jews' return to Palestine: "His Majesty's Government views with favour the establishment in Palestine of a national home for the Jewish people, and will use their best endeavors to facilitate the achievement of this object."[49] That December saw the collapse of the Ottoman Empire, the evil power identified for centuries by Christians as being in league with the Antichrist. British forces under General Edmund Allenby captured Jerusalem without a shot being fired. For the first time since the Middle Ages, the Holy City was in Christian hands.

Such events sent shock waves through premillennial circles. Dispensationalists experienced a sense of prophetic ecstasy. Scofield wrote, "Now for the first time we have a real prophetic sign." A response in the *Evangel* was euphoric: "Do not we who are looking for the coming of our Lord . . . feel a thrill go through us as we read of the dry bones coming together (Ezek. 37)?" Leading premillennialist A. B. Simpson sobbed as he read the Balfour Declaration to his church.[50]

Premillennialists also regarded war-time events in Russia as prophecy in action. Ezekiel spoke of the northern power which was to invade Israel in the last days. But prophecy enthusiasts had long differed whether this nation would be Russia or the dreaded Turks. The Russian Revolution and the collapse of the Ottoman Empire combined to settle the issue—it would be Russia. The Soviet Union was now a godless communist state and a foreboding threat—two prominent themes in premillennial thinking for most of the twentieth century.[51]

Also of great interest was the map of Europe. Long before World War I the premillennialists had articulated an end-time geopolitical scenario: The last Gentile power will be a ten-nation confederacy resembling a revived Roman Empire and led by the Antichrist. The Antichrist will forge an alliance with the Jewish state. A northern confederacy dominated by Russia will challenge the Antichrist and enlist the king of the south to fight the Antichrist in Israel. The kings of the east will also join the fray against the Western European confederacy. Thus the great powers of the world will gather in Israel for the battle of Armageddon.[52]

The dispensationalists insisted that Christians would be raptured before the events surrounding Armageddon, and that the end-time political structure would be evident before the rapture. Unfortunately, in 1914 the map of Europe gave few hints that these prophecies were unfolding.[53] However, World War I and its peace treaties redrew the European map—much to the satisfaction of the premillennialists. Germany's defeat, the collapse of Austria-Hungary, and the unraveling of the Ottoman Empire altered the boundaries of Europe and the Middle East. These changes made more feasible the rise of a Western European confederacy resembling the old Roman Empire. Moreover, after the war the Russian bear recovered from revolution, embraced Communism, and terminated its alliance with the West—thus placing it in a position to lead the northern confederacy.[54]

On the whole, the war significantly furthered the premillennial cause. It confirmed the claim that the world was getting much worse, not better. It dealt a body blow to the optimism of postmillennialism. Instead of a better tomorrow, the war indicated that the sun was setting on Western civilization. In a remarkable way World War I reordered the map of Europe and the Middle East to conform to the premillennial prophecies.[55]

After Armageddon

The 1920s witnessed a lull in end-time speculations. The fundamentalists and modernists engaged in a bitter conflict not only for the religious soul of America, but for control of several denominations. As a result, prophetic speculations tended to be put aside. Premillennialism did, however, remain alive and well during these years.[56]

The two decades between the world wars (1918–39) saw tremendous political, social, and economic turmoil. The dispensationalists interpreted these events prophetically. They viewed the League of Nations as an instrument of the Western European confederacy. Godless Communism—and even socialism by extension—was regarded as embodying the spirit of the Antichrist, and the theological liberalism that made major inroads into most mainline denominations was interpreted as the apostasy predicted for the last days. Even Franklin Roosevelt's New Deal drew suspicious scrutiny. (One prophecy enthusiast said that the National Recovery Administration might be the mark of the beast.)[57]

Yet it was the rise of totalitarianism that aroused the most prophetic speculation. Events in Germany, Italy, Russia, and Japan riveted the attention of dispensationalists. Some were so carried away that they violated a golden rule of the new premillennialism—do not make specific predictions. Most prophetic writings focused on the rise of the Antichrist and his role as world dictator in the last days. With a revived version of the Roman Empire taking shape, it now remained to identify the beast of Revelation.[58] The favorite candidates for this position were Mussolini, Hitler, Stalin, the League of Nations, Communism, socialism, and the Soviet Union. Because the term *Antichrist* can be used very loosely, the "premillenarians could speak of Communism or liberalism as embodying the spirit of Antichrist . . . while at the same time they expected a personal Antichrist."[59]

Still, Benito Mussolini took center stage. Could he be the man of sin? Most premillennialists stopped short of categorically declaring him to be the Antichrist. Instead, they mustered evidence pointing to this conclusion or regarded him as only a type of the Antichrist. Il Duce's personal characteristics, premillennialists argued, matched the biblical criteria for the beast: he was charismatic, dynamic, militaristic, power hungry, and intent on geographical expansion.[60] Furthermore, Mussolini ruled in Rome and in 1929 signed a concordat with the pope, who had been the Protestants' favorite candidate for the Antichrist since the Reformation. What clinched the matter for some people was their belief that the fascist symbol appeared on the American dime. They interpreted this as preparation for the Antichrist's global rule. A number of fundamentalist preachers were obsessed with this line of thinking. For example, Leonard Sale-Harrison, an Australian Bible teacher who held prophetic conferences in North America, predicted that the end would come in 1940 or 1941.[61]

Some prophecy buffs saw Hitler as the Antichrist. Given a predetermined numbering system, they reckoned that the letters in the name Hitler added up to 666. On a more serious level, the Nazi-Soviet nonaggression pact of 1939 electrified end-time watchers. Ezekiel 38 speaks of Gog and its ally Gomer. Dispensationalists interpreted this to mean Russia and Germany, thus making the northern confederacy a reality.[62]

Prophetic forecasters also looked beyond Europe for signs of the times. One force in the battle of Armageddon was to be the kings of the east. In the nineteenth century, premillennialists believed this power to be the Turks or the lost tribes of Israel. "Who are these kings?" asked H. A. Ironside, pastor of Chicago's Moody Church. The answer now given by most dispensationalists was Japan and China. They characterized the rising power of Japan and the growth of Communism in China as the yellow peril.[63]

America also got into the fray. Ezekiel 38:13 speaks of "the merchants of Tarshish, with all the young lions thereof," who will stand up to the power of Gog. Prophecy interpreters agreed that this referred to Great

Britain and its former colonies, including the United States. To the relief of some premillennialists, the English-speaking nations appeared to be the heroes in the end-time conflict.[64]

For a while current events seemed to bear out the premillennial interpretations. But not everything went their way. There were obvious disconfirmations—especially Mussolini's fate. Instead of being a type of the Antichrist, he died a humiliating death, and the Roman Empire never revived. And Hitler's invasion of Russia in June 1941 shattered the prophetic expectation of a great northern confederation of Germany and Russia. How did the premillennialists handle these apparent setbacks? Some were confused, others were dumbfounded. But for the most part there "seemed to be just one big awkward silence."[65] Premillennialists tended to ignore the disconfirmations.

The Appeal of Early Dispensationalism

For most of the twentieth century, the primary vehicle for apocalyptic thinking was dispensational premillennialism. But such a situation did not develop overnight. Dispensationalism came on the American scene after the Civil War. By the early twentieth century it had secured a solid base within the evangelical subculture—the first step in gaining national visibility. How did all of this happen? Why did Darby's ideas appeal to American evangelicals?

Apocalyptic thinking takes hold during times of turmoil. The century from the Civil War to World War II may not have been the most tumultuous time in Western history, but it did bring considerable stress and change. Industrialization and urbanization proceeded apace in the late nineteenth century. Immigrants from Southern, Central, and Eastern Europe poured into America. Many of these immigrants brought with them their Roman Catholic, Eastern Orthodox, or Jewish faith, so the Protestant empire came under a serious challenge. There was the additional problem of various minorities—notably blacks and Native Americans—who experienced severe discrimination. Then came World War I and the Great Depression. Such events provided fertile soil for apocalyptic ideas.

But more important was the volatile religious climate. Thanks to Darwin's ideas and theological liberalism, the historic Christian faith faced tremendous challenges. Such intellectual developments contested the authority of Scripture and the supernatural character of Christianity. Fundamentalism confronted these challenges head-on. It affirmed the historic Christian faith and looked for allies in this struggle. The dispensationalists joined the fray and became part of the fundamentalist subculture, thus receiving considerable acceptance within the evangelical community. In the process they established networks and institutions that furthered their end-time ideas.

The turn of world events played an even greater role in solidifying the credibility of dispensational eschatology. Dispensationalism abandoned the emphasis on America's millennial mission and made the Jews preeminent in God's future plans. World War I, the Balfour Declaration, and the redrawing of the European map sent dispensationalism's stock soaring. These events made possible the return of the Jews to Palestine, the rise of Russia, and a European political structure compatible with premillennial predictions. Nothing fuels the credibility of prophecy more than its apparent fulfilment. And in the minds of many evangelicals this is just what happened. Such developments set the stage for the explosion of apocalyptic ideas that would take place after the 1960s.

All of this emphasis on world events takes nothing away from dispensational eschatology itself. Not only did dispensational predictions appear to reflect current events, but they also allowed for Christ's immediate return without setting a timetable. In doing so, dispensationalism solved the problem that had plagued historicist premillennialism.

7

Rapture Fever:
The Doom Boom Has Arrived

World War I and its aftermath catapulted premillennialism to a strong position within the evangelical community. But outside of this subculture few people knew much about it. In part, this can be explained by the fact that dispensationalism was housed within separatist fundamentalism. By the 1930s fundamentalism had its own churches, schools, and publishing agencies; dispensationalism could perpetuate itself within this framework with little outside help.[1]

But all of this would change by the 1970s and 1980s. Evangelical publishers cranked out prophecy books right and left. Hal Lindsey's *Late Great Planet Earth* sold over 25 million copies—prompting the *New York Times* to declare him the best-selling author of the 1970s. Bumper stickers read "In Case of Rapture, This Car Will Be Driverless" and "Beam Me Up, Jesus." For use in churches and schools dispensationalists produced a number of Hollywood-like films with end-time themes: *The Rapture*, *A Thief in the Night*, *The Road to Armageddon*, and *Image of the Beast*.[2]

Premillennialists also jumped into the television business in a big way. Nearly all of the electronic church's big names preached the premillennial message—Jerry Falwell, Jimmy Swaggart, Pat Robertson, Jim Bakker, Oral Roberts, Kenneth Copeland, Paul Crouch, and Rex Humbard. Network and cable stations carried Christian programs which analyzed current events from a dispensational perspective: Paul Crouch's Trinity Broadcasting Network, *Jack Van Impe Presents*, Pat Robertson's *700 Club*, Charles Taylor's *Today in Bible Prophecy*, and Ray Brubaker's *God's News behind the News*.[3]

Premillennialism even reached the highest levels of the American government. In a 1981 appearance before Congress, Secretary of the Interior James Watt questioned whether humanity had many more generations left before the Lord returns. In 1984 President Reagan had several discussions with reporters in which his quasi-dispensational views came out. Of course, the news media pounced on these opportunities, running programs and articles about "Ronald Reagan and the Politics of Armageddon."[4]

How did dispensationalism come out of its subculture into the national spotlight? Most obvious is the use of the modern media. The premillennialists became masters of mass communication. They skillfully expressed their views to a popular audience through mass market paperbacks, radio, television, movies, and videocassettes.[5]

Most important, while apparent confirmations of prophecy have throughout history added fuel to the millenarian fire, in the twentieth century events appeared to jibe with biblical prophecy as never before. The long-awaited divine promise was fulfilled—Israel became a state in 1948. The premillennialists were handed a prophetic windfall of unprecedented proportions. They also saw the atomic bomb as bringing the end-time cataclysm predicted in Scripture. The total destruction of planet earth now became a real possibility. Russia had long been eyed by premillennialists as the great northern power, and now the Soviet Union had become a superpower with the capability of invading Israel.

Another factor energizing eschatological speculations was the cultural climate. The 1960s and 1970s witnessed an occult revival. The occult arts took on a new life. Americans dabbled in witchcraft and spiritualism; they speculated about UFOs and about psychic phenomena. In their thirst to know the future, Americans turned to astrology, tarot cards, and ouija boards. While there is a great gulf between premillennial theology and the occult, the curiosity regarding the future spilled over into the evangelical community. In their zeal to know when Christ will return, some evangelicals went too far. Spurred on by *The Late Great Planet Earth*, they engaged in a flood of predictions concerning the second coming and events of the last times. This preoccupation with "Christian tea leaves" became a fad among many conservative Christians.[6]

The Varieties of Dispensationalism

In the twentieth century, dispensationalism has been at the forefront in pointing to Christ's return. But dispensationalism is not a monolithic theology; not all dispensationalists are the same. Some pursue end-time events in a rabid fashion, others are more moderate.

Darrell Bock of Dallas Seminary describes three types of dispensationalism in the twentieth century—Scofieldian, revised, and progressive. The Scofieldian and revised versions are often lumped together and called classic dispensationalism. In fact, all three stripes are alike in holding to the essentials of dispensational eschatology—namely, a separation between the church and Israel, premillennialism, and the secret rapture—but there are differences.[7]

Scofieldian dispensationalism, best represented by C. I. Scofield and Lewis Sperry Chafer, rigidly separates Israel and the church. Revised dispensationalism, which developed in the mid-twentieth century, allows for more continuity between Israel and the church and between the various dispensations. Scholarly representatives of revised dispensationalism include John Walvoord, Charles Ryrie, and J. Dwight Pentecost.[8] However, this version of dispensationalism has also produced individuals who have popularized the apocalyptic books of Scripture. These popular authors have often sensationalized eschatology and yielded to date-setting or something close to it. The remainder of this chapter will largely focus on these popularizers.

The third type—progressive dispensationalism—is even more moderate. It sees considerable continuity in God's plan for humanity and avoids wild prophetic speculations. In fact, many progressive dispensationalists regard Hal Lindsey's views as an eccentric deviation from dispensationalism. But because this version has not yet filtered down to the churches and the laity, the popular authors still exert the greatest influence over end-time thinking.[9]

Prophets of the Apocalypse

"There are now in the United States almost as many prophets of doom as could ever be found in the cities of medieval Europe. . . . The fear—and more often the hope—that the world will come to a quick and violent end is still very much with us today," writes Daniel Cohen.[10] In the last forty years or so, the number of end-time prophets has increased geometrically. Most, but not all, have proclaimed a premillennial message or a twisted version thereof. Some of these self-designated prophets

117

have taken a scholarly approach to the matter, but many have engaged in pure sensationalism.

A large number of the end-time thinkers—especially the more scholarly version—have either a direct or indirect connection with Dallas Theological Seminary. Founded in 1924 as Evangelical Theological College, Dallas Seminary became the sperm bank for dispensational thought in America. According to Timothy Weber, "Dallas Seminary has been the academic and ideological 'Vatican' of the movement." It has provided the scholarly basis for dispensationalism and has been the training ground for many Bible college teachers and pastors at independent churches. Some of the ill-educated popularizers have attended a Bible college where the Dallas brand of dispensationalism has held sway.[11]

Another common trait is that, remembering the Millerite fiasco, the majority of premillennial prophets have shied away from date-setting. The postponement theory allows the dispensationalists to avoid setting dates while they continue to hold that Christ could return at any moment. Still, some come very close to making specific predictions. They may pick a time frame, but hedge their statements by using words such as "probable," "could," "perhaps," and "suggest." In this way they can extricate themselves from a corner when a chronological prediction fails.[12]

Modern prognosticators range from the sensible to the ludicrous. Most scholarly would be John F. Walvoord, long-time president of Dallas Seminary and the author of about thirty books. Best known is *Armageddon, Oil and the Middle East Crisis*, which sold over a million copies. Walvoord does not suggest any dates for Christ's return. But he believes that most events on the end-time calendar have been fulfilled and that the rapture is at hand. Except for a few nuances Walvoord does not break new turf. Rather, he presents a good general picture of classic dispensationalist eschatology.[13]

Venerable evangelist Billy Graham is a premillennialist. His *Approaching Hoofbeats* best expresses his end-time views. While he has avoided the date-setting trap, he is also convinced that humanity is living in the last days. Humankind is headed for an unprecedented cataclysm brought on by nuclear holocausts, biological warfare, chemical contamination, and pestilence.[14]

Pat Robertson—1988 presidential candidate and founder of the Christian Broadcasting Network—has made some doomsday predictions. He once implied that the tribulation would be brought on in 1982 by the Soviet Union's invasion of Israel. The Middle East would explode, with 2 billion people being killed at Armageddon. But Robertson's apocalypticism was tempered by his political ambitions. While he embraced a premillennial eschatology, he espoused something resembling the postmillennial optimism. Peace, freedom, and prosperity can be achieved in the here and now. Strictly speaking, Robertson is a premillennialist but not a dispensationalist.[15]

Jerry Falwell, the founder of Moral Majority, is a thunderous voice for biblical prophecy: "I believe in the premillennial, pretribulational coming of Christ." Prophecy, he claims, is crucial because there is no hope in this world's system. Nuclear war is inevitable. Humankind is headed for utter destruction—except for the Christians, who will be raptured before the tribulation. The greatest indicator of these coming events "is the restoration of the nation of Israel."[16]

By any estimate Hal Lindsey must be regarded as the king of the popularizers. A Dallas Seminary graduate, he has done more than anyone else to bring premillennialism to nonevangelical popular culture. Through a flood of books, tapes, and lectures he has exerted tremendous influence on American thinking. He has brought his message of biblical prophecy regarding global events to college campuses, Congress, the State Department, the Pentagon, and foreign governments. It all began with his 1970 *The Late Great Planet Earth*, which was followed up by numerous other books—all building on the same themes.[17]

In *The Late Great Planet Earth* Lindsey contributes little to standard dispensational eschatology. He simply packages it in an exciting format and adds urgency by connecting biblical prophecy with recent events— especially the return of Israel and the 1967 Six-Day War. He also comes close to setting a date for the end on the basis of the parable of the fig tree in Matthew 24:32–33: "Now learn a parable of the fig tree; When his branch is yet tender, and putteth forth leaves, ye know that summer is nigh: So likewise ye, when ye shall see all these things, know that it [the return of the Son of man] is near." Lindsey equates the fig tree with Israel: "When the Jewish people, after nearly 2,000 years of exile . . . became a nation on May 14, 1948, the 'fig tree' put forth its first leaves."[18] In verse 34 Jesus continues: "Verily I say unto you, This generation shall not pass, till all these things be fulfilled." Lindsey contends that Jesus is here connecting his second coming with the rebirth of Israel. Noting that a biblical generation was about forty years, he goes on to say that "within forty years or so of 1948, all these things could take place."[19]

Most people understood Lindsey to have predicted that the rapture would occur in or about 1988. Later on he did some backtracking, saying he had suggested 1988 as a general time frame. In *Planet Earth— 2000 A.D.* he reminds readers that he had conditioned his earlier forecast with several ifs and maybes. He also points out that "all these things" in Matthew 24:34 could be the return of Israel in 1948 or the 1967 Six-Day War. Moreover, he redefines the biblical generation as "somewhere between 40 to 100 years." Nevertheless, Lindsey does maintain that the current generation will witness the end. He expects Christ to come at any moment—"probably in your lifetime."[20]

A host of other prophets have made a splash in modern America. In *Rapture under Attack,* for instance, Tim LaHaye, a conservative activist, while cautioning about date-setting, envisions a pretribulational rapture which causes great havoc. When Christian drivers and pilots are snatched up to heaven, global chaos will occur.[21]

But some others boldly set dates. The Bible, claims Grant R. Jeffrey in *Armageddon: Appointment with Destiny,* makes it clear that the end is near—it will probably occur around the year 2000.[22] And Chuck Smith, long-time pastor of Calvary Chapel in southern California, can be regarded as a converted date-setter. In *Future Survival* (1978) he declared that "the Lord is coming for his church before the end of 1981." But ten years later Smith repented of his mistake and now condemns date-setting: "Date setting is wrong, and I was guilty of coming close to that."[23]

A more sensational end-timer is Jack Van Impe, the self-styled Walking Bible. In a 1975 newsletter he insisted that the "Soviet flag would fly over Independence Hall in Philadelphia by 1976." This prophetic misfire did not stop him. Van Impe began to address large audiences through his TV program *(Jack Van Impe Presents),* videos, cassettes, and literature. One of his 1992 videos conveyed the message that the rapture, World War III, and Armageddon would occur in about eight years.[24]

Well-known end-time specialist Salem Kirban may not have set any dates, but he has inched close to this pitfall. The invasion of the African killer bees galvanized him. As they moved through Mexico into the southern United States, he saw these insects as the locusts of Revelation 9. In the judgment sounded by the fifth trumpet, everyone without the seal of God is subjected to painful stings for five months.[25]

In recent years John Hagee has made some big waves. His book *Beginning of the End* has been described as a *Late Great Planet Earth* for the 1990s. Hagee does not pinpoint the time when Christ will rapture his people. But he does insist that contemporary events fit into God's timetable for the end. In particular, he contends that the assassination of Yitzhak Rabin will trigger a series of events leading to Christ's return. The prophetic clock is ticking fast, says Hagee. "The moment that Yigal Amir pulled the trigger will stand as a defining moment in world history."[26]

Things start to get even more bizarre. In 1983 Mary Stewart Relfe claimed that God spoke to her through dreams. On his instructions she released a chart spelling out the divine timetable: World War III would break out in 1989, the great tribulation would begin in 1990, the United States would be totally destroyed several years before Armageddon, and Christ would return in 1997 after Armageddon. A noteworthy feature is

Relfe's mid-tribulationism—the church is to witness the rise of the Antichrist before being raptured midway through the tribulation.[27]

Not to be outdone, Edgar Whisenant made even more precise predictions. He did not hedge his bets with "abouts" or "shoulds" as do most prognosticators. Instead, he painted himself into a prophetic corner. His *88 Reasons Why the Rapture Will Be in 1988,* which sold 2 million copies, dated the rapture between September 11 and 13, 1988. Jesus' statement that no one can know the day or hour of his return does not mean that we cannot know the month or year, reasoned Whisenant. He even dated the beginning of World War III (Oct. 3, 1988) and other eschatological events. When 1988 came and went, he pushed his predictions ahead by several years.[28]

"This could be the year," Charles Taylor has said repeatedly. Taylor, a popular prophecy teacher for years, may be America's ultimate date-setter. But because he has misfired so many times, his ministry is on a decline. Also, Taylor qualifies his predictions, calling them suggestions, not date-setting. Nevertheless, he suggested eleven dates from 1975 to 1989 for the rapture. These suggestions center on the main theme of his preaching—just before the tribulation Jesus will rapture the church during the Jewish Feast of Trumpets.[29]

The vast majority of the doomsday prophets are premillennialists. In many cases, they take great liberties with dispensational theology, even distorting it at times. But Harold Camping is an exception. He is a Reformed amillennialist. (Many amillennialists say the millennium is symbolic or spiritual.) Camping, the president of Family Radio, predicted the world would end in September 1994. His book *1994?* and its sequel *Are You Ready?* presented an elaborate system of dating, numerology, and allegory pointing to September 1994. The arithmetic is not based on the usual dispensational scenario, but is his own unorthodox system. Despite the obvious disconfirmation, Camping believes that Christ will return soon.[30]

There are many more popular prophets. While they may not have set dates for Christ's return, they have made other prophetic statements—often about the identity of the Antichrist. Most of these prognosticators have common characteristics. Since 1945 premillennialism has produced its serious thinkers—Donald Grey Barnhouse, Wilbur Smith, George Ladd, John Walvoord, Dwight Pentecost, Charles Ryrie, and more. But the "prophecy popularizers were rarely trained theologians, denominational leaders, or settled ministers, but were freelance writers, evangelists, or TV preachers."[31] Modern prophecy has often been done by amateurs. Some have training in science or engineering, but not in theology or history. Despite their disdain for traditional higher education, these popularizers are eager for intellectual respectability.

Whenever possible, they claim scientific or historical authority for their pronouncements. Despite deriding academia, they often fashion themselves as educated people—sometimes with honorary or even bogus doctorates.[32]

End-Time Themes

After World War II, dispensational eschatology did not change substantially. To be sure, in the late twentieth century the progressive dispensationalists have taken the apocalyptic edge off dispensational end-time ideas. They reject the mentality of many popularizers that insists on setting the date of doomsday. Yet the main outlines of dispensational eschatology have been in place since the nineteenth century. World War I and the decades thereafter simply fleshed out these themes as current events appeared to be fulfilling prophecy.

Still, end-time prophecy underwent some modifications, both in substance and in tone. As noted earlier, only two new themes can be detected—nuclear destruction and the Antichrist's use of television and computers to control the masses. But the tone changed. The more scholarly and thoughtful prophetic interpreters have taken a backseat to the popularizers, who are usually not restrained by external institutions. Many have their own organizations, television programs, and publishing houses. Therefore, as the twentieth century winds down, the popularizers have become increasingly reckless. Their predictions are often irresponsible and even laughable.

Millenarianism has always evidenced a chameleon-like character. As predictions fail, the prophets adjust their prognostications to suit another current event. This tendency has accelerated since World War II. Prophecy is now big business. And to make a big splash, a popularizer must make sensational predictions. Invariably, this reckless approach to prophecy backfires, and the interpreter usually comes up with a different prediction to match the new circumstance.

Another hallmark of premillennialism is its tendency to be pessimistic. It sees history ending in a catastrophe. And nowadays, as the popularizers preach the coming doom, the pessimism has thickened. For example, Hal Lindsey has never been an optimist in respect to world affairs. Yet in *Planet Earth—2000 A.D.* (1994) his alarmism seems to be accelerating. He addresses every conceivable topic—the crime explosion, unprecedented earthquakes and natural disasters, berserk global weather, AIDS, drug abuse, ethnic conflicts, and environmental damage.[33]

In this same vein most premillennialists see humanity as on the path to perdition. The present age is under the control of Satan and is rapidly approaching a crisis point. Yet Christians need not despair—they will be raptured before the world goes up in smoke. "We see no hope in politics, in the business world, in education, in the world of medicine. But there is hope, and it is in the Second Coming of Christ," says Jerry Falwell.[34]

By the Bomb's Early Light

Among the major themes of dispensational eschatology is worldwide destruction. The earth has already been destroyed by water. For most of the Christian Era, biblical interpreters have pointed to a second and final cataclysm—this time by fire. According to 2 Peter 3:10, "the heavens shall pass away with a great noise, and the elements shall melt with fervent heat, the earth also and the works that are therein shall be burned up." Prior to 1945 most prophecy scholars interpreted this catastrophe in natural terms—comets, volcanic eruptions, and earthquakes. Other interpreters saw it as an eschatological event attributable to God but beyond human comprehension. All of this changed with the atomic bomb: the nuclear destruction of Hiroshima and Nagasaki set off a tidal wave of apocalyptic prognostications both secular and biblical.[35]

The awesome destructive power of nuclear weapons riveted the attention of many segments of society: scientists, the popular culture, mainstream theologians, and the premillennialists. Linking the atomic bomb with biblical prophecy, the popularizers added a new wrinkle to the premillennial scenario—nuclear destruction. They combed the Scriptures for evidence that nuclear annihilation is prophesied and inevitable. In the process they faced some puzzling interpretive problems. Would this coming holocaust be a nuclear war between nations? Or would God punish humankind by using nuclear weapons? Some premillennialists, Hal Lindsey among them, worked out a detailed scenario for World War III. Others felt the need to preserve God's transcendence. John Walvoord hardly mentioned nuclear weapons. Jack Van Impe said that God does not need humankind's modern inventions to fulfil his will. A few premillennialists straddled the fence. They suggested two nuclear events—World War III and God's destruction of earth at the end of time.[36]

A second interpretive problem concerned the nature of the warfare. Would World War III actually involve the weapons envisioned by the apocalyptic writers—mounted warriors, bows and arrows, and spears? Remember, a literal interpretation of Scripture is a hallmark of dispensationalism! Some, following this principle explicitly, envisioned a disarmament or some other circumstance that will necessitate the use of primitive weapons. Salem Kirban describes the battlefield of Armageddon as "a scene from a Middle Age history book. Bows, arrows, shields, spears everywhere. Crude weaponry but highly sophisticated nuclear explosives for close-up fighting."[37] Others adopted a more figurative approach, what they called "word-pictures." Lindsey, for example, changed the spears, swords, and chariots into modern weapons, including atomic bombs.[38]

How did the premillennialists view the threat of nuclear disaster? Though opinions varied, most premillennialists said it was inevitable. The rank and file agreed with Jerry Falwell. Nuclear war is inescapable for everyone except believers, who will be raptured. But the imminent conflict will not destroy humanity; the ultimate nuclear catastrophe will come only after the millennium. Meanwhile, nuclear conflict can be delayed by evangelism and diplomacy.[39]

Pat Robertson's position evidenced more ambivalence. In the late 1970s he predicted a holocaust by 1982. But as time went on, he retreated from the nuclear abyss; "God does not want to incinerate the world," he commented. Reflecting something of a dominion theology, he urged Christians to take more responsibility for creation. Billy Graham also wavered in this regard. Though he had earlier embraced the standard premillennial fatalism, by the 1980s he was addressing the issues of social justice and world peace.[40]

The advent of the atomic age has given a new meaning to apocalypticism. All people must come to grips with the chilling possibility of a nuclear holocaust. For premillennialists the key is the secret rapture. They face the coming holocaust with a degree of confidence, in some cases even smugness. After all, they will be snatched up to heaven before the nuclear catastrophe.[41]

The Greatest Sign

"There isn't the slightest doubt but that the emergence of the nation Israel among the family of nations is the greatest piece of prophetic news that we have had in the 20th century," said William W. Orr of the Bible Institute of Los Angeles.[42] Israel is the very linchpin of premillennial eschatology. Without the establishment of the state of Israel in 1948, dispensational end-time thinking would make little sense.

For more than a century, dispensationalists had predicted the return of the Jews to Palestine. Prophecy now came true, a process that validated premillennial eschatology. "Perhaps the single most significant event that solidified in the minds of many the correctness of the dispensational scheme of the end times was the 'rebirth of the state of Israel.'"[43] The related developments of the twentieth century—the Balfour Declaration, the British capture of Jerusalem, and then the return of the Jews—gave great credibility to dispensationalism.

Israel became a state in 1948—about the same time the Soviet Union gained great power. Many dispensationalists had long seen Russia as the great northern power. According to Dwight Wilson, "the juxtaposition of events in 1948 brought in the succeeding months a sense of expectation that would not be equalled again." Since 1948 the central assertion of dispensationalism has been the return of Israel. This key event is seen as a divine act starting the prophetic clock and the countdown to the final days.[44]

"The existence of Israel revitalized premillennialism and gave it, at least in its own eyes, undeniable credibility," says Timothy Weber.[45] But more was to come. In June 1967 the Arabs and Israelis fought the Six-Day War. Israel won a resounding victory. It captured the Sinai Peninsula, the Gaza Strip, the Golan Heights, the West Bank, and, most important of all, Jerusalem. The Six-Day War sent further chills down the prophetic spines of premillennialists. The Jews were now in a position to rebuild the temple destroyed in A.D. 70—an event many believed would occur during the tribulation. Bible teacher Wilbur Smith declared, "Christians believe that the events of these recent days are part of God's plan for the ages." John Walvoord called the conquest of Jerusalem "one of the most remarkable fulfillments of biblical prophecy since the destruction of Jerusalem in A.D. 70."[46]

Of course, interest in the Jews is not new. For much of Christian history, the interpreters of prophecy have looked to the Jews and often linked them to end-time events. Some believed that the Jews had to be converted before the end could come; others insisted that Israel had to be restored before the second advent. Darby built on this tradition by placing the Jews at the center of his theological system. Other dispensationalists continued this line of thought. Then came World War I, the Balfour Declaration, the rebirth of Israel, and the Six-Day War.[47] All of these events produced a flood of interest in the Jews. Israel became the focus of prophetic speculation. As Jerry Falwell put it, "the restoration of the nation of Israel . . . is the single greatest sign indicating the imminent return of Jesus Christ." Falwell went even further: "Since the Ascension of the Lord Jesus Christ to the right hand of His Father nearly two thousand years ago, the most important date we should remember is May 14, 1948. On that day . . . Israel became a nation again." According to other popularizers, "The Jew is God's time clock," and "all prophetic truth revolves around the Jews."[48]

The restoration of Israel in 1948 became the springboard for date-setting, or something close to it. As noted earlier, the parable of the fig tree in Matthew 24 was pivotal. Dispensationalists equated the budding of the fig tree with the restoration of Israel and declared that the generation alive at the time would not pass away until the end-time events began. Most popularizers regarded a biblical generation as about forty years and did an arithmetic computation: 1948 + 40 = 1988. Or, on the assumption that the rapture would occur just before the seven-year tribulation, 1948 + 40 - 7 = 1981. Other popularizers, equating the tree's budding with the Six-Day War, offered the calculation 1967 + 40 = 2007.[49]

The premillennialists went on to insist that God had much more in store for Israel. The events of 1948 gave the Jews a homeland; those of 1967 expanded their territory. Yet even these lands fell far short of what the dispensationalists believed God had promised the Jews. As Tim LaHaye noted, "the Jews today occupy only a small portion of what God intended for them to enjoy." Most interpreters believed that a vast territory will be acquired during the millennium. Though this lies in the future, most premillennialists in America today are staunchly pro-Israeli, supporting their territorial expansion and dominance of the Palestinians.[50]

However, Israel's future also has a dark side in the view of the premillennialists. Terrible events lie ahead; Israel is destined for horrendous suffering. As if the Nazi persecution were not enough, the Jews will face a more horrible ordeal during the tribulation—Satan will pour out his hatred on them. On the other hand, many Jews will be converted during the tribulation. And during the millennium they will experience a glorious future.[51]

Satan's Global Lineup

With their attention centered on Israel, the premillennialists constructed a prophetic geopolitical scenario for the last days. Drawing from Ezekiel 38–39 and Daniel 2 and 7, they predicted the end-time drama. The main actors were Russia, the European confederacy, and Israel. The supporting cast would include the kings of the east and the king of the south. If the United States had a role, it was to be a minor one.

This prophetic outline first emerged during the nineteenth century among the early dispensationalists. In the opinion of most premillennialists, World War I confirmed this outline. They regarded the events of this era—the Balfour Declaration, the defeat of the Turks, the Russian Revolution, and the new map of Europe—as prophecy in action. Prophecy had been fulfilled, at least in part.

World War II and the years immediately following saw some equally striking developments—the atomic bomb, the Cold War, the United Nations, the North Atlantic Treaty Organization (NATO), and the European Economic Community (Common Market). The premillennialists wove these developments into their prophetic scenarios. And any current events that ran counter to their prophetic projections they either ignored or explained away.[52]

Long before the Cold War, writers on prophecy had identified Gog with Russia. Ezekiel 38 is a prophecy against "Gog, the land of Magog, the chief prince of Meshech and Tubal." While dispensational scholars identify these locations as cities in Russia, other academics disagree. Yet a similarity does exist: *Rosh* (the Hebrew word for "chief") resembles Russia; Meshech connects with Moscow. But most striking is that, according to Ezekiel, in the last days invading armies will come against Israel from the far north. Geography clinches the argument, says John Walvoord: "The reference is to Russia . . . there is no other reasonable alternative."[53]

From 1945 to the end of the Cold War, dispensational scholars and popularizers pushed the belief that Russia would invade Israel in the final days. In the 1940s Harry Rimmer and Harry Ironside said that Russia would invade Israel for its mineral wealth. Writers on the subject have valued the mineral riches in the vicinity of the Dead Sea at between 1 and 2 trillion dollars.[54] To the contrary, Salem Kirban, pointing to the Soviet Union's chronic food shortages, argues that famine will motivate Russia's invasion.[55] To other premillennialists, oil will be Russia's incentive. Conquest of Israel will be a part of Russia's strategy for controlling the oil of the Middle East. Thus Walvoord's *Armageddon, Oil and the Middle East Crisis* sees oil drawing many nations to the Middle East for a great conflict. In *The Coming Oil War* Doug Clark similarly contends that an energy shortage will precipitate a crisis leading to war.[56]

According to Ezekiel, Gog will have allies when it attacks Israel. Foremost among them is Gomer. What is Gomer? The role of Germany has perplexed prophecy buffs. A part of Germany was in the old Roman Empire and thus is a candidate for the Western confederacy that will confront Gog. The division of Germany into east and west solved the problem. East Germany fell into the Soviet orbit and thus was Gomer. But most popularizers, including Lindsey, would identify Gomer only as "part of the vast area of modern Eastern Europe."[57]

Russia has other allies. Daniel 11 mentions the king of the south. Some interpreters regard this as referring to Africa as a whole. Others see it as a pan-Arab alliance led by Egypt. According to Lindsey, "many of the African nations will be united and allied with the Russians in the invasion of Israel."[58]

The kings of the east will also invade Israel in the last days. Before and during World War II, premillennialists generally interpreted these kings to be Japan. But with the defeat of Japan and China's embrace of Communism, China came to the forefront. The Sino-Soviet alliance of the 1950s fueled this interpretation. Revelation 9:16 speaks of an army of 200 million from Asia marching on Israel. When China boasted of its ability to assemble an army of this exact size, premillennialists took notice. In *666* Salem Kirban portrayed Chinese troops marching on the Middle East. Hal Lindsey spoke of the vast hordes of the Orient, the Yellow Peril, and the Red Chinese war machine.[59]

But Russia and its allies will be confronted by another power bloc—the revived Roman Empire. Daniel 2 and 7 record two visions which have impacted prophecy interpreters through the centuries and carry particular weight in dispensational circles. These chapters describe Nebuchadnezzar's and Daniel's visions of five future world governments. The first four governments are the Babylonian, Medo-Persian, Greek, and Roman Empires. Emerging from the Roman Empire, a fifth empire is represented as having ten toes, ten horns, and ten kings—signifying a ten-nation confederacy. One horn, which is interpreted as the Antichrist, dominates the confederation.[60]

Dispensationalists had long looked for a ten-nation European confederacy to arise. In fact, a united Europe had been a dream since Charlemagne's days, a vision that never went away. The events of post–World War II Europe convinced prophetic interpreters that European unity was right around the corner. With considerable excitement they watched the establishment of the Western European Union (1948), NATO (1949), and the European Economic Community or Common Market (1957). That the treaty that paved the way for the Common Market was signed in Rome, the center of the old Roman Empire, jarred the premillennialists.[61] All of these developments caused a flutter of interpretive activity, most of it linking some European institution with Daniel's fifth empire. Arno Gaebelein interpreted NATO to be the ten kings of the revived Roman Empire. Referring to NATO and the United Nations, Harry Ironside said that "the ten kingdoms are already in process of organization."[62]

As the Common Market took a definite shape, the prophetic voices grew louder. In the 1960s and 1970s the Common Market stood at fewer than ten members. Still, prophetic interpreters saw this as the probable beginning of the revived Roman Empire of the last days. As Hal Lindsey stated in 1970, "we believe that the Common Market . . . may well be the beginning of the ten-nation confederacy predicted by Daniel and the Book of Revelation." Referring to the Common Market, Edgar C. James similarly claimed that "for the first time since the fall of the Roman Empire, a great new power is emerging in Europe—just as the Bible has long declared it would."[63]

In January 1981 the Common Market membership reached the magic number of ten. Prophecy buffs leaped for joy. However, by the 1990s the Common Market had fifteen members, which caused another problem.

Bible interpreters addressed this dilemma by citing the statement in Daniel 7:8 that the little horn destroys three horns on the beast, that is to say, the Antichrist will smash some of the nations. Other nations, Britain in particular, will probably drop out of the European union.[64]

In the 1990s the unification of Europe has continued apace. If implemented, the Maastricht Treaty will forge something close to a United States of Europe. Heading this confederacy will be the Antichrist. Based in Western Europe, he will dominate the world. For the United States will decline, and Russia will be destroyed—some say by the Antichrist, others say by God's supernatural power. Then God will demolish the Antichrist at Armageddon.[65]

The Demonic World-System

A related theme of dispensational eschatology is that there will be a new world order in the last days. Satan will orchestrate a political structure to persecute God's people, and after the rapture his demonic world-order will take hold. This frightening new order will destroy all aspects of individual autonomy—the traditional family, religious liberty, personal privacy, and economic freedom. Instead, it will impose a universal religion, a standardized economy, and totalitarian political control—all dominated by impersonal global structures. Indeed, George Orwell's *1984* is on the horizon.[66]

But before this new world order is in place, the old one has to collapse. A transition must take place. Premillennialists insist that signs of the new political order are visible—the Common Market, Russian power, and the rise of China. Likewise, they are examining the cultural landscape for indications of the new demonic order. For the premillennialists insist that Scripture has predicted not only the end-time political scenario, but cultural developments as well.

What are these prophetic signs? Premillennialists see civilizations literally disintegrating before their eyes; the disordered cosmos described in Revelation is under way. The family structure is unraveling; teenagers rebel against their parents. Violence and immorality run rampant. In religion, apostasy looms large. Premillennialists regard the National Council of Churches, the World Council, and the ecumenical movement as demonic forerunners of the apostate universal religion. Theological liberalism and Roman Catholicism also come under attack.[67]

Moreover, dispensationalists have earmarked the emerging global economy for special denunciation. The Antichrist will consolidate the world's economy by controlling energy, the financial system, and the food supply. Collectivism, socialism, and the welfare state are signs of things to come. Premillennialists point to the International Monetary

Fund, the World Bank, the Federal Reserve Board, and the Common Market as forerunners of the new global economic order.[68]

Premillennialists contend that Scripture predicts a one-world government, so the United Nations is particularly suspect. They fiercely denounce any attempt to reduce national sovereignty and place American interests under UN control. Prophecy interpreters regard the Trilateral Commission—that shadowy international organization comprising the United States, Japan, and Western Europe—as the ultimate conspiracy. Its membership consists of some of the world's most powerful political and economic leaders. Behind the scenes they pull the puppet strings, exercising immense global control.[69]

The vehicle for global political and economic control is modern technology. Computers, communications satellites, credit cards, money machines, laser-read price markings, fax machines, and much more will soon make a global system a reality. For the first time in history, global control can be achieved—so the premillennialists say. Computers will "dictate that every man, woman, and child in the world lives, works, buys, and sells under a system of code marks and numbers," says William Goetz.[70]

Basic to premillennial thinking, then, is "the belief that a demonic world order lies ahead, and that its beginnings may be discerned in contemporary world trends."[71] Through TV, radio, videocassettes, and paperbacks, dispensational premillennialists have communicated this worldview to millions of people.

Will the Real Antichrist Please Stand Up!

This new demonic world-order presupposes two things: the collapse of the old order and the appearance of the Antichrist. In premillennial thinking both concepts jumped to the forefront. Western society must face a political and economic crisis of unprecedented proportions, and then the Antichrist will take power. Signs of the decay of the old order already abound, especially in the economy. Larry Burkett's *Coming Economic Earthquake* contends that America stands on the brink of economic collapse.[72] Moral, social, and political anarchy will compound this crisis and push the old order over the edge.

The premillennialists have a scenario to accommodate this crisis. They did not invent the idea of the Antichrist. But in a secular world that tends to make light of such ideas, dispensationalism has accentuated it—sometimes in a very serious way and sometimes by reducing "it to a child's plaything."[73]

The concept of the Antichrist rests on several passages in Daniel, Revelation, Mark, 2 Thessalonians, and 1 and 2 John. Daniel 7:8 speaks of the "little horn" that sprouts from the beast. Revelation 13 portrays the Antichrist as a seven-headed beast that emerges from the sea and performs great wonders. In Mark 13:22 Jesus warns of false Christs arising in the last days, and the apostle Paul speaks of the "man of sin" or "lawless one" in 2 Thessalonians 2:3. First and Second John contain the only specific references to the Antichrist in Scripture. But John speaks of the Antichrist only as an evil force, not as an individual. Premillennialists insist that the Antichrist is a person and thus ironically do not emphasize these verses.[74]

For nearly two thousand years Christians have interpreted these passages in various ways. The result is a diverse tradition that alternately construes Antichrist as an individual, an institution, a movement, and evil in general. Some have even believed in two Antichrists—perhaps a force of evil or a blasphemous person labeled a type of the Antichrist, and then the final enemy. Before World War II a number of individuals and institutions made the list of potential Antichrists or types of the beast: Antiochus Epiphanes, Nero, a Jew from the tribe of Dan, Judas Iscariot, the papacy as an institution, individual popes, Frederick II Hohenstaufen, Napoleon, Mussolini, and Hitler. The most enduring identification of the Antichrist through history has been the papacy.[75]

After 1945 the quest for the Antichrist produced some amazing theories. Throughout history the search had often focused on finding evidence of conspiracy.[76] During the last forty years, however, this pursuit may have risen to new heights in premillennial circles. Some dispensationalists are tenaciously seeking the identity of the beast, for they believe that he is now alive somewhere in the world.

The vast majority of premillennialists believe that the Antichrist is an individual. So the popularizers have come up with name after name. But some dispensationalists see the Antichrist as a system or a movement. Other premillennialists muddy the waters. While they may hold to an individual Antichrist, they tend to see certain systems as in league with the beast. They often regard these movements and systems as demonic and make them synonymous with the Antichrist. The consensus among premillennialists seems to be that the Antichrist will be "a European, as yet unknown, who [will] rule a ten-nation revived Roman Empire, then extend his domain worldwide."[77]

The more sober dispensationalists are content with the Antichrist's anonymity. They do not feel the necessity to name him. But the prophetic popularizers feel no such restraints—they are reckless and discredit premillennialism in the process. The list of potential Antichrists reads like a who's who. Since 1945 the suggestions have included Pope Pius XII, John F. Kennedy, Pope John XXIII, Henry Kissinger, Moshe Dayan, Pope John Paul II, Anwar Sadat, Jimmy Carter, Ronald Reagan, Pat Robertson, King Juan Carlos of Spain, Sun Myung Moon, Mikhail Gorbachev, and Saddam Hussein.[78]

The popularizers seem to use one or two criteria to determine the identity of the Antichrist—the number 666 (Rev. 13:18) and evidence of a deadly wound (Rev. 13:3).[79] A person is really suspect if both criteria apply. In efforts to decipher the meaning of 666, letters of the alphabet are assigned numerical equivalents. Of course, the numbers will vary according to the language employed, and an interpreter can arbitrarily assign a particular value to each letter. As a result, if one works at it, one can find some way of associating a good many names with the number 666.

Henry Kissinger became a favorite candidate for the Antichrist. He was a Jew who orchestrated several peace initiatives. Also, ways were devised to make the letters in his name total 666. Another proposal alleged that tanks in Jimmy Carter's secret force were stamped 666. Other individuals met both tests. There are six letters in each of Ronald Wilson Reagan's names, and his house address in California was 666. Moreover, as president he was shot. When President Sadat of Egypt reopened the Suez Canal in 1975, his ship had 666 on the bow. In addition, he later received a mortal wound.[80]

Some candidates for the Antichrist primarily met the deadly wound test. Moshe Dayan, the hero of the Six-Day War, had previously lost his left eye in action. Not only did John F. Kennedy's Roman Catholic faith arouse fears of the Antichrist, but he also fell to an assassin's bullets. Some expected him to rise from the dead. Other individuals denounced Pope John Paul II as Antichrist, partly because of the attempt on his life, partly because of his endorsement of greater European economic and administrative cooperation.[81]

Many dispensationalists are fundamentalists who tend to regard the world system and even culture in general as demonic. Thus they identify a variety of elements in the global order as forces of the Antichrist. Frequently targeted are Roman Catholicism, liberal Protestantism, the global economic system, modern technology, Jews, socialism, Communism, the New Age movement, Islam, environmentalism, the Common Market, the Soviet Union, feminism, peace organizations, and rock music.[82]

The criteria most often employed by premillennialists to determine the forces in league with the Antichrist have been 666 and global control. As in identifying individuals, popularizers have devised ingenious mathematical formulas and applied them to particular institutions or movements. For example, elaborate schemes have associated both New York City and computers with 666. Premillennialists have also warned that certain international economic, political, and cultural institutions have the potential for global dominance. Such organizations will band together and enable the Antichrist to control the world.[83]

The targeting of Roman Catholicism largely subsided after 1945. Indeed, many fundamentalists now praise Catholicism's stance against Communism, feminism, and abortion, and its support of family values. Still, the old anti-Catholicism has not completely died out. Dave Hunt implies that the Catholic Church is the false prophet who will assist the Antichrist, and John Ankerberg and John Weldon connect the pope with the Antichrist's message.[84]

What is most denounced today as a force of the Antichrist is the global economic system. It is pointed out that, according to Scripture, a revived Roman Empire will wield great economic power; the beast will have absolute economic control. In order to buy and sell, in order to receive basic health services, one will need to have the mark of the beast, probably an invisible mark implanted in the body. The Antichrist will control a global credit system, which in fact is currently in place. Thus Mary Relfe says, "The '666 System' is here." The World Bank code number is 666; J. C. Penney prefixes its accounts with 666. And by using three languages, Visa can be construed to equal 666: VI is the Roman number for six; "six" in classical Greek looks like the letter S; and in Babylonian the letter A has the value of six.[85]

In the last days there will also be a global religion controlled by the Antichrist and the false prophet. The New Age movement with its pantheism and mysticism embodies this end-time religion, say some premillennialists. According to Dave Hunt, when the end comes, "millions of New Agers in thousands of network groups around the world will be sincerely implementing Antichrist's programs in the name of peace, brotherhood, and love."[86] Similarly, in *The Hidden Dangers of the Rainbow* Constance Cumbey portrays the New Age movement as a gigantic satanic conspiracy designed to control the world and force the universal worship of the Antichrist. She asserts that "for the first time in history there is a viable movement—the New Age Movement—that truly meets all scriptural requirements for the Antichrist and the political movement that will bring him on the world scene."[87]

The popularizers earmark many other institutions as in league with the Antichrist—the list is long and growing. But most important is the issue of control. These institutions and modern technology are viewed as enabling the beast to enforce his will on the entire world. Individuality and freedom in all forms will be stamped out. In fact, some popularizers have even gone so far as to suggest that the Antichrist might be a computer. Jack Van Impe theorizes that the "Antichrist will enslave and control earth's billions through a sophisticated computer fashioned in his likeness."[88]

The Shifting Sands of Prophecy

The late twentieth century witnessed a number of earthshaking events. Some seemed to disrupt the dispensational end-time scenario—especially the collapse of Communism in Eastern Europe, the unraveling of the Soviet Union, the end of the Cold War, and the reduction of the nuclear threat. On the other hand, the Persian Gulf War and the continuing move toward European unity reinvigorated dispensationalism.

How did the prophetic popularizers respond to these events? For the most part, they continued to maintain their traditional themes. After all, the main outline of their prophetic predictions remained intact. But when disconfirmations arose, the chameleon-like quality of popular dispensationalism came to the forefront. Interpretations were adapted to the shifting sands of world events.[89]

The popularizers could feel good about a number of things. Israel still existed and struggled against the Arab world. Although some observers looked with concern on Israel's peace overtures to the Palestine Liberation Movement, the centerpiece of premillennial eschatology—the Israeli state—remained intact. Further, in the 1990s European unification proceeded apace. Accordingly, some popularizers shifted their attention from the Soviet Union to an apparent prophetic confirmation—the Common Market. On the economic side, globalization accelerated. A worldwide financial system, multinational corporations, and a global information network drew the world closer. On the social ledger, human wickedness increased and morals declined—key ingredients in any last-days scenario.[90]

The Persian Gulf War of 1991 shot adrenaline into the veins of the premillennial world. The popularizers felt right at home. A flood of end-time publications rolled off the press; prophecy books boomed in sales. Some popularizers saw Saddam Hussein's invasion of Kuwait as the beginning of the end: "The nations of the world are drifting into their final formation of alliances for the Tribulation Period," declared Salem Kirban. Focusing on Revelation 18 and its predictions of the destruction of Babylon, some premillennialists believed that Saddam Hussein was about to rebuild ancient Babylon. "The Bible makes it clear that Babylon will be rebuilt," said Charles Dyer.[91] Although Iraq's rapid defeat by the United States took much of the steam out of this interest in eschatology, most popularizers viewed Saddam Hussein as a type of the Antichrist and the Persian Gulf War as a dress rehearsal for Armageddon.[92]

Still, dispensationalism's view of the end encountered some rough water—especially the collapse of the Soviet Union and the end of the Cold War. How did the prophetic popularizers respond to this apparent disconfirmation? After all, the belief that Gog will invade Israel is central to popular premillennial eschatology. There were three basic responses. Some premillennialists ignored these world happenings. Instead, they focused on apparent fulfilments of prophecy, especially European unity. They also took more notice of global problems with apocalyptic dimensions—environmental disasters, world famine, and plagues.

Most common was the second response. Many popularizers regarded the events in Eastern Europe and the Soviet Union as temporary glitches. The Bear has not been declawed, they said; it will be back. Russia's "land and naval forces remain strong," and the country "still has the basic resources to rebuild her tattered economy," warned Charles Dyer. Or, as Hal Lindsey put it, "Yes, the Evil Empire may be gone, but Russia's role in the endtimes scenario remains the same."[93] A more radical version of this second response is Grant Jeffrey's discussion of what he calls "the Great Russian Deception." Supposedly, Communism is dead and Russia is weak both militarily and economically. But "the KGB and Communist Party have embarked upon the greatest deception plan in history. . . . Glasnost, perestroika and democracy are simply disinformation designed to deceive the West."[94]

A third response seriously questions the identification of Russia with Gog. Mark Hitchcock contends that the northern power that will invade Israel is actually an Islamic confederation. The real threat to Israel comes from Islam, not Russia. The southern republics of the former Soviet Union are now independent Muslim nations. They will form an alliance with other Islamic nations, including Turkey, and become the northern confederacy that attacks Israel.[95]

Premillennialists also note other developments in current events. Although the Soviet nuclear menace is diminished, the spread of nuclear technology to smaller nations means that the threat is not over. The rise of German and Japanese economic power has also not gone unnoticed. Germany is seen as the dominant power in the western confederacy, and Japan may join China as the Asian powers that march on Israel.[96] Whatever events occur in the future, premillennialism will probably continue to demonstrate a remarkable ability to adjust its predictions to the reality of world affairs.

The Propagation of Premillennialism

By the late twentieth century, premillennial eschatology had captured the interest of millions of Americans. Why? A number of factors have contributed to this development—some religious, others political and cultural. To start, premillennialism had become entrenched within the evangelical subculture before World War II. While the evangelical faith has always occupied a significant place in American religion, since World War II it has experienced a surge in growth. Today about 25 to 30 percent of the American population can be categorized as evangelicals. Further, in the 1970s evangelicals became politically active, and one of their own (Jimmy Carter) even became president. By the 1990s they constituted an important power bloc in American politics. The mere fact that premillennialists constitute a notable presence within evangelicalism has given their end-time ideas a boost. Indeed, the vitality of the evangelical faith has provided a vehicle for promoting premillennial eschatology in the late twentieth century.[97]

Closely related is the use of the mass media by premillennialists. During the 1930s and 1940s they began to propagate their ideas by means of the radio. This small beginning turned into a flood after World War II. Along with other evangelicals the premillennialists became quite adept at using the mass media—especially television and paperback books. Premillennialist popularizers frequently preach their end-time message on television. But most important, they have mass-produced countless paperbacks for an eager audience who have gobbled them up by the millions. Indeed, the premillennial message has gotten out in a big way.

Still, there must be an audience for such ideas. And, in fact, the cultural and political climate of the late twentieth century has produced an audience with an apocalyptic mind-set. Throughout the twentieth century the dominant mood in Western society has been one of pessimism. Successive military conflicts, the specter of nuclear annihilation, energy shortages, regional famines, threats to the environment, and financial crises have cast a foreboding shadow across the future of humanity. In such an environment the premillennialist doomsday predictions appear quite credible.[98]

Of crucial importance, specific dispensational predictions appeared to be coming true right before people's eyes. This, of course, gave early dispensationalism much credibility. And the trend increased after World War II. The establishment of the Israeli state in 1948, the capture of Jerusalem in the Six-Day War, the growth of Soviet power, the development of nuclear weapons, and the organization of the European Common Market were seen as prophecy in action. And nothing gives prophecy more credibility than its apparent confirmation. One confirmation carries more weight than do several disconfirmations.

Finally, the psychological makeup of many evangelicals, especially the fundamentalist variety, may be a factor in the growth of dispensational eschatology. Throughout history socially deprived people have been vulnerable to apocalyptic ideas. But most of the contemporary premillennialists do not come from the lower social orders. They are not the powerless. In fact, they have considerable political and economic clout. Why then do they embrace apocalyptic ideas? One theory contends that they are a cognitive minority. Premillennialists embrace a supernatural worldview, a perspective that is out of step with the modern mind-set. Whether they are actually oppressed as a result is less important than how they feel. Many fundamentalists feel tyrannized by society and thus are alienated from the world. Their eagerness to embrace apocalypticism, then, is not surprising.[99]

8

Eager for the End: Messiahs and Prophets

Just before dawn on April 19, 1993, the loudspeaker blared, "This is not an assault! Do not fire!" Many of the Branch Davidians, however, "thought it was the last day of the world"; for most of them, it was.[1] This type of apocalyptic thinking is not limited to the Branch Davidians. Since 1945 a host of fringe religions have paraded across the American religious landscape, some of them with end-time visions.

Indeed, marginal religions elsewhere in the world have held apocalyptic ideas. In 1992 about twenty thousand members of the Dami sect in Korea were convinced that Christ would return on either October 20 or 28. Scores of them quit their jobs, sold their homes, and left their families; some women even underwent abortions in preparation for their trip to heaven. By 12:10 A.M. on October 29, they were disappointed. Irate members of the sect attacked those responsible for the predictions, and the leader, Lee Jang Rim, was arrested for fraud. Then in October 1994 forty-eight members of the apocalyptic Order of the Solar Temple committed suicide in Switzerland. They expected doomsday to be coming soon. The Supreme Truth, a Japanese doomsday cult, would strike in March 1995. They set off nerve gas in a Tokyo subway as the opening shot of the final world war, which they expected between 1997 and 2000. The members of the cult believed that they would be the sole survivors of this final battle in which the West attempts to destroy Japan.[2]

139

An Overview of Fringe Religions in Modern America

Throughout Western history most apocalyptic groups have existed on the margins of society and exhibited unusual theological or social characteristics. However, in some ways America has had a millennial mission; and, accordingly, apocalyptic bodies have been closer to the mainstream. Nonetheless, nineteenth-century America witnessed a number of fringe groups with a millennial orientation—the Shakers, Mormons, Oneida Community, Seventh-day Adventists, and Jehovah's Witnesses.

In this study we will use two criteria to categorize fringe religions: their orientation toward society and their point of origin. There are world-rejecting and world-affirming movements.[3] The culture-rejecting groups, usually called sects or cults, clearly state that the majority religion is inadequate or downright heretical. Such groups often exhibit apocalyptic tendencies. To them, the world is hopelessly corrupt and must experience an apocalyptic purging.[4] On the other hand, the world-affirming religions, often associated with the New Age and human potential movements, view the social order less contemptuously than do the world-rejecting groups. While the world must be improved, humanity has enormous potential to bring such change about. World-affirming movements often have a millennial mission. Looking forward to a new age, they maintain that it will not be inaugurated by a catastrophe, but will evolve gradually.[5]

Broadly speaking, the points of origin of fringe religions fall into three categories: Western Christian, occult-mystical, and Eastern.[6] Of the three, Western fringe groups are the most apocalyptic and millennial, Eastern bodies the least. Somewhere in between, occult bodies have their prophets of doom, but often foresee a golden age evolving in the near future.

In this chapter we will categorize apocalyptic fringe religions in America as Western, occult, or racist. Most of the racist groups have Christian origins, but we will treat them in a separate category. Many of the occult bodies incorporate Western apocalyptic elements.

Unfortunately, there is no clear thread that ties these diverse groups together. Unlike most dispensationalists, they do not share common themes; nor do their end-time ideas neatly fit into the pre-, post-, and amillennial categories. They even see the end differently. Some groups view it as an impending cataclysm; others see a new age evolving.

The one element that many fringe apocalyptic movements in America do have in common is the context in which they arose—the counterculture and its aftermath. The same atmosphere that fueled the apocalypticism of many premillennialists ignited the fringe groups. The years from the election of John F. Kennedy in 1960 to 1975, when Gerald Ford inaugurated the bicentennial era, were tumultuous and traumatic. These years witnessed several political assassinations. Violence erupted in the civil rights and antiwar movements. Feminism and environmentalism challenged some of the most fundamental assumptions of Western culture, namely, that men have the right to dominate women and that humanity can act with impunity toward nature. Urbanization, science, and technology brought incredible change. Indeed, American society was severely shaken and in many ways permanently transformed.[7]

The supreme catalyst for all the challenges to the American system was Lyndon Johnson's decision to escalate the Vietnam War. Cynicism toward the political establishment erupted into violence. College students and others agitated for nearly half a decade. To cap off this period, America experienced a series of traumas: Watergate, the resignation of President Nixon, and the collapse of the American-backed regime in Vietnam.[8]

All of these developments helped to foster an apocalyptic mentality in American society at large. "The invention of the atomic bomb began the . . . apocalyptic mood," which became very strong in both secular and religious sectors during the 1960s and 1970s. Widespread concern with environmental pollution was a manifestation of the apocalyptic mind-set. Apocalypticism was political as well. During the 1960s and 1970s many believed "that the American government [was] beyond reforming and must be destroyed in order for something new and better to take its place."[9]

While the apocalyptic mood could be discerned within many groups, "it was perhaps the strongest in the counterculture." As a consequence, the religious groups that emerged from the counterculture in the West tended to be radical and apocalyptic.[10] Yet by the mid-1970s the counterculture had declined and along with it many fringe religions with their end-time ideas. The new religions that rose in the late 1970s and 1980s were world-affirming groups. In particular, the human potential and New Age movements were less apocalyptic and tended to view the coming new age more in evolutionary terms.[11]

Western Fringe Groups

Of the many groups in post–World War II America that can be regarded as fringe religions, that is, sects or cults, we will look first at those that are Western in origin. They differ from Eastern and occult groups in that they generally embrace the Judeo-Christian worldview or have some historic connection with the Christian church. But they are often deviant and bizarre. Some of these groups also believe that the world or this age will end soon.

In chapter 5 we described apocalyptic groups that originated in nineteenth-century America. Several of them are alive and well in modern America—the Jehovah's Witnesses, Seventh-day Adventists, and Mormons. In this chapter we will note a few groups that have developed primarily since 1945: the People's Temple, the Jesus People, the Children of God, the Worldwide Church of God, the Unification Church, the Branch Davidians, and the Lubavitchers. We will focus on the apocalyptic characteristics of these contemporary bodies; more-complete descriptions can be found elsewhere.[12]

Nightmare at Jonestown

"Alert! Alert! Alert! Everyone to the pavilion." The Reverend Jim Jones was using the loudspeaker to summon the members of his People's Temple to their last communion. "Everyone has to die," said Jones. "If you love me as much as I love you, we must all die or be destroyed from the outside." And indeed, they did die.[13]

Perhaps the most bizarre religion-related incident of the twentieth century occurred in Jonestown, Guyana, in November 1978. Here more than nine hundred people committed suicide or were murdered because of their involvement with the People's Temple and its leader, Jim Jones.[14] What caused Jim Jones to go off the deep end? Why did over nine hundred people commit suicide?

Most government investigators and journalists interpret the Guyana situation psychologically. They say that Jones may have been insane, and the people may have been brainwashed to commit suicide by a charismatic personality who exercised immense control over them.[15] But behind the tragedy at Jonestown was an ideology or theology. As John Hall points out, the People's Temple should be regarded as an apocalyptic movement. The apocalyptic mood of American society during the 1960s had made its impact on Jones, especially the racial strife, the political unrest, and the perceived impending nuclear holocaust.[16] A predisposing factor here was Jones's own social background. Born and raised in southern Indiana, a Ku Klux Klan stronghold, he had founded the People's Temple in the 1950s "as a reaction to a cultural situation that was extremely racist." Thus the struggle against racist persecution had been a part of Jones's life from an early stage.[17]

While the roots of the People's Temple can be traced to the revivalistic evangelical tradition, by the time of Jonestown the group had come to resemble an otherworldly apocalyptic cult. They shared with other apocalyptic groups a pessimism about reforming social institutions. Though Jones supported various progressive causes, he had little hope for their success.[18] Accordingly, his prophetic views were more radical than those of most millennial groups: "he focused on an imminent apocalyptic disaster rather than on Christ's millennial salvation." His eschatology set before him the choice of either fighting the beast (the American social and economic system) or collective flight from the impending disaster to set up a kingdom of the elect. The People's Temple was more "directed toward the latter possibility."[19]

Even while in Indiana, Jones had adhered to an apocalyptic worldview. He then moved his followers to Redwood Valley in California on the assumption that this area would survive a nuclear holocaust. During these years Jones's apocalyptic vision turned to predictions of "CIA persecution and Nazi-like extermination of blacks." Like many apocalyptic sects or cults the People's Temple promised a theocratic haven on earth in which members could "escape the 'living hell' of society at large." Many of Jones's followers joined the People's Temple with such a hope in mind. For blacks in particular, the temple promised some immediate relief from persecution rather than some otherworldly hope. Gradually developing communal characteristics, "the People's Temple more and more [came] to exist as an ark of survival."[20]

In 1977 the People's Temple came under closer investigation by the media, which the church perceived as CIA persecution. As the scrutiny mounted and defectors from the temple increased, it became doubtful whether Jones could maintain his haven in the United States. He was "reduced to decrying the web of 'evil' powers" that had entrapped him and searching for another postapocalyptic sanctuary—that is, one that would survive the impending catastrophe. He went to Jonestown hoping to find such a haven. But he could not be sure that Jonestown was the promised land. Unable to "trust the Guyanese government," he was "considering seeking final asylum" in the Soviet Union or Cuba.[21]

But even this hope came unraveled when Jones became convinced that the church's enemies were about to descend on Jonestown. Without any prospect of victory over his enemies, Jones was convinced that the only recourse for the People's Temple was to "abandon the apocalyptic hell by the act of mass suicide." The opponents of the temple would then no longer be a threat; "there could be no recriminations against the dead." Moreover, this mass suicide "could achieve the otherworldly salvation Jones had promised his more religious followers."[22]

The Last Days and the Jesus People

"The last days are upon us . . . and I believe that it won't be long until we see the Second Coming of the Lord," proclaimed Chuck Smith, pastor of Calvary Chapel.[23] His words were echoed throughout the Jesus movement. Aside from the simple gospel, no doctrine characterized the Jesus People more than did the belief that the last days have arrived.

The Jesus movement refers to a social phenomenon involving numerous young people whose religious activities revolved around a strict literal interpretation of the Bible and other trappings of conservative Christianity. The phenomenon began in the mid-1960s and continued in a modified and reduced form into the 1980s. Though the Jesus movement falls largely within the framework of evangelical and fundamentalist Christianity, it has produced some deviant groups that have been labeled cults.[24]

Coming out of the counterculture, the Jesus People had characteristics shaped by that movement, namely, a subjective approach to life, an alienation from the dominant culture, and an apocalyptic hope. Smacking of fundamentalism as well, their faith was Jesus-centered, Bible-centered, and focused on the simple gospel—the message that Jesus saves.[25]

Everything in the Jesus movement—its views on evangelism, politics, culture, history, and the church—hinged on the belief that this world is in its last days. In fact, the Jesus People not only reflected the apocalyptic mentality so prevalent in the 1960s, but carried it further. Most of the Jesus People could not imagine themselves growing old and dying a natural death. They fervently believed that they were God's chosen instruments to give the world one last chance to repent.[26]

While apocalyptic hope unified the Jesus movement, there were still many differences on how and when the world would end. The Jesus People overwhelmingly embraced premillennialism, but held to three premillennial views regarding the rapture: pretribulationism, midtribulationism, and posttribulationism. All three could be found within the Jesus movement. Yet, profoundly influenced by Hal Lindsey's *Late Great Planet Earth*, most accepted the pretribulational view. However, a substantial number insisted that the church would go through the tribulation. Some even went so far as to call the pretribulational rapture a "damnable heresy."[27]

Prominent among the posttribulationalists were the Children of God (COG), the most controversial of the Jesus People groups. Born of the counterculture, they sprang from the social crises of the late 1960s. Their founder, David Berg (1919–94), took them beyond the confines of orthodox Christianity into some deviant beliefs and practices. Consequently, the mainstream of the Jesus People ostracized them.[28]

Fervently apocalyptic, the Children of God, who in 1979 changed their name to the Family of Love, were driven by their belief in the imminent end of the world. "Probably the most important COG teaching is 'End Time Prophecy,'" says Jack Sparks. "This concept is their key to understanding every part of the Christian Life."[29] Indeed, contrary to most Jesus People, the Children of God have even engaged in some date-setting.

Expecting the return of Christ and his thousand-year rule to be soon, the Children of God saw the present system, especially that of the Western world, as so corrupt that no reformation was possible. It had to end before a new order could begin. In their view the final collapse "will come when Communism takes over the western nations and paves the way for the anti-Christ." Under this individual's rule, professing Christians will deny the faith and receive the mark of the beast mentioned in the Book of Revelation. But the Children of God will stand "as God's faithful remnant of 144,000."[30]

Firmly convinced of the coming downfall of the United States, Berg had left the country by the early 1970s, and some of the Children of God followed him. One "Mo-letter" (as Berg's letters were called) warned that the comet Kohoutek would destroy America: "You in the U.S. have only until January [1974] to get out of the States before some kind of disaster." Typical of most apocalyptic groups, the Children of God went wild and insisted that the comet represented the final sign of America's doom and a fulfilment of prophecy. Though they believed that the whole world would end soon, they were obsessed with the downfall of America in particular, most likely through a Communist takeover.[31]

The Children of God expected a posttribulational rapture: the saints would be persecuted during the tribulation and drawn up into heaven at the end. In some ways "Berg's eschatology was similar to dispensational premillennialism" with its emphasis on the coming tribulation and rapture.[32] In still other ways his eschatology—especially his date-setting and exclusivism—resembled the systems of the Jehovah's Witnesses and the Worldwide Church of God. Berg's countdown to the end began with the "End of the Time of the Gentiles" in 1968. In the mid-1980s, the Antichrist would reveal himself, and the rapture would occur around 1993. After Christ's return the Children of God would serve as important officials during the millennium.[33]

145

The End according to Herbert Armstrong

Founded in the 1930s by Herbert W. Armstrong (1892–1986), the Worldwide Church of God draws its ideas from Seventh-day Adventism, the Jehovah's Witnesses, Judaism, Mormonism, and British Israelism. Until recently the Worldwide Church of God was regarded as an unorthodox religion because of its rejection of many basic Christian doctrines. Since Armstrong's death, however, the church has moved toward orthodox Christianity.[34] Moreover, repudiating its prophecy-mongering past, it now refuses to speculate when the end will come. Thus our comments will relate to the Worldwide Church of God as it existed under Herbert Armstrong.

While the Worldwide Church of God maintained a number of distinctives—Sabbath keeping, Old Testament dietary practices, and rejection of the Trinity—its teachings revolved heavily around the end times. Among the marks of Armstrong's prophetic doctrines were British Israelism, a modified dispensationalism, the belief that world history spans six thousand years, pronouncements relating to nineteenth- and twentieth-century Britons and Americans, and an emphasis on the Old Testament.

Basic to the beliefs of the Worldwide Church of God was British Israelism (or Anglo-Israelism). The central idea was that after the dispersion of the ten lost tribes of Israel, they migrated to northern Europe, where they became the ancestors of the Saxons who invaded England. Thus the people of England (and, by extension, the United States and the peoples of the British Commonwealth nations) are the literal descendants of the ten lost tribes of Israel. So Britain and the United States are special objects of God's promises and blessings.[35]

The Worldwide Church of God also "adopted the dispensational view of the history of the Church of God." The seven churches of Revelation 2–3 were considered to be the seven church ages. "The Worldwide Church identifies itself as the Church at Philadelphia, which was to appear just before the endtime events described in the Book of Revelation." It was widely believed that the tribulation would start in 1972 and that the church would have to flee the United States.[36] This belief was based on Armstrong's view of history. Like most millennialists he equated each day of creation with a thousand years. God created the world in six days and rested on the seventh, thus establishing the pattern for human history. History would extend for six thousand years and be followed by a thousand-year millennial rest. From his belief that God had created the world in 4025 B.C., Armstrong concluded that the end would come around 1975. Though he denied setting dates, he did "suggest" that certain dates fit God's time schedule.[37]

A key element in Armstrong's prophetic scheme was based on Leviticus 26:18: "I will punish you seven times more for your sins." Dating this prophecy to 717 B.C., Armstrong concluded that God would withhold his blessings from his chosen people for 2,520 years (7 years of 360 days). Subtracting 717 from 2,520, Armstrong reached the early nineteenth century. Nothing prophetic happened around 1800. However, as Armstrong pointed out, America and Britain began to grow in power and size about this time.[38] He then milked the Old Testament for anything that might match current events. Micah 5 speaks of the remnant of Jacob (which Armstrong interpreted as Britain and America) being cut off. Armstrong noted that God had continued to bless his chosen people—Britain and America—until about 1950; but after 1950 Britain's empire was nearly gone, and America did not fare well in the Korean and Vietnam Wars. "Why can't the United States whip little Vietnam?" Armstrong asked. He concluded that the decline of God's chosen people was under way, which was to take place before the beginning of the tribulation and at the hands of the ten-nation European alliance.[39]

Another quirk of Armstrong's system was his fascination with the number nineteen. Noting that the earth, moon, and sun come into near conjunction once every nineteen years, he concluded that God would work in nineteen-year cycles. That one of these cycles ended in 1972 is what led to the suggestion that the tribulation would begin in 1972. When this prediction failed, he adjusted his dates to a time in the near future. Nevertheless, the failure of this prophecy caused hardship among his followers and havoc in his empire.[40]

The Lord of the Second Advent

"We are living at a point in time unlike any since the beginning of history," declares the Unification Church. The church's leader, Sun Myung Moon (b. 1920), says that the last days are at hand. Humankind now has the opportunity to usher in the kingdom of God. Such opportunities have existed in the past, but humanity has bungled them. In terms of political power, converts, and finances, the second half of the twentieth century is a unique time to build God's kingdom on earth.[41]

The Unification Church is one of the most controversial new religions to arrive on the contemporary American scene. Its beliefs are a syncretic mixture of many religious impulses. The recipe for Moon's religion combines ingredients from Eastern and Western systems, seasoned by mysticism from Moon's own revelations.[42]

Many millennial bodies withdraw from society and have few expectations for changing the world. Not so with the Unification Church. It is a messianic movement desiring to unite all people into one religion.

147

The church aims to usher in a new age, a new moral order in which all religions are unified within itself. The church's aims are theocratic—it seems to aspire to become, either overtly or covertly, the dominant religion in the world.[43]

Like many new religious groups in modern America, the Unification Church has placed considerable emphasis on doctrines of the end times. But most other groups have promoted a version of premillennialism. Moon's church has advocated a form of postmillennialism. Instead of looking for a cataclysmic end of history, the Unification Church sees the last days as a time when human beings will turn away from the selfishness of the past to a future of God-centeredness.[44]

J. Isamu Yamamoto divides the core teachings of the Unification Church into three eras: the first Adam, the Second Adam, and the Lord of the Second Advent. The first Adam and Eve were to establish the kingdom of heaven on earth through their offspring. Instead, they fell into sin. The Second Adam, Jesus Christ, was to save humanity spiritually and physically, but his crucifixion frustrated God's plan for humanity. Jesus paid only for humankind's spiritual salvation.[45] Because Jesus failed to marry and produce the perfect family, another Messiah is needed to complete the physical aspect of salvation. This is the job of the Lord of the Second Advent, who must come to establish the kingdom on earth. Although the *Divine Principle*, the church's scripture, does not state that Moon is the Messiah, it does establish conditions which only Moon fulfils. The Unification Church is, then, "a millennial Christian movement with the interesting twist that the anticipated Second Coming of Christ will have little to do with Jesus of Nazareth."[46]

The *Divine Principle* also places great emphasis on the number two thousand. God took the two thousand years from Abraham to Jesus to prepare the world for the first Messiah; for the last two thousand years God has been preparing the world for the second Messiah. The *Divine Principle* implies that the second Messiah could come at any moment, if he has not already.[47] For the kingdom of God will be ushered in when the Unification Church has brought sufficient change to the world. "The Kingdom of Heaven cannot be realized by supernatural miracles but only by man's fulfilling his responsibility to solve all of the problems in a realistic way." In the 1960s Moon predicted that the kingdom would be achieved in 1967. Later he revised this figure to 1981. Because the world was still not ready for the kingdom, Moon postponed the date to 2000.[48] Its coming will be an age of harmony, not a catastrophe.

The Messiah of Waco

"Fueled by kerosene," flames quickly consumed Ranch Apocalypse, killing "86 Branch Davidians—including 17 children."[49] How could this happen? In part, the religious freedom guaranteed by the First Amendment leads to such bizarre action. "If people want to follow Donald Duck, so be it. The First Amendment guarantees neither taste nor truth," says Leo Sandon, professor of religion at Florida State. But when Donald Duck turns out to be Jim Jones, Charles Manson, or David Koresh, people die—as they did at Waco in April of 1993.[50]

But religious freedom can account for only part of the story. Psychological explanations abound. David Koresh, the leader of the Branch Davidians, had obvious mental problems, especially a messianic delusion. Others have used less charitable terms to describe him—"a religious psycho" or "the wacko from Waco."[51]

Koresh's chosen names and title betray his obvious messianic delusion. He changed his name from Vernon Howell to David Koresh, declaring himself to be prefigured by two kings mentioned in the Old Testament. From Koresh or Cyrus the Great, the leader of the Persian Empire, he gained his ruling authority. David, of course, referred to King David. This placed Koresh in the line of Christ. But the title "The Lamb of the Book of Revelation" is even more outrageous. Rather than identify the Lamb with Christ, he declared, "I am the Branch . . . the Lamb," thus reinforcing his claim to have ultimate truth.[52]

Koresh's puppetlike followers also had obvious psychological problems. They submitted themselves to the total control of a ninth-grade dropout with a charismatic personality and were willing to die for their cause.[53] That his followers were only a handful must have been a blow to the ego of someone who believed himself to be a prophet. This situation may have made it easier for him to lead his flock into a final inferno.

But psychology cannot provide all the answers. The Branch Davidians had a history and a theology. They were a split-off from a split-off. In 1959 the Branch Davidians splintered from the Davidian Seventh-day Adventists, who had broken from the mainline Seventh-day Adventists thirty years earlier.[54] The long-standing millennial tradition of Adventism significantly influenced the Branch Davidians and Koresh's ideas. Through the years, of course, the mainstream Seventh-day Adventists had lowered their expectations of an impending end-time and opted for institutional development instead. But some of the split-offs maintained and even accelerated the apocalypticism of earlier Adventism. In addition, from the time of William Miller and Ellen G. White, Adventism has housed a number of prophetic voices. In David Koresh the apocalyptic extremes of this tradition came home to roost.[55] In all fairness, however, it must be noted that the Branch Davidians distorted the broader Adventist tradition. The cultic trademarks of the Branch Davidians—widespread intimidation and abuse, a perverted view of sex and marriage, and military-like discipline—cannot be found in mainstream Adventism.[56]

In professing his lineage from King David, Koresh had established himself as a messianic figure on a divine mission—namely, to open the seven seals of Revelation. These seven seals were the core of Koresh's eschatology. He embraced something resembling a premillennial post-tribulational view of the end. Koresh believed that humanity had already entered the tribulation prophesied in Revelation. The tribulation was a necessary purging prior to the second coming of Christ and the millennium.[57] In addition, the opening of the seven seals would precede the end of the world. With the opening of each seal, the Lamb would unleash another judgment upon the world. His disciples saw themselves as God's faithful remnant, chosen to rule with the Messiah during the millennium.[58]

More specifically, Koresh saw himself as carrying out the judgment of the sixth seal. The sixth seal of Revelation 6:12–17 involves several cataclysmic events. When government agents surrounded the Branch Davidians in their compound at Mt. Carmel, Koresh interpreted this confrontation with the government as one of the events associated with the opening of the sixth seal. The government agents, who were part of the evil world order (Babylon), were simply carrying out their prophesied role. Their attack on Mt. Carmel would trigger the end of the world.[59] We know the rest of the story. Koresh and his followers went to a fiery death. The confrontation may not have been the fiery sixth seal destroying the world—but it certainly was for the Branch Davidians.

A Jewish Messiah in New York

As we saw in chapters 6 and 7, many fundamentalist Christians believe in the impending return of Christ. They view the establishment of the Israeli state and the Six-Day War as the fulfilment of prophecy. Some even insist that the Jewish temple must be rebuilt in Jerusalem before Christ will return.

Orthodox Judaism maintains similar ideas. More liberal Jews depersonalize the messianic concept, seeing it as an era of peace rather than an individual. Not so with the Orthodox Jews. They view the Old Testament as literally as Christian fundamentalists do the entire Bible. Refusing to believe that Jesus Christ has fulfilled the Old Testament prophecies, they look for a future Messiah.[60]

Orthodox Judaism has its ultraorthodox wing, the Hasidic Jews. A conservative branch of the Hasidic Jews is the Chabad Lubavitch movement. According to the Lubavitch tradition, during every generation there lives at least one righteous Jew who meets the qualifications for the Messiah. In recent years the Lubavitchers have even gone so far as to set up a toll-free Messiah hotline and to carry beepers so that they can be reached immediately when the Messiah arrives. They tapped their leader Menachem Mendel Schneerson of Brooklyn as the prime candidate for Messiah.[61]

A prominent rabbi, Schneerson had an outstanding Jewish pedigree: a brilliant scholar in Jewish law, math, and science; a student of seventeen languages; a descendant of the founder of Hasidism; and a rabbi's son. Like the Christian fundamentalists he saw current events—the establishment of the Israeli state, the collapse of the Soviet Union, and the Persian Gulf War—as the final events preceding the Messiah's arrival.[62] In particular, he used the Persian Gulf War to stir up apocalyptic expectations, for, according to a Midrashic prophecy, the Messiah would come in the year of a great confrontation in the Arabian Gulf. In fact, Schneerson predicted that the Messiah would come by September 1991. Despite this misfire Lubavitchers still looked for the Messiah, probably Schneerson himself. But disaster struck—Schneerson died in 1994. Some Lubavitchers still did not give up on Schneerson—they expected him to be raised from the dead as the Messiah.[63]

Occult and New Age Predictions

The end could come in any one of many forms. Occult prophets and New Age seers provide us with a variety of options. End-time predictions "range from a violent apocalypse, floods, pestilence, and utter chaos to utopian visions of technological breakthrough and peace for the Age of Aquarius."[64] On the whole, the occult prophets foresee an impending catastrophe, but many New Agers view the future as an era of enlightenment and progress.

Prophets of Doom

"The future is frightening," said Marie Julie in 1880. "The Earth will be like a vast cemetery. Corpses of the impious and the just will cover it. The Earth will tremble to its foundations, then great waves will agitate the sea and invade the continents."[65] This view of the future, especially the years around 2000, is shared by most occult prophets. These doomsday seers could fill an entire volume, but we will note only three—Nostradamus, Edgar Cayce, and Jeane Dixon.

Nostradamus may be the world's most famous prophet. We encountered him in chapter 4. Michel de Notredame lived in the sixteenth century, but his prophecies address issues ranging from his day to the late twentieth century and beyond. In particular, his predictions regarding the end of the twentieth century have intrigued millions, catapulting his writings to record sales.

How accurate are his predictions? Nostradamus's vague quatrains are subject to varied interpretations. His supporters claim an 85 to 90 percent accuracy rate for his prophecies. But according to Daniel Cohen, "his followers usually credit the master with predicting whatever it is they already believe." Detractors such as James Randi claim his quatrains are either inaccurate or allegorical nonsense.[66]

Whether seer or charlatan, current interest in Nostradamus rests on his prophecies regarding the modern world. He has been credited with predicting Communism, the creation of the state of Israel, nuclear warfare, the AIDS epidemic, and the Persian Gulf War. But most important, his prediction of a cataclysm at the end of this millennium sends chills through the spines of those who believe his prophecies:[67]

> In the year 1999 and seven months
> The great King of Terror will come from the sky.
> He will bring back to life the great king of the Mongols.
> Before and after war reigns happily unrestrained.

Nostradamus expected the world to go beyond 1999. Although the world will be shattered by global conflict, famine, and pestilence, despair will give way to hope. Eventually there will come a gradual reawakening and world peace. Nostradamus's end-time scenario bears some resemblance to Christian eschatology, namely, destruction followed by a golden age. And he even refers to an Antichrist.[68] But on the whole, Nostradamus brings us an end without God; political and military activities—not divine intervention—determine the end-time events.

Edgar Cayce (1877–1945) is well known for many occult activities, including his prophecies. This so-called sleeping prophet founded the Association for Research and Enlightenment in 1931; it still continues his work, especially by promoting his writings on physical healing, astrology, diet, reincarnation, and prophecy, including interpretations of biblical prophecy. While in a self-induced trance, Cayce would make pronouncements on many subjects. Some events he predicted successfully include the Great Depression, the union of Austria and Germany, the death of two American presidents while in office, the Russian-German clash, and the end of World War II in 1945.[69]

Before his death in 1945, Cayce prophesied many catastrophic events that would begin in 1958 and run to the end of the century. While he did not predict doomsday, the magnitude of the disasters he prophesied point in that direction. Much of the North American continent will break up and slide into the sea; Japan will experience a similar fate; rising oceans will inundate coastal areas throughout the globe; earthquakes and volcanoes will wreak terrible havoc; and the lost civilization of Atlantis will rise again, probably in the Caribbean Sea.[70]

While Cayce twisted the prophetic scriptures, the Bible—especially Daniel and Revelation—heavily influenced his thinking. In fact, he put a Christian veneer on many of his prophecies. He believed that the natural disasters coming around 2000 point to the second coming of Christ and will be followed by the millennium and a new age.[71]

During the 1960s Jeane Dixon became an American legend, largely because she had forecast the assassination of John F. Kennedy. She had a number of other successful predictions, along with many misfires. Of particular interest is her disclosure relative to end-time events. On February 5, 1962, the day of the great Aquarian conjunction, a child of the East was born. Dixon saw this child as revolutionizing the world's religions and governments. His power would reach its zenith in 1999, "when a terrible holocaust will shock the world's peoples into a true renewal." At first Dixon regarded this child as a new Messiah, but then she decided that he was the Antichrist.[72]

The predictions of many more prophets could be noted. But their message is basically the same, even a bit repetitious: "We are heading into a time of tremendous upheaval—what some seers have described as the 'end of the world.' . . . Yet along with this foreboding is the promise of a new and far better world to be built beyond."[73]

The New Age Movement

The New Age movement became visible in the early 1970s; during the 1980s New Age ideas penetrated American culture. The New Age can be seen as a cultural shift with social and religious dimensions. Gordon Melton regards it as "a social, religious, political, and cultural convergence between the new Eastern and mystical religions and the religious disenchantment of many Westerners."[74] The New Age is a meeting of three cultural forces: the Judaic and Christian traditions, Western occult mysticism, and Eastern religions.

The New Age is also a transformational or millennial movement. It regards humanity as standing between two ages in human history—the Age of Pisces and the Age of Aquarius.[75] The heart of the New Age vision is the spiritual and psychological transformation of individual people. But this is only the first step. The New Age, as the name indicates, envisions a new world, a new era in human history. For this change to begin, a number of influential individuals must experience transformation and then actively work for social change.[76]

Barbara Hargrove sees New Age apocalypticism as different from that of similar post–World War II movements, namely, the Jesus People and fundamentalist premillennialism. The Jesus People took a dim view of the future and were absolutely convinced that Jesus would come in their lifetime. Fundamentalist premillennialism, as represented in Hal Lindsey's *Late Great Planet Earth*, "holds that social and moral corruption will increase until Jesus returns to take up his faithful." Unlike this pessimistic apocalypticism, New Age millennialism is "characterized by love and light." More like postmillennialists than premillennialists, the New Age groups have a "more positive interpretation of the end of the Age."[77]

The writings of prominent New Age advocate David Spangler reflect this positive view. He contends that the world is entering a new age, a cycle when humanity will become the "world savior," a time when light will enter the planet and the world will experience an "occult redemption." The New Age is to be "the age of communication" when humanity, nature, Christ, and God effectively communicate and come to realize their unity and oneness.[78]

The coming New Age will be based not on some doomsday scenario, but on a paradigm shift. "A paradigm is a scheme for understanding and explaining certain aspects of reality," writes New Age spokesperson Marilyn Ferguson. "A paradigm shift is a distinctly new way of thinking about old problems." While a new paradigm will include old truth, a paradigm shift has taken place when people begin to think differently.[79]

New Ager Fritjof Capra believes that the modern Western world is in a state of crisis brought on by the old paradigm that was formed by the rationalism of René Descartes, Isaac Newton's physics, and the Judeo-Christian tradition. Cartesian rationalism promoted linear reason and pushed mysticism aside. Newtonian physics gave the West a mechanized worldview. The Judeo-Christian tradition desacralized creation by removing God from it and opened the door to the exploitation of nature. The old paradigm also produced a patriarchal order, an authoritarian and centralized political system, and a hierarchical social organization.[80]

Based on a new paradigm, the New Age will be different. While elements of the old order will be retained, there will be a convergence of East and West. Rationalism will be balanced by intuition. God, humanity, and nature will no longer be regarded as distinct entities. The environment will be nurtured because humanity will be one with nature. A holistic view of science will replace Newtonian physics. Men and women will have an equal status. Society will be less hierarchical, and the political systems will be decentralized. Internationalism will replace nationalism in global relations. Crime and war will be greatly reduced. Also, there will be one world religion, based on common mystical assumptions drawn from the religions of the world. Finally, instead of competition which fragments the world, cooperation will reign supreme.[81]

While most New Agers are working toward a new world order, some connect the New Age with the coming of Christ. Of course, the Christ of the New Age is not the Jesus of orthodox Christianity. In fact, the New Age movement separates the human Jesus from the office of Christ or the divine Christ-spirit, which has indwelt many great religious leaders throughout history (e.g., Rama, Krishna, Buddha, and Jesus). In fact, because Christ is divine and divinity indwells all people, Christ is within each person.[82]

When will this New Age arrive? When will the paradigm shift occur? On the whole, New Agers are vague about this issue, suggesting a range of several centuries. According to astrologers, however, an equinox shift occurs about every two thousand years, and one is due anytime now. Such a change in the stars ushers in a new age in human history. Thus many New Agers expect a change around the year 2000. On the basis of Mayan and Aztec beliefs, David Spangler sees an age of harmony beginning about 2000. Ken Carey regards 2000 as a kind of psychic watershed. On the other side lies a utopian society.[83]

Still, most New Agers do not specify when the golden age will arrive. They speak of the coming of Christ in only a very general sense—he manifests himself in all humanity.[84] However, other New Age teachers have become involved in specific predictions, date-setting, and even doomsday forecasts. Many Theosophists believed that a world savior had come in the person of Jiddu Krishnamurti. When he renounced this role in 1929, Alice Bailey predicted the reappearance of the Christ, whom some called Lord Maitreya. Several groups and individuals emerging from her Arcane School continued this line of prediction.[85]

Most prominent of these individuals was Benjamin Creme. He said that in 1945 Christ announced that he would return if certain global conditions were met (peace, economic sharing, human goodwill, and reduction of authoritarianism). In July 1977 Maitreya informed Creme that he had taken a body and would descend from the Himalayas. Creme intensified his traveling and speaking on the matter, and in 1982 took out full-page ads in major newspapers to announce the coming of Maitreya.[86]

The Harmonic Convergence of 1987 was an event that prompted an end-of-the-world prediction. In his book *The Mayan Factor* José Arguelles contended that according to ancient Mayan calendars August 17, 1987, would be the beginning of the end. On that day three planets would line up with the moon, and a twenty-five-year period of trouble would begin, culminating in a catastrophe in 2012. This period could be headed off only if 144,000 believers would gather at various sites around the world "to resonate in harmony" for a new age of peace and unity. Thousands of people did meet on that date.[87]

The "11:11 Doorway" movement made a similar prophecy. Humankind is now in a twenty-year period of opportunity to end the conflict on planet earth. The doorway will open only once—from January 11, 1992, to December 31, 2011. During this time frame a unified humanity can pass through the door into new realms of consciousness, perhaps opening a "major planetary activation."[88]

The New Age movement has several prophets who believe that violence and destruction will usher in the new era. One of the better-known doomsday prophets is Ruth Montgomery. In her view the Age of Aquarius will be a time of love and brotherhood, but the transition from the Piscean Age to the Aquarian Age will be a time of purging. The evils of the old age will be eradicated by wars and natural disasters, including a shift in the earth's axis. Montgomery even contends that the Antichrist is currently alive and will reveal himself as the final shift in the axis occurs.[89]

Another New Age doomsday prophet is Elizabeth Clare Prophet, known as Guru Ma. She leads the Church Universal and Triumphant, a syncretistic mixture of Western occult and Eastern spirituality. Prophet claims to be "God's chosen earthly messenger for direct dictations [channeled messages] from a host of ascended masters including Buddha, Jesus, Saint Germain, [and] Pope John XXIII."[90]

Guru Ma comes close to predicting the end of the world. On April 23, 1990, the world entered a twelve-year period of negative karma. Thus from 1990 to 2002 all kinds of disasters—including nuclear war and earthquakes—will befall planet earth. In particular, a Soviet nuclear strike will devastate the United States.[91]

The Church Universal and Triumphant's headquarters is a 63,000-acre ranch in Montana. Here Guru Ma's followers have built underground bunkers and stockpiled food, fuel, and weapons. She likens her shelter to Noah's ark in the earth. Others fear another Jonestown in the making. When Armageddon did not come as she anticipated and the Cold War ended, she denied making any specific predictions regarding a catastrophe. She even took some credit for the turn of events by attributing the lessening of international tensions to her church's rapid-fire prayer chants.[92]

156

The Apocalypse and Flying Saucers

William Ferguson claims to have been picked up by a spacecraft. He describes his conversation with the space beings, in this case the oligarchies of the planet Venus: "They [the oligarchies] told me to tell the people of the planet Earth, that all unidentified flying objects are here to help the planet Earth . . . at the time when it is approaching its next evolutionary step." Does this have a New Age ring to it? During the 1980s unidentified flying objects (UFOs) became popular in the New Age subculture.[93]

The UFO movement, which began in the 1940s, can be divided into two categories. First are the ufologists, who believe that flying saucers are real and that the political establishments have suppressed evidence proving their existence. But the scientific proof being meager, what began as science has sometimes turned into religion. Out of this development came the UFO cults. Rather than discuss UFOs in a scientific framework, the cultists spiritualize the phenomena, relying on inward states of mind and occult information.[94]

It was in 1952, when George Adamski claimed that a UFO occupant met and talked with him, that the UFO sightings took on another dimension. Some of the people who claimed to have been contacted by UFO occupants sought scientific answers about the nature of UFO visitors. But a second group viewed the UFOs from an occult perspective. Having made contact with what they claimed to be extraterrestrial beings, they committed themselves to telling others the message of the space people. The movement had acquired a religious dimension.[95] While the message articulated by the space people varied in the specifics, the general thrust was the same. The space people were more highly evolved beings who were coming to aid the occupants of Earth. "They brought a message of concern about the course of man, whose materialism is leading him to destruction." But the space people also offered a means of salvation: humankind could avoid the coming destruction by following the message of love.[96]

On the whole, the UFO movement must be regarded as a worldaffirming religion. The message coming from the aliens from space is essentially redemptive. They will cure all diseases, deliver humanity from nuclear holocaust, and even provide transportation to another planet where there are happiness and security. In sum, salvation is to come through the intervention of the space beings, who will lead humanity to a higher stage of evolution.[97]

Still, some UFO messages are starkly apocalyptic, predicting catastrophes that will bring an end to history. Some speak of an economic collapse; others point to natural disasters, perhaps a depletion of the ozone or pollution of the oceans. Yet humanity "will survive, either by being transplanted to some safe planet to live . . . or through becoming one with the aliens through their process of hybridization," writes John Whitmore. (Hybridization refers to the union of a space being with a human, a process through which the superior knowledge and moral strength of the alien raise humankind to a higher level.)[98]

Among examples of UFO apocalypticism is Marian Keech, who, as the leader of a small saucer cult in the 1950s, claimed to have received channeled messages from space beings. These communications spoke of the world's being destroyed by a great flood. Confident that flying saucers would rescue her group and transport them to another planet, she gathered her flock. Well, the deadline came, but the flying saucers did not. The only flood was one of tears. So the group disbanded.[99]

In true apocalyptic fashion Augusta Almeida brought disaster and triumph together. Merging the concepts of UFOs, Jesus, and the rapture, she claimed that Jesus was an extraterrestrial and the leader of a large space force. In what she called the Grand Lift, the earth was to be "evacuated" between 1993 and 1997 so it could be repaired. After the repairs Jesus would return, and Earth would again be a paradise: "People will then be returned to live in peace on it for a thousand years."[100]

The Aetherius Society also belongs to the apocalyptic wing of the flying saucer movement. This society has shifted its focus from saucer phenomena to direct communication with celestial beings. According to the society, the earth is at a crisis point as it enters the Aquarian Age. There is a lot of negative karma around, and evil magicians from the lower astral realms are attempting to enslave humanity. They will employ bacterial and nuclear warfare as well as terrible mental illusions to do the job. But Operation Karmalight will save humanity. Interplanetary Adepts will come to Earth, even to the pits of hell, to battle the forces of darkness and free humankind.[101]

In March 1997 UFO apocalypticism took a bizarre and deadly twist—thirty-nine members of the Heaven's Gate cult committed mass suicide in southern California. "Planet earth [is] about to be recycled. Your only chance to survive [is to] leave with us," said Marshall Herff Applewhite, the group's leader. In what was the worst mass suicide on American soil, his followers then "killed themselves in order to hook up with a UFO."[102]

But this sad story began years earlier. It started in the 1970s with a UFO cult known by several names—the Human Individual Metamorphosis, the UFO People, and eventually Heaven's Gate. Its leaders, Applewhite and Bonnie Nettles, went by several names: Bo and Peep, Pig and Sow, Do and Ti. Borrowing from Gnosticism, Christianity, and Theosophy, they preached a "strange brew of Christian theology, castration, science fiction [and] belief in UFO's."[103] Convinced that they

158

were the two witnesses prophesied by the Book of Revelation, Apple-white and Nettles proclaimed a flying saucer gospel for years, largely in the Western states. Their UFO gospel, which was never set in stone and which in fact underwent several shifts, claimed that Bo and Peep had come to Earth in a spacecraft with a mission and a message: "Only escape from our planet, doomed by pollution and decay, [can] save the human race." Salvation meant moving up to the kingdom of God, which is a physical place outside the earth's atmosphere. The saved will be "beamed up by a flying saucer and transformed into a higher level, that of resurrected people." But prospective members had to prepare themselves, that is, renounce their desires and possessions.[104]

During the 1970s and 1980s Applewhite and Nettles moved through the West, exhorting potential enlistees to give up friends, families, and jobs in the hope of getting beamed up by a flying saucer to the next level. At one point Bo and Peep disappeared only to reappear and reinvigorate the UFO group with a new message: "the doors of the next level are closed," and few will be eligible to enter God's kingdom. At this time the group became more regimented internally and isolated from the world.[105]

By the 1990s the message of the UFO cult evidenced a more dramatic apocalyptic tone. In 1985 Nettles had "left her human vehicle." By 1987 the practice of castration had been introduced. In the early 1990s the group believed that the lift-off might take place in the next two years. They even took out an advertisement in *USA Today* stating that "the Earth's present civilization is about to be recycled—spaded under."[106] They were making their final bid for recruits. As they awaited the end, along came the Hale-Bopp comet. For most people it was a celestial wonder. But to the Heaven's Gate group it signaled the end. The tail of Hale-Bopp, they believed, concealed the UFO that would lift them up. But to be beamed up to the next level they had to leave their human containers. And this they did by swallowing a dose of lethal drugs.[107]

The Racist Apocalypse

According to the Bible, we are redeemed by grace. Several racist groups, however, both black and white, drop the "g." They say that we are saved by race. In particular, the Christian Identity movement and the Black Muslims take this tack. But while focusing on race, they are also millennial groups with an apocalyptic worldview.

The Christian Identity movement and the Black Muslims are obviously poles apart—one regarding non-Aryans as either subhuman or children of the devil, the other speaking of the Caucasian devils. Yet they

159

have much in common. They are both world-rejecting movements, believing that society is hopelessly corrupt. Also, they fervently maintain an apocalyptic and dualistic worldview: the forces of good and evil are on a collision course. Exuding pessimism, both movements have adopted a twisted version of premillennialism. They also share other convictions—namely, every government is by nature evil, they are the chosen people, and other races are inferior.

The Christian Identity Movement

The Jews are a "half-breed, race-mixed, polluted people not of God. . . . They are not God's creation." Rather, they are "the children of Satan," "the serpent seed line" that came from Cain.[108] Does this sound like something Adolf Hitler would say? Actually, these are the words of leaders of the Christian Identity movement.

What is Christian Identity? It is an extreme right-wing militant movement that believes only Caucasians are God's people. It is also an umbrella term for a number of independent religious groups and congregations most of which were at one time led by a "prominent minister who frequently combine[d] the roles of congregational leader, writer, and radio-TV spokesperson." However, the leadership of these groups rapidly passed to a number of extreme right-wing political organizations, the best-known being the Aryan Nations, the Order, Posse Comitatus, and the Ku Klux Klan.[109]

Founded after World War II, Christian Identity is a mutation of British Israelism, which we encountered when examining Herbert Armstrong's Worldwide Church of God. This ideology, which began in nineteenth-century Britain, maintained that "the Anglo-Saxon-Celtic peoples are in reality the 'ten lost tribes of Israel.'"[110] Though both movements insisted that the lost tribes of Israel migrated to northern Europe, where they eventually became the British people, Christian Identity constructed an elaborate anti-Semitic ideology that was totally foreign to British Israelism. While contending that the tribes of Israel migrated to northwest Europe and that nearly all non-Slavic European peoples are Israelites, Christian Identity denies that there is a link between the Jews and Israel. Instead, the Jews descended from the Khazars, a people from the Black Sea area who in the seventh century converted to Judaism but could not assimilate into Western culture.[111] In fact, Christian Identity contends that the Jews are ultimately the devil's offspring, the result of Satan's sex act with Eve in the Garden of Eden. White Aryans are the true descendants of the tribes of Israel and have been chosen to do God's work on earth; all other races were planted on earth before the Aryans and are inferior.[112]

Christian Identity is also a millennial movement with an apocalyptic worldview. But its end-time perspective differs significantly from that of contemporary dispensationalism, which it holds in utter contempt. Both movements believe that the last days are upon us, but the similarity ends there. Dispensationalism points to the return of Israel, moral decay, apostasy, and certain political events as signs of the times. While Christian Identity may mention such developments, its focus is on what it perceives to be the destruction of the white race. Because the white Aryans are God's chosen people, this is an apocalyptic event.[113] The assault on the white race is being led by a Jewish conspiracy, which controls the American government ("Zionist Occupation Government"). Remember, in dispensationalism the Jews are the centerpiece; they occupy the key position in God's future plans, especially the millennium. No wonder dispensationalism is anathema to the Christian Identity movement, which regards the Jews as the children of Satan, not God's chosen people.[114]

Christian Identity utterly rejects the pretribulational rapture, which it regards as a cowardly notion. Christians will not be taken out of the tribulation. Instead, they must participate in the final apocalyptic struggle between good and evil, which will be a racial conflict. The chosen of God, the white Aryans, must do battle against the forces of Satan, that is, Jews and other non-Aryans. Thus a survival mentality pervades the Christian Identity movement. Its adherents have moved to remote areas and stockpiled guns and food for Armageddon, which will take place in the United States, not Israel.[115] In this struggle the destruction of the white race will be narrowly averted. The Jesus-led Aryan forces will defeat the Jewish and nonwhite armies. Following this violent struggle will come the New Order—the Christian Identity version of the millennium. Jesus Christ will return and establish his earthly rule in Jerusalem. During this golden age Jesus will reunite the twelve tribes of Israel, and the Aryans will rule as the spiritual and racial elite.[116]

The Black Muslims

The Black Muslims constitute a protest movement closely related to the urbanization of blacks, racial tensions, and the spirit of black nationalism. Though the group is also known as the Nation of Islam, Eric Lincoln regards it as more an expression of social protest than a religious movement. E. U. Essien-Udom sees the Black Muslims as primarily a black nationalist movement.[117] To be sure, the Nation of Islam is both a social protest and black nationalist movement. But these two expressions are cast in an apocalyptic context. The primary drawing card of the Nation of Islam is the opportunity to identify with a group

161

strong enough to cast off the domination of the white race—and perhaps even subordinate it in turn. This basic appeal has apocalyptic and millennial overtones. For Black Muslims the end means the end of the present white civilization.[118]

The Black Muslims developed primarily in two periods: the 1920s and the 1930s, which gave birth to the movement; and the 1950s and 1960s, which provided the catalyst for its greatest growth. During the early years leadership came primarily from Timothy Drew and Wallace D. Farad. But after World War II Elijah Muhammad (1897–1975) became the dominant figure and the primary source for Black Muslim apocalypticism.[119]

Because Black Muslims despise white society, they must be regarded as a world-rejecting movement. The Nation of Islam rejects "the whole value construct of white Christian society." Instead, it seeks to establish a new nation of blacks with a black god, new values, and a new creed.[120] This hatred for white society has fueled Black Muslim apocalypticism and provided the basis for regarding Caucasian civilization as the work of the devil. Black Muslims take two approaches to American society— separation and expectancy. They erect a rigid dualism between the devil society and themselves. Since the white civilization is evil and doomed to destruction, there is no need to integrate with it or to reform it. Rather, it must be destroyed. Allah will destroy this devilish Caucasian civilization and usher in a millennial age where blacks dominate.[121]

In spelling out this millennial vision, Elijah Muhammad turned traditional American values upside down, namely, the belief in Anglo-Saxon superiority and the idea of America as the Redeemer Nation.[122] His writings teach that the Nation of Islam will lead the blacks of North America to their "true inheritance as members of the ancient tribe of Shabazz," of which Abraham was the patriarch and to which the nonwhite people of the world belong. "Caucasian people are an inferior, latter-day offshoot of the Black Asiatic Nation." Consequently, African-Americans' self-hatred and negative regard for black culture must be replaced with a strong positive image and a sense of triumphant nationhood.[123]

Despite shunning Christianity, the leaders of the Nation of Islam drew support for their eschatology from the Book of Revelation. According to Elijah Muhammad, Revelation prophesies the downfall of the white devils. Their demise, he claimed, began in World War I, the "War of the Antichrists," but Allah gave them a fifty-year grace period. Furthermore, "the years 1965 and 1966 are going to be fateful for America." They will bring a "showdown to determine who will live on earth. The survivor is to build a nation of peace to rule the people forever."[124] When America did not fall in 1965 or 1966, the Black Muslims responded to Elijah Muhammad's failed prediction with silence. References to America's fall disappeared from their publications. The subject did return in a few years, but in a much subdued way. Elijah Muhammad gradually de-eschatologized Black Muslim doctrine by pointing to a distant date for the end.[125]

Still, Black Muslim doctrine—at least under Elijah Muhammad—must be regarded as millennial. It insists that God has already come. In addition, there is no life after death, and "heaven and hell are only two contrasting earthly conditions." The hereafter, which will begin about A.D. 2000, is but the end of the present "civilization of the Caucasian usurpers, including the Christian religion." This age will be followed "by the redemption of the Black Nation" and its glorious dominion over the world.[126]

With the death of Elijah Muhammad in 1975, his son Wallace Muhammad assumed the Nation's leadership. He further de-eschatologized his father's doctrine and reduced his strident racism, in effect moving the Nation of Islam more toward the mainline Islamic tradition and American culture. The "white devil" doctrine has been dropped, and the Nation's racist apocalypticism has been significantly modified. The new leadership has also ignored Elijah Muhammad's designation of the year 2000 as the date for the end of the white civilization.[127]

After Elijah Muhammad's death the Nation of Islam began to call itself the Bilalian Muslims, and in 1976 it adopted a new name, the World Community of Islam in the West. All of this Americanization and Islamization was too much for some Black Muslims. Louis Farrakhan left the organization and in 1978 formed his own Muslim movement, which still uses the original name, the Nation of Islam. Farrakhan has remained true to the literal teachings of Elijah Muhammad, including a combative racism and black separation.[128]

American Culture and Fringe Apocalypticism

Most fringe religions have been shaped extensively by the cultural milieu out of which they arose. Some adopt the traits of the dominant culture. Others are influenced in a different way: they strongly reject the dominant culture. Whatever direction the influence runs, such fringe groups usually exaggerate cultural trends. And this response is reflected in how fringe groups view the end of the world. They exaggerate the various apocalyptic tendencies found in society.

Since World War II the end-time ideas of nontraditional religions have run in two directions—the catastrophic and the utopian. These differences are largely due to cultural shifts and to the orientations of the particular groups. The fringe religions coming out of the counterculture

163

have quite naturally taken a doomsday outlook, for they are products of the turmoil ignited by the developments of the counterculture years—political assassinations; the civil rights, feminist, and environmental movements; and the Vietnam War. Added to the proliferation of nuclear weapons and the Cold War these developments prompted considerable apocalyptic excitement among both nontraditional religions and Christian premillennialists. That is to say, what stirred up the Christian fundamentalists also ignited the fringe religions—often in an exaggerated way.

Like similar groups throughout history the nontraditional religions today usually exist on the margins of society and are subject to apocalyptic pressures. Most often they originated in the West, where apocalyptic ideas have been the strongest. The apocalyptic visions of such bodies often bear a vague resemblance to Christian eschatology, especially a twisted version of premillennialism.

Not all end-time ideas associated with fringe religions sprang from the counterculture. The counterculture had wound down by the mid-1970s, but end-time visions did not. Instead, they took a different shape—one more conducive to the therapeutic milieu of the 1980s and 1990s with its emphasis on self-improvement. Such end-time ideas were usually less apocalyptic and more utopian. If humankind will reverse their destructive behavior, a new age will dawn in the not-too-distant future. But if humankind fails to do so, dire consequences lie ahead. New Age and occult prognostications are a mixed bag containing both utopian and catastrophic elements.

It is clear that Christianity does not have a corner on apocalyptic visions. Some of the counterculture groups and nearly all of the New Age and occult bodies have drawn their end-time views from sources other than Scripture. At times their terminal visions resemble Christian eschatology, but usually in a muddled way. In other cases end-time ideas approximate a secular millennialism or are closely connected with occult prophecies.

The End without God:
The Secular Apocalypse

How will the world end? With a bang or with a whimper? asked writer T. S. Eliot. By fire or by ice? wondered poet Robert Frost. "Is there hope for men?" asked economist Robert Heilbroner in *An Inquiry into the Human Prospect* (1980).[1] It is clear from *The Population Bomb* (1968) that doomsday ecologist Paul Ehrlich didn't think so: "The battle to feed all humanity is over. In the 1970s the world will undergo famines—hundreds of millions of people will starve to death." The population explosion, he contended, would be halted by "three of the four apocalyptic horsemen—war, pestilence, and famine."[2] Elsewhere Ehrlich was even more pessimistic. In a 1969 publication he pointed to a series of catastrophes to befall humanity during the 1970s. His hypothetical scenario envisioned the end of the oceans as coming in the summer of 1979: "By September 1979, all important animal life in the ocean was extinct. . . . Earlier in the year, the bird population was decimated." Humans do not escape these calamities—people die of malnutrition, pollution kills millions, diseases increase, and chaos breaks out.[3]

If this is not bad enough, consider what a few more scientists have said. In *Cosmos* (1980) astronomer Carl Sagan warned that "we may have only a few decades until Doomsday."[4] In 1975 biologist George Wald described himself as "one of those scientists who . . . still finds it difficult to see how the human race will get itself much past the year

2000."[5] In *Famine—1975! America's Decision: Who Will Survive?* William and Paul Paddock painted a grim picture: "Catastrophe is foredoomed . . . now it is too late."[6]

Does all of this sound like something in a doomsday sermon? Well, it did not come from Hal Lindsey, Jerry Falwell, or Pat Robertson. Instead, by the 1950s members of the scientific and economic communities began to use apocalyptic rhetoric—"the last days," "day of judgment," "the horsemen of the apocalypse," "atonement," and more.[7] As with religious people, not all scientists believe that doomsday is approaching. Still, many do. What's more, like prophets of the apocalypse, scientists differ over what the end will bring—total or limited destruction. Some see the end of all life on earth; others see a more limited catastrophe—segments of humanity will survive.

Thus in the late twentieth century the apocalyptic mind-set is no longer "the fringe phenomenon of a few marginalized people which we can ignore." Instead, people who "sit in seats of political and economic power" are embracing an apocalyptic worldview.[8] Also, end-time ideas are being accepted by members of the scientific and literary communities. Warren Wagar has examined the end-time ideas of over one hundred fiction authors, at least one-third of whom are generally regarded as men and women of the literary mainstream.[9]

For at least two thousand years there have been countless predictions regarding the end of the world. But now such prognostications are taken more seriously, largely because they are grounded in science. Our age is different from previous ages: "predictions of imminent catastrophe are far more justified [because they] are based on scientific observation rather than on religious inspiration."[10] In fact, in recent years the most significant apocalyptic outbreaks have been secular.[11]

What Is the Secular Apocalyptic?

Some scholars see great continuity between the sacred and secular apocalypses; others regard them as strikingly different. As a general statement, it would seem that the secular apocalyptic grew out of the sacred, and that until the early twentieth century there existed considerable interaction between the two.[12] Even today the differences are not always clear. Consider, for example, that the end can come by any one of three types of causes—divine, natural, and human. Some prophets see God employing earthquakes and floods to punish humanity. Other people attach no eschatological significance to such events. Were a comet to destroy the earth, they would say that it just happened; God did not cause it. To a lesser degree, the same dilemma applies to human disasters. Will God use nuclear weapons, environmental pollution, or over-population to destroy humankind? Or will humanity be fool enough to do it to themselves?

However, differences do exist between the sacred and secular apocalyptic. Religion no longer has a corner on eschatology. While new to the game, science has exerted considerable impact on end-time thinking. It has given us a depersonalized end: there will be no redemption, no survivors, and no paradise. Scientists warn us that forces are at work in the universe that can literally blow us out of existence.[13]

Like religious predictions, there is an extensive menu of scientific end-time projections. These doomsday scenarios wax and wane in popularity. In the 1950s and 1960s, nuclear destruction ranked first on the list. By the 1980s, environmental issues began to jump to the forefront. The greenhouse effect may melt the polar caps, drowning us all. Or perhaps the planet will experience another ice age. Another possibility is that doomsday may be brought on by pollution or the depletion of rain forests. The betting odds are that at some time Earth will be hit by another celestial body—this has happened before, but next time it may be far more catastrophic. Consider too that in the developing world humans are still breeding like rabbits. As a result, overpopulation may bring famine. Or pestilence could do us in: something like AIDS or the Ebola virus may get out of control, killing us all. Others talk of a global financial disaster ushering humankind into hopelessness and despair.[14]

No matter how the end will come, secular prophets take a different approach. Strictly defined, apocalypse connotes both disaster and triumph. Accordingly, most religious millenarians see doomsday as being followed by a golden age. At times they tend to get carried away with the impending calamity. Still, they maintain that recovery and victory will come. Secular prophets of doom, on the other hand, come up a bit short on the positive aspect. Their apocalyptic visions have "tended to be clearer and stronger on the coming catastrophe than on the new world that will arise from it." In fact, many scientists bleakly insist that the problems of the physical world are irreversible—no redemption will come forth. Some modern fiction writers have picked up on similar themes.[15]

Religious and secular thinkers also differ as to the cause of apocalyptic events. From a religious perspective, "the end of history will be brought about through external, divine intervention." The last days are tied to a divine design. Wars and natural disasters do not occur randomly, but are part of a divine plan "to separate good from evil."[16] Secularists move down a different path. Rather than regard a nuclear war, an environmental crisis, or natural disaster as being directed by God, secular prophets regard these events in themselves as potential causes of doomsday. Human beings and natural forces, not God, are behind these events. This secular apocalypticism "grows out of a naturalistic world view, indebted to science and to social criticism rather than to theology."[17]

The secular apocalypse sprang from a growing disillusionment with the belief in progress, the notion that civilization would steadily advance. Sometime between the mid-seventeenth and early nineteenth centuries, the modern world arrived. Along with it came great optimism. Scientists and philosophers believed that science and human reason could improve the lot of humanity. Advances in agriculture, science, commerce, and industry bolstered such contentions and countered arguments that the world would end because of human evil.[18] By the nineteenth century the belief in progress had taken root in the Western world. It helped to justify humankind's dominance and exploitation of nature. Intoxicated with tremendous improvements in living standards brought on by the Industrial Revolution, most people did not notice the downside, namely, the potential for environmental disasters.[19]

But this gradually began to change. By the 1930s scientists, theologians, philosophers, novelists, and social critics warned about uncontrolled industrial growth. Unless humanity put limits on economic development, they would face extinction. Life on earth could be saved only by rejecting faith in the idea of progress.[20]

Thus was born the secular apocalypse. A number of scientists and social critics in the 1960s and 1970s built on this beginning. They warned that humanity's faith in science and industrial development was actually irrational, not scientific. This misguided faith came from a faulty understanding of the relationship between humankind and nature, an understanding that allowed humanity to exploit the environment with impunity.[21]

In some ways the sacred and secular apocalypses mirror each other. Millennial movements often grow out of disasters, social dislocations, and dashed expectations. The same seems to be true for the secular apocalypse. The hopes that the progress of science and industry would usher in a golden age (a secularized version of the Christian millennium) were dashed, and out of this disillusionment grew the secular apocalypse. Radical events in America during the 1960s and 1970s produced apocalyptic excitement that went beyond the religious community. Scientists and economists also joined in by depicting terrible end-time calamities—nuclear destruction, ecological disasters, financial collapse, and racial conflict. Indeed, many secular prophets were as gloomy as were some fundamentalists—but they did not have the rapture to bail them out.[22]

Some scientists came close to being date-setters. They insisted that life on earth could not survive beyond a particular year. Fortunately for their reputations, most of their projected dates for the end still lie in the future. Also, the secular prophets have not been quite as specific as some Christian date-setters have. Nevertheless, some of the years designated by scientists for global destruction have come and gone. On the whole, society has been more charitable to such disconfirmations than it has to similar failures by religious prophets.

Imaginary Apocalypses

Most of the ideas of how the world will end have come from the Bible, science, or the occult. But eschatology—particularly secular eschatology—has also been conveyed through fiction, especially novels and films. This is not totally surprising, for the imagination is not pure invention. It connects with one's perception of reality, or what one believes reality will be in the future. Perception fuels the imagination, and in turn imagination fuels ideas. So as perception changes, the imagination and ideas change. Novels and films with end-time themes signal something about their writers—they believe the world will come to a disastrous end in the future. Indeed, "the bulk of eschatological fictions . . . can be read as indicators of a growing consciousness within modern Western culture that its end is in view" and that a new civilization will replace it.[23]

By the late seventeenth century the notion of progress had pushed end-of-the-world ideas into the background. But during the nineteenth century things began to change. The Romantic movement cherished nature and resented what the industrial world was doing to it. Forms of irrationalism reared their heads and embraced apocalyptic ideas. Economist Thomas Malthus painted a dire picture regarding overpopulation and humankind's future. Charles Darwin's theory of evolution shook everyone's beliefs and in the mind of some people diminished God's power. Prominent philosophers such as Arthur Schopenhauer and Friedrich Nietzsche expressed pessimistic and irrational ideas. Following the boom in science came a rapid growth of science fiction, the major genre for eschatological fiction. Then World War I provided a real apocalypse for the imagination to feed on.[24]

Eschatological fiction began to pop up during the nineteenth century. For "it was in the nineteenth century in the West, that the vision of the total end of man appeared for the first time in a systematic and repeated fashion."[25] And fiction served as a major vehicle for communicating these end-time ideas. Prior to 1914 it was the forces of nature, not humankind, that were depicted as causing the collapse of civilization: "the world most often ended in imagination because of some natural catastrophe."[26]

In 1805 a French priest, Jean-Baptiste Cousin de Grainville, published *Le Dernier Homme* (The last man). The world ends by a natural catastrophe—soil exhaustion and human sterility. Mary Shelley published *The Last Man* in 1826, the story of a plague that kills off all of humanity except three people. Two of them then die in a storm and the third is left to wander the earth in vain.[27]

In the first half of the nineteenth century end-time themes crossed the Atlantic. During this time several comets excited America, including the most famous of them all, Halley's comet. Inspired by these and other events, Edgar Allan Poe wrote three end-time stories. In "The Conversation of Eiros and Charmion" (1839), a comet strikes the earth, and humankind perishes in great agony. In "The Masque of the Red Death" (1842), a plague is the vehicle for destruction. Finally, in "The Colloquy of Monos and Una," the world ends because humankind, obsessed with the idea of progress, attempts to control nature instead of obeying natural law.[28]

During the middle decades of the nineteenth century few secular eschatological works were written. But apocalyptic excitement heated up by the 1890s. From the 1890s to the late twentieth century, Western civilization has been embroiled in serious problems—wars, economic crises, totalitarianism, and even psychological issues that damage self-esteem. Such a climate lends itself to doomsday thinking.[29]

The king of apocalyptic writers was English novelist H. G. Wells (1866–1946). He published numerous novels and stories regarding the future, many of them pointing to doomsday. In *The Time Machine* (1895), the world ends in three ways: biological degeneration, class conflict, and the dying of the sun. The short story "The Star" (1897) tells about a runaway star causing great havoc on Earth, killing all but a few people. In *The War of the Worlds* (1898), humankind is nearly obliterated by technologically superior Martian invaders. An early atomic bomb ends civilization in *The World Set Free* (1914), and *All Aboard for Ararat* (1941) describes a modern Noah.[30]

In eschatological fiction before 1914, natural forces were the usual means of destroying humankind. However, around 1900 a shift could be detected. Nature continued to perform its evil deeds, but more often humanity became the chief cause of world-ending catastrophes. Of these human-made disasters, most were brought on by world wars fought with doomsday weapons.[31] Wells's *Shape of Things to Come* (1933) envisioned a new order after a global war that wrecked civilization. In Edward Shanks's *People of the Ruins* (1920), the cause of humanity's downfall is a global series of socialist revolutions. Shaw Desmond's *Ragnarok* (1926) and Stephen Southwold's *Gas War of 1940* (1931) focus on the horrors of modern weaponry. In J. B. Priestley's *Doomsday Men* (1938), a mad scientist nearly blows up the world.[32]

Annihilation by war became the subject of many modern films as well, especially in the 1950s and 1960s. Nikita Khrushchev's threat to bury the United States precipitated a flurry of movies. *On the Beach* (1959) shows us an Australia where people wait for a nuclear war's radiation to reach them. In *The Day the Earth Caught Fire* (1962), accidental nuclear detonations by the United States and the Soviet Union knock the earth into a lower orbit around the sun. *Dr. Strangelove* (1963) portrays the way in which the final war begins. *The Planet of the Apes* (1967) and *Beneath the Planet of the Apes* (1969) depict how nuclear war wipes out civilization first on Earth and then on a future earth.[33]

Several other films follow the theme of nuclear destruction but take a different approach. In some, radiation enlarges animals or insects to monster proportions and they terrorize humanity. Examples include *Food of the Gods* (wasps, rats), *Them* (ants), and *Night of the Lepus* (rabbits). Other films portray a morally slack postnuclear world in which roving bands rule. Some examples are *The Road Warrior, Mad Max: Beyond Thunderdome,* and *Lord of the Flies.* Apocalyptic themes can be found in many other films: *Star Wars, The Poseidon Adventure, Battlestar Galactica, Earthquake,* the *Star Trek* series, *The Towering Inferno, The Invasion of the Body Snatchers, Judgment Day, The Omen* films, the *Terminator* series, *Waterworld, Outbreak, Independence Day,* and *Asteroid.*[34]

To sum up, the modern world has been a time of unprecedented social change. The Industrial Revolution and now the postindustrial world have brought new hopes, new fears, and new visions of the end. And literature and the film industry responded quickly and with great imagination. Among their plot lines are that aliens will turn us into pod-people, computers will take over the world, scientists will mess up the natural order, and our robots will run amok.[35]

The Big-Bang Theory

The world may not have begun with a big bang, but it could certainly end with one. Consider what some people have to say. "As the bomb fell over Hiroshima and exploded, we saw an entire city disappear. . . . 'My God, what have we done?'" wrote Robert C. Lewis, an American aviator.[36] According to Andrei Sakharov, Soviet nuclear scientist: "All-out nuclear war would mean the destruction of contemporary civilization."[37] And as J. Robert Oppenheimer, father of the nuclear bomb, watched the first mushroom-shaped cloud over the New Mexico desert, he was heard to say: "I am become death, the destroyer of the world."[38]

Revelation 6 speaks of the four horsemen of the apocalypse. The red horse denotes war. Of course, war is not new, and today humans are not more evil or cruel. In fact, people have fought wars of unspeakable ferocity since ancient times. The nature of war has changed, however; weapons are far more efficient. The most sadistic Roman soldier could not have killed in a lifetime what a modern pilot can do on one mission. And on August 6, 1945, warfare became even more efficient as the United States dropped the first atomic bomb on Hiroshima.[39]

In searing heat and a blinding light, the nuclear age opened with awesome destructiveness. From 100,000 to 200,000 people died directly or indirectly at Hiroshima. But even worse, those early bombs look like firecrackers when compared to modern weapons. Today, one bomb is from five to fifty times more powerful, and ten or more can be fired from a multiple warhead missile.[40]

While everybody agrees that a nuclear war would be cataclysmic, the inevitability of nuclear war is subject to debate. The probability of such a conflict has waxed and waned since 1945. The bomb ended World War II in short order. We had won the war, and only we had the bomb; no one would dare attack us. But this sense of euphoria ended in 1949 when the Soviets tested their first nuclear weapon. The United States and the Soviet Union were already embroiled in the Cold War, and many thought a nuclear war inevitable. At various levels of intensity this feeling prevailed until the late 1980s. About fifty thousand nuclear weapons existed, and somebody was bound to use them—so many people thought.[41]

Then came the end of the Cold War. The upheaval of 1989 ended Soviet rule in Eastern Europe, and the Soviet Union came unraveled in 1991. In the minds of many, nuclear war was no longer likely. The hands of the Doomsday Clock in Chicago, where 12:00 symbolizes the dreaded nuclear apocalypse, were moved back from 11:58 to 11:43—the farthest the hands had been from midnight since the clock was introduced in 1947.[42]

The specter of a nuclear war has disappeared, so many believe. The red horse of the apocalypse has faded to a shade of pink. Yet the world still has about fifty thousand nuclear weapons, and the technology to make more continues to exist. To some extent the mushroom-shaped cloud still hangs over the world. Doomsday may only have been postponed. With all these weapons around, some madman will probably push the button.[43] The big questions are who, when, why, and where.

The most devastating nuclear holocaust would come in an American-Russian conflict. The old Soviet Union may be dead, but Russia still possesses thousands of nuclear weapons. In the late 1990s, Russian nationalism is on the rise. Also, Russia has tremendous natural resources and massive potential strength. While a resurgence of Russian power may not come in the near future, it is possible somewhere down the road. And along with this recovery will come a renewed possibility of a nuclear confrontation.

But Russia is merely the most obvious threat. A small power or a terrorist group could also provoke a nuclear confrontation. The technical know-how to build nuclear weapons is here to stay. Despite well-meaning arms-control treaties and sanctions, this technology has spread. Officially, five nations have the bomb; but many smaller nations either have secret nuclear weapons or the capability to build them in short order. And most frightening, nations like Iraq, Libya, and Iran have had very unstable rulers—modern-day Neros who would push the button with no regard for the consequences.[44] In *Thinking about the Unthinkable* nuclear-war expert Herbert Kahn presents a scenario in which a smaller power or even a terrorist group provokes the larger powers into a nuclear exchange. The renegade launches a first-strike nuclear attack in the hope of drawing the major powers into the conflict. They go for the bait and proceed to demolish each other. Meanwhile, the rogue power is left standing and gains control after the war.[45]

Or a nuclear debacle could come by an accident. The world has seen a number of lesser episodes such as the 1979 partial meltdown at Three Mile Island, Pennsylvania. The worst nuclear disaster came at the Chernobyl power plant in the Soviet Union. This and perhaps a future meltdown could have devastating consequences. Humanity lives in fear of such an accident. And even if such a catastrophe does not happen, we still have the problem of nuclear waste, the most dangerous pollutant on earth. Currently we have no safe way to dispose of it, and it takes thousands of years to lose its radioactivity. Even in minute amounts plutonium—the waste product of nuclear fuel—can be deadly to human, animal, and plant life.[46]

Still, the most likely scenario for a nuclear holocaust is war. War is endemic to the modern world-system. Despite much idealism and efforts to curb belligerence, war will continue to be a fact of life. If a conflict ever escalates to merely the use of "low-yield 'tactical' or 'battlefield' nuclear weapons, limiting its further escalation up the ladder to thermonuclear doomsday" may be impossible.[47]

How destructive would a nuclear war be? This would depend on the nations involved, the number of warheads detonated, their destructive power, and the targets selected. Still, even best-case scenarios are catastrophic. Moreover, students of nuclear war agree that the long-term effects will be at least as disastrous as the immediate destructiveness of the nuclear weapons themselves.[48]

In the first few days, millions of people will perish. The initial blast, firestorms, heat, radiation, hurricane-strength winds, and choking smoke and dust will cause an unprecedented number of casualties. Even if civilian centers are not targeted, the deaths will be in the millions, for military, industrial, and government centers are often in densely populated areas.[49] In the worst-case scenarios far more people will die in the months and years thereafter. Almost all urban centers will be destroyed. While not everyone will perish, a large percentage of the total population will be burned or poisoned by radiation. The very fabric of life might unravel. With transportation and communication systems severed, power plants destroyed, governments incapacitated, and medical supplies unavailable, the necessities of life will be lacking in many regions. And if several industrial nations were destroyed, there would be little chance of aid from the outside, just as there was after World War II. Indeed, with farmers no longer growing food or unable to transport it to urban areas, the Western world would be threatened by famine, pestilence, and civil disorder not seen since the Middle Ages.[50]

But even worse is the "nuclear winter" scenario, which has come under attack by respected scientists. However, if the doomsday ecologists are on target, global temperatures would plunge, especially in the Northern Hemisphere, to at least –10° F. The world would be in an artificial winter from three months to two years. As a result, the food cycle would be disrupted and millions of people would die.[51]

The Wrath of Mother Nature

"Oh, my God! Los Angeles has vanished! . . . Wait a minute. There's more. Orange County is gone too. And most of San Diego. And . . ." So goes the book *The Last Days of the Late Great State of California* (1968) by Curt Gentry, a California journalist.[52]

Will the end come at the hands of Mother Nature? Today very few scientists believe that natural causes—earthquakes, volcanoes, floods—can precipitate a global catastrophe. To be sure, nature can still get angry and cause great havoc on a regional level. Thousands of people could still die because of one of these upheavals. And for others caught up in such a calamity, their world may in effect come to an end.

Throughout history people have viewed nature with great awe. Earthquakes, volcanoes, tidal waves, floods, and the like have roused terror. Most often the forces of nature were viewed as the instruments of God, but some people saw nature as acting without God. Today a collection of scientists, prophets, psychics, astrologers, and eccentrics predict widespread natural catastrophes, if not the absolute end of humanity. The calamities that most frequently arouse an apocalyptic excitement include earthquakes, volcanoes, an ice age, and a polar shift.

Earthquakes head the list. Why? A sense of the havoc they can wreak is deeply imbedded in the human psyche. In the Middle East, where much of our thinking is rooted, earthquakes are the most common natural disaster. The Old Testament prophets, Jesus, and John of Revelation spoke of them, as did Nostradamus. And in our day a host of soothsayers including Edgar Cayce and Jeane Dixon have predicted them. Semiscientific seers like Jeffrey Goodman and Immanuel Velikovsky refer to them apocalyptically.[53]

History has witnessed a number of devastating earthquakes. The most deadly earthquake occurred in central China in 1556; approximately 830,000 people perished. The Lisbon earthquake of 1755 killed about 60,000 people. The 1811–12 quake in New Madrid, Missouri, killed few people because of the sparse population. But it shifted the topography of the entire area. Chile experienced a major earthquake in 1960, killing 3,000 people and sinking about 5,000 square miles of land. The worst natural disaster of the twentieth century occurred in Tangshan, China, in 1976 when 242,000 people perished.[54]

Could earthquakes endanger life on earth? Probably not. But one theory conjectures that gigantic earthquakes could impact the rotation of the earth. Scientists know that the earth's rotation wobbles and that this wobble is related to earthquakes and volcanoes. Moreover, even minor variations in the rotation axis can affect climate on the earth's surface and stresses within the earth. But scientists don't know whether an axis shift causes earthquakes or earthquakes cause axis shifts, which could be catastrophic. If the latter, an earthquake might well be indirectly connected with the end of the world.[55]

Volcanoes may be nature's most spectacular expression, but they have not evoked much apocalyptic excitement. While they had a role in the end-time scenario of the Norseman, they play little role in the Christian and Western traditions. Moreover, unlike earthquakes, which strike without warning, volcanoes send a clear signal before erupting. Thus, if humans perish, it is usually because they failed to evacuate the area.[56]

Still, there have been at least two doomsday explosions in modern times. Perhaps the most devastating eruption took place in 1883 on Krakatoa, an island in what is now Indonesia. The explosion could be heard nearly 3,000 miles away, and about 37,000 people perished. In 1902 Mount Pelée blew up on Martinique in the Caribbean. About 40,000 died, largely because they failed to heed the ample warnings.[57]

175

A more likely but far more distant threat to world survival is ice. Scientists say that ice ages occur in cycles that last perhaps 100,000 years. Between these ice ages are balmy interludes, but they are the exception not the rule. Geologists insist that a new ice age is all but inevitable; sheets of ice will again spread over much of the Northern Hemisphere.[58] We are now about halfway through the warm interlude. In about ten to fifteen thousand years a new cycle will begin. Ironically, there must first be a warming for ice to soften and move south. Because the greenhouse effect may quicken the process, some scientists believe that a new ice age will be upon us within two thousand years. They disagree, however, as to the effects of this new ice age. Some scientists believe it will be devastating, but humanity will survive. Others say no one will survive. Regardless, we ought not lose any sleep over it—it's still thousands of years away.[59]

The Quiet Apocalypse

The end of the world may be sneaking up on us, say some environmentalists. We are committing global suicide. Global warming, spilled oil, poisoned seas, ozone depletion, radioactive soil, acid rain, and toxic waste are "combining to bring the earth to the brink of apocalypse." Thus the "coming end will be a strictly do-it-yourself apocalypse."[60] No one is doing it to us; we are doing it to ourselves!

Nearly all scientists view the rape of the environment with extreme concern. Unless we do an about-face in the near future, humanity will face serious problems. But there is disagreement as to whether the environmental damage can be reversed. The pessimists "warn of doom within a century unless mankind mends its ways. Pshaw, say the skeptics. But they, too, see a need for change."[61] The doomsday environmentalists—those that believe the planet is near death—view the greatest threat as coming from three related problems. Global warming, deforestation, and the depletion of the ozone—especially global warming—could bring us to the brink of a secular Armageddon.

The greenhouse effect (or global warming) has many environmentalists up in arms. The earth's temperature is rising because the upper atmosphere contains too much carbon dioxide, which comes from the burning of fossil fuels (oil, gasoline, and coal). Such substances serve as a blanket trapping the earth's heat. Up to a point this is normal. But excessive gases cause a gradual warming of the earth's temperature.[62]

The greenhouse effect had its beginnings in the nineteenth century. With industrialization and later the automobile, tremendous amounts of fossil fuel were burnt, emitting enormous quantities of carbon dioxide into the atmosphere. Such emissions have accelerated rapidly in the twentieth century, bringing the world to a crisis point.[63] Global warming threatens the climate equilibrium. Temperatures could rise from three to thirty degrees Fahrenheit. Even a change of a few degrees would dramatically affect life on earth. Weather patterns in every part of the globe would change. Some areas would be drier, significantly reducing the food supply. Others would experience monsoons and floods. Even a rise in temperature of a few degrees would melt the polar ice caps; the oceans would rise, submerging coastal areas throughout the globe. Most of the world's major cities would be inundated. And we have said nothing about a rise of twenty to thirty degrees. This would be unimaginably disastrous.[64]

Doomsday by deforestation! Could it happen? In *Earth in the Balance* Vice-President Al Gore says that the destruction of the rain forests and the living species found therein "represent[s] the single most serious damage to nature now occurring."[65] Forests and the plant and animal life they house are the key to biodiversity. And without a hospitable ecosystem "the remaining tenure of the human race would be nasty and brief."[66]

What if we lose some species? Who needs these birds, insects, and plants anyway? We do! Our ecosystem cannot be altered significantly without impacting human life. On a more direct level, the forests provide humanity with pharmaceuticals, fibers, petroleum substitutes, timber, and other essential products.[67]

Deforestation is also an aspect of the greenhouse effect—it magnifies global warming. Carbon dioxide levels in the atmosphere are higher because of the mass destruction of the world's forests. Trees consume much carbon dioxide, which they need for photosynthesis. Therefore, the fewer trees, the more carbon dioxide in the atmosphere, and the greater the global warming.[68] And we know what a catastrophe this will cause.

The third environmental problem with the potential for worldwide disaster is the depletion of the ozone. The earth's atmosphere has a thin ozone layer which protects us from harmful ultraviolet sunlight. Unfortunately, chlorofluorocarbons (CFCs), which are used in refrigeration systems, some aerosol sprays, fertilizers, jets, and the production of foam packaging, contain ozone-destroying chemicals.[69] Some governments have taken steps to greatly reduce CFCs. Yet scientists tell us that a hole in the ozone about the size of the United States exists over Antarctica. Another one might be developing over the heavily populated Northern Hemisphere. Without this ozone shield all kinds of problems will develop—genetic abnormalities, skin cancers, cataracts, and damage to marine life. In fact, some scientists even contend that the increase in radiation could destroy all plant and animal life. Could a hole in the ozone bring doomsday? Probably not. But southern Chile, where an ozone hole exists, has experienced some ominous phenomena—blind cattle and sheep, withered trees and cactus, severe sunburns, and strange spots on animals. One farmer even tried to put sunglasses on his sheep.[70]

Standing Room Only

Planet earth is small, and at this time we have no place else to go. Eventually, we will run out of space and the ability to feed ourselves. The end will come because of overpopulation and lack of food. In *The Population Bomb* (1968), scientist Paul Ehrlich said we would cross this threshold by the 1970s: "At this late date nothing can prevent a substantial increase in the world death rate." Despite crash programs to feed people, millions will starve. Such "programs will only provide a stay of execution" unless there are successful efforts to control the population.[71]

Ehrlich's first prediction misfired, but like many religious prognosticators he did not recant. He has continued to make similar forecasts. His 1991 book *The Population Explosion* says that our runaway population will result in "a billion or more deaths from starvation and disease." Moreover, society as we know it will dissolve.[72]

Of course, not all scientists agree with Ehrlich's doomsday predictions. Some starry-eyed optimists see the world supporting from 25 to 30 billion people. They see most of the world improving its agricultural productivity to something approximating that of North America and Europe. More-realistic scientists set the limits at around 15 billion.[73]

Scientists also disagree as to when, if ever, humanity will reach the limits. The optimists point to the slow population growth in the industrial nations and say that the whole world will emulate this pattern. The world's population should stabilize within tolerable limits, somewhere between 10 and 15 billion. Other scientists point to the runaway population growth in the developing world. Barring a nuclear war or a devastating plague, the upper limits will be reached around 2100. Mother Earth will snap. Billions will die from starvation and disease.[74] There will also be incredible tension, for lack of food brings out the animal instincts in humans. It will be survival of the fittest. With the lack of space prohibiting privacy, people will become unsociable and hostile. Poverty will run rampant. Even if humanity survives, much of the world will be crowded into metropolises like Mexico City, São Paulo, and Calcutta.[75]

Awareness of the population peril goes back as far as English economist Thomas Malthus and his 1798 *Essay on the Principle of Population:* "The power of population is indefinitely greater than the power in the earth to produce subsistence for man." Malthus believed that the population would grow until checked by a lack of food. For a while, people accepted Malthus's ideas. But improved agricultural methods came along, allowing fewer people to produce more food on less land. As a result, the world population grew from about 1 billion in Malthus's day to about 6 billion in 2000.[76]

But Malthus may eventually prove to be right. Improved agricultural methods have increased the food supply—only to be outstripped by an exploding population. Today much of the world is not being fed properly and mass famines are common. Unless the world's population is drastically limited in the next one hundred years, the crash will come. Indeed, the rider on the black horse (famine) may stalk humanity once again. And this is to say nothing about the environmental problems caused by overpopulation. The more people polluting nature and cutting down trees, the greater the chance for environmental catastrophe.[77]

Plague and Pestilence

The pale horse of the apocalypse—representing death by plague and disease—has stalked humanity through history. Quite often it has been associated with end-of-the-world panics or divine judgment. In Matthew 24:7 Jesus speaks of "famines, and pestilences, and earthquakes" as signs of the end. Revelation 8–16 tells of God's pouring out his judgment at the end of the world in the form of pestilences and plagues.

Horror of horrors—the Black Death terrified Western society as no plague ever has. During the Middle Ages it killed about one-third of Europe's population. No one knew what caused it. "Some say that it descended upon the human race through the influence of the heavenly bodies," wrote Giovanni Boccaccio in his *Decameron*. A grand conjunction of Saturn, Jupiter, and Mars in March 1345 was thought by some enlightened scientists of the day to have corrupted the earth's atmosphere and caused the plague. Many said that it was "a punishment signifying God's righteous anger at our iniquitous way of life." Still other Europeans blamed it on the Jews, insisting that they had poisoned the wells.[78]

Most people connected the Black Death with some form of divine judgment or end-of-the-world scenario. But when the plague continued for centuries, people gradually began to think in terms of natural causes. By the early twentieth century they figured out that bacilli from rat fleas had caused the epidemic.[79]

The Black Death illustrates how pestilences relate to end-of-the-world thinking. Religious people see plagues as a divine instrument for punishing humanity for its evil and as a sign of the end. To secular thinkers epidemics have natural causes—sometimes unknown. They may also view plagues apocalyptically, but not as the end of the world, for plagues are usually local in scope. A new pestilence, however, adds to the horror. People become particularly terrified when an unknown disease—one they don't understand—attacks.[80]

To a large extent modern medicine has curbed the specter of widespread epidemics, but not completely. During World War I more than 3 million Russians died of typhus. In 1918 an influenza epidemic killed 20 million people throughout the world. But this attack did not set off an end-of-the-world panic, for influenza was a known disease that could be treated.[81]

Then came AIDS. By the 1980s it had surfaced in America, largely among homosexuals. As long as it was confined to the gay community, it did not set off a major crisis. But when AIDS began to go mainstream, it stirred up considerable apocalyptic excitement, for the disease has no known cure. Once contracted it usually proves fatal.[82]

The chief causes of AIDS are homosexual or promiscuous heterosexual activity and the exchange of needles for taking drugs, all of which most Christians consider to be immoral. Thus some Christians declared AIDS to be God's judgment for sin. By the mid-1980s the spread of AIDS had begun to arouse some apocalyptic excitement. Jerry Falwell said, "AIDS is God's judgment on a society that does not live by his rules."[83] Then Jack Van Impe really stirred matters up. Quoting Revelation 16, he related AIDS to the sin of bestiality. In Africa's jungles men committed sex with monkeys carrying the virus and thus catapulted the disease to global proportions. In the belief that AIDS could wipe out civilization, Van Impe declared that by 2020 the disease might kill the last human on earth.[84] Citing a CIA study, Hal Lindsey estimated that by the mid-1990s 75 percent of sub-Saharan Africa could be infected by AIDS.[85]

But such apocalyptic talk is not confined to the doomsaying preachers. Millions will obviously die if a cure is not found. In 1992 the World Health Organization estimated that 40 million people will be HIV-infected by 2000. And as AIDS spreads among heterosexuals, the crisis will grow worse unless a cure is developed.[86]

Could much of the world wind up like Uganda, which currently represents the worst-case scenario? Estimates in 1992 said that half of Uganda's population of 18 million had contracted HIV and that many could die in the near future. British journalist Dan Wooding feared that Uganda might become "so decimated that it will not be able to exist as a nation." While AIDS is not as bad elsewhere, it has destabilized other countries in the developing world by inflicting especially the young adults in the prime of life.[87]

In the mid-1990s a measure of medical progress with HIV helped to reduce the hysteria over AIDS. But along came the gruesome Ebola virus. Having first surfaced in Sudan in 1976, it lay dormant for about sixteen years, only to arise in 1995 to kill again—this time in Zaire. It is one of the most elusive, mysterious, and deadly pathogens in the world. The Ebola virus ravages the human body by destroying the immune system and causing massive bleeding that usually ends in a horrible death.[88] True, most scientists say that the Ebola virus is ill suited to bring about doomsday. It cannot be transmitted by a sneeze or cough; it kills its victims so quickly that they don't have much chance to infect others. Still, if a mysterious disease without a cure ever got loose in a major urban center, a catastrophe would result.[89]

Futurists envision two other plague-related nightmares—biological warfare and diseases from outer space. Even small powers can develop a stock of devastating bacteriological weapons. Such weapons could also be launched by a clandestine organization. However, for a global doomsday to be a real possibility, a major power with missiles and planes would probably have to get involved. More far-fetched is the possibility of unknown germs entering Earth from a spacecraft. If humans ever begin to explore other planets, such a scenario will be a realistic concern.[90]

Big Scary Things from the Sky

Suppose we come to our senses and eliminate nuclear, chemical, and biological weapons. Suppose we also solve our environmental problems, and medical science learns to control all communicable diseases. Would the possibility of doomsday then be eliminated? Not entirely! Planet earth could still be bombarded by a comet or asteroid. Or we could experience some other cosmic disaster such as the sun exploding.[91]

"During a human lifetime, there's roughly a 1-in-10,000 chance that Earth will be hit by something big enough to wipe out crops worldwide and possibly force survivors to return to the ways of Stone Age hunter-gatherers," writes Sharon Begley. Those odds are about the same as one's dying in a car crash during any six-month period, getting cancer from breathing automobile exhaust in Los Angeles, or dying from anesthesia during surgery. The fact is that "killer asteroids and comets are out there. And someday, one will be on a collision course with Earth." The only question is when. If life on Earth goes on long enough, scientists believe that such a fate is inevitable.[92]

Before proceeding we need to define some terms. What is the difference between comets, meteors, meteorites, and asteroids? Comets consist of frozen gases. Like planets, they travel around the sun, but in irregular orbits. Meteors are small particles entering the earth's atmosphere, where they burn up and are seen as shooting stars. The remains of these shooting stars are called meteorites, solid objects of metal and stone that actually reach the earth. Asteroids are large meteoroids whose usual orbit lies between Mars and Jupiter.[93]

For several millennia people have watched cosmic objects—comets, meteor showers, and asteroids—with great fascination. They saw them as strange and unnatural events and as omens for good or ill. "These signs forerun the death or fall of kings," says a minor character in Shakespeare's *Richard II*. Christians more often view such cosmic activities as signs of God's wrath rather than his favor. But while they may be omens, they do not always point to the end of the world.[94]

Of the various astronomical phenomena comets have generated the most end-of-the-world excitement. The appearance of a comet in 1843 swelled the ranks of the Millerite movement, convincing many that Christ would return shortly. In 1910 Halley's comet prompted an endtime panic. Many people believed that it would collide with the earth and smash it to bits. To no avail scientists pointed out that Halley's movement had been known for two centuries and that it would miss the earth by millions of miles. In 1910 Halley disappointed the doomsdayers; its reappearance in 1986 prompted no apocalyptic excitement.[95]

Are comets merely omens of doom, or could they become agents of doom? Could a collision with a large comet destroy planet earth? This possibility has been the grist for many science fiction stories. And, in fact, some astronomers contend that a huge comet smashed into the earth 65 million years ago, killing the dinosaurs and about two-thirds of all life. (Other scientists believe that even worlds could collide.)[96]

In June 1908 a huge fireball streaked across the Siberian sky. What scientists believe was a comet leveled 80 million trees in a circle about twentyfive miles in diameter. Scientists theorize that the comet, which was several miles in diameter and about 10 million tons in weight, exploded in the atmosphere right before reaching the ground. Thus it created no large crater. But the people in Siberia thought that the world had ended.[97]

In our day the Swift-Tuttle comet concerns some scientists. Most comets originate in far space beyond Pluto. Gravity pulls some of them toward the sun, and at times they cross the earth's orbit. About two hundred visit the earth's environs every two centuries. Swift-Tuttle (named after the two astronomers who first saw it) passed within 110 million miles of Earth in 1862. Astrophysicist Brian Marsden calculates that Swift-Tuttle will come much closer to the earth in August 2126. And if it goes slightly off course, it might even hit the earth. The odds are 1 in 10,000.[98]

Meteorites constantly bombard Earth, but they are usually small and do little damage. Fortunately, the larger asteroids, which could devastate Earth, are fewer in number. But so much for the friendly skies. Earth has taken some major hits: scientists have verified 139 craters, and erosion has undoubtedly erased many more. Meteor Crater, which is near Winslow, Arizona, has a 3-mile circumference. The 30-mile-wide Vredefort Ring in South Africa may have been a meteorite. The largest one in recent years struck Siberia in 1947.[99]

Actually, the near misses have caused more anxiety than have the hits. The asteroid Hermes passed Earth by 500,000 miles in October 1937. If it had crashed, Hermes would have packed more punch than all the nuclear weapons in the world. In August 1972 an asteroid with five times the power of the Hiroshima bomb passed over Wyoming. Another asteroid missed Earth by 700,000 miles in March 1989. Had it arrived six hours later, civilization might have been destroyed. In 1992 the asteroid Toutatis came within 2 million miles of Earth. It will be back, swooping less than 1 million miles away in 2004, says Gareth Williams of the Smithsonian Astrophysical Observatory.[100]

If the comet misses, the friendly skies have other ways to do us in. Scientists tell us that the days on Earth are getting one second longer every sixty thousand years because the moon is gradually pulling away from the earth. As this occurs, the earth's rotation slows down and oceanic tides are disrupted. In about 10 billion years each day and night will equal fifty of our current days. Such a climatic change will have a drastic effect on plant and animal life.[101]

In addition, if a comet or asteroid doesn't strike this planet, a star might. Our Milky Way is hurtling toward its nearest neighbor—the galaxy Andromeda—at about seventy miles a second. In about 5 to 10 billion years they will collide. And since Andromeda is two to three times larger, the Milky Way will get the worse of the collision. Our galaxy will be destroyed and consumed.[102]

But before Andromeda gets us, our own sun may do us in. Planet earth may well get cooked by its own star. The sun is now about 4.5 billion years old, making it a middle-aged star. Its fuel supply is moving to its outer edges. As a result, the sun is gradually getting bigger and brighter. In about 2 billion years Earth will feel the effects; for example, winters in New England will hit about 90° Fahrenheit. In about 7 billion years, the oceans will boil, and the sun will get so large that it engulfs the inner planets of Mercury and Venus and chars Earth into a cinder. But this will be the last hurrah for the sun. It will run out of fuel and become a dwarf star. It will then be too cold for any form of life in our solar system to survive.[103]

183

The Secularization of the Four Horsemen

The four horsemen portrayed in the Book of Revelation symbolize a catastrophic end to the world. For most of Western history, people have believed that the end would come at the hands of God. But God now has some competition—humanity might destroy itself. To be sure, the sacred and secular apocalypses overlap at points. In fact, given a particular view of divine providence, Christians can interpret secular disasters as being directed by God. Traditionally, natural calamities—earthquakes, volcanoes, and such—have been seen as the work of God. Some Christians even attribute manmade catastrophes—wars and the rape of the environment—to divine providence.

This chapter, however, has focused on a different perspective—that there will be a natural and secular end to the world. While the sacred and secular apocalypses are often muddled together, they differ at two points—the end results and the causes. In a strict sense, apocalyptic thinking entails both disaster and triumph. The secular apocalypse places little emphasis on triumph. No golden age will follow a nuclear war or an environmental catastrophe. At best, humankind will pull back from the edge of a precipice and avert a calamity. But this can hardly be viewed as a triumph, let alone a golden age.

The major point of divergence concerns causes. Who or what causes wars, earthquakes, famine, pestilence, environmental crises? Or, should the ultimate disaster, a nuclear holocaust, occur, who would be responsible? Christians may not say that God has caused these calamities, but they will say that he has permitted them. Conversely, secular thinkers look to natural or human causes. While they may not be irreligious people, they focus on secondary factors, that is, human beings or nature, rather than the ultimate cause, God. They emphasize what can be observed or scientifically validated. Such thinking has its roots in the late Middle Ages. While the vast majority of the people attributed the Black Death to divine judgment, some individuals began to look for natural causes. As the modern world emerged in the eighteenth and nineteenth centuries, the notion of a secular apocalypse began to gain momentum. But it was not until the post–World War II era that such thinking took off: humanity does not need God to destroy the world; they can do it themselves!

We have seen that the end without God can come in several ways. If doomsday comes via an environmental crisis or a plague, there will be a quiet apocalypse. Or, as T. S. Eliot put it, "This is the way the world ends, not with a bang but a whimper." On the other hand, if the end comes by means of a nuclear war or a cosmic collision, it may be with a bang after all.[104]

2000 and a Few Afterthoughts

Our study has briefly examined how people in Western culture have viewed the end of the world. In this all too short of a journey, two concepts have risen to the surface: apocalyptic thinking has been highly adaptable, and, as a result, it has persisted through two thousand years of Western history. These two characteristics—elasticity and persistence—have marked end-time thinking in the West for nearly two millennia. Both the great minds and the rank and file of the Christian church have thought about how the world will end—often with strikingly different conclusions. Such apocalyptic expressions show no sign of abating; they are alive and well as we approach 2000.

The Persistent Apocalypse

To be sure, apocalyptic expressions have had their peaks and valleys. Endism, as Charles Strozier calls it, "has ebbed and flowed in significance within the self and culture, depending on historical circumstances." At times it has been repressed by church and society only to break out in full fury on other occasions. Peter Stearns has likened the persistence of apocalyptic thinking to a dormant virus—it resides in the body only to break out periodically, especially in sectarian groups.[1]

"The crowding out of apocalyptic into sectarian circles has characterized church history since its beginnings," writes Ulrich Körtner. Apocalyptic expressions can be found in the New Testament, the Didache, and other writings of the early church. Groups such as the Montanists anticipated that the world would end soon. The early church even had a date-setter in Hippolytus, who said the world would end in A.D. 500.[2]

But when the church became incorporated into the Roman Empire, the situation changed. Thanks to Augustine's rejection of crass millennialism and his identification of the church on earth with the kingdom of heaven, the church now worked to serve the world—not to oppose it and separate from it. The secular state and the church cooperated to restrain evil and further God's kingdom. Such thinking dominated the medieval church. Still, an apocalyptic expression remained alive, usually underground. It burst forth in the prophetic vision of Joachim of Fiore and in groups such as the Hussites and Taborites.[3]

During the Reformation the official churches attempted to stifle apocalyptic thinking. Nevertheless, it did play an important role during this time, even with Martin Luther. Radicals such as Thomas Müntzer, Melchior Hofmann, and the people at Münster behaved recklessly in the belief that the end was at hand and they were God's instruments to purge a fallen world. Apocalyptic thinking may have reached new heights in seventeenth-century England as the turmoil of the English Civil War ignited an explosion of end-time excitement.[4]

Apocalyptic expressions came to a standstill by the eighteenth century, however. The Enlightenment and the notion of progress repressed the apocalypse, though it did remain alive. End-time thinking was then awakened by events like the Lisbon earthquake and the French Revolution, and would later erupt in the Millerite movement and other nineteenth-century fringe groups.[5]

In our day apocalyptic thinking has roared back, says Stephen O'Leary: "The appeal of apocalyptic prophecy has endured through the ages; but its popularity has undergone a remarkable resurgence in the latter half of the twentieth century." He gives two reasons for this revival—the development of nuclear weapons and the establishment of the state of Israel.[6] Charles Strozier puts it in a different way: "It takes an act of imagination *not* to ponder end-time issues" in a day when human history could end by nuclear destruction or environmental degradation.[7]

Several theories have attempted to explain the ups and downs of apocalyptic ideas, but as Bernard McGinn notes, none fully accounts for the phenomenon. The ascendancy of end-time thinking has been variously seen as an attempt to understand the meaning of disasters, as a way for people to deal with social and economic deprivation, as a form of paranoia, and as the response of a cognitive minority.[8] What is clear is that a crisis mentality seems to promote an apocalyptic mind-set. And in the modern world, anxiety is certainly in the air. The twentieth century has seen two world wars, a depression, the holocaust, the advent of the nuclear age, a tense Cold War, the threat of environmental disaster, and the social upheavals of the 1960s. As Hillel Schwartz notes, the twentieth century "has often been regarded as a century less to celebrate than to survive." And the anxieties brought on by its turmoil have produced a doomsday mind-set and even a belief that the world might end.[9] Catherine Keller sees the apocalyptic pattern emerging today as entailing four basic beliefs: (1) the world is "unacceptable and pervasively corrupt"; (2) "an imminent and unavoidable catastrophe" will bring it to an end; (3) individuals "proclaiming the end" have a prophetic calling; and (4) the "final showdown" will be followed by a new age in which justice reigns and nature is renewed.[10]

The Elastic Apocalypse

The second concept rising to the forefront is the adaptability of apocalyptic ideas. Indeed, end-time thinking has been incredibly elastic. It has been molded and shaped to the events of at least two thousand years of Western history. Prophets and soothsayers have predicted the end countless times. And their batting average has been a perfect zero. But apocalyptic thinking has withstood many disconfirmations and is still going strong.

"Apocalypse can be disconfirmed without being discredited," explains Frank Kermode. It has an extraordinary resilience; it can "absorb changing interests [and] rival apocalypses." The apocalypse is "patient of change" and "allows itself to be diffused." When a prediction misfires, the failure "can be attributed to an error of calculation, either in arithmetic or allegory." With such freedom the prophet can "manipulate data" in order to achieve a desired result. Thus the end can "occur at pretty well any desired date." Similarly, Peter Stearns sees the apocalyptic vision as having "proved immune to repeated failures in predictions" because "it provide[s] people with an alternative to the rigid, rationalistic scientific framework that dominates our culture."[11]

Shifting Millennial Interpretations

Although millennial and apocalyptic ideas are not identical, they are related, and the various millennial views often connect with how people perceive the end of the world. Not surprisingly, then, millennial patterns generally approximate the ebb and flow, and the elasticity, of apocalyptic expressions. Most millennial ideas roughly fit into one of three positions—premillennialism, amillennialism, and postmillennialism. End-of-the-world speculations are generally most at home with, though not limited to, premillennialism. And many apocalyptists thus tend to be premillennialists. But it must be remembered that pre-, post-, and amillennialism are relatively modern terms. Thus these expressions can be used only as rough approximations of earlier millennial positions.

While most millennial interpretations can be found throughout Christian history, certain positions predominated at various times. During the first three centuries of Christian history, an end-time expectancy was commonplace. Thus a version of premillennialism prevailed. Its adherents included Justin Martyr, Papias, Tertullian, Irenaeus, Hippolytus, and Lactantius.[12] By the fourth century the church became incorporated into the Roman Empire. Visions of an impending end had largely waned, for Christians reinterpreted the millennium to refer to the church. Their equating Christ's thousand-year rule with the entire history of the church on earth negated the hope of a future millennium. The allegorical or amillennial position became the official position of the medieval Catholic Church. Its most famous spokesperson was Augustine. But chiliasm continued on the fringes of society, usually associated with apocalyptic movements.

Despite some apocalyptic inclinations the Protestant Reformers largely embraced a form of the amillennial position. At the same time medieval millennialism spilled over into the sixteenth century, energizing some radical groups to lash out at society. Such extremes encouraged the Reformers to condemn millennial beliefs, but premillennialism came back in the seventeenth century. In the chaos of the English Civil War, radical Puritan groups espoused premillennialism.

Still, the situation would change in the eighteenth century. Radical Puritanism had discredited premillennialism, and the Enlightenment fostered an optimistic view of the world contrary to premillennialism. Thus in came postmillennialism, the eschatological interpretation that would dominate during the eighteenth and nineteenth centuries. According to this perspective, the world would be converted to Christ, and peace, happiness, and righteousness would reign for a thousand years.

But along came John Nelson Darby and the birth of a new version of premillennialism. As the nineteenth century progressed, this dispensational premillennialism gained steam and came to dominate the older variations of premillennialism. In the twentieth century, thanks to popularizers such as Hal Lindsey, it may be the dominant view within evangelical circles, although a substantial number of evangelicals embrace amillennialism. Postmillennialism with its optimistic view of the world has to a substantial degree been stilled by the wars, turmoil, and atrocities of the twentieth century. Yet in the Reconstructionist or Dominion movement it is staging a comeback.[13] Indeed, apocalyptic expressions have been similarly repressed through much of Western history only to break out at certain times. The late twentieth century is one such occasion. Thanks to the persistence and chameleon-like quality of the apocalypse, end-time thinking is surging as we approach 2000.

The Countdown to 2000

The year 2000 is upon us. Is the end near? Yes say widely dissimilar categories of people—dispensational fundamentalists, devotees of Our Lady of Fatima, some environmentalists, UFO cultists, and interpreters of Nostradamus and the Mayan calendar. Will the approach of the year 2000 unleash a flood of doomsday prophecies? Probably. But this is not certain. In A.D. 1000 an apocalyptic mood existed, but not to the extent once believed; it was not widespread. In 1999, then, the apocalyptic activities could be less than anticipated. However, if the last thirty years of the twentieth century are any indication, there will be intense apocalyptic expectations. These years have witnessed a surge of predictions from several quarters—Christians, New Agers, psychics, environmentalists, and Native Americans. Yes, apocalyptic thinking is in the air. And as we approach 2000, forewarnings, prophecies, and "suggestions" will probably increase.[14]

As Hillel Schwartz notes, the end of a century prompts an apocalyptic stir. So much more so for 2000. It stands at the end of a millennium, not just another century. It is widely expected that "when the world's odometer ticks over to three zeros, it will have cosmic significance," says Ted Daniels, editor of *Millennial Prophecy Report*.[15] Richard Erdoes tells us that in our day people are speaking of the "Second Coming—the coming of Christ, of the anointed Messiah, of the Tenth Imam, of the Mahdi, even of Buddha." Some neo-Nazis are eagerly awaiting the reappearance of the Führer from outer space. A collection of individuals and groups on the margins of society, including "Neo-Nostradamians, Paracelsians, Cagliostroans, Saucerians, Pyramidians, followers of Edgar Cayce the Sleeping Prophet, of Wanda the Ultra-Aquarian, of Joseph the Hairstyling Augur, and of other sooth-or-gloom-sayers," predict that some cosmic cataclysm will destroy the world or a portion of it.[16]

But it is no longer only the eccentrics walking the streets with placards "proclaiming the end of the world who think that this puny planet of ours might not survive the twentieth century." Perfectly rational people, including scientists and Nobel laureates, "predict humankind's demise due to overpopulation, famines, deforestation, pollution, depletion of the earth's ozone layer, or simply the collapse of civilization due to the exhaustion of essential, nonrenewable raw materials."[17] An apocalyptic mentality is pervasive in strange and sane individuals. On the other hand, the collapse of Communism and the diminished possibility of a nuclear holocaust have encouraged a degree of optimism. Such a positive outlook fits into the predictions of many New Age groups, which anticipate not the end of the world but a new and improved age.

Why 2000?

Why the frenzy over 2000? It is a subjective date with no significance in the Bible, ancient writings, or science. In fact, the third millennium will begin in 2001, not 2000. Yet the world will go wild on December 31, 1999. Millennial parties were completely booked years in advance. Major gatherings will take place at Stonehenge, the Great Wall of China, the Great Pyramid, the Eiffel Tower, the Taj Mahal, the Acropolis, Red Square, and aboard the *Queen Elizabeth II*.[18]

Other dates have inspired an end-of-the-world excitement—999, 1013, 1300, 1600, 1666, 1844, and 1914. Still, 2000 is different. It excites perhaps an unparalleled passion. A nice round number, 2000 marks the end of a century and a millennium and has a tremendous psychological appeal. And thanks to a global calendar and modern technology, nearly the whole world will celebrate the dawn of a new millennium simultaneously. The year 2000 just seems like a time when something momentous should happen, something like the end of the world.[19]

Beyond the usual eschatological frenzy that a string of zeroes can arouse, there exist several other psychological factors. Curt Suplee lists five of them: (1) in the twenty years preceding 2000 there have been a lot of natural and unnatural disasters—perhaps not more than in past years, but we are more aware of them; (2) a deep numerological determinism grips many people; they see historical epochs coming in tens and groups of tens; (3) people have a growing appetite for the weird, especially in religion; witness the strange activities in many fringe religions; (4) in the decades before 2000 America has experienced tremendous social change, and social change often prompts people to expect a great cosmic change; and (5) American society is gripped with a sense of inadequacy; the problems seem overwhelming. In such a climate people look for some ultimate calamity.[20]

Also of tremendous importance is the view of the date of creation. Through the centuries Christians have believed that God created the world in six days and rested on the seventh. And according to 2 Peter 3:8, a day with the Lord is as a thousand years. Thus the millennium or the end of time must come six thousand years after creation. Such a scenario has provided the grist for much date-setting. When the world was created, however, is a matter of speculation. Thus prophets have

190

considerable flexibility—at least until A.D. 2000. Inasmuch as no one claims a date for creation later than 4000 B.C., A.D. 2000 is somewhat of a dead end.[21]

Recent events also point to 2000—so some people think. "Since 1945 it began to be technologically feasible to end life on this planet," notes philosopher Michael Grosso.[22] Either a nuclear holocaust or an environmental disaster could do us in. "It is the age of terror," writes Ulrich Körtner. "The catastrophic and its possibilities have obtained hitherto unimagined dimensions in our century."[23] While conditions do not lock us into the year 2000, they make it appear likely as an approximate date.

The overall irrationality of the age also points to 2000. There exists no rational basis for endowing the year 2000 with end-time significance. Apocalyptic thinking, however, always involves a certain amount of irrationality, which the focus on 2000 has raised to another level. Predictions regarding 2000 have no biblical or scientific basis. Rather, they rest largely on psychic vibrations, dreams, astrological projections, and so forth.

Christian Prophets and 2000

What predictions point to the year 2000? Actually, there are fewer than one might suppose. Rather, there exists more of an apocalyptic mood than a rash of specific predictions. Christians have made many end-time predictions for the late twentieth century, but few earmark the year 2000. Scientists, economists, and sociologists may see 2000 as a benchmark year, but they usually do not endow it with any apocalyptic significance. Actually, the vast majority of the prophecies regarding 2000 come from the fringe religions—astrologers, freelance prophets, soothsayers, New Agers, and psychics—many of whom base their end-time scenarios on a combination of sources, including the occult, ancient writings, and the Bible.[24]

Most of the Christian references to 2000 or thereabouts came several centuries before that date. A noteworthy example occurred in the early Protestant apocalyptic tradition, which rested on three sources: the books of Daniel and Revelation and the Prophecy of Elias. This prophecy divided history into three periods: before the law, under the law, and of the Messiah. Each period was allotted two thousand years, and thus the duration of the world was six thousand years. If creation came about 4000 B.C., as many suggested, the end would be about A.D. 2000.[25]

But most Protestant apocalyptic thinkers in the sixteenth and seventeenth centuries believed that God in his mercy would shorten the last age. This old world is so evil that it cannot last another four or five hundred years—so they thought. This led them to set dates much earlier than 2000, often close to their own day. For example, Martin Luther initially mentioned 2000, but later believed that the end would come around 1600.[26]

In early modern Europe most references to the end were more immediate. But at least two individuals pointed to the end of the millennium. Archbishop James Ussher—famous for dating creation at 4004 B.C.—believed the duration of the world to be six thousand years. This placed the world's end in 1996. Jansenism, an austere version of French Catholicism, produced a radical apocalyptic group—the Convulsionaries. Most Convulsionaries looked for an immediate doomsday, but one of their ranks, Jacques-Joseph Duguet (d. 1733), set 2000 as the date for Christ's second coming. He believed that many developments—including the conversion of Jews—had to occur before that event.[27]

Colonial and early national America heard at least two references to 2000. Most premillennialists at that time looked for a much earlier date for the second advent, but the postmillennialists felt that more time was needed for the world to be ready for the millennium. Jonathan Edwards regarded his own age, the First Great Awakening, as the vanguard of the millennium. Given the conversions during that period of revival, conditions would improve and the world would be ready for the millennium to begin by 2000.[28] Timothy Dwight made a similar prediction. Living during the Second Great Awakening, he regarded the revivals and perfectionism of his day as preparation for the millennium, which he too saw as beginning by 2000.[29]

One would expect the premillennialist popularizers to be gushing with proclamations about the year 2000. Many are in fact in a state of intense expectancy as the twentieth century winds down, but few have made specific predictions regarding 2000. Why? First, as Timothy Weber notes, premillennialists live in "the tension of the now/not yet." Whereas no event needs to be fulfilled before the second advent, they take us to the very edge of the now. But they usually hold up and do not make a specific prediction about the not yet. However, some popularizers have yielded to this temptation and made predictions. Others have "suggested" a date for the end.[30]

Second, many premillennial popularizers have already shot their prophetic cannon and had less than spectacular results. Their suggestions regarding the 1980s and 1990s have largely misfired. Two factors set off these prognostications. Hal Lindsey suggested that Christ would come one generation (forty years) after the establishment of the state of Israel (1948). Many prognosticators followed in the train of Lindsey's suggestion and made predictions for the 1980s and 1990s. Then, too, the long arm of Ussher's influence reached the late twentieth century. If the duration of human history is 6,000 years and creation took place in

192

4004 B.C., the end, it was reasoned, would come in 1996. Subtracting 7 years for the tribulation yielded a date in the late 1980s or early 1990s.[31]

Among the popularizers who have mentioned 2000 as a time of eschatological significance, if not the end of the world, was Lester Sumrall of LeSEA Broadcasting. In his book *I Predict 2000 A.D.* he declared: "I predict the absolute fullness of man's operation on planet Earth by the year 2000 A.D. Then Jesus Christ shall reign from Jerusalem for 1000 years."[32] Relying on the 6,000-year theory and Ussher's dates, other popularizers have inched toward 2000. In his *End Times News Digest* James McKeever said that Christ could return anytime between 1983 and 2030. That the 2,000-year Messianic Age could have begun with Christ's resurrection in A.D. 29 accounts for the terminus ad quem of 2030.[33] Canadian Grant Jeffrey argues that the early church accepted the 6,000-year theory and believed Christ would return around 2000. He also notes that 2000 is the target that groups like the New World Order and the New Agers have set for the imposition of a one-world government.[34] Jack Van Impe says that Christ will return "right around 2000." The sixth day will not "conclude until the year 2000, and perhaps as far ahead as the year 2012."[35]

The year 2000 rings a bell in other ways for some evangelicals. Reflecting Reconstructionist tendencies, Pat Robertson sees major changes by 2000.[36] A number of mission groups are targeting 2000 for completion of the task of world evangelization.[37] To others the German reunification in 1990, the collapse of the Soviet Union in 1991, and the furtherance of European unification all point to an apocalyptic event—the establishment of a single European currency by 2000.[38]

Secular Prophets and 2000

Secular doomsdayers have even less to say about the year 2000, although there is no shortage of secular doomsday predictions. Scientists tell us that humanity could be destroyed by a nuclear war or an environmental catastrophe. Economists point to a global financial collapse. Still, most of these secularists do not earmark 2000. A few scientists like Paul Ehrlich have issued warnings that pointed to years prior to 2000. Others give humanity another seventy-five to one hundred years. And while the predicted economic disasters may be catastrophic, it is not believed that they will bring the end of the world.

Yet a few secular prognosticators do mention the years around 2000 or tell us what the new millennium will bring. Their visions of the future are not always negative; in fact, some are utopian. About a hundred years ago, several prognosticators said a secular millennium would dawn by 2000. Edward Bellamy looked forward to a cooperative utopia,

Winnifred Cooley to a feminist welfare state, Friedrich Bilz to a universal nature cure, William Morris to a socialist revolution, and Edward Berwick to a vegetarian farmers'-paradise.[39]

As we approach the end of the millennium, other secularists are caught up with endism. In 1960 sociologist Daniel Bell paved the way when he proclaimed *The End of Ideology*. Other such books include *The End of Affluence, The End of Christendom, The End of Law, The End of Organized Capitalism*, and *The End of Nature*. Francis Fukuyama set Washington abuzz with his article "The End of History?" and a subsequent book *The End of History and the Last Man*. In these writings Fukuyama is not predicting the end of the world, but argues that liberal democracy has triumphed over all other ideologies—monarchy, fascism, and Communism. As a result, "history understood as a single, coherent, evolutionary process" has come to an end.[40]

Charles Berlitz's *Doomsday: 1999 A.D.* (1981) is not for the faint of heart. His brew of scientific, occultic, and psychic elements points directly to doomsday. He speaks of nuclear annihilation and environmental suicide. Pseudoscientist Berlitz is different from most secular prophets in that he says that all of this could happen by 2000. He places great emphasis on the direct alignment of Jupiter, Saturn, Uranus, Neptune, the sun, and the moon with the earth. This alignment, which occurred in 1982, could produce all kinds of geological changes by the year 2000—tidal waves, earthquakes, a polar flip, and a collision with a planetoid.[41]

Several economists forecast financial disasters around 2000. Most of these predictions, however, fall short of an economic apocalypse. Most specific and pessimistic is Peter Jay and Michael Stewart's *Apocalypse 2000*, which speaks of a catastrophic economic breakdown and the suicide of democracy by 2000. In the United States poverty, despair, and violence will have become endemic. "Life in America in 2000 [will be like] Lebanon in the mid-1980s." Conditions in Europe will not be much better.[42]

Some other economists use apocalyptic language but do not earmark 2000. In *The Great Depression of 1990* Ravi Batra forecasts a global financial Armageddon. However, this catastrophe will be followed by a moral regeneration in which people come to their senses and condemn immorality and great wealth.[43] Robert Heilbroner uses some Frankensteinian language to describe the future—sprawling urban blight, starving masses, revolution, and war.[44]

While not pointing to doomsday, some other economic forecasters note serious problems beginning around 2000. In *Millennium* Jacques Attali sees the United States in a decline and a world dominated by Europe and Japan.[45] Paul Kennedy predicts a similar future for America. In *The Rise and Fall of the Great Powers* he argues that America may be a great military power, but its economic base is rotting away. In *Preparing for the Twenty-First Century* he addresses global issues—scarce resources, food production, AIDS, and an exploding population.[46] C. Owen Paepke's *Evolution of Progress* tells us that the age of economic growth is over.[47]

The Psychics and 2000

The psychics tell us that all kinds of disasters will happen by 2000. Ruth Montgomery, for example, describes a polar shift: "After a period of churning seas and frightful wind velocities the turbulence will cease, and those in the north will live in a tropical clime, and vice versa. Before the year 2000 it will come to pass."[48] Other expected disasters include earthquakes, wars, pestilence, and collisions with celestial bodies. Many say that a new age of peace and tranquility will emerge after such calamities.

While the year 2000 has no apocalyptic importance for the Bible or science, it has a magical appeal for psychics, soothsayers, and astrologers, who expect momentous happenings around 2000. The source of their knowledge is usually dreams, trances, visions, ancient writings, or channeling sessions. Some occultists regard the Great Pyramid as a source of prophecy. Western esoteric schools have long regarded its dimensions and the symbols found in its passageways as keys to the future. One inch, for example, is regarded as equal to a year of time. Interpretations of the pyramid vary. According to occultist Max Toth, a kingdom of the spirit will emerge between 1995 and 2025. The year 2040 will see Christ's physical reincarnation, and great human achievements will mark the years between 2055 and 2080. The predictions go on until 2979, the last date indicated by the pyramid.[49]

A number of seers, mystics, and psychics have told stories of disaster and triumph for the end of the millennium. Heading the list is Nostradamus. Close behind is Edgar Cayce. The list also includes Jeane Dixon, Ruth Montgomery, Rudolf Steiner, Elizabeth Clare Prophet, Carl Jung, Madame Blavatsky, Djwhal Khul, Sun Bear, Alice Bailey, and José Arguelles. Of course, their individual predictions differ. But most of them would agree that the years around 2000 will experience floods, a polar shift, earthquakes, catastrophes brought on by a planetary alignment, famine, pestilence, droughts, fires, overpopulation, political repression, international terrorism, wars, and other horrors. "Great afflictions will come. . . . Nations will end in flames, and famine will annihilate millions," said Princess Billante of Savoy in the early twentieth century.[50]

Still, in true apocalyptic fashion triumph usually follows disaster. Many occultists see a new age dawning sometime after 2000. Humankind will survive the unprecedented upheavals. The world will be ushered into an era of peace, justice, and spiritual harmony. Because Christianity has lost its influence, inspiration will be drawn from various spiritual sources including Eastern wisdom and Native American religions. Spiritually, philosophically, economically, politically, scientifically, and artistically, all people will be integrated into a new world order.[51]

Along with this coming new age will be the arrival of a world savior or avatar. The major world religions all point to the coming of such an individual. Hindus await Kalki, Buddhists Maitreya, the Jews the Messiah, the Muslims Muntazar, and Christians the Christ. According to many psychics, he will arrive at the beginning of the twenty-first century and inaugurate a true golden age. But before this new age the world will be purged by many catastrophes. Many occult prophets do not in fact conceive of an absolute end of the world, but "merely a kind of purification" that is to come during the 1990s.[52]

Many seers see the future of humankind hanging in the balance. According to John Hogue, "all prophetic cycles throughout history pinpoint the 1990s as a turning point." Their collective vision foresees "humankind either destroyed by an outer fire or transformed by an inner one." From Nostradamus and Edgar Cayce to the Spirit Guides of Ruth Montgomery and the Center for Strategic and International Studies, "saints, seers, and authorities have indicated that our present historical moment is at the crossroads of utter doom or utopian splendor."[53]

It is intriguing that while the Bible does not endow the year 2000 with any particular significance, many psychics and seers employ the basic outline of Christian eschatology—impending catastrophes, a period of purging, the deeds of an Antichrist or evil one, the arrival of a great religious leader, and the coming of a golden age. Psychics adapt these concepts to their own situation and say that they will come to fulfilment around 2000.[54]

How Shall We Then Live?

We can be thankful that historians are not expected to sermonize or predict the future. Yet while hoping to avoid such pitfalls, one is tempted to make a few personal statements after looking at two thousand years of end-time thinking.

The belief that the world as we know it will end is deeply embedded in the Western psyche; it is part of our religious and cultural heritage. For centuries people have considered our world so hopelessly messed up that it must end soon. Evil—whether it be immorality, the spread of nuclear weapons, or pollution—is so ingrained that it cannot be reversed. Consequently, some people may even welcome the end. The world is so bad that it deserves to be destroyed. Or perhaps they are convinced that they will be rescued from the coming holocaust. At any rate, they seem to savor the thought of the apocalypse.[55]

End-time thinking has its ups and downs. But it will not go away—at least not until the real apocalypse occurs. So we must live with it. And this may not be all that bad. For apocalyptic thinking can have its positive as well as negative aspects. Moreover, we should keep in mind that prophecy occupies an important place in Christian theology.

Given the inevitability of apocalyptic thinking, it will help to see it as a product of its historical context. People tend to regard the problems of their age as the worst ever: morals are always on a decline; earthquakes and other natural disasters seem to be ever increasing; current events can be interpreted as the fulfilment of prophecy; and evil political and religious leaders who can be identified as the Antichrist are never wanting. But as the historical context shifts, so do the specific interpretations of prophecy. At most points in history it is possible to identify particular events and people as fulfilments of prophecy. Given this historical understanding of apocalyptic thinking, we can remain calm. People have been predicting the end of the world for two millennia. And sometime the end will come. But every time someone sounds an alarm, we don't have to quit our jobs or sell our houses.

It also helps to keep in mind that Christianity is not the sole source of end-time thinking. Though not as prevalent as in Western culture, apocalyptic visions also appear in non-Western religious traditions. Even within the Western tradition, Christianity does not have a corner on endism. To be sure, Christianity has led the way in producing apocalyptic scenarios. But through the centuries psychics and seers have voiced their projections. And in the last thirty years or so, the scientists have joined in.

Therefore, informed people must relate to at least three apocalyptic traditions—the Christian, occult, and scientific. Christians will want to distance themselves from occult apocalypticism. Still, it is all around us. Projections by Nostradamus and Edgar Cayce are taken seriously by many people. More than that, for centuries occult and Christian apocalypticism have been muddled together. Psychics have frequently used the broad contours of Christian eschatology for predictions. And Christians have employed the occult arts—astrology, pyramidalism, and numerology—in their projections.[56]

On the other hand, we should not readily dismiss the dire predictions of many scientists. Some doomsday scientists may have been precipitate. The greenhouse effect and mass starvations probably will not overwhelm us before 2000. But even the more conservative scientists are sending out warnings—something must be done about our exploding population, environmental problems, and the spread of nuclear weapons. If not, humankind has a bleak future. We must not allow our eschatological position to sedate us to such problems. The hope of Christ's imminent return should not deter Christians from working to prevent an environmental or nuclear apocalypse.

Christians must also relate to other Christians who have differing eschatological views. To be sure, the personal and visible return of Jesus Christ is an inescapable biblical truth. Christians also agree on the major issues of judgment, heaven, and hell. But within the Christian community there is no consensus regarding the chronology of most end-time events—the second advent, the tribulation, and the millennium. In fact, some Christians reject the concept of a literal golden age on earth. We must keep in mind that there is room for legitimate differences regarding the interpretation of the prophetic passages of Scripture, and that apocalyptic thinking is shaped by its historical context. We must, then, work to eliminate intolerance toward those who differ with us over the chronology of end-time events, an intolerance that arises in part out of an apocalyptic worldview that leaves little room for shades of gray. We should focus instead on working together to further the coming of the kingdom of God.[57]

Pitfalls to Avoid

In respect to end-time thinking, two common mistakes are made. On one hand, some Christians have become obsessed with it, especially the chronology of Christ's return. They see nearly every twist and turn of current events as the fulfilment of prophecy. Prophecy books become best-sellers, and prophecy sermons pack the sanctuary. On the other hand, some Christians pay scant attention to Bible prophecy. In doing so, they are ignoring an important part of God's Word. They have seen the excesses of apocalyptic thinking and want no part of it. We cannot know when Christ will return, they correctly reason; but then they completely ignore the subject of prophecy.[58]

Eschatology is a broad subject. Unfortunately, end-time thinking focuses primarily on only one aspect of it—the chronology of the end. The order of events surrounding Christ's return is not the most important dimension in the Christian teaching regarding the end of the world. Yet it has taken center stage. Why? Humans crave to know the future, and in particular when the end will come.

This intense appetite to know when the end will come has led to the worst problem of all—date-setting. True, many end-time prophets will not admit to date-setting. They may call their predictions suggestions or condition their prognostications with the words "if," "ought," and "should." Those who merely suggest a time for the end have been called implicit date-setters.[59]

Such date-setting (or suggestions if you please) grows out of several trends, especially a misreading of the signs of the times and the imposition of current events on Scripture. In Matthew 24:3 Jesus' disciples pose the question that has been asked for centuries: "What shall be the sign of thy coming, and of the end of the world?" They impatiently wanted a sign. So do we.

And Jesus proceeded to give them a sign—two chapters of signs as a matter of fact. He described all kinds of dire scenarios. For starters there will be famines, earthquakes, wars, and pestilences in many places. But before the end there will also be false prophets showing "great signs and wonders" and misleading many. As a result, in Jesus' day people misread the signs. People today make the same mistake.[60]

Jesus gave his disciples clues, in other words, hints as to when the end would come. He did not give them an exact blueprint or a timetable for the end of the world. But like the people of old, Christians today are not satisfied with clues; they want a precise road map.[61]

Moreover, having labeled the signs that he gave his disciples "the beginning of sorrows," Jesus also made clear that "the end is not yet" (Matt. 24:6, 8). The signs began in Jesus' time, especially with the fall of Jerusalem, but they will not be completed until his second coming. The last days began in Jesus' day, not when Israel became a nation in 1948. And they have run the course of Christian history. The death and resurrection of Jesus were eschatological events. Thus, to believe that the last days began in 1948 or 1967 locks one into an illegitimate timetable and the unwarranted belief that the present generation cannot pass away without the return of Christ. Prophecy has an "already/not yet" dimension. Many prophecy buffs neglect the "already" aspect.[62]

End-time hysteria results not only from a misreading of the signs, but also from a faulty method of biblical interpretation. Popularizers view many current events as the final fulfilment of end-time prophecies. They do not interpret Scripture in the context of its day, that is, "from a historical, cultural, grammatical and theological perspective."[63] Rather, they use a *pesher*-like hermeneutic. The *pesher* (Aramaic for "interpretation") method assumes that biblical prophecy is being fulfilled in the interpreter's own day. For example, modern doomsday prophets read current events back into Ezekiel, Daniel, and Revelation. But do the biblical prophets really speak of Cobra helicopters, AIDS, tanks, nuclear weapons, African killer-bees, computers, oil, and a unified Europe?[64] To read current events back into Scripture actually intensifies the chameleon-like character of prophecy. As modern prophets scrutinize every jot and tittle of current events, they may maintain the major outline of their eschatological position, but must frequently switch the details as circumstances change. When contemporary trends disconfirm their predictions, they quietly forget their earlier position. Indeed, as Mark Noll states, the modern end-time prophets tend to be "blown about by every wind of apocalyptic speculation."[65]

All of these problems are compounded by two trends within American evangelicalism—a strident populism and anti-intellectualism. Few of the prophecy popularizers have any serious theological training. In their view, anyone can interpret the Bible, even the difficult prophetic passages. The popularizers are often proud of their lack of academic credentials—they are not among the academic elite. Instead, God has given them a special insight into Scripture. But they usually manhandle the Bible and twist biblical passages out of their context.[66]

Mark Noll and Os Guinness have noted the anti-intellectualism within American evangelicalism. Evangelicals seldom engage in substantive biblical or theological studies. What they want out of church is to feel good. Books that sell well zero in on sensational or subjective subjects—Satan, demons, prophecy, conspiracies, or personal growth. In such a climate apocalyptic speculations and eschatological titillations will continue to thrive. Indeed, there is a ready-made audience for apocalyptic sensationalism.[67]

Thy Kingdom Come

However, we do not want to end this history on a sour note. Eschatology and even apocalypticism have their positive aspects, especially if they are interpreted from a Christian framework. Apocalyptic entails both disaster and triumph. Unfortunately, through time the catastrophic element has gripped the popular mind. Eschatology, a broader concept, includes some glorious subjects—Christ's return, the millennium, and heaven.

Eschatology bears on both the present and the future. The last days began in the first century A.D. Christians were called then and are called now to focus on Christ, not the signs of the times. Still, they must be prepared for Christ's second coming. This preparation includes obeying the call to holiness, right living, and evangelism as well as combating evil. Christians know what the future holds—the triumphant return of Christ and the universal rule of God—and they are to live in the present with that in mind.[68]

Regarding the future, the most important aspect of biblical eschatology is not what has captivated popular thinking, namely, the chronology of the end. Rather, the key aspect is the consummation of the kingdom of God. Eschatology also focuses on some weighty philosophical matters: the flow and significance of history, the sovereignty of God, and the future of the world.[69]

From the Christian perspective, history is going somewhere. It is not a static process, nor is it a story of randomness and unrelated events. The Christian believes that God is in control of history and that it is following a path of development. This path began with creation. The central event was the life and death of Jesus Christ. The culmination of the divine program for history will be the second coming of Christ and his magnificent rule. Our goal should not be to satisfy our human curiosity as to when these events will occur, but to better understand them and to live in their glorious light.[70]

Notes

Chapter 1. The End Is upon Us

1. Ken Baker, "Preachers Proclaiming 'The End Is Near,'" *Wichita Eagle*, 4 February 1995, p. 7c.

2. Daniel Cohen, *Waiting for the Apocalypse* (Buffalo: Prometheus, 1983), 7–8.

3. Lance Morrow, "A Cosmic Moment," *Time*, Fall 1992 (special issue), 6; Alvin P. Sanoff, "The Faces of Doomsday," *U.S. News and World Report*, 19 October 1992, 73; Jeffrey Kaplan, *Radical Religion in America* (Syracuse: Syracuse University Press, 1997), vii.

4. Joe Maxwell, "Prophecy Books Become Big Sellers," *Christianity Today*, 11 March 1991, 60; Peter Steinfels, "Gulf War Proving Bountiful for Some Prophets of Doom," *New York Times*, 1 February 1991, pp. 1, 10; Kenneth L. Woodward, "The Final Days Are Here Again," *Newsweek*, 18 March 1991, 55.

5. The quotes are from Hillel Schwartz, "Fin-de-Siècle Fantasies," *New Republic*, 30 July and 6 August 1990, 22.

6. Ibid., 22–24. See also Hillel Schwartz, *Century's End* (New York: Doubleday, 1990); Edwin McDowell, "New Year's Eve Hot Spots Already Booked—for 99," *Wichita Eagle*, 18 December 1995, pp. 1A, 7A; Peter N. Stearns, *Millennium III, Century XXI* (Boulder, Colo.: Westview, 1996), vii, 4.

7. Frank Palmeri, "Apocalypse: Then and Now," *Humanist*, January-February 1983, 26.

8. The quote is from Robert Jewett, "Coming to Terms with the Doom Boom," *Quarterly Review* 4.3 (Fall 1984): 9. See also Bill Lawren, "Are You Ready for Millennial Fever?" *Utne Reader*, March-April 1990, 91–92; G. Clark Chapman Jr., "Falling in Rapture before the Bomb," *Reformed Journal* 37 (June 1987): 13.

9. Richard Kyle, *The Religious Fringe* (Downers Grove, Ill.: InterVarsity, 1993), 366; Ron Rhodes, "Millennial Madness," *Christian Research Journal* 13.2 (Fall 1990): 39; Michael Barkun, "Reflections after Waco: Millennialists and the State," *Christian Century*, 2–9 June 1993, 596.

10. Bill Lawren, "Apocalypse Now?" *Psychology Today* 23.5 (May 1989): 42; Dick Teresi and Judith Hooper, "The Last Laugh?" *Omni* 12.4 (Jan. 1990): 43.

11. Cullen Murphy, "The Way the World Ends," *Wilson Quarterly* 14.1 (Winter 1990): 54; Teresi and Hooper, "The Last Laugh?" 43.

12. William F. Allman, "Fatal Attraction:

Why We Love Doomsday," *U.S. News and World Report*, 30 April 1990, 13.

13. Charles Krauthammer, "Apocalypse, with and without God," *Time*, 22 March 1993, 82 (quote); Samuel McCracken, "Apocalyptic Thinking," *Commentary*, October 1971, 61.

14. Krauthammer, "Apocalypse," 82; Ray Corelli, "Boom Time for Futurists," *World Press Review*, December 1989, 28.

15. Ibid.

16. See, e.g., Ravi Batra, *The Great Depression of 1990* (New York: Simon and Schuster, 1987); Krauthammer, "Apocalypse," 82; Corelli, "Boom Time," 27–28.

17. Bernard McGinn, *Visions of the End* (New York: Columbia University Press, 1979), 3; Stephen D. O'Leary, *Arguing the Apocalypse* (New York: Oxford University Press, 1994), 10.

18. Lois Parkinson Zamora, ed., *The Apocalyptic Vision in America* (Bowling Green, Ohio: Bowling Green University Popular Press, 1982), 2–3.

19. George E. Ladd, "Apocalyptic," in *Evangelical Dictionary of Theology*, ed. Walter A. Elwell (Grand Rapids: Baker, 1984), 63; H. H. Rowley, *The Relevance of Apocalyptic* (Greenwood, S.C.: Attic, 1980), 54ff.; Lester L. Grabbe, "The Social Setting of Early Jewish Apocalypticism," *Journal for the Study of Pseudepigrapha* 4 (April 1989): 27–47.

20. Zamora, ed., *Apocalyptic Vision*, 3, 14 (quote); Jewett, "Coming to Terms with the Doom Boom," 10; Walter Schmithals, *The Apocalyptic Movement* (Nashville: Abingdon, 1975), 18, 21–24.

21. O'Leary, *Arguing the Apocalypse*, 5–6; Barry Brummett, *Contemporary Apocalyptic Rhetoric* (New York: Praeger, 1991), 7; Frank Kermode, *The Sense of an Ending* (New York: Oxford University Press, 1967); Catherine Keller, *Apocalypse Now and Then* (Boston: Beacon, 1996), 20.

22. McGinn, *Visions of the End*, 4 (quote); Ladd, "Apocalyptic," 63.

23. Robert G. Clouse, "Views of the Millennium," in *Evangelical Dictionary of Theology*, ed. Elwell, 714; "Millenarianism," in *Oxford Dictionary of the Christian Church*, ed. F. L. Cross, 2d ed. (New York: Oxford University Press, 1974), 916.

24. Stanley J. Grenz, *The Millennial Maze* (Downers Grove, Ill.: InterVarsity, 1992), 24–26, 149–52; Clouse, "Views of the Millen-

nium," 715; Robert G. Clouse, ed., *The Meaning of the Millennium* (Downers Grove, Ill.: InterVarsity, 1977), 7; Grant Underwood, *The Millenarian World of Early Mormonism* (Urbana: University of Illinois Press, 1993), 4, 6.

25. Russell Chandler, *Doomsday* (Ann Arbor: Servant, 1993), 34–35; Otto Friedrich, *The End of the World: A History* (New York: Fromm International, 1986), 17–19.

26. Cohen, *Waiting for the Apocalypse*, 78–82; Friedrich, *End of the World*, 20–21.

27. Cohen, *Waiting for the Apocalypse*, 57.

28. Donald V. Gawronski, *History: Meaning and Method* (Glenview, Ill.: Scott, Foresman, 1975), 24–25; Chandler, *Doomsday*, 15–16; D. W. Bebbington, *Patterns in History* (Downers Grove, Ill.: InterVarsity, 1979), 21–42; Keller, *Apocalypse Now and Then*, 12; Stearns, *Millennium III*, 12–13.

29. Brummett, *Contemporary Apocalyptic Rhetoric*, 32–33; Bebbington, *Patterns in History*, 43–67.

30. W. Warren Wagar, *Terminal Visions* (Bloomington: Indiana University Press, 1982), 34–35; Brummett, *Contemporary Apocalyptic Rhetoric*, 32–33; Debra Bergofen, "The Apocalyptic Meaning of History," in *Apocalyptic Vision in America*, ed. Zamora, 13–29; Catherine Keller, "Why Apocalypse Now?" *Theology Today* 49.2 (1992): 184.

31. Cohen, *Waiting for the Apocalypse*, 83; Daniel Cohen, *Prophets of Doom* (Brookfield, Conn.: Millbrook, 1992), 15.

32. John G. Gager, *Kingdom and Community* (Englewood Cliffs, N.J.: Prentice Hall, 1975); Gerd Theissen, *Sociology of Early Palestinian Christianity* (Philadelphia: Fortress, 1978). The quote is from D. H. Williams, "The Origins of the Montanist Movement: A Sociological Analysis," *Religion* 19 (1989): 334.

33. Norman Cohn, *The Pursuit of the Millennium*, rev. ed. (New York: Oxford University Press, 1974), 281–82.

34. Marjorie Reeves, *The Influence of Prophecy in the Later Middle Ages* (New York: Oxford University Press, 1969), 314–17 (Reeves refers to an earlier edition of *Pursuit of the Millennium* [1957 or 1961]). McGinn, *Visions of the End*, 2, 36, 145–48; Bernard McGinn, "Introduction: John's Apocalypse and the Apocalyptic Mentality," in *The Apocalypse in the Middle Ages*, ed. Richard K. Emmerson and Bernard McGinn (Ithaca, N.Y.:

Cornell University Press, 1992), 11.

35. Michael Barkun, *Disaster and the Millennium* (New Haven: Yale University Press, 1974), 6.

36. For a refinement of Barkun's ideas see his *Crucible of the Millennium* (Syracuse: Syracuse University Press, 1986).

37. James H. Moorhead, "Searching for the Millennium in America," *Princeton Seminary Bulletin* 8.2 (1987): 17–33; Brummett, *Contemporary Apocalyptic Rhetoric*, 29; David L. Rowe, "Millerites: A Shadow Portrait," in *The Disappointed*, ed. Ronald L. Numbers and Jonathan M. Butler (Knoxville: University of Tennessee Press, 1993), 7–8.

38. O'Leary, *Arguing the Apocalypse*, 9; Robert G. Clouse, "The New Christian Right, America, and the Kingdom of God," *Christian Scholar's Review* 12 (1983): 3–16; Erling Jorstad, *The Politics of Moralism* (Minneapolis: Augsburg, 1981).

39. Kenneth A. Myers, "Fear and Frenzy on the Eve of A.D. 2000," *Genesis* 3.1 (Jan. 1990): 1, 3; Curt Suplee, "Apocalypse Now: The Coming Doom Boom," *Washington Post*, 17 December 1989, pp. B1–B2.

40. Ibid.

Chapter 2. Apocalypse Postponed

1. "The Epistle of Ignatius to the Ephesians," in *The Ante-Nicene Fathers*, 10 vols. (Grand Rapids: Eerdmans, 1960), 1:54.

2. Yuri Rubinsky and Ian Wiseman, *A History of the End of the World* (New York: Morrow, 1982), 24.

3. Ibid., 24–25; A. H. M. Jones, *Augustus* (New York: Norton, 1970), 153ff.; Peter Arnott, *The Romans and Their World* (New York: St. Martin's, 1970), 186ff.

4. Russell Chandler, *Doomsday* (Ann Arbor: Servant, 1993), 32; Rubinsky and Wiseman, *End of the World*, 27; George John Hoynacki, "Messianic Expectations in Non-Christian Religious Traditions," *Asia Journal of Theology* 5 (Oct. 1991): 381–82.

5. W. S. LaSor, "Zoroastrianism," in *Evangelical Dictionary of Theology*, ed. Walter A. Elwell (Grand Rapids: Baker, 1984), 1202; Hoynacki, "Messianic Expectations," 381.

6. Stanley J. Grenz, *The Millennial Maze* (Downers Grove, Ill.: InterVarsity, 1992), 32–33. See also Paul D. Hanson, "Old Testament Apocalyptic Reexamined," in *Visionar-*

ies and Their Apocalypses, ed. Paul D. Hanson (Philadelphia: Fortress, 1983).

7. H. H. Rowley, *The Relevance of Apocalyptic* (Greenwood, S.C.: Attic, 1980), 13–27; Grenz, *Millennial Maze*, 33. See also Lester L. Grabbe, "The Social Setting of Early Jewish Apocalypticism," *Journal for the Study of Pseudepigrapha* 4 (April 1989): 27–47.

8. Rubinsky and Wiseman, *End of the World*, 31; Rowley, *Relevance of Apocalyptic*, 35–37.

9. Paul Boyer, *When Time Shall Be No More* (Cambridge, Mass.: Harvard University Press, 1992), 27; Rubinsky and Wiseman, *End of the World*, 32.

10. See Roland K. Harrison, *Introduction to the Old Testament* (Grand Rapids: Eerdmans, 1969), 1105–34; and Gleason L. Archer Jr., *A Survey of Old Testament Introduction* (Chicago: Moody, 1964), 365–79. Among the popularizers who see Daniel's visions as relevant for the late twentieth century are Hal Lindsey, *The Late Great Planet Earth* (Grand Rapids: Zondervan, 1970); Salem Kirban, *Guide to Survival* (Chattanooga: AMG, 1990); and Jimmy Swaggart, *Armageddon: The Future of Planet Earth* (Baton Rouge: Jimmy Swaggart Ministries, 1987).

11. Rowley, *Relevance of Apocalyptic*, 55–56; Boyer, *When Time Shall Be No More*, 31. See also Bernhard W. Anderson, *Understanding the Old Testament*, 2d ed. (Englewood Cliffs, N.J.: Prentice Hall, 1966), 536–40; James King West, *Introduction to the Old Testament* (New York: Macmillan, 1971), 409–27.

12. West, *Introduction to the Old Testament*, 422–23; Anderson, *Understanding the Old Testament*, 544–45.

13. Anderson, *Understanding the Old Testament*, 549–50; Boyer, *When Time Shall Be No More*, 31–32; West, *Introduction to the Old Testament*, 423–24.

14. Rubinsky and Wiseman, *End of the World*, 33; Boyer, *When Time Shall Be No More*, 32.

15. Rubinsky and Wiseman, *End of the World*, 34; Rowley, *Relevance of Apocalyptic*, 54–57.

16. Walter Schmithals, *The Apocalyptic Movement* (Nashville: Abingdon, 1975), 13–28.

17. Rowley, *Relevance of Apocalyptic*, 54ff.; Rubinsky and Wiseman, *End of the World*, 34.

18. Rowley, *Relevance of Apocalyptic*, 85; Boyer, *When Time Shall Be No More*, 32.

19. Rowley, *Relevance of Apocalyptic*, 90–92; Boyer, *When Time Shall Be No More*, 32–33; Michael J. St. Clair, *Millenarian Movements in Historical Context* (New York: Garland, 1992), 35–37.

20. Quoted in Jaroslav Pelikan, *The Emergence of the Catholic Tradition* (Chicago: University of Chicago Press, 1971), 123.

21. Robert A. Cole, *The Gospel according to St. Mark* (Grand Rapids: Eerdmans, 1976), 197; Boyer, *When Time Shall Be No More*, 34.

22. Cole, *St. Mark*, 198–203; Boyer, *When Time Shall Be No More*, 34.

23. Boyer, *When Time Shall Be No More*, 35.

24. Lindsey, *Late Great Planet Earth*, 53–54.

25. Rubinsky and Wiseman, *End of the World*, 44.

26. Ibid., 46; Rowley, *Relevance of Apocalyptic*, 140–42.

27. Leon Morris, *The Revelation of St. John* (Grand Rapids: Eerdmans, 1969), 16–17; David Ewert, *The Church under Fire* (Winnipeg: Kindred, 1988), ii–iii.

28. Ewert, *Church under Fire*, ii–iii; Morris, *Revelation of St. John*, 17.

29. Morris, *Revelation of St. John*, 17–18; Ewert, *Church under Fire*, iii–iv.

30. Rowley, *Relevance of Apocalyptic*, 148.

31. M. Eugene Boring, *Revelation* (Louisville: John Knox, 1989), 202; Morris, *Revelation of St. John*, 234.

32. Boyer, *When Time Shall Be No More*, 45.

33. Ibid.

34. St. Clair, *Millenarian Movements*, 60.

35. Pelikan, *Emergence of the Catholic Tradition*, 122.

36. J. C. De Smidt, "Chiliasm: An Escape from the Present into an Extra-Biblical Apocalyptic Imagination," *Scriptura* 45 (1993): 83–84; Grabbe, "Social Setting of Early Jewish Apocalypticism," 27–47.

37. St. Clair, *Millenarian Movements*, 65; Robert M. Grant, *Early Christianity and Society* (New York: Harper, 1977), 79–84.

38. Pelikan, *Emergence of the Catholic Tradition*, 125.

39. Grenz, *Millennial Maze*, 38; Avihu Zakai and Anya Mali, "Time, History and Eschatology: Ecclesiastical History from Euse-bius to Augustine," *Journal of Religious History* 17.4 (Dec. 1993): 403–4.

40. Russell Chandler, *Doomsday* (Ann Arbor: Servant, 1993), 39; Grenz, *Millennial Maze*, 39; Zakai and Mali, "Time, History and Eschatology," 403.

41. Cited in Eusebius *Ecclesiastical History* 3.39. See also Grenz, *Millennial Maze*, 39; Pelikan, *Emergence of the Catholic Tradition*, 124.

42. St. Clair, *Millenarian Movements*, 77; Grenz, *Millennial Maze*, 41; J. N. D. Kelly, *Early Christian Doctrines*, rev. ed. (New York: Harper, 1978), 463.

43. William C. Weinrich, "Antichrist in the Early Church," *Concordia Theological Quarterly* 49.2–3 (1985): 139; Bernard McGinn, *Antichrist* (San Francisco: Harper, 1994), 58–60; Grenz, *Millennial Maze*, 40; St. Clair, *Millenarian Movements*, 78; Pelikan, *Emergence of the Catholic Tradition*, 124.

44. Grenz, *Millennial Maze*, 39; St. Clair, *Millenarian Movements*, 78.

45. Rubinsky and Wiseman, *End of the World*, 56; St. Clair, *Millenarian Movements*, 78; Kelly, *Early Christian Doctrines*, 467–69; Ernest Lee Tuveson, *Millennium and Utopia* (New York: Harper, 1964), 11.

46. Rubinsky and Wiseman, *End of the World*, 56; Justo L. Gonzalez, *History of Christian Thought*, vol. 1 (Nashville: Abingdon, 1970), 235–37; Jeffery L. Sheler, "The Christmas Covenant," *U.S. News and World Report*, 19 December 1994, 64; Chandler, *Doomsday*, 39; Bernard McGinn, *Visions of the End* (New York: Columbia University Press, 1979), 51; Peter N. Stearns, *Millennium III, Century XXI* (Boulder, Colo.: Westview, 1996), 16.

47. David F. Wright, "The Montanists," in *Eerdmans' Handbook to the History of Christianity*, ed. Tim Dowley (Grand Rapids: Eerdmans, 1977), 74; St. Clair, *Millenarian Movements*, 79–82; D. H. Williams, "The Origins of the Montanist Movement: A Sociological Analysis," *Religion* 19 (1989): 338–45; W. H. C. Frend, "Montanism: A Movement of Prophecy and Regional Identity in the Early Church," *Bulletin of the John Rylands University of Manchester* 70 (Autumn 1988): 29–34.

48. Grenz, *Millennial Maze*, 42; Kelly, *Early Christian Doctrines*, 464–65; McGinn, *Antichrist*, 70–75; Catherine Keller, *Apocalypse Now and Then* (Boston: Beacon, 1996), 97.

49. Zakai and Mali, "Time, History and Eschatology," 406; Kelly, *Early Christian Doctrines*, 464–65; Robert M. Grant, *Augustus to Constantine* (San Francisco: Harper, 1990), 51; Tuveson, *Millennium and Utopia*, 14.

50. Kelly, *Early Christian Doctrines*, 41–48; Grenz, *Millennial Maze*, 42; Pelikan, *Emergence of the Catholic Tradition*, 124–25.

51. Kelly, *Early Christian Doctrines*, 469–79; Pelikan, *Emergence of the Catholic Tradition*, 125; Boyer, *When Time Shall Be No More*, 47; De Smidt, "Chiliasm," 84–85; Robert L. Wilken, "Early Christian Chiliasm, Jewish Messianism, and the Idea of the Holy Land," *Harvard Theological Review* 79.1–3 (1986): 302–4.

52. Zakai and Mali, "Time, History and Eschatology," 401–2; Keller, *Apocalypse Now and Then*, 97.

53. St. Clair, *Millenarian Movements*, 88–89; Zakai and Mali, "Time, History and Eschatology," 413.

54. Boyer, *When Time Shall Be No More*, 48; Grenz, *Millennial Maze*, 42–43; Paula Fredriksen, "Tyconius and Augustine on the Apocalypse," in *The Apocalypse in the Middle Ages*, ed. Richard K. Emmerson and Bernard McGinn (Ithaca, N.Y.: Cornell University Press, 1992), 24; Keller, *Apocalypse Now and Then*, 102–3.

55. Peter Brown, *Augustine of Hippo* (Berkeley: University of California Press, 1969), 140, 272; Gerald Bonner, "Augustine's Thoughts on This World and Hope for the Next," *Princeton Seminary Bulletin*, supplementary issue 3 (1994): 94–99; Grenz, *Millennial Maze*, 45; Fredriksen, "Tyconius and Augustine," 20–24, 136, 140; Bruce W. Speck, "Augustine's Tale of Two Cities: Teleology/Eschatology in *The City of God*," *Journal of Interdisciplinary Studies* 8.1–2 (1996): 104–30.

56. Augustine *City of God* 20.9. See Bonner, "Augustine's Thoughts," 102; Fredriksen, "Tyconius and Augustine," 31.

57. Zakai and Mali, "Time, History and Eschatology," 411.

58. Grenz, *Millennial Maze*, 44; Rubinsky and Wiseman, *End of the World*, 59; Robert E. Lerner, "The Medieval Return to the Thousand-Year Sabbath," in *The Apocalypse in the Middle Ages*, ed. Emmerson and McGinn, 52.

59. Zakai and Mali, "Time, History and Eschatology," 416–17; Boyer, *When Time Shall Be No More*, 49; St. Clair, *Millenarian*

Movements, 87; Grenz, *Millennial Maze*, 44; Fredriksen, "Tyconius and Augustine," 35–36.

Chapter 3. The Slumbering Apocalypse

1. Ernest Lee Tuveson, *Millennium and Utopia* (New York: Harper, 1964), 20–21.

2. Walter Klaassen, *Living at the End of the Ages* (Lanham, Md.: University Press of America, 1992), 4–5; J. C. De Smidt, "Chiliasm: An Escape from the Present into an Extra-Biblical Apocalyptic Imagination," *Scriptura* 45 (1993): 85. See also Beryl Smalley, *The Study of the Bible in the Middle Ages* (Notre Dame, Ind.: University of Notre Dame Press, 1964).

3. Klaassen, *Living at the End of the Ages*, 5.

4. Yuri Rubinsky and Ian Wiseman, *A History of the End of the World* (New York: Morrow, 1982), 28; George John Hoynacki, "Messianic Expectations in Non-Christian Religious Traditions," *Asia Journal of Theology* 5 (Oct. 1991): 378–79.

5. Daniel Cohen, *Waiting for the Apocalypse* (Buffalo: Prometheus, 1983), 36–38.

6. Bernard McGinn, *Visions of the End* (New York: Columbia University Press, 1979), 51.

7. Norman Cohn, *Pursuit of the Millennium*, rev. ed. (New York: Oxford University Press, 1974), 35–36; Bernard McGinn, *Antichrist* (San Francisco: Harper, 1994), 80–81, 87–90; Otto Friedrich, *The End of the World* (New York: Fromm International, 1986), 27–64.

8. H. H. Rowley, *The Relevance of Apocalyptic* (Greenwood, S.C.: Attic, 1980), 75–76.

9. McGinn, *Visions of the End*, 40–50; Rubinsky and Wiseman, *End of the World*, 60.

10. Rubinsky and Wiseman, *End of the World*, 58.

11. Cohn, *Pursuit of the Millennium*, 30–31; McGinn, *Antichrist*, 88–92; Richard K. Emmerson, *Antichrist in the Middle Ages* (Seattle: University of Washington Press, 1981), 48–50.

12. McGinn, *Antichrist*, 108; Rubinsky and Wiseman, *End of the World*, 60.

13. McGinn, *Antichrist*, 90 (quote); Klaassen, *Living at the End of the Ages*, 6; Paul J. Alexander, "Medieval Apocalypses as Historical Sources," *American Historical Review* 73.4 (1968): 998–99.

14. McGinn, *Antichrist*, 90; idem, *Visions of the End*, 70.

15. Rubinsky and Wiseman, *End of the World*, 62; McGinn, *Antichrist*, 92.

16. Emmerson, *Antichrist in the Middle Ages*, 35–58; McGinn, *Antichrist*, 58–70; Rubinsky and Wiseman, *End of the World*, 63.

17. McGinn, *Antichrist*, 102; Emmerson, *Antichrist in the Middle Ages*, 76–83; Rubinsky and Wiseman, *End of the World*, 63.

18. The quote is from Richard Erdoes, "The Year 1000," *Psychology Today* 23.5 (May 1989): 44. See also idem, *A.D. 1000: Living on the Brink of Apocalypse* (New York: Harper and Row, 1988).

19. See Hillel Schwartz, *Century's End* (New York: Doubleday, 1990), 6; idem, "Fin-de-Siècle Fantasies," *New Republic*, 30 July and 6 August 1990, 23; Howard G. Chua-Eoan, "Life in 1999: A Grim Struggle," *Time*, Fall 1992 (special issue), 18; McGinn, *Antichrist*, 100; idem, *Visions of the End*, 89; Peter N. Stearns, *Millennium III, Century XXI* (Boulder, Colo.: Westview, 1996), 21–34.

20. McGinn, *Antichrist*, 100.

21. Stearns, *Millennium III*, 21–37.

22. Stanley J. Grenz, *The Millennial Maze* (Downers Grove, Ill.: InterVarsity, 1992), 46.

23. Michael J. St. Clair, *Millenarian Movements* (New York: Garland, 1992), 95–96.

24. Ibid., 97; Rubinsky and Wiseman, *End of the World*, 73, 75; Hans E. Mayer, *The Crusades* (New York: Oxford University Press, 1972), 28–31; Friedrich, *End of the World*, 111–42.

25. Robert E. Lerner, "The Black Death and Western European Eschatological Mentalities," *American Historical Review* 86.3 (1981): 534 (quote). See also Philip Ziegler, *The Black Death* (New York: Harper and Row, 1969); Barbara W. Tuchman, *A Distant Mirror: The Calamitous 14th Century* (New York: Ballantine, 1978); Schwartz, *Century's End*, 65–74.

26. McGinn, *Visions of the End*, 94; St. Clair, *Millenarian Movements*, 96; Grenz, *Millennial Maze*, 46. See also Steven Ozment, *The Age of Reform, 1250–1550* (New Haven: Yale University Press, 1980).

27. Emmerson, *Antichrist in the Middle Ages*, 56–57; Grenz, *Millennial Maze*, 46.

28. Emmerson, *Antichrist in the Middle Ages*, 7; Grenz, *Millennial Maze*, 47; Robert E. Lerner, "The Medieval Return to the Thou-sand-Year Sabbath," in *The Apocalypse in the Middle Ages*, ed. Richard K. Emmerson and Bernard McGinn (Ithaca, N.Y.: Cornell University Press, 1992), 70–71.

29. Emmerson, *Antichrist in the Middle Ages*, 54–55.

30. McGinn, *Visions of the End*, 180; C. Warren Hollister, *The Making of England: 55 B.C. to 1399*, 4th ed. (Lexington, Mass.: D. C. Heath, 1983), 205.

31. McGinn, *Visions of the End*, 180.

32. Rubinsky and Wiseman, *End of the World*, 80.

33. Cohn, *Pursuit of the Millennium*, 108; McGinn, *Visions of the End*, 126; Catherine Keller, *Apocalypse Now and Then* (Boston: Beacon, 1996), 107.

34. Marjorie Reeves, *Joachim of Fiore and the Prophetic Future* (New York: Harper and Row, 1976), i–ii; St. Clair, *Millenarian Movements*, 99.

35. Cohn, *Pursuit of the Millennium*, 109; Marilyn Ferguson, *The Aquarian Conspiracy* (Los Angeles: J. P. Tarcher, 1980); Richard Kyle, *The New Age Movement in American Culture* (Lanham, Md.: University Press of America, 1995), 21.

36. E. Randolph Daniel, "Joachim of Fiore: Patterns of History in the Apocalypse," in *Apocalypse in the Middle Ages*, ed. Emmerson and McGinn, 73.

37. Reeves, *Joachim of Fiore*, 1–28; McGinn, *Visions of the End*, 127; Grenz, *Millennial Maze*, 46; Keller, *Apocalypse Now and Then*, 108.

38. Cohn, *Pursuit of the Millennium*, 109–10; Reeves, *Joachim of Fiore*, 6–17.

39. Bernard McGinn, "Angel Pope and Papal Antichrist," *Church History* 47.2 (1978): 160–61; Rubinsky and Wiseman, *End of the World*, 77–78.

40. Cohn, *Pursuit of the Millennium*, 109–10; Daniel, "Joachim of Fiore," 84; McGinn, *Antichrist*, 140–41; Reeves, *Joachim of Fiore*, 22; McGinn, "Angel Pope and Papal Antichrist," 158–59.

41. McGinn, *Visions of the End*, 134; Rubinsky and Wiseman, *End of the World*, 78; Klaassen, *Living at the End of the Ages*, 13; Schwartz, *Century's End*, 52–53.

42. Daniel, "Joachim of Fiore," 87; Reeves, *Joachim of Fiore*, 5–7.

43. Daniel, "Joachim of Fiore," 87.

44. St. Clair, *Millenarian Movements*,

101–2; McGinn, *Visions of the End*, 146.

45. Malcolm Lambert, *Medieval Heresy* (New York: Holmes and Meier, 1977), 190; McGinn, *Antichrist*, 155; Gordon Leff, "Heresy and the Decline of the Medieval Church," in *Religious Dissent in the Middle Ages*, ed. Jeffrey B. Russell (New York: Wiley, 1971), 104–8.

46. Reeves, *Joachim of Fiore*, 32–33; Cohn, *Pursuit of the Millennium*, 110; Rubinsky and Wiseman, *End of the World*, 80; McGinn, *Visions of the End*, 160.

47. St. Clair, *Millenarian Movements*, 104; McGinn, *Antichrist*, 159–60.

48. McGinn, *Visions of the End*, 205 (quote); Lambert, *Medieval Heresy*, 190; Emmerson, *Antichrist in the Middle Ages*, 69.

49. St. Clair, *Millenarian Movements*, 106–7; McGinn, *Visions of the End*, 234; Lambert, *Medieval Heresy*, 184–86.

50. McGinn, *Antichrist*, 152; idem, *Visions of the End*, 168; Cohn, *Pursuit of the Millennium*, 111.

51. Cohn, *Pursuit of the Millennium*, 111; Marjorie Reeves, *The Influence of Prophecy in the Later Middle Ages* (New York: Oxford University Press, 1969), 104, 123–26, 166, 307–13.

52. McGinn, *Antichrist*, 156; Cohn, *Pursuit of the Millennium*, 117.

53. Cohn, *Pursuit of the Millennium*, 111–12; McGinn, *Visions of the End*, 168; idem, *Antichrist*, 154.

54. St. Clair, *Millenarian Movements*, 108–9; Rubinsky and Wiseman, *End of the World*, 82; Friedrich, *End of the World*, 125–33; Cohn, *Pursuit of the Millennium*, 127–33.

55. Ziegler, *Black Death*, 192; Cohn, *Pursuit of the Millennium*, 136–39; Lerner, "Black Death," 537.

56. Lerner, "Black Death," 537; St. Clair, *Millenarian Movements*, 109–10; Cohn, *Pursuit of the Millennium*, 136, 140.

57. McGinn, *Visions of the End*, 259, 261.

58. Ibid.; Matthew Spinka, *John Hus* (Westport, Conn.: Greenwood, 1979).

59. Cohn, *Pursuit of the Millennium*, 208–9; McGinn, *Visions of the End*, 258; St. Clair, *Millenarian Movements*, 122–23; Spinka, *John Hus*, 306; Lambert, *Medieval Heresy*, 307–10.

60. St. Clair, *Millenarian Movements*, 128–30; Cohn, *Pursuit of the Millennium*, 210.

61. McGinn, *Visions of the End*, 262; St. Clair, *Millenarian Movements*, 130–31; Rubinsky and Wiseman, *End of the World*, 88.

62. Cohn, *Pursuit of the Millennium*, 211–14; St. Clair, *Millenarian Movements*, 130–31.

63. Cohn, *Pursuit of the Millennium*, 219–20; St. Clair, *Millenarian Movements*, 145–47.

64. Cohn, *Pursuit of the Millennium*, 219–20; St. Clair, *Millenarian Movements*, 145–47.

65. McGinn, *Visions of the End*, 277–78.

66. St. Clair, *Millenarian Movements*, 112–13; McGinn, *Visions of the End*, 277–79; Schwartz, *Century's End*, 78–79.

67. McGinn, *Visions of the End*, 277–79; St. Clair, *Millenarian Movements*, 112–13.

68. Robert G. Clouse, ed., *The Meaning of the Millennium* (Downers Grove, Ill.: InterVarsity, 1977), 9–10.

Chapter 4. The On-Again, Off-Again Apocalypse

1. Martin Luther, *Dr. Martin Luthers Sämmtliche Schriften*, ed. Johann Georg Walch, 23 vols. (St. Louis: Concordia, 1881–1910), 22:1334.

2. See Keith Thomas, *Religion and the Decline of Magic* (New York: Scribner, 1971).

3. See Michael Barkun, *Disaster and the Millennium* (New Haven: Yale University Press, 1974).

4. See W. Warren Wagar, *Terminal Visions* (Bloomington: Indiana University Press, 1982), 54–61; Frank Kermode, *The Sense of an Ending* (New York: Oxford University Press, 1967), 93–124.

5. Yuri Rubinsky and Ian Wiseman, *A History of the End of the World* (New York: Morrow, 1982), 90.

6. Ibid.

7. Pauline Moffitt Watts, "Prophecy and Discovery: On the Spiritual Origins of Christopher Columbus's 'Enterprise of the Indies,'" *American Historical Review* 90.1 (1985): 90–94; Hillel Schwartz, *Century's End* (New York: Doubleday, 1990), 84–85; Bernard McGinn, *Visions of the End* (New York: Columbia University Press, 1979), 284; Catherine Keller, *Apocalypse Now and Then* (Boston: Beacon, 1996), 159–62.

8. Watts, "Prophecy and Discovery," 94.

9. McGinn, *Visions of the End*, 284;

Schwartz, *Century's End*, 84–85; Watts, "Prophecy and Discovery," 98–100.

10. Walter Klaassen, *Living at the End of the Ages* (Lanham, Md.: University Press of America, 1992), 20, 23.

11. See George H. Williams, *The Radical Reformation* (Philadelphia: Westminster, 1962); George H. Williams and Angel M. Mergal, eds., *Spiritual and Anabaptist Writers* (Philadelphia: Westminster, 1957), 19–38; William R. Estep, *The Anabaptist Story* (Grand Rapids: Eerdmans, 1975); Leonard Verduin, *The Reformers and Their Stepchildren* (Grand Rapids: Eerdmans, 1964).

12. Walter Klaassen, "Apocalypticism," in *The Mennonite Encyclopedia*, ed. Cornelius J. Dyck and Dennis D. Martin, vol. 5 (Scottdale, Pa.: Herald, 1990), 29 (quote); idem, *Living at the End of the Ages*, 20–21.

13. Michael J. St. Clair, *Millenarian Movements in Historical Context* (New York: Garland, 1992), 155.

14. Williams and Mergal, eds., *Spiritual and Anabaptist Writers*, 32; Klaassen, *Living at the End of the Ages*, 34; Steven E. Ozment, *Mysticism and Dissent* (New Haven: Yale University Press, 1973), 79–89; Otto Friedrich, *The End of the World* (New York: Fromm International, 1986), 156. See also Eric W. Gritsch, *Thomas Müntzer: A Tragedy of Errors* (Minneapolis: Fortress, 1989); Abraham Friesen, *Reformation and Utopia: The Marxist Interpretation of the Reformation and Its Antecedents* (Wiesbaden: F. Steiner, 1974).

15. Norman Cohn, *The Pursuit of the Millennium* (New York: Oxford University Press, 1970), 235–36; Richard Bailey, "The Sixteenth Century's Apocalyptic Heritage and Thomas Müntzer," *Mennonite Quarterly Review* 57.1 (1983): 36–38; Thomas Nipperdey, "Thomas Müntzer: Theologian and Revolutionary," in *The Anabaptists and Thomas Müntzer*, ed. James M. Stayer and Werner O. Packull (Dubuque: Kendall/Hunt, 1980), 105–17.

16. Cohn, *Pursuit of the Millennium*, 245–46; Paul Boyer, *When Time Shall Be No More* (Cambridge, Mass.: Harvard University Press, 1992), 58; James M. Stayer, *Anabaptists and the Sword* (Lawrence, Kans.: Coronado, 1972), 80; Williams, *Radical Reformation*, 59–84; Friedrich, *End of the World*, 158–59.

17. Hans-Jürgen Goertz, "Thomas Müntzer: Revolutionary between the Middle Ages and Modernity," *Mennonite Quarterly Review* 64.1 (1990): 27–31; Bailey, "Sixteenth Century's Apocalyptic Heritage," 37–43; Cohn, *Pursuit of the Millennium*, 240–42. See also Abraham Friesen, *Thomas Muentzer, a Destroyer of the Godless* (Berkeley: University of California Press, 1990).

18. Stayer, *Anabaptists and the Sword*, 80–90; Boyer, *When Time Shall Be No More*, 58; Williams, *Radical Reformation*, 81–84; Keller, *Apocalypse Now and Then*, 187–88.

19. Stayer, *Anabaptists and the Sword*, 212–19; St. Clair, *Millenarian Movements*, 170–71.

20. Klaassen, *Living at the End of the Ages*, 28–29; Stayer, *Anabaptists and the Sword*, 217–22; St. Clair, *Millenarian Movements*, 170–71; Werner O. Packull, "Melchior Hoffman's First Two Letters," *Mennonite Quarterly Review* 64.2 (1990): 140–59.

21. Klaassen, *Living at the End of the Ages*, 45–46; Stayer, *Anabaptists and the Sword*, 230–36; Williams, *Radical Reformation*, 355–61; St. Clair, *Millenarian Movements*, 173–75.

22. Williams, *Radical Reformation*, 368–72; Klaassen, *Living at the End of the Ages*, 47–49; St. Clair, *Millenarian Movements*, 175–77.

23. Stayer, *Anabaptists and the Sword*, 255–74; St. Clair, *Millenarian Movements*, 177–84; Williams, *Radical Reformation*, 371–75; Keller, *Apocalypse Now and Then*, 191–92.

24. St. Clair, *Millenarian Movements*, 184–85.

25. Bernard McGinn, *Antichrist* (San Francisco: Harper, 1994), 201–2; idem, "Angel Pope and Papal Antichrist," *Church History* 47.2 (1978): 155–73; Stanley J. Grenz, *The Millennial Maze* (Downers Grove, Ill.: InterVarsity, 1992); John M. Headley, *Luther's View of Church History* (New Haven: Yale University Press, 1963), 198; Robin B. Barnes, *Prophecy and Gnosis* (Stanford, Calif.: Stanford University Press, 1988), 42–44.

26. McGinn, *Antichrist*, 206; Harvey Buchanan, "Luther and the Turks 1519–1529," *Archiv für Reformationsgeschichte* 47 (1956): 145–60; Paul Althaus, *The Theology of Martin Luther* (Philadelphia: Fortress, 1966), 421.

27. Althaus, *Theology of Martin Luther*,

418–21; Bryan W. Ball, *A Great Expectation: Eschatological Thought in English Protestantism to 1660* (Leiden: E. J. Brill, 1975), 15–16.

28. Althaus, *Theology of Martin Luther*, 419; Grenz, *Millennial Maze*, 51.

29. T. F. Torrance, "The Eschatology of the Reformation," *Scottish Journal of Theology*, occasional papers 2 (1953): 43–44; Headley, *Luther's View of Church History*, 240–65; Barnes, *Prophecy and Gnosis*, 40–47.

30. Barnes, *Prophecy and Gnosis*, 1–3; Schwartz, *Century's End*, 92.

31. John Knox, *The Works of John Knox*, ed. David Laing, 6 vols. (Edinburgh: Bannatyne Club, 1846–64), 1:190. See also Richard Kyle, *The Mind of John Knox* (Lawrence, Kans.: Coronado, 1984), 227–32; idem, "John Knox and Apocalyptic Thought," *Sixteenth Century Journal* 15.4 (1984): 449–69.

32. Rodney L. Petersen, *Preaching in the Last Days* (New York: Oxford University Press, 1993), 136–37; Le Roy E. Froom, *The Prophetic Faith of Our Fathers*, 4 vols. (Washington, D.C.: Review and Herald, 1946–54), 2:342–44.

33. McGinn, *Antichrist*, 226.

34. Ibid., 228–29.

35. Dava Sobel, "The Resurrection of Nostradamus," *Omni* 16.3 (Dec. 1993): 44, 48; Daniel Cohen, *Prophets of Doom* (Brookfield, Conn.: Millbrook, 1992), 62–64; Peter Lorie, *Nostradamus: The Millennium and Beyond* (New York: Simon and Schuster, 1993), 12–18.

36. James Randi, *The Mask of Nostradamus* (Buffalo: Prometheus, 1993), 17–19; Cohen, *Prophets of Doom*, 66–68; Sobel, "Resurrection of Nostradamus," 48; Lorie, *Nostradamus*, 18–19.

37. Rubinsky and Wiseman, *End of the World*, 89; Sobel, "Resurrection of Nostradamus," 48; Russell Chandler, *Doomsday* (Ann Arbor: Servant, 1993), 64.

38. Randi, *Mask of Nostradamus*, 30–38; Rubinsky and Wiseman, *End of the World*, 89; Chandler, *Doomsday*, 64–65.

39. Rubinsky and Wiseman, *End of the World*, 89.

40. St. Clair, *Millenarian Movements*, 200.

41. Christopher Hill, *Antichrist in Seventeenth-Century England*, rev. ed. (London: Verso, 1990), 9, 13, 31–32, 62, 77, 131.

42. Bernard Capp, "The Fifth Monarchists and Popular Millenarianism," in *Radical Religion in the English Revolution*, ed. J. F. McGregor and B. Reay (New York: Oxford University Press, 1984), 176–78, 185–86; Katharine R. Firth, *The Apocalyptic Tradition in Reformation Britain, 1530–1645* (Oxford: Oxford University Press, 1979), 5; Cohen, *Prophets of Doom*, 56–57.

43. Capp, "Popular Millenarianism," 176, 178.

44. Ibid.; Bernard Capp, *Astrology and the Popular Press* (Boston: Faber, 1979); Thomas, *Religion and the Decline of Magic*, 358–432.

45. Paul Christianson, *Reformers and Babylon* (Toronto: University of Toronto Press, 1978), 15–30; Grenz, *Millennial Maze*, 54; Ball, *Great Expectation*, 15–88.

46. Firth, *Apocalyptic Tradition*, 195; Ball, *Great Expectation*, 55–88; Robert G. Clouse, "John Napier and Apocalyptic Thought," *Sixteenth Century Journal* 5.1 (1974): 101–14.

47. St. Clair, *Millenarian Movements*, 191, 197–98; Keller, *Apocalypse Now and Then*, 193–94.

48. Capp, "Popular Millenarianism," 167–68; Ball, *Great Expectation*, 55–88; Peter Toon, ed., *Puritans, the Millennium and the Future of Israel* (Greenwood, S.C.: Attic, 1970), 19–22.

49. Capp, "Popular Millenarianism," 168–69; Michael R. Watts, *The Dissenters* (Oxford: Clarendon, 1985), 14–76. See also Christopher Hill, *Society and Puritanism* (New York: Schocken, 1967); idem, *Puritanism and Revolution* (New York: Schocken, 1964).

50. Ball, *Great Expectation*, 89–125; Capp, "Popular Millenarianism," 168–69. See also William Haller, *The Rise of Puritanism* (New York: Columbia University Press, 1938); Christopher Hill, *The World Turned Upside Down* (New York: Viking, 1972); J. F. Maclear, "New England and the Fifth Monarchy: The Quest for the Millennium in Early American Puritanism," *William and Mary Quarterly* 32 (April 1975): 223–60.

51. Firth, *Apocalyptic Tradition*, 144–203; Grenz, *Millennial Maze*, 52–53; Toon, ed., *Puritans*, 23–41; Christianson, *Reformers and Babylon*, 97–113.

52. Robert G. Clouse, "The Rebirth of Millenarianism," in *Puritans*, ed. Toon, 42, 62–64; Capp, "Popular Millenarianism," 167.

53. Grenz, *Millennial Maze*, 53–54; Clouse, "Rebirth of Millenarianism," 64; Ball, *Great Expectation*, 163–71.

54. Ball, *Great Expectation*, 171 (quote); Grenz, *Millennial Maze*, 53–54.

55. George Rosen, "Social Change and Psychopathology in the Emotional Climate of Millennial Movements," *American Behavioral Scientist* 16.2 (1972): 159; Capp, "Popular Millenarianism," 165; Hill, *World Turned Upside Down*, 148–207; idem, *Antichrist in Seventeenth-Century England*, 88–116.

56. B. S. Capp, "Extreme Millenarianism," in *Puritans*, ed. Toon, 65–68; St. Clair, *Millenarian Movements*, 192–93; Ball, *Great Expectation*, 183–89; Ernest Lee Tuveson, *Millennium and Utopia* (New York: Harper, 1964), 89.

57. Rubinsky and Wiseman, *End of the World*, 93; Capp, "Popular Millenarianism," 181.

58. St. Clair, *Millenarian Movements*, 192–93.

59. Capp, "Extreme Millenarianism," 71, 85–89; St. Clair, *Millenarian Movements*, 213–15; Ball, *Great Expectation*, 187–97; Schwartz, *Century's End*, 114–15.

60. Hill, *Antichrist in Seventeenth-Century England*, 146–47; McGinn, *Antichrist*, 230–36.

61. Boyer, *When Time Shall Be No More*, 66–69; J. F. C. Harrison, *The Second Coming: Popular Millenarianism, 1780–1850* (New Brunswick, N.J.: Rutgers University Press, 1979), 3–7.

62. James West Davidson, *The Logic of Millennial Thought* (New Haven: Yale University Press, 1977), 87–88; Boyer, *When Time Shall Be No More*, 67; Tuveson, *Millennium and Utopia*, 131–32.

63. Perry Miller, *Errand into the Wilderness* (Cambridge, Mass.: Harvard University Press, 1964), 222–32; Boyer, *When Time Shall Be No More*, 67. See also Saul Friedländer, "Themes of Decline and End in Nineteenth-Century Western Imagination," in *Visions of Apocalypse*, ed. Saul Friedländer et al. (New York: Holmes and Meier, 1985), 61–80.

64. Tuveson, *Millennium and Utopia*, 1; Harrison, *Second Coming*, 6–7.

65. John Meyendorff, *The Orthodox Church*, rev. ed. (Crestwood, N.Y.: St. Vladimir's Seminary Press, 1981), 107; McGinn, *Antichrist*, 233; Thomas Robbins, "Religious Mass Suicide before Jonestown: The Russian Old Believers," *Sociological Analysis* 47.1 (Spring 1986): 7.

66. Robbins, "Russian Old Believers," 3; Meyendorff, *Orthodox Church*, 110; McGinn, *Antichrist*, 234; Alexander Schmemann, *Historical Road of Eastern Orthodoxy* (Crestwood, N.Y.: St. Vladimir's Seminary Press, 1977), 329–30.

67. Robbins, "Russian Old Believers," 3, 7.

68. Ibid., 2–3.

69. McGinn, *Antichrist*, 242; St. Clair, *Millenarian Movements*, 224; Clarke Garrett, *Respectable Folly* (Baltimore: Johns Hopkins University Press, 1975), 12–14.

70. Harrison, *Second Coming*, 5–7; St. Clair, *Millenarian Movements*, 223–32.

71. Clarke Garrett, *Spirit Possession and Popular Religion: From the Camisards to the Shakers* (Baltimore: Johns Hopkins University Press, 1987), 16–20; St. Clair, *Millenarian Movements*, 224; Harrison, *Second Coming*, 25.

72. St. Clair, *Millenarian Movements*, 227.

73. Garrett, *Spirit Possession and Popular Religion*, 18–24; St. Clair, *Millenarian Movements*, 226; Harrison, *Second Coming*, 25; Rosen, "Social Change and Psychopathology," 157.

74. St. Clair, *Millenarian Movements*, 226–27; Garrett, *Spirit Possession and Popular Religion*, 31–34.

75. St. Clair, *Millenarian Movements*, 228–29; Garrett, *Spirit Possession and Popular Religion*, 10–11.

76. McGinn, *Antichrist*, 242; Garrett, *Respectable Folly*, 12–13.

77. Garrett, *Respectable Folly*, 10, 21–27; St. Clair, *Millenarian Movements*, 230–31; McGinn, *Antichrist*, 243–45.

78. Richard Kyle, *The Religious Fringe* (Downers Grove, Ill.: InterVarsity, 1993), 49; Harrison, *Second Coming*, 73.

79. Kyle, *Religious Fringe*, 49; Harrison, *Second Coming*, 73. See also Emanuel Swedenborg, *Divine Love and Wisdom* (London: Swedenborg Society, 1969); idem, *Apocalypse Revealed* (New York: Swedenborg Foundation, 1855); and *Emanuel Swedenborg*, ed. Michael Stanley (New York: Sterling, 1989).

80. Ernest R. Sandeen, *The Roots of Fundamentalism* (Chicago: University of Chicago Press, 1970), 4–5.

81. St. Clair, *Millenarian Movements*,

239–40; Deborah M. Valenze, "Prophecy and Popular Literature in Eighteenth-Century England," *Journal of Ecclesiastical History* 29.1 (1978): 75–92; Harrison, *Second Coming*, 6–7.

82. David Bebbington, "The Advent Hope in British Evangelicalism since 1800," *Scottish Journal of Religious Studies* 9.2 (Autumn 1988): 104; Sandeen, *Roots of Fundamentalism*, 5–7; Harrison, *Second Coming*, 6–7.

83. St. Clair, *Millenarian Movements*, 240–41. See also Frank E. Manuel, *The Religion of Isaac Newton* (Oxford: Clarendon, 1974); I. B. Cohen, "Newton, Isaac," in *Dictionary of Scientific Biography*, ed. Charles Coulston Gillespie, 14 vols. (New York: Scribner, 1974), 10:81–83.

84. St. Clair, *Millenarian Movements*, 240–41.

85. Garrett, *Spirit Possession and Popular Religion*, 46–48; St. Clair, *Millenarian Movements*, 242–43; Harrison, *Second Coming*, 23, 27, 29.

86. Garrett, *Spirit Possession and Popular Religion*, 45–50; St. Clair, *Millenarian Movements*, 246–52.

87. Garrett, *Respectable Folly*, 134–35; McGinn, *Antichrist*, 243–44; Bebbington, "Advent Hope in British Evangelicalism," 104–5; Sandeen, *Roots of Fundamentalism*, 5–7.

88. Harrison, *Second Coming*, 57–85; Rubinsky and Wiseman, *End of the World*, 112.

89. Harrison, *Second Coming*, 86–94; St. Clair, *Millenarian Movements*, 256–58.

90. Harrison, *Second Coming*, 96–99; Rubinsky and Wiseman, *End of the World*, 112; St. Clair, *Millenarian Movements*, 258.

91. Clarence B. Bass, *Backgrounds to Dispensationalism* (Grand Rapids: Eerdmans, 1960), 19–23; Charles C. Ryrie, *Dispensationalism Today* (Chicago: Moody, 1965), 22–47.

92. Timothy P. Weber, *Living in the Shadow of the Second Coming* (New York: Oxford University Press, 1979), 22; Bass, *Backgrounds to Dispensationalism*, 17–18. For more information on Darby and the Plymouth Brethren see Harold H. Rowdon, *The Origins of the Brethren* (London: Pickering and Inglis, 1967); F. Roy Coad, *History of the Brethren Movement* (Grand Rapids: Eerdmans, 1968); George T. Stokes, "John Nelson Darby," *Contemporary Review* 48 (Oct. 1885):

537–52; Henry M. King, "The Plymouth Brethren," *Baptist Review* 3 (1881): 438–65; Thomas Corskery, "The Plymouth Brethren," *Princeton Review*, n.s. 1 (1872): 48–77.

93. Sandeen, *Roots of Fundamentalism*, 59–60 (quote); Weber, *Living in the Shadow of the Second Coming*, 14–15; "Dates and Date-Setting," *Millennial Prophecy Chart*, May 1994, 9.

94. Sandeen, *Roots of Fundamentalism*, 63–64.

95. Bass, *Backgrounds to Dispensationalism*, 129.

96. Boyer, *When Time Shall Be No More*, 88.

97. Richard P. McBrien, *Catholicism*, rev. ed. (San Francisco: Harper, 1989), 1089–90; St. Clair, *Millenarian Movements*, 233–34.

98. McBrien, *Catholicism*, 1092; St. Clair, *Millenarian Movements*, 234–35.

99. Mary Lee Nolan and Sidney Nolan, *Christian Pilgrimage in Modern Western Europe* (Chapel Hill: University of North Carolina Press, 1989), 199; St. Clair, *Millenarian Movements*, 235; McBrien, *Catholicism*, 1092; Elliot Miller and Kenneth R. Samples, *The Cult of the Virgin* (Grand Rapids: Baker, 1992), 90–92.

100. McBrien, *Catholicism*, 1093; Chandler, *Doomsday*, 205; Rubinsky and Wiseman, *End of the World*, 122; Miller and Samples, *Cult of the Virgin*, 93–97.

101. Rubinsky and Wiseman, *End of the World*, 122; Chandler, *Doomsday*, 205–6; Kenneth L. Woodward, "Going to See the Virgin Mary," *New York Times Book Review*, 11 August 1991, p. 22.

102. Chandler, *Doomsday*, 211; Rubinsky and Wiseman, *End of the World*, 122.

103. Friedrich, *End of the World*, 179–212; Chandler, *Doomsday*, 115.

104. Friedrich, *End of the World*, 227–334; Chandler, *Doomsday*, 121–22.

Chapter 5. America and the Great Millennial Hope

1. Ernest R. Sandeen, *The Roots of Fundamentalism* (Chicago: University of Chicago Press, 1970), 42; Catherine Albanese, *America: Religions and Religion*, 2d ed. (Belmont, Calif.: Wadsworth, 1992); Sidney E. Mead, *The Nation with the Soul of a Church* (New York: Harper and Row, 1975); Ernest Lee Tuveson, *Redeemer Nation: The Idea of America's*

Millennial Role (Chicago: University of Chicago Press, 1968).

2. Ira V. Brown, "Watchers for the Second Coming: The Millenarian Tradition in America," *Mississippi Valley Historical Review* 39 (Dec. 1952): 445.

3. Robert C. Fuller, *Naming the Antichrist* (New York: Oxford University Press, 1995), 42–43.

4. James West Davidson, *The Logic of Millennial Thought* (New Haven: Yale University Press, 1977), 75; Ruth H. Bloch, *Visionary Republic* (New York: Cambridge University Press, 1985), 12.

5. Davidson, *Logic of Millennial Thought,* 63, 262, 281; Bloch, *Visionary Republic,* 12.

6. J. F. Maclear, "New England and the Fifth Monarchy: The Quest for the Millennium in Early American Puritanism," *William and Mary Quarterly* 32 (April 1975): 225–26; Brown, "Watchers for the Second Coming," 445; Michael J. St. Clair, *Millenarian Movements in Historical Context* (New York: Garland, 1992), 268.

7. Paul Boyer, *When Time Shall Be No More* (Cambridge, Mass.: Harvard University Press, 1992), 69.

8. Robert Middlekauff, *The Mathers: Three Generations of Puritan Intellectuals, 1596–1728* (New York: Oxford University Press, 1976), 323.

9. Fuller, *Naming the Antichrist,* 45–47. See also James Alan Patterson, "Changing Images of the Beast: Apocalyptic Conspiracy Theories in American History," *Journal of the Evangelical Theological Society* 31 (Dec. 1988): 443–44.

10. Davidson, *Logic of Millennial Thought,* 62–63; Boyer, *When Time Shall Be No More,* 69–70; Middlekauff, *Mathers,* 342–43, 346.

11. Davidson, *Logic of Millennial Thought,* 62; Boyer, *When Time Shall Be No More,* 75, 88.

12. Brown, "Watchers for the Second Coming," 446–50; Davidson, *Logic of Millennial Thought,* 13–16, 60–63.

13. Timothy L. Smith, "Righteousness and Hope: Christian Holiness and the Millennial Vision in America, 1800–1900," *American Quarterly* 31.1 (Spring 1979): 21–27; Russel Blaine Nye, *Society and Culture in America, 1830–1860* (New York: Harper and Row, 1974), 36, 289–92; William G. McLoughlin Jr., *Modern Revivalism* (New York: Ronald,

1959), 102–3.

14. See Jean B. Quandt, "Religion and Social Thought: The Secularization of Postmillennialism," *American Quarterly* 25 (Oct. 1973): 390–409; James H. Moorhead, "Between Progress and Apocalypse: A Reassessment of Millennialism in American Religious Thought, 1800–1880," *Journal of American History* 71.3 (1984): 524–42; idem, "The Erosion of Postmillennialism in American Religious Thought, 1865–1925," *Church History* 53.1 (1984): 61–77; Rush Welter, "The Idea of Progress in America," *Journal of the History of Ideas* 14 (1955): 401–15.

15. Christopher M. Beam, "Millennialism and American Nationalism, 1740–1800," *Journal of Presbyterian History* 54 (Spring 1976): 182; Boyer, *When Time Shall Be No More,* 70; Nathan O. Hatch, "The Origins of Civil Millennialism in America," in *Reckoning with the Past,* ed. D. G. Hart (Grand Rapids: Baker, 1995), 88, 90.

16. C. C. Goen, "Jonathan Edwards: A New Departure in Eschatology," *Church History* 28.1 (1959): 26 (quote); Leonard I. Sweet, "Millennialism in America: Recent Studies," *Theological Studies* 40 (Sept. 1979): 513; Tuveson, *Redeemer Nation,* 99–101.

17. Fuller, *Naming the Antichrist,* 66–67; Goen, "Jonathan Edwards," 29; Patterson, "Changing Images of the Beast," 444; Perry Miller, *Errand into the Wilderness* (Cambridge, Mass.: Harvard University Press, 1964), 233.

18. St. Clair, *Millenarian Movements,* 270; Albanese, *America,* 425.

19. Hatch, "Origins of Civil Millennialism," 91–95; Robert G. Clouse, "The New Christian Right, America, and the Kingdom of God," *Christian Scholar's Review* 12 (1983): 5; Melvin B. Endy Jr., "Just War, Holy War, and Millennialism in Revolutionary America," *William and Mary Quarterly* 42 (Jan. 1985): 3–5.

20. Fuller, *Naming the Antichrist,* 68–70; Clouse, "New Christian Right," 5; Hatch, "Origins of Civil Millennialism," 98; Bloch, *Visionary Republic,* 46–48.

21. Clouse, "New Christian Right," 5–6; Hatch, "Origins of Civil Millennialism," 105.

22. Fuller, *Naming the Antichrist,* 71–72; Bloch, *Visionary Republic,* 79–86; Endy, "Just War, Holy War," 15–17; Harry S. Stout, "Preaching the Insurrection," *Christian His-*

tory 15.2 (1996): 14–15.

23. Beam, "Millennialism and American Nationalism," 185; Patterson, "Changing Images of the Beast," 445.

24. Boyer, *When Time Shall Be No More*, 72.

25. N. Gordon Thomas, "The Second Coming: A Major Impulse of American Protestantism," *Adventist Heritage* 3 (1976): 4; Brown, "Watchers for the Second Coming," 449.

26. Clouse, "New Christian Right," 6; Patterson, "Changing Images of the Beast," 445; Bloch, *Visionary Republic*, 103–4; Tuveson, *Redeemer Nation*, 125–31.

27. Clouse, "New Christian Right," 6–7; Fuller, *Naming the Antichrist*, 72–73; Dawn Glanz, "The American West as Millennial Kingdom," in *The Apocalyptic Vision in America*, ed. Lois Parkinson Zamora (Bowling Green, Ohio: Bowling Green University Popular Press, 1982), 141; Albanese, *America*, 426–27; Moorhead, "Erosion of Postmillennialism," 62–72; idem, "Between Progress and Apocalypse," 526–27; Tuveson, *Redeemer Nation*, 131, 162–63; Quandt, "Religion and Social Thought," 391–92.

28. Richard Kyle, *The Religious Fringe* (Downers Grove, Ill.: InterVarsity, 1993), 62, 72, 74.

29. Ibid., 74–75; Rosabeth M. Kanter, *Commitment and Community: Communes and Utopias in Sociological Perspective* (Cambridge, Mass.: Harvard University Press, 1972), 1–8; Alice Felt Tyler, *Freedom's Ferment* (New York: Harper and Row, 1944), 108–10.

30. Robert S. Ellwood Jr., *Alternative Altars* (Chicago: University of Chicago Press, 1979), 70; Tyler, *Freedom's Ferment*, 115–16; Kyle, *Religious Fringe*, 80; Ruth Tucker, *Another Gospel* (Grand Rapids: Zondervan, 1989), 42.

31. Sydney Ahlstrom, *A Religious History of the American People* (New Haven: Yale University Press, 1972), 495–96; Kyle, *Religious Fringe*, 80; Tyler, *Freedom's Ferment*, 115–16.

32. St. Clair, *Millenarian Movements*, 276; Kyle, *Religious Fringe*, 80–81; Catherine Keller, *Apocalypse Now and Then* (Boston: Beacon, 1996), 234–35.

33. Edward Deming Andrews, *The People Called Shakers* (New York: Dover, 1963); Henri Desroche, *The American Shakers: From Neo-Christianity to Presocialism* (Amherst:

University of Massachusetts Press, 1971); Marguerite Fellows Melcher, *The Shaker Adventure* (Cleveland: Western Reserve University Press, 1968); Stephen J. Stein, *The Shaker Experience in America* (New Haven: Yale University Press, 1992).

34. William M. Kephart, *Extraordinary Groups*, 2d ed. (New York: St. Martin's, 1982), 224; Ellwood, *Alternative Altars*, 74; Albanese, *America*, 155–56; Tyler, *Freedom's Ferment*, 146–47; Warren Lewis, "What to Do after the Messiah Has Come Again and Gone: Shaker 'Premillennial' Eschatology and Its Spiritual Aftereffects," in *The Coming Kingdom*, ed. M. Darrol Bryant and Donald W. Dayton (Barrytown, N.Y.: International Religious Foundation, 1983), 74.

35. St. Clair, *Millenarian Movements*, 292 (quote); Suzanne Youngerman, "Shaking Is No Foolish Play: An Anthropological Perspective on the American Shakers—Person, Time, Space, and Dance-Ritual," Ph.D. diss., Columbia University, 1983, 78.

36. Lewis, "What to Do," 74; Clarke Garrett, *Spirit Possession and Popular Religion: From the Camisards to the Shakers* (Baltimore: Johns Hopkins University Press, 1987), 164–65; Tyler, *Freedom's Ferment*, 146–47; J. F. C. Harrison, *The Second Coming: Popular Millenarianism, 1780–1850* (New Brunswick, N.J.: Rutgers University Press, 1979), 166; Lawrence Foster, "Had Prophecy Failed?" in *The Disappointed*, ed. Ronald L. Numbers and Jonathan M. Butler (Knoxville: University of Tennessee Press, 1993), 177.

37. Lawrence Foster, *Religion and Sexuality: The Shakers, the Mormons, and the Oneida Community* (Urbana: University of Illinois Press, 1984), 21–24; Yuri Rubinsky and Ian Wiseman, *A History of the End of the World* (New York: Morrow, 1982), 110.

38. Kephart, *Extraordinary Groups*, 224–25; Ellwood, *Alternative Altars*, 77–78; Tyler, *Freedom's Ferment*, 146–47.

39. Quoted in Harrison, *Second Coming*, 180.

40. See Klaus J. Hansen, *Mormonism and the American Experience* (Chicago: University of Chicago Press, 1981), 1–44; David Brion Davis, "The New England Origins of Mormonism," in *Mormonism and American Culture*, ed. Marvin S. Hill and James B. Allen (New York: Harper and Row, 1972), 13–28; Leonard J. Arrington and Davis Bitton, *The*

Mormon Experience (New York: Knopf, 1979); Jan Shipps, *Mormonism* (Urbana: University of Illinois Press, 1985).

41. Albanese, *America*, 141–42 (quote); Thomas F. O'Dea, *The Mormons* (Chicago: University of Chicago Press, 1957), 22–40; Robert Flanders, "To Transform History: Early Mormon Culture and the Concept of Time and Space," *Church History* 40.1 (1971): 111; Duane S. Crowther, *The Prophecies of Joseph Smith* (Bountiful, Utah: Horizon, 1983), 155–202; Bruce R. McConkie, *The Millennial Messiah* (Salt Lake City: Deseret, 1982), 182–205.

42. R. Laurence Moore, *Religious Outsiders and the Making of Americans* (New York: Oxford University Press, 1986), 44–46; Tuveson, *Redeemer Nation*, 179–86; Albanese, *America*, 143–44; Harrison, *Second Coming*, 176–92; Tyler, *Freedom's Ferment*, 95–96.

43. Tuveson, *Redeemer Nation*, 179–86; Albanese, *America*, 143–44. The ambivalence in Mormon millennialism has produced disagreement among scholars. See Grant Underwood, "Early Mormon Millenarianism: Another Look," *Church History* 54.1 (1985): 215–29; Timothy L. Smith, "The Book of Mormon in a Biblical Culture," *Journal of Mormon History* 7 (1980): 3–21; Klaus J. Hansen, *Quest for Empire: The Political Kingdom of God and the Council of Fifty* (East Lansing: Michigan State University Press, 1967); McConkie, *Millennial Messiah*, 282–96.

44. Grant Underwood, *The Millenarian World of Early Mormonism* (Urbana: University of Illinois Press, 1993), 8–9, 40–41.

45. Rubinsky and Wiseman, *End of the World*, 114 (quote); Underwood, *Millenarian World of Early Mormonism*, 32–33; Harry Benjamin Gray, "Eschatology of the Millennial Cults," Th.D. diss., Dallas Theological Seminary, 1956, 110–17; McConkie, *Millennial Messiah*, 399–405.

46. Leonard Bernstein, "The Ideas of John Humphrey Noyes, Perfectionist," *American Quarterly* 5 (March 1953): 157–65; Ernest R. Sandeen, "John Humphrey Noyes as the New Adam," *Church History* 40.1 (1971): 83–87; Kephart, *Extraordinary Groups*, 94–95; Ahlstrom, *Religious History of the American People*, 498–99; Foster, *Religion and Sexuality*, 16, 76–78, 90–93; Spencer Klaw, *Without Sin: The Life and Death of the Oneida Community* (New York: Penguin, 1993).

47. Michael Barkun, *Crucible of the Millennium* (Syracuse: Syracuse University Press, 1986), 64–65; idem, "The Wind Sweeping over the Country," in *The Disappointed*, ed. Numbers and Butler, 156–58; Kyle, *Religious Fringe*, 78–79.

48. St. Clair, *Millenarian Movements*, 285–87; Tyler, *Freedom's Ferment*, 121–28; Daniel Cohen, *Prophets of Doom* (Brookfield, Conn.: Millbrook, 1992), 21–22; K. J. R. Arndt, *George Rapp's Harmony Society, 1785–1847*, rev. ed. (Philadelphia: University of Pennsylvania Press, 1972).

49. St. Clair, *Millenarian Movements*, 291; Brown, "Watchers for the Second Coming," 453.

50. St. Clair, *Millenarian Movements*, 290–91; Tyler, *Freedom's Ferment*, 203–4.

51. Bryan R. Wilson, *Religious Sects* (New York: McGraw-Hill, 1970), 103, 107; Tucker, *Another Gospel*, 46; Charles H. Lippy, *The Christadelphians in North America* (Lewiston, N.Y.: Edwin Mellen, 1989).

52. Bryan R. Wilson, *Sects and Society* (Berkeley: University of California Press, 1961), 246–47; idem, *Religious Sects*, 103, 106–7; Richard Kyle, "Christadelphians," in *Encyclopedia U.S.A.*, ed. Archie P. McDonald (Gulf Breeze, Fla.: Academic International, 1989), 11:72; Lippy, *Christadelphians in North America*, 133, 135, 156, 299.

53. Daniel Cohen, *Waiting for the Apocalypse* (Buffalo: Prometheus, 1983), 13.

54. Quoted in J. Gordon Melton, *The Encyclopedia of American Religions*, 2 vols. (Wilmington, N.C.: McGrath, 1978), 1:460.

55. Sandeen, *Roots of Fundamentalism*, 50. See also Ronald L. Numbers and Jonathan M. Butler, eds., *The Disappointed*, xv.

56. Jonathan M. Butler, "From Millerism to Seventh-day Adventism: 'Boundlessness to Consolidation,'" *Church History* 55.1 (1986): 53–54; Numbers and Butler, eds., *The Disappointed*, xviii; James Moorhead, "Searching for the Millennium in America," *Princeton Seminary Bulletin* 8.2 (1987): 21.

57. Clouse, "New Christian Right," 8; Sandeen, *Roots of Fundamentalism*, 5–11.

58. Sandeen, *Roots of Fundamentalism*, 50–53; Barkun, *Crucible of the Millennium*, 36; Louis Billington, "The Millerite Adventists in Great Britain, 1840–1850," in *The Disappointed*, ed. Numbers and Butler, 59–70.

59. Barkun, *Crucible of the Millennium*, 50, 52; Eric Anderson, "The Millerite Use of Prophecy," in *The Disappointed*, ed. Numbers and Butler, 79–80.

60. Barkun, *Crucible of the Millennium*, 54–56, 107–17; Fuller, *Naming the Antichrist*, 104; Stephen D. O'Leary, *Arguing the Apocalypse* (New York: Oxford University Press, 1994), 93, 98. See also Whitney R. Cross, *The Burned-Over District* (New York: Harper, 1965); David L. Rowe, "A New Perspective on the Burned-Over District: The Millerites in Upstate New York," *Church History* 47.4 (1978): 409.

61. Ruth Alden Doan, "Millerism and Evangelical Culture," in *The Disappointed*, ed. Numbers and Butler, 122.

62. Butler, "From Millerism to Seventh-day Adventism," 53; Sandeen, *Roots of Fundamentalism*, 51–53; Doan, "Millerism and Evangelical Culture," 118–20; Moore, *Religious Outsiders*, 131. See also William G. McLoughlin, "Pietism and the American Character," *American Quarterly* 17.1 (1965): 163–86; Ruth Alden Doan, *The Miller Heresy, Millennialism, and American Culture* (Philadelphia: Temple University Press, 1987).

63. St. Clair, *Millenarian Movements*, 306; Barkun, *Crucible of the Millennium*, 35–36; Tyler, *Freedom's Ferment*, 70; Cohen, *Prophets of Doom*, 23; Rowe, "New Perspective," 411–12.

64. Harrison, *Second Coming*, 200–201; Anderson, "Millerite Use of Prophecy," 78–89; Sandeen, *Roots of Fundamentalism*, 59; Tyler, *Freedom's Ferment*, 71; David T. Arthur, "Millerism," in *The Rise of Adventism*, ed. Edwin Gaustad (New York: Harper and Row, 1974), 154.

65. O'Leary, *Arguing the Apocalypse*, 100; Sandeen, *Roots of Fundamentalism*, 53–58.

66. Harrison, *Second Coming*, 194; C. Marvin Pate and Calvin B. Haines Jr., *Doomsday Delusions* (Downers Grove, Ill.: InterVarsity, 1995), 93; Brown, "Watchers for the Second Coming," 453–54.

67. St. Clair, *Millenarian Movements*, 306; Anderson, "Millerite Use of Prophecy," 80; Pate and Haines, *Doomsday Delusions*, 93–94; Harrison, *Second Coming*, 194; Russell Chandler, *Doomsday* (Ann Arbor: Servant, 1993), 85.

68. Harrison, *Second Coming*, 194; Chandler, *Doomsday*, 85; St. Clair, *Millenarian Movements*, 306.

69. Barkun, *Crucible of the Millennium*, 36–37; Harrison, *Second Coming*, 192–93; St. Clair, *Millenarian Movements*, 308; Chandler, *Doomsday*, 85–86.

70. David T. Arthur, "Joshua V. Himes and the Cause of Adventism," in *The Disappointed*, ed. Numbers and Butler, 39–47; idem, "Millerism," 155–56; Barkun, *Crucible of the Millennium*, 38; Tyler, *Freedom's Ferment*, 72.

71. Moorhead, "Searching for the Millennium in America," 19; David L. Rowe, "Millerites: A Shadow Portrait," in *The Disappointed*, ed. Numbers and Butler, 4–5, 9; O'Leary, *Arguing the Apocalypse*, 131; Michael Barkun, *Disaster and the Millennium* (New Haven: Yale University Press, 1974), 11–33; St. Clair, *Millenarian Movements*, 311–12.

72. Doan, "Millerism and Evangelical Culture," 123; Pate and Haines, *Doomsday Delusions*, 95–96; Arthur, "Joshua V. Himes," 43.

73. Wayne R. Judd, "William Miller," in *The Disappointed*, ed. Numbers and Butler, 27; Fuller, *Naming the Antichrist*, 105; St. Clair, *Millenarian Movements*, 313–14; Tyler, *Freedom's Ferment*, 74–75; Butler, "From Millerism to Seventh-day Adventism," 57; Arthur, "Millerism," 162–63.

74. Quoted in Francis D. Nichol, *The Midnight Cry* (Washington, D.C.: Review and Herald, 1945), 171.

75. Cohen, *Waiting for the Apocalypse*, 28.

76. Le Roy E. Froom, *The Prophetic Faith of Our Fathers*, 4 vols. (Washington, D.C.: Review and Herald, 1946–54), 4:812; O'Leary, *Arguing the Apocalypse*, 106; Tyler, *Freedom's Ferment*, 76.

77. St. Clair, *Millenarian Movements*, 314; Cohen, *Waiting for the Apocalypse*, 28–29; Harrison, *Second Coming*, 194.

78. Harrison, *Second Coming*, 195; Chandler, *Doomsday*, 81–82; St. Clair, *Millenarian Movements*, 315.

79. Harrison, *Second Coming*, 195.

80. Lawrence Foster, "Had Prophecy Failed?" 175–84; Jonathan M. Butler, "The Making of a New Order," in *The Disappointed*, ed. Numbers and Butler, 189–205; St. Clair, *Millenarian Movements*, 317; Chandler, *Doomsday*, 88–89; Pate and Haines, *Doomsday Delusions*, 126–27.

81. Boyer, *When Time Shall Be No More*, 82.

82. Melton, *Encyclopedia of American Religions*, 1:481 (quote); Leon Festinger, Henry W. Riecken, and Stanley Schachter, *When Prophecy Fails* (New York: Harper and Row, 1964), 3–32.

83. Godfrey T. Anderson, "Sectarianism and Organization, 1846–1864," in *Adventism in America*, ed. Gary Land (Grand Rapids: Eerdmans, 1986), 47; Butler, "From Millerism to Seventh-day Adventism," 59.

84. Butler, "From Millerism to Seventh-day Adventism," 50, 59. See also Wilson, *Religious Sects*, 101.

85. Butler, "Making of a New Order," 200 (quote); Kenneth R. Samples, "From Controversy to Crisis," *Christian Research Journal* 11.1 (Summer 1988): 11; Gray, "Eschatology of the Millennial Cults," 156–57.

86. Butler, "Making of a New Order," 200 (quote); St. Clair, *Millenarian Movements*, 320; Samples, "From Controversy to Crisis," 11; Moore, *Religious Outsiders*, 133; Gray, "Eschatology of the Millennial Cults," 164–65.

87. P. Gerard Damsteegt, "Foundations of the Seventh-Day Adventist Message and Mission," *Missiology* 8.1 (1980): 75–76; Samples, "From Controversy to Crisis," 11; Roy Adams, *The Sanctuary Doctrine: Three Approaches in the Seventh-day Adventist Church* (Berrien Springs, Mich.: Andrews University Press, 1981); Gray, "Eschatology of the Millennial Cults," 173.

88. Douglas Morgan, "Adventism, Apocalyptic, and the Cause of Liberty," *Church History* 63.2 (1994): 237–39; Damsteegt, "Foundations of the Seventh-Day Adventist Message," 76–78; St. Clair, *Millenarian Movements*, 320–21; Albanese, *America*, 232; Anderson, "Sectarianism and Organization," 39–40.

89. Jonathan M. Butler, "Adventism and the American Experience," in *Rise of Adventism*, ed. Gaustad, 180–81; Damsteegt, "Foundations of the Seventh-Day Adventist Message," 75–77; Morgan, "Adventism, Apocalyptic, and the Cause of Liberty," 237–39; St. Clair, *Millenarian Movements*, 322; Albanese, *America*, 232; Wilson, *Religious Sects*, 102; E. G. White, *America in Prophecy* (Jemison, Ala.: Inspiration Books East, 1988).

90. Quoted in M. James Penton, "The Eschatology of Jehovah's Witnesses: A Short, Critical Analysis," in *The Coming Kingdom*, ed. Bryant and Dayton, 184.

91. M. James Penton, *Apocalypse Delayed: The Story of the Jehovah's Witnesses* (Toronto: University of Toronto Press, 1985), 7.

92. Chandler, *Doomsday*, 91, 96; Melvin D. Curry, *Jehovah's Witnesses: The Millenarian World of the Watch Tower* (New York: Garland, 1992), 5–8; Brown, "Watchers for the Second Coming," 455–56.

93. Joseph F. Zygmunt, "Prophetic Failure and Chiliastic Identity: The Case of Jehovah's Witnesses," *American Journal of Sociology* 75 (1970): 933–34; Gray, "Eschatology of the Millennial Cults," 193.

94. Melton, *Encyclopedia of American Religions*, 1:481–91; J. Gordon Melton, *Encyclopedic Handbook of Cults in America* (New York: Garland, 1986), 62–67; Kyle, *Religious Fringe*, 155–56; Moore, *Religious Outsiders*, 137.

95. Kyle, *Religious Fringe*, 156; Fuller, *Naming the Antichrist*, 152.

96. Tucker, *Another Gospel*, 123; Penton, "Eschatology of Jehovah's Witnesses," 175–79; idem, *Apocalypse Delayed*, 18–22; St. Clair, *Millenarian Movements*, 325; Edward H. Abrahams, "The Pain of the Millennium: Charles Taze Russell and the Jehovah's Witnesses, 1879–1916," *American Studies* 18 (Spring 1977): 57–71.

97. St. Clair, *Millenarian Movements*, 325; Chandler, *Doomsday*, 92; Gray, "Eschatology of the Millennial Cults," 206; Curry, *Jehovah's Witnesses*, 101–3.

98. Kyle, *Religious Fringe*, 156; Tucker, *Another Gospel*, 123; Chandler, *Doomsday*, 123; St. Clair, *Millenarian Movements*, 325; David A. Reed, "Whither the Watchtower? An Unfolding Crisis for Jehovah's Witnesses," *Christian Research Journal* 16.1 (Summer 1993): 26.

99. Tucker, *Another Gospel*, 124; Penton, "Eschatology of Jehovah's Witnesses," 178; idem, *Apocalypse Delayed*, 24–29; Reed, "Whither the Watchtower?" 26.

100. St. Clair, *Millenarian Movements*, 326; Chandler, *Doomsday*, 93.

101. Chandler, *Doomsday*, 93–94; Moore, *Religious Outsiders*, 137; Timothy White, *A People for His Name* (New York: Vantage, 1967), 95–96.

102. Raymond Franz, *Crisis of Con-

science: The Struggle between Loyalty to God and Loyalty to One's Religion (Atlanta: Commentary, 1983), 343–44 (quote); Gray, "Eschatology of the Millennial Cults," 218; Curry, *Jehovah's Witnesses*, 108–12; White, *A People for His Name*, 86–88.

103. St. Clair, *Millenarian Movements*, 328 (quote); Chandler, *Doomsday*, 95; Penton, "Eschatology of Jehovah's Witnesses," 180; Curry, *Jehovah's Witnesses*, 113–14; Wilson, *Religious Sects*, 112–13; Charles S. Braden, *These Also Believe* (New York: Macmillan, 1957), 374–75.

104. St. Clair, *Millenarian Movements*, 328–29; Chandler, *Doomsday*, 95; Curry, *Jehovah's Witnesses*, 113–15; Penton, *Apocalypse Delayed*, 44–46.

105. Melvin D. Curry Jr., "Jehovah's Witnesses: The Effects of Millenarianism on the Maintenance of a Religious Sect," Ph.D. diss., Florida State University, 1980, 243.

106. Chandler, *Doomsday*, 96; Penton, "Eschatology of Jehovah's Witnesses," 182; idem, *Apocalypse Delayed*, 48–56; White, *A People for His Name*, 221–25.

107. Zygmunt, "Prophetic Failure and Chiliastic Identity," 936–37; Chandler, *Doomsday*, 96; Reed, "Whither the Watchtower?" 28; Penton, "Eschatology of Jehovah's Witnesses," 182; Gray, "Eschatology of the Millennial Cults," 225–26; Curry, *Jehovah's Witnesses*, 115–18; White, *A People for His Name*, 251–58.

108. Penton, *Apocalypse Delayed*, 58 (quote); Tucker, *Another Gospel*, 125–28; Kyle, *Religious Fringe*, 157.

109. Chandler, *Doomsday*, 97–98; St. Clair, *Millenarian Movements*, 329; Penton, "Eschatology of Jehovah's Witnesses," 183; idem, *Apocalypse Delayed*, 99–101; Curry, *Jehovah's Witnesses*, 119–20; Rick Townsend, "When Christians Meet Jehovah's Witnesses," *Christian Herald*, April 1988, 38; Kenneth L. Woodward, "Are They False Witnesses?" *Newsweek*, 20 July 1981, 75; W. C. Stevenson, *Year of Doom, 1975* (London: Hutchinson, 1967).

110. Tucker, *Another Gospel*, 140; Chandler, *Doomsday*, 98; Curry, *Jehovah's Witnesses*, 124–26; Penton, *Apocalypse Delayed*, 99–101; Kenneth L. Woodward, "Apocalypse Later," *Newsweek*, 18 December 1995, 59; "Sect Postpones Armageddon," *Christianity Today*, 5 February 1996, 106.

111. Charles H. Lippy, "Waiting for the End: The Social Context of American Religion," in *Apocalyptic Vision in America*, ed. Zamora, 50–51; Keller, *Apocalypse Now and Then*, 200–201.

112. Lippy, "Waiting for the End," 50; Rubinsky and Wiseman, *End of the World*, 103–7.

113. Michael Harner, *The Way of the Shaman* (San Francisco: Harper, 1990), 54; Rubinsky and Wiseman, *End of the World*, 103–5.

114. Thomas W. Overholt, *Channels of Prophecy* (Minneapolis: Fortress, 1989), 27; Lippy, "Waiting for the End," 49.

115. Overholt, *Channels of Prophecy*, 27–28 (quote); idem, "The Ghost Dance of 1890 and the Nature of the Prophetic Process," *Ethnohistory* 21 (1974): 37–63; Barkun, *Disaster and the Millennium*, 15; J. Mooney, "The Ghost-Dance Religion and the Sioux Outbreak of 1890," *Annual Report of the Bureau of American Ethnology* 14 (Washington, D.C.: Government Printing Office, 1896); William Willoya and Vinson Brown, *Warriors of the Rainbow* (Happy Camp, Calif.: Naturegraph, 1962), 61–64.

116. Overholt, *Channels of Prophecy*, 28; Albanese, *America*, 44.

117. Lippy, "Waiting for the End," 50; Overholt, *Channels of Prophecy*, 28; Chandler, *Doomsday*, 194–96.

118. Lippy, "Waiting for the End," 37–39.

Chapter 6. Rapture Fever

1. Michael Barkun, "The Language of Apocalypse: Premillennialists and Nuclear War," in *The God Pumpers*, ed. Marshall W. Fishwick and Ray B. Browne (Bowling Green, Ohio: Bowling Green State University Popular Press, 1987), 159 (quote); Robert Jewett, "Coming to Terms with the Doom Boom," *Quarterly Review* 4.3 (Fall 1984): 18.

2. Alvin P. Sanoff, "The Faces of Doomsday," *U.S. News and World Report*, 19 October 1992, 73; Paul Boyer, "A Brief History of the End of Time," *New Republic*, 17 May 1993, 30–33; Jeffery L. Sheler, "The Christmas Covenant," *U.S. News and World Report*, 19 December 1994, 62.

3. George Marsden, *Fundamentalism and American Culture* (New York: Oxford University Press, 1980), 44.

4. George Marsden, "Fundamentalism," in *Eerdmans' Handbook to Christianity in America*, ed. Mark Noll et al. (Grand Rapids: Eerdmans, 1983), 384.

5. Ernest R. Sandeen, "Towards a Historical Interpretation of the Origins of Fundamentalism," *Church History* 36.1 (1967): 82; idem, "Fundamentalism and American Identity," *Annals of the American Academy of Political and Social Science* 387 (Jan. 1970): 57–58; George Marsden, "Fundamentalism as an American Phenomenon: A Comparison with English Evangelicalism," *Church History* 46.2 (1977): 225–26; idem, *Fundamentalism and American Culture*, 5, 224.

6. Timothy P. Weber, "Happily at the Edge of the Abyss: Popular Premillennialism in America," *Ex Auditu* 6 (1991): 87.

7. This general information can be found in a number of contemporary dispensational sources: Hal Lindsey, *The Late Great Planet Earth* (Grand Rapids: Zondervan, 1970); John F. Walvoord, *Armageddon, Oil and the Middle East Crisis*, rev. ed. (Grand Rapids: Zondervan, 1990); Jimmy Swaggart, *Armageddon: The Future of Planet Earth* (Baton Rouge: Jimmy Swaggart Ministries, 1987); Billy Graham, *Approaching Hoofbeats* (New York: Avon, 1983). Aspects of our summary were taken from Russell Chandler, *Doomsday* (Ann Arbor: Servant, 1993), 228–30.

8. James H. Moorhead, "The Erosion of Postmillennialism in American Religious Thought, 1865–1925," *Church History* 53.1 (1984): 61.

9. Ibid., 63–75; Robert G. Clouse, "The New Christian Right, America, and the Kingdom of God," *Christian Scholar's Review* 12 (1983): 6–8.

10. Timothy P. Weber, *Living in the Shadow of the Second Coming* (New York: Oxford University Press, 1979), 41–42.

11. Douglas W. Frank, *Less than Conquerors* (Grand Rapids: Eerdmans, 1986), 68–69.

12. Ernest R. Sandeen, *The Roots of Fundamentalism* (Chicago: University of Chicago Press, 1970), 54, 59; Stanley D. Walters, "The World Will End in 1919," *Asbury Theological Journal* 44.1 (1989): 29–37.

13. Weber, *Living in the Shadow*, 16–17; Sandeen, *Roots of Fundamentalism*, 62–64. See also George E. Ladd, *The Blessed Hope* (Grand Rapids: Eerdmans, 1956), 35–40.

14. Chandler, *Doomsday*, 103; Sandeen, *Roots of Fundamentalism*, 64.

15. Weber, *Living in the Shadow*, 46–48.

16. Weber, "Happily at the Edge of the Abyss," 89; idem, *Living in the Shadow*, 19; *Scofield Reference Bible* (New York: Oxford University Press, 1909), 914–15. See also Alva McClain, *Daniel's Prophecy of the Seventy Weeks* (Grand Rapids: Zondervan, 1940), 12–15.

17. Martin Marty, *Modern American Religion: The Irony of It All, 1893–1919* (Chicago: University of Chicago Press, 1986), 224; Daniel P. Fuller, "The Hermeneutics of Dispensationalism," Th.D. diss., Northern Baptist Seminary, 1957, 287–337; Weber, *Living in the Shadow*, 19–20.

18. Weber, *Living in the Shadow*, 19–20 (quote); Clarence B. Bass, *Backgrounds to Dispensationalism* (Grand Rapids: Eerdmans, 1960), 129–31.

19. Sandeen, *Roots of Fundamentalism*, 62–64; Bass, *Backgrounds to Dispensationalism*, 38–39.

20. J. Gordon Melton, *The Encyclopedia of American Religions*, 2 vols. (Wilmington, N.C.: McGrath, 1978), 1:415–16.

21. Jon R. Stone, *A Guide to the End of the World: Popular Eschatology in America* (New York: Garland, 1993), 34; Sandeen, *Roots of Fundamentalism*, 74–76.

22. Paul Boyer, *When Time Shall Be No More* (Cambridge, Mass.: Harvard University Press, 1992), 90–91.

23. Sir Robert Anderson, *The Coming Prince* (Grand Rapids: Kregel, 1986 reprint), 3, 124, 131; McClain, *Daniel's Prophecy of the Seventy Weeks*.

24. Stanley N. Gundry, *Love Them In: The Proclamation Theology of D. L. Moody* (Chicago: Moody, 1976), 179–89; James F. Findlay Jr., *Dwight L. Moody: American Evangelist, 1837–1899* (Grand Rapids: Baker, 1973), 125–28, 260–61.

25. Weber, *Living in the Shadow*, 32–33; Chandler, *Doomsday*, 104, 106; Gundry, *Love Them In*, 180–81; Marsden, *Fundamentalism and American Culture*, 46–47; Roger Martin, *R. A. Torrey* (Murfreesboro, Tenn.: Sword of the Lord, 1976), 88–100.

26. Boyer, *When Time Shall Be No More*, 92; Weber, *Living in the Shadow*, 33–34; William V. Trollinger Jr., *God's Empire: William Bell Riley and Midwestern Funda-*

mentalism (Madison: University of Wisconsin Press, 1990), 84; Marsden, *Fundamentalism and American Culture*, 32–39; James Davidson Hunter, *American Evangelicalism* (New Brunswick, N.J.: Rutgers University Press, 1983), 27; David A. Rausch, "Arno C. Gaebelein (1861–1945): Fundamentalist Protestant Zionist," *American Jewish History* 68 (Sept. 1978): 44–55.

27. Sandeen, *Roots of Fundamentalism*, 132–43; C. Norman Kraus, *Dispensationalism in America: Its Rise and Development* (Chicago: Moody, 1965), 71–80; Weber, *Living in the Shadow*, 26–28; Stone, *Guide to the End of the World*, 47–48; Frank, *Less than Conquerors*, 69, 75.

28. See William R. Hutchison, *The Modernist Impulse in American Protestantism* (Durham, N.C.: Duke University Press, 1992), 76–110; Kenneth Cauthen, *The Impact of American Religious Liberalism* (New York: Harper and Row, 1962), 209–20.

29. Marsden, *Fundamentalism and American Culture*, 118–23; C. Allyn Russell, *Voices of American Fundamentalism* (Philadelphia: Westminster, 1976), 18–19; Sandeen, *Roots of Fundamentalism*, 188–207. See also Louis Gasper, *The Fundamentalist Movement* (The Hague: Mouton, 1968); S. G. Cole, *The History of Fundamentalism* (New York: R. R. Smith, 1931).

30. Weber, *Living in the Shadow*, 27–42; Marsden, *Fundamentalism and American Culture*, 124–25; Sandeen, *Roots of Fundamentalism*, 162–64; Frank, *Less than Conquerors*, 92–93; "Our Future Hope: Eschatology and Its Role in the Church," *Christianity Today*, 6 February 1987, 6–1.

31. James Barr, *Fundamentalism* (Philadelphia: Westminster, 1977), 45. See also Marty, *Modern American Religion*, 219–20; Robert C. Fuller, *Naming the Antichrist* (New York: Oxford University Press, 1995), 125–26.

32. For more on Scofield's life see J. M. Canfield, *The Incredible Scofield and His Book* (Vallecito, Calif.: Ross House, 1988); Charles G. Trumbull, *The Life Story of C. I. Scofield* (New York: Oxford University Press, 1920); William A. BeVier, "C. I. Scofield: Dedicated and Determined," *Fundamentalist Journal* 2.9 (Oct. 1983): 37–39, 56.

33. C. I. Scofield, *Rightly Dividing the Word of Truth* (Neptune, N.J.: Loizeaux, n.d.);

BeVier, "C. I. Scofield," 39; John D. Hannah, "Cyrus Ingerson Scofield," in *Dictionary of Christianity in America*, ed. Daniel G. Reid et al. (Downers Grove, Ill.: InterVarsity, 1990), 1057–58.

34. Melton, *Encyclopedia of American Religions*, 1:416–17; Boyer, *When Time Shall Be No More*, 97–98; C. W. Whiteman, "Scofield Reference Bible," in *Dictionary of Christianity in America*, ed. Reid et al., 1058; Fuller, *Naming the Antichrist*, 125.

35. Sandeen, *Roots of Fundamentalism*, 222; Boyer, *When Time Shall Be No More*, 98; Chandler, *Doomsday*, 106.

36. Sandeen, *Roots of Fundamentalism*, 222 (quote); Stanley J. Grenz, *The Millennial Maze* (Downers Grove, Ill.: InterVarsity, 1992), 93.

37. *Scofield Reference Bible*, 5. See also Kraus, *Dispensationalism in America*, 114.

38. Marty, *Modern American Religion*, 220–21; C. I. Scofield, *What Do the Prophets Say?* (Philadelphia: Sunday School Times, 1918), 161; Boyer, *When Time Shall Be No More*, 98–99; Fuller, *Naming the Antichrist*, 128–29.

39. Reuben A. Torrey, *The Return of the Lord Jesus* (Los Angeles: Bible Institute of Los Angeles, 1913), 89.

40. Weber, *Living in the Shadow*, 105.

41. Boyer, *When Time Shall Be No More*, 102; Sandeen, *Roots of Fundamentalism*, 224–26.

42. Joel Carpenter, "A Shelter in the Time of Storm: Fundamentalist Institutions and the Rise of Evangelical Protestantism, 1929–1942," *Church History* 49.1 (1980): 62–75; Weber, "Happily at the Edge of the Abyss," 90; Marsden, *Fundamentalism and American Culture*, 192–95; Sandeen, *Roots of Fundamentalism*, 219–22.

43. Dwight Wilson, *Armageddon Now! The Premillenarian Response to Russia and Israel since 1917* (Grand Rapids: Baker, 1977), 37–39; Boyer, *When Time Shall Be No More*, 100–101; Weber, *Living in the Shadow*, 105–6, 115; Sandeen, *Roots of Fundamentalism*, 233. For a description of the early events of World War I, see Barbara Tuchman, *The Guns of August* (New York: Dell, 1962).

44. Weber, *Living in the Shadow*, 105–6.

45. Wilson, *Armageddon Now!* 36–38; *Weekly Evangel*, 10 April 1917, 3; C. I. Scofield, "The War in the Light of Prophecy," *Weekly*

Evangel, 28 October 1916, 6–7.

46. See Clarence Larkin, *Dispensational Truth*, 11th ed. (Philadelphia: Clarence Larkin, 1918), 86–96; Weber, *Living in the Shadow*, 130–31; Charles C. Ryrie, *Dispensationalism Today* (Chicago: Moody, 1965), 159–61.

47. William E. Blackstone, *Jesus Is Coming* (New York: Revell, 1908), 165, 171–72; William B. Riley, *The Evolution of the Kingdom* (New York: Charles C. Cook, 1913), 48; Weber, *Living in the Shadow*, 131; I. M. Haldeman, *The Coming of Christ* (New York: Charles C. Cook, 1906), 205.

48. David A. Rausch, "Zionism" and "Zionism, Christian," in *Evangelical Dictionary of Theology*, ed. Walter A. Elwell (Grand Rapids: Baker, 1984), 1200–1202; idem, *Zionism within Early American Fundamentalism, 1878–1919* (Lewiston, N.Y.: Edwin Mellen, 1980); F. B. Nelson, "Zionism and American Christianity," in *Dictionary of Christianity in America*, ed. Reid et al., 1303–4; Ruth Mouly and Roland Robertson, "Zionism in American Premillenarian Fundamentalism," *American Journal of Theology and Philosophy* 4.3 (1983): 98–102. See also Yona Malachy, *American Fundamentalism and Israel* (Jerusalem: Hebrew University, 1978); L. J. Epstein, *Zion's Call: Christian Contributions to the Origins and Development of Israel* (Lanham, Md.: University Press of America, 1984).

49. Quoted in Wilson, *Armageddon Now!* 42. See also David Bebbington, "The Advent Hope in British Evangelicalism since 1800," *Scottish Journal of Religious Studies* 9.2 (Autumn 1988): 107–8; T. DeCourcy Rayner, "Hidden Hands in Palestine," *Moody Monthly* 48.4 (Dec. 1947): 282.

50. *Weekly Evangel*, 19 May 1917, 17; Wilson, *Armageddon Now!* 37–46, 67; Charles G. Trumbull, *Prophecy's Light on Today* (New York: Revell, 1937), 67; Larkin, *Dispensational Truth*, 63–64.

51. Wilson, *Armageddon Now!* 48–50; Boyer, *When Time Shall Be No More*, 102; James M. Gray, *A Text-Book on Prophecy* (New York: Revell, 1918), 192; James Alan Patterson, "Changing Images of the Beast: Apocalyptic Conspiracy Theories in American History," *Journal of the Evangelical Theological Society* 32 (Dec. 1988): 449–50.

52. *Scofield Reference Bible*, 1341–42.

53. Weber, *Living in the Shadow*, 108.

54. Wilson, *Armageddon Now!* 50–54; Weber, *Living in the Shadow*, 112.

55. Stone, *Guide to the End of the World*, 93.

56. Wilson, *Armageddon Now!* 67–68; Boyer, *When Time Shall Be No More*, 104–5; Weber, *Living in the Shadow*, 160–61.

57. Stone, *Guide to the End of the World*, 93–94; Wilson, *Armageddon Now!* 77–81; Boyer, *When Time Shall Be No More*, 107; Sandeen, *Roots of Fundamentalism*, 239–69; Marsden, *Fundamentalism and American Culture*, 153–59; Louis S. Bauman, "The Blue Eagle and Our Day as Christians," *Sunday School Times*, 16 September 1933, 583–84; Fuller, *Naming the Antichrist*, 148–60.

58. Stone, *Guide to the End of the World*, 93–94; Boyer, *When Time Shall Be No More*, 108; Wilson, *Armageddon Now!* 82–85.

59. Wilson, *Armageddon Now!* 81 (quote); Fuller, *Naming the Antichrist*, 148–60; Stone, *Guide to the End of the World*, 93–94.

60. Timothy P. Weber, *Living in the Shadow of the Second Coming*, rev. ed. (Chicago: University of Chicago Press, 1987), 178–81; Boyer, *When Time Shall Be No More*, 108; Wilson, *Armageddon Now!* 82–83. See also Oswald J. Smith, *Is the Antichrist at Hand?* 5th ed. (Toronto: Tabernacle, 1926); Arno C. Gaebelein, *As It Was—So Shall It Be* (New York: Our Hope, 1937); J. M. Ritchie, *Prophetic Highlights* (New York: Revell, 1935).

61. Robert G. Clouse, "The Danger of Mistaken Hopes," in *Dreams, Visions and Oracles*, ed. Carl E. Armerding and W. Ward Gasque (Grand Rapids: Baker, 1977), 33–35; Boyer, *When Time Shall Be No More*, 108; D. Brent Sandy, "Did Daniel See Mussolini?" *Christianity Today*, 8 February 1993, 34; Leonard Sale-Harrison, *The Resurrection of the Old Roman Empire* (London: Leonard Sale-Harrison, 1939).

62. Wilson, *Armageddon Now!* 114–17; Boyer, *When Time Shall Be No More*, 109; Arthur I. Brown, *The Eleventh "Hour"* (Findlay, Ohio: Fundamental Truth, 1940), 77; Louis S. Bauman, "Russia and Armageddon," *King's Business*, 29 September 1938, 286.

63. H. A. Ironside, "The Kings of the East," *King's Business*, 29 January 1938, 9; Wilson, *Armageddon Now!* 118–19; Boyer, *When Time Shall Be No More*, 109; Louis T. Talbot, "The Army of Two Hundred Million," *King's Business*, 23 October 1932, 424.

64. Boyer, *When Time Shall Be No More*, 108.

65. Wilson, *Armageddon Now!* 146 (quote); Sandy, "Did Daniel See Mussolini?" 34; Weber, *Living in the Shadow*, rev. ed., 183.

Chapter 7. Rapture Fever

1. Timothy P. Weber, "Happily at the Edge of the Abyss: Popular Premillennialism in America," *Ex Auditu* 6 (1991): 90; Joel Carpenter, "Fundamentalist Institutions and the Rise of Evangelical Protestantism, 1929–1942," *Church History* 49.1 (1980): 63–75.

2. Joe Maxwell, "Prophecy Books Become Big Sellers," *Christianity Today*, 11 March 1991, 60; Timothy P. Weber, *Living in the Shadow of the Second Coming*, rev. ed. (Chicago: University of Chicago Press, 1987), 211; idem, "Happily at the Edge of the Abyss," 92.

3. Michael Barkun, "The Language of Apocalypse: Premillennialists and Nuclear War," in *The God Pumpers*, ed. Marshall W. Fishwick and Ray B. Browne (Bowling Green, Ohio: Bowling Green State University Popular Press, 1987), 159; Weber, "Happily at the Edge of the Abyss," 92; Jeffery L. Sheler, "The Christmas Covenant," *U.S. News and World Report*, 19 December 1994, 62; Erik Davis, "Spiritual Warfare: Televangelists Stay Tuned for the End," *Village Voice*, 19 February 1991, 49–50.

4. Robert Jewett, "Coming to Terms with the Doom Boom," *Quarterly Review* 4.3 (Fall 1984): 9; G. Clark Chapman Jr., "Falling in Rapture before the Bomb," *Reformed Journal* 37 (June 1987): 13; Weber, "Happily at the Edge of the Abyss," 93–94; David Douglas, "God, the World and James Watt," *Christianity and Crisis*, 5 October 1981, 258, 269–70; Ronnie Dugger, "Does Reagan Expect a Nuclear Armageddon?" *Washington Post*, 8 April 1984, pp. C1, C4.

5. Barkun, "Language of Apocalypse," 159; Weber, "Happily at the Edge of the Abyss," 92–93; Maxwell, "Prophecy Books Become Big Sellers," 60.

6. Richard Kyle, *The Religious Fringe* (Downers Grove, Ill.: InterVarsity, 1993), 258–63; Terry Tremaine, "Global Fortune-Telling and Bible Prophecy," *Skeptical Inquirer*, Winter 1994, 166–69.

7. Darrell L. Bock, "Charting Dispensationalism," *Christianity Today*, 12 September 1994, 26–29.

8. Ibid., 27–28. For examples of revised dispensationalism see J. Dwight Pentecost, *Things to Come* (Grand Rapids: Zondervan, 1958); Charles C. Ryrie, *Dispensationalism Today* (Chicago: Moody, 1965); John F. Walvoord, *Armageddon, Oil and the Middle East Crisis*, rev. ed. (Grand Rapids: Zondervan, 1990).

9. Sheler, "Christmas Covenant," 70; Bock, "Charting Dispensationalism," 28–29; Stanley J. Grenz, *The Millennial Maze* (Downers Grove, Ill.: InterVarsity, 1992), 94; C. Marvin Pate and Calvin B. Haines Jr., *Doomsday Delusions* (Downers Grove, Ill.: InterVarsity, 1995). See also Craig A. Blaising and Darrell L. Bock, *Progressive Dispensationalism* (Wheaton, Ill.: Victor/Bridgepoint, 1993); Robert L. Saucy, *The Case for Progressive Dispensationalism* (Grand Rapids: Zondervan, 1993).

10. Daniel Cohen, *Waiting for the Apocalypse* (Buffalo: Prometheus, 1983), back cover.

11. Weber, *Living in the Shadow*, 238–39. See also John D. Hannah, "Dallas Theological Seminary," in *Dictionary of Christianity in America*, ed. Daniel G. Reid et al. (Downers Grove, Ill.: InterVarsity, 1990), 338.

12. Russell Chandler, *Doomsday* (Ann Arbor: Servant, 1993), 253.

13. Walvoord, *Armageddon, Oil and the Middle East Crisis*, 17–30.

14. Billy Graham, *Approaching Hoofbeats* (New York: Avon, 1983). See also idem, *World Aflame* (Garden City, N.Y.: Doubleday, 1965).

15. See Pat Robertson, *Perspective* (newsletter), February-March 1980, 5; idem, *The New World Order* (Dallas: Word, 1991); idem, *The New Millennium* (Dallas: Word, 1990); Mark G. Toulouse, "Pat Robertson: Apocalyptic Theology and American Foreign Policy," *Journal of Church and State* 31.1 (Winter 1989): 73–99; Stephen D. O'Leary and Michael McFarland, "The Political Use of Mythic Discourse: Prophetic Interpretation in Pat Robertson's Presidential Campaign," *Quarterly Journal of Speech* 75.4 (Nov. 1989): 431–52; Andrew G. Lang, "Armageddon: The Religious Doctrine of Survivable Nuclear War," *Japanese Christian Quarterly* 5 (Spring 1987): 106.

16. Jérry Falwell, "The Twenty-first Century and the End of the World," *Fundamentalist Journal* 7.5 (May 1988): 10–11; idem, *Nuclear War and the Second Coming of Jesus Christ* (Lynchburg, Va.: Old Time Gospel Hour, 1983).

17. Chandler, *Doomsday*, 248–49. See Hal Lindsey, *The Late Great Planet Earth* (Grand Rapids: Zondervan, 1970); idem, *The Road to Holocaust* (New York: Bantam, 1989); idem, *The 1980s: Countdown to Armageddon* (New York: Bantam, 1981); idem, *There's a New World Coming* (New York: Bantam, 1973); idem, *Planet Earth—2000 A.D.* (Palos Verdes Estates, Calif.: Western Front, 1994); Chapman, "Falling in Rapture before the Bomb," 12.

18. Lindsey, *Late Great Planet Earth*, 53–58.

19. Ibid., 54.

20. Chandler, *Doomsday*, 251; Roy Rivenburg, "Is the End Still Near?" *Los Angeles Times*, 30 July 1992, pp. E-1, E-2; Russell Chandler and John Dart, "Visions of Apocalypse Rise Again: Prophets of Doom Link Bible Predictions to Current Events," *Los Angeles Times*, 26 July 1976, p. A-14; Jewett, "Coming to Terms with the Doom Boom," 17; Lindsey, *Planet Earth—2000 A.D.*, 3, 6.

21. Tim LaHaye, *Rapture under Attack: Can We Still Trust the Pre-Trib Rapture?* (Sisters, Ore.: Multnomah, 1992). See also idem, *No Fear of the Storm* (Sisters, Ore.: Multnomah, 1992); idem, *The Beginning of the End* (Wheaton, Ill.: Tyndale, 1972).

22. Grant R. Jeffrey, *Armageddon: Appointment with Destiny* (Toronto: Frontier Research, 1988), 193.

23. Chuck Smith, *Future Survival* (Costa Mesa, Calif.: Calvary Chapel, 1978), 20; idem, *The Last Days, the Middle East, and the Book of Revelation* (Tarrytown, N.Y.: Chosen, 1991); William A. Alnor, *Soothsayers of the Second Advent* (Old Tappan, N.J.: Revell, 1989), 41–42.

24. *Has Russia Really Changed? America's Next President—and World War III?* (Troy, Mich.: Jack Van Impe Ministries International, 1992); Ed Hindson, "The End Is Near . . . or Is It?" *World*, 24 November 1990, 12; Gary DeMar, *Last Days Madness* (Brentwood, Tenn.: Wolgemuth and Hyatt, 1991), 38; Kenneth L. Woodward, "The Final Days Are Here Again," *Newsweek*, 18 March 1991, 55; Jack Van Impe, *2001: On the Edge of Eternity* (Dallas: Word, 1996).

25. Salem Kirban, *Countdown to Rapture* (Irvine, Calif.: Harvest House, 1977), 33; Tom Gorman, "San Diego Prepares Tactics to Battle Killer Bee Swarms," *Los Angeles Times*, 10 September 1992, pp. A-1, A-19; Chandler, *Doomsday*, 255. See also Salem Kirban, *666* (Wheaton, Ill.: Tyndale, 1970); idem, *Guide to Survival* (Chattanooga: AMG, 1990).

26. John Hagee, *Beginning of the End* (Nashville: Nelson, 1996), 4. See also H. Wayne House, "A Summary Critique: *Beginning of the End*," in *Christian Research Journal* 19.3 (1997): 50.

27. Mary Stewart Relfe, *Economic Advisor* (newsletter), 28 February 1983; Alnor, *Soothsayers of the Second Advent*, 35; Weber, *Living in the Shadow*, 225.

28. Edgar C. Whisenant, *88 Reasons Why the Rapture Will Be in 1988*, rev. ed. (Nashville: World Bible Society, 1988), 3, 36, 56; idem, *On Borrowed Time* (Nashville: World Bible Society, 1988), 48; idem, *The Final Shout: Rapture Report* (Nashville: World Bible Society, 1989), 24; Paul Boyer, *When Time Shall Be No More* (Cambridge, Mass.: Harvard University Press, 1992), 130; Alnor, *Soothsayers of the Second Advent*, 35–36; Dean C. Halverson, "88 Reasons: What Went Wrong," *Christian Research Journal* 11.2 (Fall 1988): 15–16.

29. Charles R. Taylor, *Get All Excited—Jesus Is Coming Soon* (Redondo Beach, Calif.: Today in Bible Prophecy, 1975), introduction, 89, 93; idem, *Those Who Remain* (Orange, Calif.: Today in Bible Prophecy, 1980), 70–71; Alnor, *Soothsayers of the Second Advent*, 134–35.

30. Harold Camping, *1994?* (New York: Vantage, 1992); Joe Maxwell, "End-times Prediction Draws Strong Following," *Christianity Today*, 20 June 1994, 46–47; idem, "Camping Misses End-times Deadline," *Christianity Today*, 24 October 1994, 84; Perucci Ferraiuolo, "Could '1994' Be the End of Family Radio?" *Christian Research Journal* 16.1 (Summer 1993): 5–6.

31. Boyer, *When Time Shall Be No More*, 304–5.

32. Ibid., 305, 310–11. For a broader view of anti-intellectualism in evangelical circles see Mark A. Noll, *The Scandal of the Evangelical Mind* (Grand Rapids: Eerdmans, 1994); idem, "The Scandal of the Evangelical Mind," *Christianity Today*, 25 October 1993,

29–32; Os Guinness, *Fit Bodies, Fat Minds: Why Evangelicals Don't Think and What to Do about It* (Grand Rapids: Baker, 1994).

33. Lindsey, *Planet Earth—2000 A.D.* See also John M. Werly, "Premillennialism and the Paranoid Style," *American Studies* 18 (Spring 1977): 39–55.

34. Falwell, "Twenty-first Century," 10. See also Lang, "Armageddon," 107.

35. Wilbur M. Smith, *This Atomic Age and the Word of God* (Boston: Wilde, 1948), 45, 52; Boyer, *When Time Shall Be No More,* 115–16. See also Paul Boyer, *By the Bomb's Early Light* (New York: Pantheon, 1985).

36. Merrill F. Unger, *Beyond the Crystal Ball* (Chicago: Moody, 1973), 113, 115; LaHaye, *Beginning of the End,* 9; Jack Van Impe, *Signs of the Times* (Royal Oak, Mich.: Jack Van Impe Ministries, 1979), 66; Boyer, *When Time Shall Be No More,* 131; Harold Lindsell, *The Armageddon Spectre* (Westchester, Ill.: Crossway, 1984), 16, 18; G. Clarke Chapman Jr., "American Theology in the Shadow of the Bomb," *Union Seminary Quarterly Review* 41.3–4 (1987): 25–38.

37. Kirban, *666,* 136. See also Boyer, *When Time Shall Be No More,* 132; Richard W. De Haan, *Israel and the Nations in Prophecy* (Grand Rapids: Zondervan, 1968), 140–41.

38. Lindsey, *Late Great Planet Earth,* 146–68; Boyer, *When Time Shall Be No More,* 133; S. Maxwell Coder, *The Final Chapter* (Wheaton, Ill.: Tyndale, 1984), 97.

39. Falwell, *Nuclear War and the Second Coming of Jesus Christ;* idem, "Twenty-first Century," 11; Boyer, *When Time Shall Be No More,* 137; Barkun, "Language of Apocalypse," 160.

40. Robertson, *Perspective,* 5; Toulouse, "Pat Robertson," 73–99; Boyer, *When Time Shall Be No More,* 138–40; Danny Collum, "Armageddon Theology as a Threat to Peace," *Faith and Mission* 4.1 (1986): 63–64; David Edwin Harrell Jr., *Pat Robertson: A Personal, Religious, and Political Portrait* (San Francisco: Harper and Row, 1987); Graham, *World Aflame,* 246–52; idem, *Approaching Hoofbeats,* 127–59.

41. Charles B. Strozier, *Apocalypse: On the Psychology of Fundamentalism in America* (Boston: Beacon, 1994); Stephen D. O'Leary, *Arguing the Apocalypse* (New York: Oxford University Press, 1994), 141; Michael R. Cosby, "The Danger of Armageddon Theol-ogy," *Covenant Quarterly* 51.3 (1993): 40–41; Chapman, "Falling in Rapture before the Bomb," 11.

42. Louis T. Talbot and William W. Orr, *The Nation of Israel and the Word of God!* (Los Angeles: Bible Institute of Los Angeles, 1948), 8.

43. Grenz, *Millennial Maze,* 92.

44. Dwight Wilson, *Armageddon Now! The Premillenarian Response to Russia and Israel since 1917* (Grand Rapids: Baker, 1977), 123. See also Grenz, *Millennial Maze,* 92–93; Hagee, *Beginning of the End,* 91–94.

45. Weber, *Living in the Shadow,* 204.

46. Wilbur M. Smith, *Israeli/Arab Conflict and the Bible* (Glendale, Calif.: Regal, 1967), preface; John F. Walvoord, "The Amazing Rise of Israel," *Moody Monthly,* October 1967, 22. See also John F. Walvoord, *Israel in Prophecy* (Grand Rapids: Zondervan, 1962); idem, *Armageddon, Oil and the Middle East Crisis,* 31–51.

47. Boyer, *When Time Shall Be No More,* 181–84; David Dolan, *Holy War for the Promised Land* (Nashville: Nelson, 1991).

48. Falwell, "Twenty-first Century," 10; Jack Van Impe with Roger F. Campbell, *Israel's Final Holocaust* (Nashville: Nelson, 1979), 9.

49. Lindsey, *Late Great Planet Earth,* 53–58; David Webber and Noah W. Hutchings, *Is This the Last Century?* (Nashville: Nelson, 1979), 45–47; Wim Malgo, *Russia's Last Invasion* (West Columbia, S.C.: Midnight Call, 1980), 59; Boyer, *When Time Shall Be No More,* 190.

50. Walvoord, *Israel in Prophecy,* 63–79; Boyer, *When Time Shall Be No More,* 194–97; Tim LaHaye, *The Coming Peace in the Middle East* (Grand Rapids: Zondervan, 1984), 26; Robert G. Clouse, "The New Christian Right, America, and the Kingdom of God," *Christian Scholar's Review* 12 (1983): 11–12. See also Steven R. David, "Bosom of Abraham: America's Enduring Affection for Israel," *Policy Review* 55 (Winter 1991): 57–59; Moishe Rosen, *Overture to Armageddon* (San Bernardino, Calif.: Here's Life, 1991), 114–16.

51. Walvoord, *Israel in Prophecy,* 101–4; idem, *Armageddon, Oil and the Middle East Crisis,* 169–75; Pentecost, *Things to Come,* 275–313.

52. Boyer, *When Time Shall Be No More,* 159–60; Wilson, *Armageddon Now!* 152.

53. John Walvoord, "Russia: King of the North," *Fundamentalist Journal* 3.1 (Jan. 1984): 37. See also Boyer, *When Time Shall Be No More*, 155; Wilson, *Armageddon Now!* 152; Tim LaHaye, "Will God Destroy Russia?" in Texe Marrs et al., *Storming toward Armageddon* (Green Forest, Ark.: New Leaf, 1994), 260–64.

54. Harry Rimmer, *The Shadow of Coming Events* (Grand Rapids: Eerdmans, 1946), 42–44; Boyer, *When Time Shall Be No More*, 163; Harry A. Ironside, *Expository Notes on Ezekiel the Prophet* (Neptune, N.J.: Loizeaux, 1949), 267.

55. Kirban, *Guide to Survival*, 181; Boyer, *When Time Shall Be No More*, 163; LaHaye, "Will God Destroy Russia?" 265–66.

56. Walvoord, *Armageddon, Oil and the Middle East Crisis*, 26–29; Doug Clark, *The Coming Oil War* (Irvine, Calif.: Harvest House, 1980). See also Charles H. Dyer, *World News and Bible Prophecy* (Wheaton, Ill.: Tyndale, 1993), 115–23.

57. Lindsey, *Late Great Planet Earth*, 70; Boyer, *When Time Shall Be No More*, 166; Wilson, *Armageddon Now!* 180; Walvoord, "Russia: King of the North," 37.

58. Lindsey, *Late Great Planet Earth*, 68; idem, *Planet Earth—2000 A.D.*, 171–83; Boyer, *When Time Shall Be No More*, 166–67; Walvoord, *Armageddon, Oil and the Middle East Crisis*, 179; James M. Boice, "Are We Nearing the Last Holocaust?" *Eternity*, December 1972, 59.

59. Kirban, *666*, 234; Boyer, *When Time Shall Be No More*, 167–69; Lindsey, *Late Great Planet Earth*, 81–87; idem, *The 1980s*; idem, *There's a New World Coming*, 124.

60. This view is common in dispensational circles. See *Scofield Reference Bible* (New York: Oxford University Press, 1909), 900–902, 909–11; LaHaye, *Beginning of the End*, 156–58; Lindsey, *Late Great Planet Earth*, 94–97; Clarence Larkin, *Dispensational Truth*, 11th ed. (Philadelphia: Clarence Larkin, 1918), 119–21; Steve Terrell, *The 90's: Decade of the Apocalypse* (South Plainfield, N.J.: Bridge, 1994), 1–26.

61. Herbert H. Ehrenstein, "The Common Market and Bible Prophecy," *Eternity*, March 1962, 18–20, 34; Boyer, *When Time Shall Be No More*, 276–77.

62. *Our Hope* 55 (1948–49): 673; H. A. Ironside, "Setting the Stage for the Last Act of the Great World Drama," *Our Hope* 56 (1949–50): 20. The quote is from Wilson, *Armageddon Now!* 157.

63. Lindsey, *Late Great Planet Earth*, 94; Edgar C. James, "Prophecy and the Common Market," *Moody Monthly*, March 1974, 24; Ehrenstein, "Common Market," 18–20, 34; Boice, "Are We Nearing the Last Holocaust?" 18–20, 59; J. Vernon McGee, "The Prophetic Word in Europe," in *The Prophetic Word in Crisis Days*, ed. Paul Bauman (Findlay, Ohio: Durham, 1961), 78.

64. Lindsey, *Planet Earth—2000 A.D.*, 225–35; Boyer, *When Time Shall Be No More*, 277; Jack Van Impe, *11:59 and Counting* (Royal Oak, Mich.: Jack Van Impe Ministries, 1983), 106; William R. Goetz, *Apocalypse Next and the New World Order* (Camp Hill, Pa.: Horizon, 1991), 117–27; Terrell, *The 90's*, xx–xxi, 11–15; Noah W. Hutchings, *The Revived Roman Empire* (Oklahoma City: Hearthstone, 1993).

65. Kirban, *Guide to Survival*, 16–62; Boyer, *When Time Shall Be No More*, 254–55; Robertson, *New World Order*, 26–34; idem, *New Millennium*, 163–80; LaHaye, *Beginning of the End*, 87–134; Lindsey, *Planet Earth—2000 A.D.*, 11–25; Dyer, *World News and Bible Prophecy*, 185–206; John Ankerberg and John Weldon, *One World: Biblical Prophecy and the New World Order* (Chicago: Moody, 1991), 21–28; Fiammetta Rocco, "The Antichrist of the Berlaymont," *Spectator*, 19 September 1992, 15–17.

66. Boyer, *When Time Shall Be No More*, 254–55; Edgar Z. Friedenberg, "George Orwell's Neglected Prophecy," *Dalhousie Review* 69.1 (1989): 270–75; Jack Van Impe, *2001*, 85–92; Hagee, *Beginning of the End*, 117–20.

67. For these general conditions see William T. James, "Characteristics of End-Time Man," in Marrs et al., *Storming toward Armageddon*, 21–45; Ray Brubaker, "The Unmistakable Evidence Mounts: Christ's Return Is Imminent," in *Storming toward Armageddon*, 47–62; Kirban, *Guide to Survival*, 48–91; Robertson, *New Millennium*, 183–200; Goetz, *Apocalypse Next*, 223–48; Graham, *World Aflame*, 1–49; idem, *Approaching Hoofbeats*, 83–105; LaHaye, *Beginning of the End*, 125–33; Robert Van Kampen, *The Sign* (Wheaton, Ill.: Crossway, 1992), 145–56; Dave Hunt and T. A. McMahon, *The Seduction of Christianity* (Eugene, Ore.: Harvest House,

1985).

68. For these general conditions see Mary Stewart Relfe, *When Your Money Fails* (Montgomery: Ministries, Inc., 1981); Dave Hunt, *Peace, Prosperity and the Coming Holocaust* (Eugene, Ore.: Harvest House, 1983), 155–86; Texe Marrs, *Millennium* (Austin: Living Truth, 1990), 115–75; Grant R. Jeffrey, *Prince of Darkness* (Toronto: Frontier Research, 1994), 146–56; "Signs of the Times," *This Week in Bible Prophecy Magazine*, June 1994, 4–5.

69. Marrs, *Millennium*, 35–66; Joseph R. Chambers, "The Rise of Babylon," in Marrs et al., *Storming toward Armageddon*, 100–102; Lindsey, *Planet Earth—2000 A.D.*, 47–63; Hunt, *Peace, Prosperity and the Coming Holocaust*, 47–60; Robertson, *New World Order*, 95–115; Goetz, *Apocalypse Next*, 191–220; Jeffrey, *Prince of Darkness*, 103–11; Gary H. Kah, *En Route to Global Occupation* (Lafayette, La.: Huntington House, 1992), 120–40; Norman N. Franz, "One World Government," *Monetary and Economic Review*, March 1993, 1, 11–13; Larry Bates, "New World Order—Phase II," *Monetary and Economic Review*, May 1993, 1, 11–13.

70. Goetz, *Apocalypse Next*, 202; Relfe, *When Your Money Fails*, 115–29; William T. James, "The Computer Messiah Comes Forth!" in Marrs et al., *Storming toward Armageddon*, 71–92; Jeffrey, *Prince of Darkness*, 91–102; Robertson, *New Millennium*, 209–23.

71. Boyer, *When Time Shall Be No More*, 266, 268–70 (quote); Hagee, *Beginning of the End*, 117–30; Van Impe, *2001*, 86–90.

72. Larry Burkett, *The Coming Economic Earthquake* (Chicago: Moody, 1991). See also Norman N. Franz, "The World Financial System," *Monetary and Economic Review*, April 1994, 1, 9, 15.

73. Bernard McGinn, *Antichrist: Two Thousand Years of the Human Fascination with Evil* (San Francisco: Harper, 1994), 253.

74. The key biblical passages on the Antichrist include Daniel 2:41; 7:7; 8:24; 9:26–27; 11:31; Matt. 24:15–16, 23–24; Mark 13:22; 2 Thess. 2:3; 1 John 4:3; 2 John 1:7; and Rev. 13:1, 5; 17:12. See D. A. Hubbard, "Antichrist," in *Evangelical Dictionary of Theology*, ed. Walter A. Elwell (Grand Rapids: Baker, 1984), 55–56; Paul Lee Tan, *The Interpretation of Prophecy* (Winona Lake, Ind.: BMH, 1974); Walter K. Price, *The Coming Antichrist*

(Chicago: Moody, 1974).

75. See Bernard McGinn, *Antichrist*; idem, *Visions of the End* (New York: Columbia University Press, 1979); James Alan Patterson, "Changing Images of the Beast: Apocalyptic Conspiracy Theories in American History," *Journal of the Evangelical Theological Society* 31 (Dec. 1988): 443–52; Norman Cohn, *Pursuit of the Millennium*, rev. ed. (New York: Oxford University Press, 1970); Walter Klaassen, *Living at the End of the Ages* (Lanham, Md.: University Press of America, 1992); Michael J. St. Clair, *Millenarian Movements in Historical Context* (New York: Garland, 1992).

76. See Brooks Alexander, "The Final Threat: Apocalypse, Conspiracy, and Biblical Faith," *SCP Newsletter*, January-February 1984, 7–8; Patterson, "Changing Images of the Beast," 447–49; William T. Still, *New World Order: The Ancient Plan of Secret Societies* (Lafayette, La.: Huntington House, 1990).

77. Boyer, *When Time Shall Be No More*, 276 (quote); see Jimmy Swaggart, *Armageddon: The Future of Planet Earth* (Baton Rouge: Jimmy Swaggart Ministries, 1987), 130–34.

78. See William Martin, "Waiting for the End," *Atlantic Monthly*, June 1982, 35–36; McGinn, *Antichrist*, 259–61; Raymond L. Cox, "Will the Real Antichrist Please Stand Up!" *Eternity*, May 1974, 15–17, 60; Boyer, *When Time Shall Be No More*, 275–78; Robert Faid, "Gorby the Antichrist," *Harper's Magazine*, January 1989, 24–26. Other candidates have included Kurt Waldheim, Willy Brandt, and Muammar el-Qaddafi.

79. Cox, "Will the Real Antichrist Please Stand Up!" 15–16.

80. Martin, "Waiting for the End," 35; Cox, "Will the Real Antichrist Please Stand Up!" 17; Robert C. Fuller, *Naming the Antichrist* (New York: Oxford University Press, 1995), 166; Relfe, *When Your Money Fails*, 31, 138; Tom Sine, "Bringing Down the Final Curtain," *Sojourners* 13.6 (June-July 1984): 12–13.

81. Fuller, *Naming the Antichrist*, 160; Boyer, *When Time Shall Be No More*, 274–77; Cox, "Real Antichrist," 15–16; "Paisley and the Pope," *Time*, 24 October 1988, 62.

82. Fuller, *Naming the Antichrist*, 134–90.

83. Relfe, *When Your Money Fails*, 15–40; Boyer, *When Time Shall Be No More*, 282–83;

Fuller, *Naming the Antichrist*, 179–84; Hutchings, *Revived Roman Empire*, 121–30.

84. Dave Hunt, *Global Peace and the Rise of the Antichrist* (Eugene, Ore.: Harvest House, 1990), 99–111; Ankerberg and Weldon, *One World*, 19. See also Lindsey, *Planet Earth—2000 A.D.*, 231; Boyer, *When Time Shall Be No More*, 275; Fuller, *Naming the Antichrist*, 145–48; Ken Klein, *The False Prophet* (Eugene, Ore.: Winterhaven, 1993).

85. Relfe, *When Your Money Fails*, 18–22; McGinn, *Antichrist*, 261; Patterson, "Changing Images of the Beast," 451; Fuller, *Naming the Antichrist*, 185; Marrs, *Millennium*, 84–87, 177–80; Jeffrey, *Prince of Darkness*, 103–9; Sylvia J. Michaelson, *The New World Order: The Mark ($) of the Beast* (Helena, Mont.: Ministering Angel, 1991); Van Impe, *2001*, 123–29.

86. Hunt, *Peace, Prosperity and the Coming Holocaust*, 35, 52, 68, 80, 108, 122, 145, 180, 198, 232. See also Boyer, *When Time Shall Be No More*, 233–34; Fuller, *Naming the Antichrist*, 183–84; Marrs, *Millennium*, 181–82.

87. Constance Cumbey, *The Hidden Dangers of the Rainbow*, rev. ed. (Lafayette, La.: Huntington House, 1983), 7. See also Richard Kyle, *The New Age Movement in American Culture* (Lanham, Md.: University Press of America, 1995), 202.

88. James, "Computer Messiah Comes Forth!" 71–92; Boyer, *When Time Shall Be No More*, 283; Van Impe, *11:59 and Counting*, 119, 121, 208; idem, *2001*, 124–28; Relfe, *When Your Money Fails*, 115–29; Ankerberg and Weldon, *One World*, 141–48; Jeffrey, *Prince of Darkness*, 110–11.

89. Boyer, *When Time Shall Be No More*, 325–26.

90. See "As It Was in the Days of Noah," *Midnight Call*, September 1992, 4–10; "Signs of the Times," 4–6; Norman H. Franz, "The Truth about NAFTA," *Monetary and Economic Review*, July 1994, 13–15; idem, "World Financial System," 1, 9, 15; idem, "PLO Wants Israel," *Monetary and Economic Review*, September 1993, 1, 7, 13; Arno Froese, "Europe: Beyond 2000—and the USA," *Midnight Call*, May 1994, 7–15; Jeffrey, *Prince of Darkness*, 103–21, 142–43; Dyer, *World News and Bible Prophecy*, 185–206; David Breese, "Europe and the Prince That Shall Come," in Marrs et al., *Storming toward Armageddon*, 173–201.

91. Kenneth L. Woodward, "The Final Days Are Here Again," *Newsweek*, 18 March 1991, 55; David Jeremiah, "Prophecy and the Persian Gulf," *Christian Herald*, November 1990, 8; Peter Steinfels, "Gulf War Proving Bountiful for Some Prophets of Doom," *New York Times*, 2 February 1991, pp. 1, 10; Jeffery L. Sheler, "A Revelation in the Middle East," *U.S. News and World Report*, 19 November 1990, 67–68; Boyer, *When Time Shall Be No More*, 328 (Kirban quote); Charles H. Dyer, *The Rise of Babylon* (Wheaton, Ill.: Tyndale, 1991), cover; John F. Burns, "New Babylon Is Stalled by a Modern Upheaval," *New York Times*, 11 October 1990.

92. Molly Guthrey, "Prelude to Armageddon?" *Minnesota Daily*, 16 January 1991, pp. 1, 14; Russell Chandler, "Persian Gulf Threat Inspires New Warnings of Fiery Armageddon," *Minneapolis Star Tribune*, 21 September 1990, p. 17A; Sheler, "Revelation in the Middle East," 67–68; Dyer, *World News and Bible Prophecy*, 140.

93. Dyer, *World News and Bible Prophecy*, 104; Lindsey, *Planet Earth—2000 A.D.*, 190. See also Scot Overbey, *Vladimir Zhirinovsky: The Man Who Would Be God* (Oklahoma City: Hearthstone, 1994); Van Impe, *2001*, 41–53.

94. Jeffrey, *Prince of Darkness*, 161.

95. Mark Hitchcock, *After the Empire: The Fall of the Soviet Union and Bible Prophecy* (Oklahoma City: Hearthstone, 1992), 6–7.

96. Dominique Lagarde, "The Highest Bidder Gets the Weapons," *World Press Review*, December 1991, 11; "Germany: The Next Super Power?" *Midnight Call*, June 1992, 15; "End-time Destruction," *God's News behind the News*, July-August 1994, 6–7; "Hands of Doomsday Clock Are Moved Up Three Minutes," *Wichita Eagle*, 9 December 1995, p. 7A.

97. Boyer, *When Time Shall Be No More*, 293–94.

98. Grenz, *Millennial Maze*, 20–22.

99. O'Leary, *Arguing the Apocalypse*, 8–10; Boyer, *When Time Shall Be No More*, 293.

Chapter 8. Eager for the End

1. Barbara Kantrowitz, "Day of Judgment," *Newsweek*, 2 May 1993, 22.

2. "South Koreans Disappointed by a New Day," *Wichita Eagle*, 29 October 1992, pp. 1A,

7A; "So Much for Doomsday, South Koreans Find," *Wichita Eagle*, 3 November 1992, p. 3A; Tom Post, "Mystery of the Solar Temple," *Newsweek*, 17 October 1994, 42–44; Steven Strasser, "A Cloud of Terror—and Suspicion," *Newsweek*, 3 April 1995, 36–37; David Van Biema, "Prophet of Poison," *Time*, 3 April 1995, 28–33.

3. Max Weber, *The Sociology of Religion* (Boston: Beacon, 1963), 46–117, 166–83; Ernst Troeltsch, *The Social Teaching of the Christian Churches*, 2 vols. (New York: Harper, 1960), 1:331–43; J. Milton Yinger, *Religion, Society and the Individual* (New York: Macmillan, 1957).

4. Bryan R. Wilson, *Religion in Sociological Perspective* (New York: Oxford University Press, 1982), 101–5, 121ff.

5. Roy Wallis, *The Elementary Forms of the New Religious Life* (Boston: Routledge and Kegan Paul, 1984), 9–37; idem, *The Rebirth of the Gods: Reflections on the New Religions in the West* (Belfast: University of Belfast, 1978), 6–10.

6. For more-detailed ways to classify fringe religions see Richard Kyle, *The Religious Fringe* (Downers Grove, Ill.: InterVarsity, 1993), 29–30; Ron Enroth, *The Lure of the Cults* (Chappaqua, N.Y.: Christian Herald, 1979), 23–35; J. Gordon Melton and Robert L. Moore, *The Cult Experience* (New York: Pilgrim, 1982), 19–20.

7. Richard Kyle, "The Cults: Why Now and Who Gets Caught?" *Journal of the American Scientific Affiliation* 33.2 (1981): 95; idem, *Religious Fringe*, 183–84; Sydney E. Ahlstrom, "The Traumatic Years: American Religion and Culture in the 60's and 70's," *Theology Today* 36.4 (1980): 510–11; idem, "The Radical Turn in Theology and Ethics: Why It Occurred in the 1960s," *Annals of the American Academy of Political and Social Sciences* 387 (Jan. 1970): 9, 12; Ronald B. Flowers, *Religion in Strange Times* (Macon, Ga.: Mercer University Press, 1984), 1–27.

8. Ahlstrom, "Radical Turn," 11–12; idem, "Traumatic Years," 512–13; Kyle, *Religious Fringe*, 185–86.

9. Ronald Enroth, Edward E. Ericson Jr., and C. Breckinridge Peters, *The Jesus People* (Grand Rapids: Eerdmans, 1972), 182.

10. Enroth et al., *Jesus People*, 182.

11. Martin E. Marty, "As the New Religions Grow Older," in *Encyclopaedia Britan-*

nica, 1986 Book of the Year, ed. Daphne Daume and J. E. Davis (Chicago: Encyclopaedia Britannica, 1986), 371; Kyle, *Religious Fringe*, 187.

12. For more general descriptions of fringe groups in modern America see Kyle, *Religious Fringe*; Ruth Tucker, *Another Gospel* (Grand Rapids: Zondervan, 1989); J. Gordon Melton, *Encyclopedic Handbook of Cults in America* (New York: Garland, 1986).

13. Quoted in Tom Mathews, "The Cult of Death," *Newsweek*, 4 December 1978, 38.

14. For more on the Jonestown story see Judith M. Weightman, *Making Sense of the Jonestown Suicides* (Lewiston, N.Y.: Edwin Mellen, 1983); Philip Kerns, *People's Temple, People's Tomb* (Plainfield, N.J.: Logos, 1979); Marshall Kilduff and Ron Javers, *The Suicide Cult* (New York: Bantam, 1978); Kenneth Wooden, *The Children of Jonestown* (New York: McGraw-Hill, 1981); Ethan Feinsod, *Awake in a Nightmare* (New York: Norton, 1981).

15. James T. Richardson, "People's Temple and Jonestown: A Corrective Comparison and Critique," *Journal for the Scientific Study of Religion* 19.3 (1980): 240; Kyle, *Religious Fringe*, 351.

16. John R. Hall, "The Apocalypse at Jonestown," in *In Gods We Trust*, ed. Thomas Robbins and Dick Anthony (New Brunswick, N.J.: Transaction, 1981), 248; Kyle, *Religious Fringe*, 351; Stephen C. Rose, *Jesus and Jim Jones* (New York: Pilgrim, 1979), 93–94.

17. Richardson, "People's Temple and Jonestown," 241–42 (quote); H. Paul Chalfant, Robert E. Beckley, and C. Eddie Palmer, *Religion in Contemporary Society* (Sherman Oaks, Calif.: Alfred, 1981), 276; "Messiah from the Midwest," *Time*, 4 December 1978, 22.

18. Hall, "Apocalypse at Jonestown," 174–75; Kyle, *Religious Fringe*, 351; Richardson, "People's Temple and Jonestown," 249.

19. Hall, "Apocalypse at Jonestown," 175–76 (quote); Kyle, *Religious Fringe*, 351.

20. Hall, "Apocalypse at Jonestown," 175–76, 186–89 (quote); Kyle, *Religious Fringe*, 352, 354; "Messiah from the Midwest," 22; Robert S. Ellwood and Harry B. Partin, *Religious and Spiritual Groups in Modern America*, 2d ed. (Englewood Cliffs, N.J.: Prentice Hall, 1988), 300.

21. Hall, "Apocalypse at Jonestown,"

186–89 (quote); Kyle, *Religious Fringe,* 354; Kenneth Labich, "Ghosts of Jonestown," *Newsweek,* 11 December 1978, 29.

22. Hall, "Apocalypse at Jonestown," 186–89 (quote); Kyle, *Religious Fringe,* 354; "Nightmare in Jonestown," *Time,* 4 December 1978, 19.

23. Quoted in Enroth et al., *Jesus People,* 179.

24. Chalfant, Beckley, and Palmer, *Religion in Contemporary Society,* 267. For a general description of the Jesus People see Enroth et al., *Jesus People*; Michael McFadden, *The Jesus Revolution* (New York: Harper and Row, 1972); Edward E. Plowman, *The Jesus Movement in America* (Elgin, Ill.: David C. Cook, 1971); Robert S. Ellwood Jr., *One Way: The Jesus Movement and Its Meaning* (Englewood Cliffs, N.J.: Prentice Hall, 1973).

25. James T. Richardson and Rex Davis, "Experiential Fundamentalism: Revisions of Orthodoxy and the Jesus Movement," *Journal of the American Academy of Religion* 5 (1983): 398; Christopher R. Stones, "The Jesus People: Fundamentalism and Changes in Factors Associated with Conservatism," *Journal for the Scientific Study of Religion* 17.1 (1978): 155–58; Enroth et al., *Jesus People,* 161–64; McFadden, *Jesus Revolution,* 7–10; Jack Balswick, "The Jesus Movement: A Generational Interpretation," *Journal of Social Issues* 30.3 (1994): 23–27.

26. Ellwood, *One Way,* 186–93; Enroth et al., *Jesus People,* 179–87; "The New Rebel Cry: Jesus Is Coming," *Time,* 21 June 1971, 59; Richardson and Davis, "Experiential Fundamentalism," 399–400.

27. Enroth et al., *Jesus People,* 186–88; Ellwood, *One Way,* 90–92; David Gordon, "The Jesus People: An Identity Synthesis," *Urban Life and Culture* 3.2 (1974): 162–63.

28. Melton, *Encyclopedic Handbook of Cults in America,* 154; Kyle, *Religious Fringe,* 361; Daniel Cohen, *The New Believers* (New York: Ballantine, 1975), 3. For a general description of the Children of God see David E. Van Zandt, *Living in the Children of God* (Princeton, N.J.: Princeton University Press, 1991); Ellwood, *One Way,* 101.

29. Jack Sparks, *The Mindbenders* (Nashville: Nelson, 1979), 166; Ellwood, *One Way,* 101.

30. Tucker, *Another Gospel,* 240 (quote); Melton, *Encyclopedic Handbook of Cults in America,* 156; Roy Wallis, "Observations on the Children of God," *Sociological Review* 24.4 (1976): 818–19; Ellwood, *One Way,* 102.

31. Lowell D. Streiker, *The Cults Are Coming* (Nashville: Abingdon, 1978), 52 (quote); Roy Wallis, *Salvation and Protest* (New York: St. Martin's, 1979), 58–59; idem, "Observations on the Children of God," 814; Leon McBeth, *Strange New Religions,* rev. ed. (Nashville: Broadman, 1977), 51; Rex Davis and James T. Richardson, "The Organization and Functioning of the Children of God," *Sociological Analysis* 37.4 (1976): 325–26.

32. Tucker, *Another Gospel,* 240–41 (quote); Van Zandt, *Living in the Children of God,* 24; Kyle, *Religious Fringe,* 363.

33. David G. Bromley and Anson D. Shupe Jr., *Strange Gods* (Boston: Beacon, 1981), 29–31; Wallis, "Observations on the Children of God," 818–19; Tucker, *Another Gospel,* 240–41; Kyle, *Religious Fringe,* 366.

34. J. Gordon Melton, *The Encyclopedia of American Religions,* 2 vols. (Wilmington, N.C.: McGrath, 1978), 1:471; William J. Whalen, *Strange Gods* (Huntington, Ind.: Our Sunday Visitor, 1981), 28–29; "Worldwide Church of God Edges toward Orthodoxy," *Christianity Today,* 9 November 1992, 57; Mark A. Kellner, "Move toward Orthodoxy Causes Big Income Loss," *Christianity Today,* 24 April 1995, 53; David Neff, "The Road to Orthodoxy," *Christianity Today,* 2 October 1995, 15; Ruth Tucker, "From the Fringe to the Fold," *Christianity Today,* 15 July 1996, 26–32. For general information on the Worldwide Church of God see Joseph Hopkins, *The Armstrong Empire* (Grand Rapids: Eerdmans, 1974); Herman Hock, *A True History of the Church* (Pasadena, Calif.: Ambassador College, 1959); Marion J. McNair, *Armstrongism: Religion . . . or Rip-off?* (Orlando: Pacific Charters, 1977); David Robinson, *Herbert Armstrong's Tangled Web* (Tulsa: Hadden, 1980).

35. Melton, *Encyclopedic Handbook of Cults in America,* 100; Hopkins, *Armstrong Empire,* 66–88; Tucker, *Another Gospel,* 207–8; Horton Davies, *Christian Deviations* (Philadelphia: Westminster, 1985), 74–85; Whalen, *Strange Gods,* 32–33.

36. Melton, *Encyclopedic Handbook of Cults in America,* 100 (quote); Hopkins, *Armstrong Empire,* 89–100; "Worldwide Church of God Edges toward Orthodoxy," 57.

37. Herbert W. Armstrong and Garner Ted Armstrong, *The Wonderful World of Tomorrow* (Pasadena, Calif.: Ambassador College, 1966), 3; Tucker, *Another Gospel*, 208.

38. Herbert W. Armstrong, *The United States and Britain in Prophecy* (New York: Everest House, 1980), 130–60; Tucker, *Another Gospel*, 208–9; Hopkins, *Armstrong Empire*, 84–85.

39. Armstrong, *United States and Britain in Prophecy*, 187–96; Tucker, *Another Gospel*, 210; Hopkins, *Armstrong Empire*, 84–85 (quote).

40. Herbert W. Armstrong, *The Incredible Human Potential* (Pasadena, Calif.: Worldwide Church of God, 1980), 123; Tucker, *Another Gospel*, 210–11; William Martin, "Waiting for the End," *Atlantic Monthly*, June 1982, 35; Tom Sine, "Bringing Down the Final Curtain," *Sojourners* 13.6 (June-July 1984): 12.

41. *Outline of the Divine Principle: Level 4* (New York: Holy Spirit Association for the Unification of World Christianity, 1980), 214 (quote); Bromley and Shupe, *Strange Gods*, 34.

42. John Newport, *Christ and the New Consciousness* (Nashville: Broadman, 1978), 122; McBeth, *Strange New Religions*, 11; Whalen, *Strange Gods*, 55.

43. Arthur S. Parsons, "Messianic Personalism: A Role Analysis of the Unification Church," *Journal for the Scientific Study of Religion* 25.2 (1986): 141–42; Whalen, *Strange Gods*, 57; Kyle, *Religious Fringe*, 330; Flowers, *Religion in Strange Times*, 105–6. See also David G. Bromley and Anson D. Shupe Jr., *Moonies in America* (Beverly Hills, Calif.: Sage, 1979), 243, 256.

44. Tucker, *Another Gospel*, 255; Mose Durst, *To Bigotry, No Sanction: The Reverend Sun Myung Moon and the Unification Church* (Chicago: Regnery Gateway, 1984), 42; Kyle, *Religious Fringe*, 337; Gordon L. Anderson, "The Unification Vision of the Kingdom of God on Earth," in *The Coming Kingdom*, ed. M. Darrol Bryant and Donald W. Dayton (Barrington, N.Y.: International Religious Foundation, 1983), 209–20.

45. J. Isamu Yamamoto, "Unification Church," in *A Guide to Cults and New Religions*, ed. Ronald Enroth et al. (Downers Grove, Ill.: InterVarsity, 1983), 156–57; George Braswell Jr., *Understanding Sectarian Groups in America* (Nashville: Broadman,

1986), 113; Melton, *Encyclopedic Handbook of Cults in America*, 195; Newport, *Christ and the New Consciousness*, 122–23.

46. Bromley and Shupe, *Strange Gods*, 35 (quote); *Outline of the Divine Principle*, 199–214; Newport, *Christ and the New Consciousness*, 123–24; Yamamoto, "Unification Church," 158–59; Tucker, *Another Gospel*, 251; Young Oon Kim, *Unification Theology* (New York: Holy Spirit Association for the Unification of World Christianity, 1980), 183; Braswell, *Understanding Sectarian Groups*, 120–21; James Bjornstad, *The Moon Is Not the Son* (Minneapolis: Bethany Fellowship, 1976), 58–59.

47. Yamamoto, "Unification Church," 158–59; Newport, *Christ and the New Consciousness*, 124; Braswell, *Understanding Sectarian Groups*, 120–21; Frederick Sontag, *Sun Myung Moon and the Unification Church* (Nashville: Abingdon, 1977), 78–79.

48. *Outline of the Divine Principle*, 204 (quote); Bromley and Shupe, *Strange Gods*, 34–35.

49. "The Killing Ground," *Newsweek*, 3 May 1993, 20.

50. Kenneth L. Woodward, "Cultic America: A Tower of Babel," *Newsweek*, 15 March 1993, 60.

51. Stephen D. O'Leary, *Arguing the Apocalypse* (New York: Oxford University Press, 1994), 227; James Ridgeway, "Armies of God," *Valley Voice*, 14 May 1993, 16.

52. Kenneth R. Samples et al., *Prophets of the Apocalypse* (Grand Rapids: Baker, 1994), 60, 69–70; James M. Wall, "Eager for the End," *Christian Century*, 5 May 1993, 475.

53. Barbara Kantrowitz, "The Messiah of Waco," *Newsweek*, 15 March 1993, 56–58; Melinda Beck, "Children of the Cult," *Newsweek*, 17 May 1993, 48–53; Mark E. DeVries, "David Koresh and the Apocalyptic Imagination," *Perspectives*, June 1993, 3.

54. William L. Pitts Jr., "Davidians and Branch Davidians, 1929–1987," in *Armageddon in Waco*, ed. Stuart A. Wright (Chicago: University of Chicago Press, 1995), 20–38; Samples et al., *Prophets of the Apocalypse*, 29–30; "Apocalypse in Waco," *America*, 22 May 1993, 3.

55. David G. Bromley and Edward D. Silver, "The Davidian Tradition," in *Armageddon in Waco*, ed. Wright, 56–57; Samples et al., *Prophets of the Apocalypse*, 36–37, 98–119;

231

Pitts, "Davidians and Branch Davidians," 30–36.

56. Raymond Contrell, "History and Fatal Theology of the Branch Davidians," *Adventist Today,* May-June 1993, 5–7; Samples et al., *Prophets of the Apocalypse,* 97.

57. Bromley and Silver, "Davidian Tradition," 58; Paul Boyer, "A Brief History of the End of Time," *New Republic,* 17 May 1993, 30.

58. Bromley and Silver, "Davidian Tradition," 59; Samples et al., *Prophets of the Apocalypse,* 79.

59. Samples et al., *Prophets of the Apocalypse,* 80–81; Kantrowitz, "Messiah of Waco," 57; George J. Church, "The End Is Near?" *Time,* 26 April 1993, 32.

60. Russell Chandler, *Doomsday* (Ann Arbor: Servant, 1993), 214; Arthur Hertzberg, ed., *Judaism* (New York: George Braziller, 1962), 210–20.

61. "Zealots for the Television Age," *New Statesman and Society,* 15 May 1992, 21; Chandler, *Doomsday,* 213; Os Guinness, *Fit Bodies, Fat Minds* (Grand Rapids: Baker, 1994), 66.

62. Allen Lesser, "Waiting for the End of the World," *Humanist,* September 1992, 19; Chandler, *Doomsday,* 214.

63. Lesser, "Waiting for the End of the World," 19; Chandler, *Doomsday,* 214–15; "Zealots for the Television Age," 21; "Lubavitcher Rabbi Schneerson Dies," *Christian Century,* 29 June 1994, 636.

64. John Hogue, *The Millennium Book of Prophecy* (San Francisco: Harper, 1994), inside cover.

65. Quoted in Hogue, *Millennium Book of Prophecy,* 83.

66. Daniel Cohen, *Waiting for the Apocalypse* (Buffalo: Prometheus, 1983), 248; James Randi, *The Mask of Nostradamus* (Buffalo: Prometheus, 1993), 235–44; Chandler, *Doomsday,* 67.

67. Daniel Cohen, *Prophets of Doom* (Brookfield, Conn.: Millbrook, 1992), 71; Jean-Charles de Fontbrune, *Nostradamus into the Twenty-First Century* (New York: Holt, 1982), 133–54; A. T. Mann, *Millennium Prophecies* (Rockport, Mass.: Element, 1992), 63–64; Dava Sobel, "The Resurrection of Nostradamus," *Omni* 16.3 (Dec. 1993): 48; Peter N. Stearns, *Millennium III, Century XXI* (Boulder, Colo.: Westview, 1996), 39–41.

68. Peter Lorie, *Nostradamus* (New York: Simon and Schuster, 1993), 66, 98–105; Cohen, *Prophets of Doom,* 71–72; *Prophecies on World Events by Nostradamus,* ed. Stewart Robb (New York: Liveright, 1961), 135–40.

69. See Jess Stearn, *Edgar Cayce: The Sleeping Prophet* (New York: New American Library, 1969), 16–32; Richard Woods, *The Occult Revolution* (New York: Herder and Herder, 1971), 160–65; James Bjornstad, *Twentieth Century Prophecy* (Minneapolis: Dimension Books, 1969), 84–89; Kyle, *Religious Fringe,* 269; John Godwin, *Occult America* (Garden City, N.Y.: Doubleday, 1972), 100–111.

70. Mann, *Millennium Prophecies,* 86–88; Stearn, *Edgar Cayce,* 64–80, 224–41; Edgar Cayce, *Modern Prophet* (New York: Gramercy, 1990), 39–62; Samuel McCracken, "Apocalyptic Thinking," *Commentary,* October 1971, 65–66; Moira Timms, *Prophecies and Prediction* (Santa Cruz, Calif.: Unity, 1980), 153–56; Martin Ebon, *Prophecy in Our Time* (New York: New American Library, 1968), 35–36.

71. Mann, *Millennium Prophecies,* 90–91; Cohen, *Prophets of Doom,* 73–74; Bjornstad, *Twentieth Century Prophecy,* 113–26; Charles Berlitz, *Doomsday: 1999 A.D.* (Garden City, N.Y.: Doubleday, 1981), 52–53.

72. Woods, *Occult Revolution,* 165–68 (quote); Ruth Montgomery, *A Gift of Prophecy* (New York: Bantam, 1965), 103, 155, 164, 176; Kyle, *Religious Fringe,* 269–70; Jeane Dixon, *The Call to Glory* (New York: Bantam, 1971), 160–84; Bjornstad, *Twentieth Century Prophecy,* 46–54.

73. Joey R. Jochmans, *Rolling Thunder: The Coming Earth Changes* (Santa Fe: Sun, 1980), 16.

74. Melton, *Encyclopedic Handbook of Cults in America,* 107–8. For general information on the New Age movement see Richard Kyle, *The New Age Movement in American Culture* (Lanham, Md.: University Press of America, 1995); Russell Chandler, *Understanding the New Age* (Dallas: Word, 1988); Douglas Groothuis, *Unmasking the New Age* (Downers Grove, Ill.: InterVarsity, 1986); Karen Hoyt, ed., *The New Age Rage* (Old Tappan, N.J.: Revell, 1987); James R. Lewis and J. Gordon Melton, eds., *Perspectives on the New Age* (Albany: State University of New York Press, 1992); Elliot Miller,

Crash Course on the New Age Movement (Grand Rapids: Baker, 1989); Ted Peters, *The Cosmic Self* (San Francisco: Harper, 1989).

75. Tucker, *Another Gospel*, 335; Robert Burrows, "A Vision for a New Humanity," in *New Age Rage*, ed. Hoyt, 33.

76. Ted Peters, "Post Modern Religion," *Update* 8.1 (1984): 23; J. Gordon Melton et al., *New Age Almanac* (Detroit: Visible Ink, 1991), 3; Richard Kyle, "The Political Ideas of the New Age Movement," *Journal of Church and State* 37.4 (Autumn 1995): 831–32; idem, *Religious Fringe*, 286; Martin Green, *Prophets of a New Age* (New York: Scribner, 1992), 213–26.

77. Barbara Hargrove, "New Religious Movements and the End of the Age," *Iliff Review* 39.2 (Spring 1982): 42–46; Martin, "Waiting for the End," 34–36; Kyle, *New Age Movement*, 77.

78. David Spangler, *Reflections on the Christ* (Findhorn, Scotland: Findhorn, 1978), 11, 19. See also idem, *Revelation: The Birth of a New Age* (Middleton, Wis.: Lorian, 1976); idem, *Emergence: The Rebirth of the Sacred* (New York: Delta, 1984); Kyle, *New Age Movement*, 57–58.

79. Marilyn Ferguson, *The Aquarian Conspiracy* (Los Angeles: J. P. Tarcher, 1980), 26–28. See also Thomas Kuhn, *The Structure of Scientific Revolutions* (Chicago: University of Chicago Press, 1962).

80. Fritjof Capra, *The Turning Point* (New York: Bantam, 1982), 53–74, 101–22; Kyle, *New Age Movement*, 78; Robert J. L. Burrows, "Americans Get Religion in the New Age," *Christianity Today*, 16 May 1986, 18–19. See also Fritjof Capra, *The Tao of Physics*, 3d ed. (Boston: Shambhala, 1991); Michael Talbot, *Beyond the Quantum* (New York: Bantam, 1986); Paul Davies, *God and the New Physics* (New York: Simon and Schuster, 1983).

81. Many New Age sources promote these general views; examples include Capra, *Turning Point*; Ferguson, *Aquarian Conspiracy*; and Spangler, *Emergence*. See also Kyle, *New Age Movement*, 78–79.

82. Spangler, *Reflections on the Christ*, 4, 6–10, 40–41; Benjamin Creme, *The Reappearance of the Christ and the Masters of Wisdom* (North Hollywood, Calif.: Tara Center, 1980), 28, 46–48; Shirley MacLaine, *Out on a Limb* (New York: Bantam, 1983), 91. For a critique of the New Age view of Christ see

Ron Rhodes, *The Counterfeit Christ of the New Age Movement* (Grand Rapids: Baker, 1990); Norman Geisler, "The New Age Movement," *Bibliotheca Sacra* 144, no. 573 (1987): 91–92; Douglas Groothuis, "The Shamanized Jesus," *Christianity Today*, 29 April 1991, 20–23.

83. Chandler, *Doomsday*, 183; Tucker, *Another Gospel*, 335; Robert Muller, *The New Genesis* (New York: Image, 1984), 186; Hillel Schwartz, "Fin-de-Siècle Fantasies," *New Republic*, 30 July and 6 August 1990, 22.

84. Spangler, *Reflections on the Christ*, 4–10; George Trevelyan, *Visions of the Aquarian Age* (Walpole, N.H.: Stillpoint, 1984), 137; Ron Rhodes, "The Christ of the New Age Movement," *Christian Research Journal* 12.1 (1989): 9–14; 12.2 (1989): 15–20.

85. Melton et al., *New Age Almanac*, 10; Tucker, *Another Gospel*, 335. See also Alice Bailey, *The Externalization of the Hierarchy* (New York: Lucis, 1957); Jonathan Adolph, "What Is New Age?" *Guide to New Age Living* 1 (1988): 9.

86. Creme, *Reappearance of the Christ*, 31–32, 55–56; Melton et al., *New Age Almanac*, 316; Tucker, *Another Gospel*, 336–37; Kyle, *New Age Movement*, 79.

87. Bill Barol, "The End of the World (Again)," *Newsweek*, 17 August 1987, 70–71; Martha Smilgis, "A New Age Dawning," *Time*, 31 August 1987, 83; Tucker, *Another Gospel*, 335–36; Kyle, *New Age Movement*, 79–80; Dick Teresi and Judith Hooper, "The Last Laugh?" *Omni* 12.4 (Jan. 1990): 82; Stearns, *Millennium III*, 12–13.

88. Charles B. Strozier, *Apocalypse* (Boston: Beacon, 1994), 231; Ashtar Command, "11:11 Doorway," *Connecting Link*, n.d.; Chandler, *Doomsday*, 185; *Millennial Prophecy Report*, May 1994, 13–14.

89. Ruth Montgomery, *Strangers among Us* (New York: Fawcett, 1979), 30–35, 38, 52, 64, 191–205, 220–21; Strozier, *Apocalypse*, 230–31.

90. Chandler, *Understanding the New Age*, 63 (quote); Melton, *Encyclopedic Handbook of Cults in America*, 137; Kyle, *New Age Movement*, 71; Samples et al., *Prophets of the Apocalypse*, 153–54; Holger Jensen, "Trouble in Paradise," *Maclean's*, 7 May 1990, 34; Marjorie Lee Chandler, "Churches Wary of 'New Age' Neighbors," *Moody Monthly*, September 1987, 95–96; Bill Shaw and Maria Wilhelm, "The Cloud over Paradise Valley," *People's*

Weekly, 4 June 1990, 48–53.

91. Chandler, *Doomsday,* 186; Samples et al., *Prophets of the Apocalypse,* 152–53; Jensen, "Troubles in Paradise," 33–35; Timothy Eagan, "Guru's Bomb Shelter Hits Legal Snag," *New York Times,* 24 April 1990, pp. A16–A17; "Weapons, Arrests and 'Doomsday Talk' Shroud Church Universal and Triumphant," *Christian Research Journal* 12.3 (Winter–Spring 1990): 27; Walter Kirn, "Apocalypse Later," *Village Voice,* 14 August 1990, 45; Ron Rhodes, "Millennial Madness," *Christian Research Journal* 13.2 (Fall 1990): 39.

92. Jensen, "Trouble in Paradise," 33, 35; Chandler, *Doomsday,* 186; Samples et al., *Prophets of the Apocalypse,* 152–53; Eagan, "Guru's Bomb Shelter," A16–A17.

93. John A. Saliba, "Religious Dimensions of UFO Phenomena," in *The Gods Have Landed,* ed. James R. Lewis (Albany: State University of New York Press, 1995), 48 (quote); William Alnor, "UFO Cults Are Flourishing in New Age Circles," *Christian Research Journal* 13.1 (1990): 5.

94. David M. Jacobs, "UFO's and Scientific Legitimacy," in *The Occult in America,* ed. Howard Kerr and Charles Crow (Urbana: University of Illinois Press, 1983), 219, 228–29; Alnor, "UFO Cults Are Flourishing in New Age Circles," 5–6; "UFO Believers Demand End to Cosmic Cover-up," *Wichita Eagle,* 6 July 1993, p. 10A; Mark Albrecht and Brooks Alexander, "UFOs: Is Science Fiction Coming True?" *SCP Journal,* August 1977, 14–16; Elizabeth L. Hillstrom, *Testing the Spirits* (Downers Grove, Ill.: InterVarsity, 1995), 200–204.

95. Robert W. Balch and David Taylor, "Salvation in a UFO," *Psychology Today* 10.5 (Oct. 1976): 58–66; idem, "Seekers and Saucers: The Role of the Cultic Milieu in Joining a UFO Cult," *American Behavioral Scientist* 20.6 (1977): 839–60; Jacobs, "UFO's and Scientific Legitimacy," 219, 228–29.

96. Melton, *Encyclopedia of American Religions,* 2:199 (quote); Chandler, *Understanding the New Age,* 92–93; Ted Peters, *UFOs—God's Chariots? Flying Saucers in Politics, Science and Religion* (Atlanta: John Knox, 1977); Melton et al., *New Age Almanac,* 143.

97. Saliba, "Religious Dimensions of UFO Phenomena," 48; Ellwood and Partin, *Religious and Spiritual Groups in Modern America,* 126.

98. John Whitmore, "Religious Dimensions of the UFO Abductee Experience," in *The Gods Have Landed,* ed. Lewis, 73. See also Strozier, *Apocalypse,* 235.

99. John A. Saliba, "UFO Contactee Phenomena from a Sociopsychological Perspective: A Review," in *The Gods Have Landed,* ed. Lewis, 222–23; Chandler, *Doomsday,* 188; Cohen, *Prophets of Doom,* 91–94; Michael J. St. Clair, *Millenarian Movements in Historical Context* (New York: Garland, 1992), 331–35; Leon Festinger, Henry W. Riecken, and Stanley Schachter, *When Prophecy Fails* (New York: Harper and Row, 1964), 139–73.

100. Strozier, *Apocalypse,* 237–38.

101. Ellwood and Partin, *Religious and Spiritual Groups in Modern America,* 126–28.

102. Elizabeth Gleick, "The Marker We've Been . . . Waiting For," *Time,* 7 April 1997, 30–31 (quote); "Toll at 39 in California Mass Suicide," *Wichita Eagle,* 27 March 1997, pp. 1A, 4A; William Booth and William Claiborne, "Suicide the Final Step in Leaving It All Behind," *Wichita Eagle,* 29 March 1997, pp. 1A, 6A.

103. Saliba, "Religious Dimensions of UFO Phenomena," 31; Evan Thomas et al., "The Next Level," *Newsweek,* 7 April 1997, 26–28 (quote); Stephen J. Hedges, "WWW.MASSSUICIDE.COM," *U.S. News and World Report,* 7 April 1997, 26; Richard Lacayo, "The Lure of the Cult," *Time,* 7 April 1997, 46; Kenneth Woodward, "Christ and Comets," *Newsweek,* 7 April 1997, 42.

104. Robert W. Balch, "Waiting for the Ships," in *The Gods Have Landed,* ed. Lewis, 137–39; Saliba, "Religious Dimensions of UFO Phenomena," 31 (quote); Hedges, "WWW.MASSSUICIDE.COM," 28; Thomas et al., "Next Level," 32.

105. Balch, "Waiting for the Ships," 153–54 (quote); Joel Achenbach and Laurie Goodstein, "Web-connected Doomsayers Left for 'Next Level,'" *Wichita Eagle,* 28 March 1997, p. 4A.

106. Howard Chua-Eoan, "The Faithful among Us," *Time,* 14 April 1997, 45–46; Balch, "Waiting for the Ships," 163–64 (quote); Gleick, "Marker," 42; Thomas et al., "Next Level," 32–38; T. Trent Gegax, "The Unkindest Cut of All," *Newsweek,* 7 April 1997, 39.

107. Hedges, "WWW.MASSSUICIDE.-

COM," 26–30; Achenbach and Goodstein, "Web-connected Doomsayers Left for 'Next Level,'" 1A; Thomas et al., "Next Level," 35.

108. Quoted in Michael Barkun, *Religion and the Racist Right* (Chapel Hill: University of North Carolina Press, 1994), 191. See also Jarah B. Crawford, *Last Battle Cry: Christianity's Final Conflict with Evil* (Knoxville: Jann, 1984), 7, 321, 333–40, 346.

109. Melton, *Encyclopedic Handbook of Cults in America*, 57 (quote); Barkun, *Religion and the Racist Right*, 3; John George and Laird Wilcox, *American Extremists* (Amherst, N.Y.: Prometheus, 1996), 340–49; Richard Abanes, *American Militias* (Downers Grove, Ill.: InterVarsity, 1996), 44, 154–55.

110. Harry Benjamin Gray, "Eschatology of the Millennial Cults," Th.D. diss., Dallas Theological Seminary, 1956, 11 (quote); Jeffrey Kaplan, *Radical Religion in America* (Syracuse: Syracuse University Press, 1997), 1.

111. Michael Barkun, "Racist Apocalypse," *American Studies* 31.2 (Fall 1990): 123; Melton, *Encyclopedic Handbook of Cults in America*, 55, 60; George and Wilcox, *American Extremists*, 340–42; "Freedmen's Beliefs Roadblock to Peace," *Wichita Eagle*, 3 April 1996, p. 8A; Abanes, *American Militias*, 155–56.

112. Barkun, "Racist Apocalypse," 123–24; George and Wilcox, *American Extremists*, 340–42; Barkun, *Religion and the Racist Right*, 188–89; Kaplan, *Radical Religion in America*, 2, 47–48; Richard Abanes, "America's Patriot Movement," *Christian Research Journal* 19.3 (1997): 15; idem, *American Militias*, 162–63.

113. Barkun, *Religion and the Racist Right*, 104–5; idem, "Racist Apocalypse," 126–28; Kaplan, *Radical Religion in America*, 4; Abanes, "America's Patriot Movement," 10–12.

114. Barkun, "Racist Apocalypse," 126–28; idem, *Religion and the Racist Right*, 103–5; John Coleman, "Who Are the Jews, and Where Do They Come From?" *Christian Vanguard* 131 (Nov. 1982): 1–2; Abanes, *American Militias*, 166–67; Kaplan, *Radical Religion in America*, 48.

115. Barkun, "Racist Apocalypse," 126–27; idem, *Religion and the Racist Right*, 104, 106; Samples et al., *Prophets of the Apocalypse*, 154; Abanes, *American Militias*,

166–67; Kaplan, *Radical Religion in America*, 4.

116. Barkun, "Racist Apocalypse," 131–32; idem, *Religion and the Racist Right*, 108–11; Kaplan, *Radical Religion in America*, 4.

117. C. Eric Lincoln, *The Black Muslims in America*, rev. ed. (Boston: Beacon, 1973), 29; E. U. Essien-Udom, *Black Nationalism: A Search for an Identity in America* (Chicago: University of Chicago Press, 1962).

118. Perry E. Gianakos, "The Black Muslims: An American Millennialistic Response to Racism and Cultural Deracination," *Centennial Review* 23 (Fall 1979): 435–38; Sydney Ahlstrom, *A Religious History of the American People* (New Haven: Yale University Press, 1972), 1068; Peter W. Williams, *Popular Religion in America* (Englewood Cliffs, N.J.: Prentice Hall, 1980), 52.

119. Kyle, *Religious Fringe*, 240.

120. Lincoln, *Black Muslims*, xxvii–xxx (quote); Richard Kyle, "Black Muslims," in *Encyclopedia U.S.A.*, ed. Archie P. McDonald (Gulf Breeze, Fla.: Academic International, 1985), 6:137; idem, *Religious Fringe*, 242–43.

121. Gianakos, "Black Muslims," 435–39. See also Martha Lee, *The Nation of Islam: An American Millenarian Movement* (Syracuse: Syracuse University Press, 1996).

122. Gianakos, "Black Muslims," 435, 439–42; Ernest Lee Tuveson, *Redeemer Nation: The Idea of America's Millennial Role* (Chicago: University of Chicago Press, 1968).

123. Ahlstrom, *Religious History*, 1068 (quote); Williams, *Popular Religion*, 50–52; Kyle, "Black Muslims," 138; Henry J. Young, *Major Black Religious Leaders since 1940* (Nashville: Abingdon, 1979).

124. Quoted in Martha Lee, "The Black Muslims and the Fall of America: An Interpretation Based on the Failure of Prophecy," *Journal of Religious Studies* 16.1–2 (1990): 145.

125. Ibid., 146.

126. Ahlstrom, *Religious History*, 1068 (quote); Gianakos, "Black Muslims," 436, 440–42; Elijah Muhammad, *Message to the Blackman in America* (Chicago: Muhammad Mosque of Islam no. 2, 1965); idem, *The Fall of America* (Chicago: Muhammad's Temple of Islam no. 2, 1973); Kyle, *Religious Fringe*, 242.

127. Gianakos, "Black Muslims," 436,

449–50; Kyle, *Religious Fringe,* 244–45; Lee, "Black Muslims," 147–48.

128. Braswell, *Understanding Sectarian Groups,* 347–48; William J. Whalen, *Minority Religions in America* (New York: Alba, 1981), 30–31; Lawrence H. Mamiya, "From Black Muslim to Bilalian," *Journal for the Scientific Study of Religion* 21.2 (1982): 141–44, 149; David Gates, "The Black Muslims: A Divided Flock," *Newsweek,* 9 April 1984, 15; George and Wilcox, *American Extremists,* 320–21; Lee, "Black Muslims," 148–49.

Chapter 9. The End without God

1. Robert L. Heilbroner, *An Inquiry into the Human Prospect,* rev. ed. (New York: Norton, 1980), 11. See also Cullen Murphy, "The Way the World Ends," *Wilson Quarterly* 14.1 (Winter 1990): 50.
2. Paul R. Ehrlich, *The Population Bomb* (New York: Ballantine, 1968), 11.
3. Paul R. Ehrlich, "Eco-Catastrophe," *Ramparts* 8.3 (Sept. 1969): 24–31.
4. Carl Sagan, *Cosmos* (New York: Random House, 1980), 328.
5. George Wald, "There Isn't Much Time," *The Progressive* 39 (Dec. 1975): 22.
6. William and Paul Paddock, *Famine—1975! America's Decision: Who Will Survive?* (Boston: Little, Brown, 1967), 9.
7. Chris H. Lewis, "Science, Progress, and the End of the Modern World," *Soundings* 75.2 (Summer-Fall 1992): 307–8.
8. Paul D. Hanson, "The Apocalyptic Consciousness," *Quarterly Review* 4.3 (1984): 26.
9. W. Warren Wagar, *Terminal Visions* (Bloomington: Indiana University Press, 1982), 10.
10. Michael Emsley, "The Evolution and Imminent Extinction of an Avaricious Species," in *The Apocalyptic Vision in America,* ed. Lois Parkinson Zamora (Bowling Green, Ohio: Bowling Green University Popular Press, 1982), 183.
11. Charles Krauthammer, "Apocalypse, with and without God," *Time,* 22 March 1993, 82.
12. For two different opinions see Michael Barkun, "Divided Apocalypse: Thinking about the End in Contemporary America," *Soundings* 66.3 (Fall 1983): 257–80; and Lewis, "Science, Progress, and the End of the Modern World," 307–31.

13. Russell Chandler, *Doomsday* (Ann Arbor: Servant, 1993), 127; Yuri Rubinsky and Ian Wiseman, *A History of the End of the World* (New York: Morrow, 1982), 133.
14. Such ideas are found in many sources, including Hanson, "Apocalyptic Consciousness," 24–27; Murphy, "Way the World Ends," 54–55; Chandler, *Doomsday,* 128–36; Peter Shaw, "Apocalypse Again," *Commentary,* 4 April 1989, 50–52; Dick Teresi and Judith Hooper, "The Last Laugh?" *Omni* 12.4 (Jan. 1990): 43–44, 78.
15. Thomas R. DeGregori, "Apocalypse Yesterday," in *Apocalyptic Vision in America,* ed. Zamora, 214 (quote); Chandler, *Doomsday,* 127–28; Catherine Keller, *Apocalypse Now and Then* (Boston: Beacon, 1996), 142.
16. Barkun, "Divided Apocalypse," 271.
17. Lewis, "Science, Progress, and the End of the Modern World," 308 (quote); Barkun, "Divided Apocalypse," 263, 271–72.
18. Wagar, *Terminal Visions,* 132–34; Lewis, "Science, Progress, and the End of the Modern World," 313. See also W. Warren Wagar, *The Idea of Progress since the Renaissance* (New York: Wiley, 1969); Ulrich H. J. Körtner, *The End of the World: A Theological Interpretation* (Louisville: Westminster/John Knox, 1995), 2–3.
19. Lewis, "Science, Progress, and the End of the Modern World," 315–16; Wagar, *Terminal Visions,* 132–37.
20. Lewis, "Science, Progress, and the End of the Modern World," 325–26; Heilbroner, *Human Prospect,* 47. See also Herbert Marcuse, *One-Dimensional Man* (Boston: Beacon, 1964).
21. Barkun, "Divided Apocalypse," 274–75; Lewis, "Science, Progress, and the End of the Modern World," 326–28; Shaw, "Apocalypse Again," 51–52.
22. Debra Bergoffen, "The Apocalyptic Meaning of History," in *Apocalyptic Vision in America,* ed. Zamora, 33–34; Lewis, "Science, Progress, and the End of the Modern World," 308–9; Barkun, "Divided Apocalypse," 274–75; Wagar, *Terminal Visions,* 118–19. See also Charles Reich, *The Greening of America* (New York: Random House, 1970).
23. Wagar, *Terminal Visions,* 204 (quote); Rubinsky and Wiseman, *End of the World,* 136.
24. For general sources see Roland N. Stromberg, *An Intellectual History of Modern*

Europe, 2d ed. (Englewood Cliffs, N.J.: Prentice Hall, 1975); W. Warren Wagar, *World Views: A Study in Comparative History* (Hinsdale, Ill.: Dryden, 1977); Franklin L. Baumer, *Modern European Thought* (New York: Macmillan, 1977); Crane Brinton, *The Shaping of Modern Thought* (Englewood Cliffs, N.J.: Prentice Hall, 1950).

25. Saul Friedländer, "Themes of Decline and End in Nineteenth-Century Western Imagination," in *Visions of Apocalypse*, ed. Saul Friedländer et al. (New York: Holmes and Meier, 1985), 61.

26. Wagar, *Terminal Visions*, 24.

27. I. F. Clarke, *The Pattern of Expectation, 1644–2001* (New York: Basic, 1979), 43–44; Wagar, *Terminal Visions*, 13–16; Lewis, "Science, Progress, and the End of the Modern World," 315–16.

28. Burton R. Pollin, *Discoveries in Poe* (Notre Dame, Ind.: University of Notre Dame Press, 1970), ch. 5; Wagar, *Terminal Visions*, 17; Lewis, "Science, Progress, and the End of the Modern World," 316.

29. Wagar, *Terminal Visions*, 19–20.

30. Wagar, *Terminal Visions*, 20; Rubinsky and Wiseman, *End of the World*, 140–41. See also W. Warren Wagar, ed., *H. G. Wells: Journalism and Prophecy, 1893–1946* (Boston: Houghton Mifflin, 1964), 441–42; H. G. Wells, *The War of the Worlds* (New York: Harper, 1898); idem, *The Time Machine* (New York: New American Library, 1984); idem, *All Aboard for Ararat* (New York: Alliance, 1941).

31. Wagar, *Terminal Visions*, 24; Friedländer, "Themes of Decline," 80.

32. Wagar, *Terminal Visions*, 24–25; H. G. Wells, *The Shape of Things to Come* (New York: Macmillan, 1933); Edward Shanks, *The People of the Ruins* (New York: Stokes, 1920); Shaw Desmond, *Ragnarok* (London: Duckworth, 1926); Stephen Southwold, *The Gas War of 1940* (London: Partridge, 1931); J. B. Priestley, *The Doomsday Men* (New York: Harper, 1938).

33. John Wiley Nelson, "The Apocalyptic Vision in American Popular Culture," in *Apocalyptic Vision in America*, ed. Zamora, 173–74; Harvey Elliott, "Apocalypse Eventually," *Video*, 3 June 1986, 77–79, 150–51.

34. Nelson, "Apocalyptic Vision in American Popular Culture," 173–74; Elliott, "Apocalypse Eventually," 77–79, 150–51; Rick Marin, "Alien Invasion!" *Newsweek*, 8 July 1996, 48–53; Chandler, *Doomsday*, 276–77.

35. Nelson, "Apocalyptic Vision in American Popular Culture," 179; Rubinsky and Wiseman, *End of the World*, 136; Paul Gray, "The Astonishing 20th Century," *Time*, Fall 1992 (special issue), 27–29.

36. Quoted in Arthur M. Katz, *Life after Nuclear War* (Cambridge, Mass.: Ballinger, 1982), xxi.

37. Quoted in Carl Sagan, "Nuclear War and Climatic Catastrophe: Some Policy Implications," *Foreign Affairs* 62.2 (Winter 1983–84): 257.

38. Quoted in Anthony Hunter, *The Last Days* (London: Anthony Blond, 1958), 231. See also Chandler, *Doomsday*, 145; Richard Rhodes, *The Making of the Atomic Bomb* (New York: Simon and Schuster, 1995).

39. W. Warren Wagar, *Next Three Futures: Paradigms of Things to Come* (New York: Praeger, 1991), 98–99; Daniel Cohen, *Waiting for the Apocalypse* (Buffalo: Prometheus, 1983), 165; idem, *Prophets of Doom* (Brookfield, Conn.: Millbrook, 1992), 123.

40. Wagar, *Next Three Futures*, 103; Paul R. Ehrlich et al., *The Nuclear Winter* (London: Sidgwick, 1984), 6–7.

41. Cohen, *Waiting for the Apocalypse*, 165–66; Sagan, "Nuclear War and Climatic Catastrophe," 260–61; Philip Morrison, "The Actuary of Our Species: The End of Humanity Regarded from the Viewpoint of Science," in *Visions of Apocalypse*, ed. Friedländer et al., 256–58.

42. "Hands of Doomsday Clock Are Moved Up Three Minutes," *Wichita Eagle*, 9 December 1995, p. 7A; Chandler, *Doomsday*, 147; *National and International Religion Report*, 16 December 1991, 1.

43. Bruce W. Nelan, "How the World Will Look in 50 Years," *Time*, Fall 1992 (special issue), 37; Sagan, "Nuclear War and Climatic Catastrophe," 260–61; "Apocalypse Right Now?" *Psychology Today* 27.1 (Jan. 1994): 27–31.

44. Rubinsky and Wiseman, *End of the World*, 156; Ignace Lepp, "Fear of Collective Death," in *Endtime: The Doomsday Catalog*, ed. William Griffin (New York: Macmillan, 1979), 59; Chandler, *Doomsday*, 148–49; Nelan, "How the World Will Look in 50 Years," 37; Dominique Lagarde, "The Highest Bidder Gets the Weapons," *World Press Review*, December 1991, 11.

45. Herman Kahn, *Thinking about the Unthinkable* (New York: Horizon, 1962); Chandler, *Doomsday*, 148–49; Rubinsky and Wiseman, *End of the World*, 158.

46. David H. Hopper, *Technology, Theology, and the Idea of Progress* (Louisville: Westminster/John Knox, 1991), 17; Cohen, *Waiting for the Apocalypse*, 184–85; Chandler, *Doomsday*, 149–50; Rubinsky and Wiseman, *End of the World*, 152.

47. Wagar, *Next Three Futures*, 103 (quote); Sagan, "Nuclear War and Climatic Catastrophe," 261–62.

48. Wagar, *Next Three Futures*, 104; Katz, *Life after Nuclear War*, 41–68.

49. L. S. Stavrianos, *The Promise of the Coming Dark Age* (San Francisco: Freeman, 1976), 190; Wagar, *Next Three Futures*, 104; Sagan, "Nuclear War and Climatic Catastrophe," 262–63; Otto Friedrich, *The End of the World* (New York: Fromm International, 1986), 344–47; Katz, *Life after Nuclear War*, 41–78; Herman Kahn, *On Thermonuclear War* (Princeton, N.J.: Princeton University Press, 1960), 40–54.

50. Stavrianos, *Coming Dark Age*, 190; Wagar, *Next Three Futures*, 104; Sagan, "Nuclear War and Climatic Catastrophe," 261–62; Katz, *Life after Nuclear War*, 48–68; Kahn, *On Thermonuclear War*, 57–74; Magnus Clarke, *The Nuclear Destruction of Britain* (London: Croom Helm, 1982), 29–37; Jonathan Schell, *The Fate of the Earth* (New York: Avon, 1982), 56–76; Paul R. Ehrlich et al., "Long-Term Biological Consequences of Nuclear War," *Science*, 22 December 1983, 1293–97.

51. Wagar, *Next Three Futures*, 105; Ehrlich et al., *Nuclear Winter*, 3–43; idem, "Long-Term Biological Consequences of Nuclear War," 1297–98; R. P. Turco et al., "Nuclear Winter: Global Consequences of Multiple Nuclear Explosions," *Science*, 22 December 1983, 1283–89.

52. Curt Gentry, *The Last Days of the Late Great State of California* (New York: Putnam, 1968); Cohen, *Waiting for the Apocalypse*, 193.

53. Chandler, *Doomsday*, 138; Cohen, *Waiting for the Apocalypse*, 197; Charles Berlitz, *Doomsday: 1999 A.D.* (Garden City, N.Y.: Doubleday, 1981), 57–59.

54. Berlitz, *Doomsday*, 41; Chandler, *Doomsday*, 139; Cohen, *Waiting for the Apocalypse*, 189; *The World Almanac and Book of Facts: 1992*, ed. Mark S. Hoffman (New York: Pharos, 1991), 546; Gordon Rattray Taylor, *The Doomsday Book* (Greenwich, Conn.: Fawcett, 1970), 39; Friedrich, *End of the World*, 179–212.

55. Cohen, *Waiting for the Apocalypse*, 200–202; Chandler, *Doomsday*, 140–41; Moira Timms, *Prophecies and Predictions* (Santa Cruz, Calif.: Unity, 1980), 80.

56. Cohen, *Waiting for the Apocalypse*, 206–7.

57. Chandler, *Doomsday*, 142; Edward O. Wilson, "The Diversity of Life," *Discover*, September 1992, 48–50; Cohen, *Waiting for the Apocalypse*, 207–8; John Zajac, *The Delicate Balance* (Lafayette, La.: Prescott, 1990), 92–93; Richard W. Noone, *5/5/2000* (New York: Harmony Books, 1983), 306.

58. Gregg Easterbrook, "Return of the Glaciers," *Newsweek*, 23 November 1992, 62–63; Cohen, *Waiting for the Apocalypse*, 216–17; Chandler, *Doomsday*, 142–43; Al Gore, *Earth in the Balance: Ecology and the Human Spirit* (Boston: Houghton Mifflin, 1992), 61–62.

59. Easterbrook, "Return of the Glaciers," 62–63; Chandler, *Doomsday*, 142–43; Cohen, *Waiting for the Apocalypse*, 216–17; Taylor, *Doomsday Book*, 62–63; Rubinsky and Wiseman, *End of the World*, 162.

60. Chandler, *Doomsday*, 163 (quote); "Doom Hotline: Hang It Up," *United Methodist Reporter*, 5 October 1990, 2.

61. Sharon Begley, "Is It Apocalypse Now?" *Newsweek*, 1 June 1992, 37–42 (quote); William Lowther, "A Threat to Human Life," *Maclean's*, 30 June 1996, 43; Robert Silverberg, "The Greenhouse Effect: Apocalypse Now or Chicken Little?" *Omni* 13.10 (July 1991): 50–54, 86; Robert J. Samuelson, "The End Is Not at Hand," *Newsweek*, 1 June 1992, 43; Robert M. White, "The Great Climate Debate," *Scientific American*, July 1990, 36–37; Morrison, "Actuary of Our Species," 250–54.

62. George F. Sanderson, "Climate Change," *Futurist*, March-April 1992, 35–36; Michael Oppenheimer and Robert H. Boyle, *Dead Heat* (New York: Basic, 1990), 2–3; Wagar, *Next Three Futures*, 61; Silverberg, "Greenhouse Effect," 52–53; Burkhard Bilger, *Global Warming* (New York: Chelsea, 1992), 33–38; Bill McKibben, *The End of Nature* (New York: Random House, 1989), 11–12.

63. Wagar, *Next Three Futures*, 61; White, "Great Climate Debate," 37–38; Bilger, *Global Warming*, 14–15; Leslie A. Chambers, "Air Pollution in Historical Perspective," in *Environmental Decay in Its Historical Context*, ed. Robert Detweiler et al. (Glenview, Ill.: Scott, Foresman, 1973), 114–18.

64. Lowther, "Threat to Human Life," 43; Wagar, *Next Three Futures*, 62; Sanderson, "Climate Change," 35–37; Oppenheimer and Boyle, *Dead Heat*, 8–17; McKibben, *End of Nature*, 23–32.

65. Gore, *Earth in the Balance*, 116, 119; Chandler, *Doomsday*, 168–69.

66. Wilson, "Diversity of Life," 65–68 (quote); Chandler, *Doomsday*, 168.

67. Jamie Murphy, "The Quiet Apocalypse," *Time*, 13 October 1986, 80; Chandler, *Doomsday*, 168–69; Barry Commoner, *The Closing Circle* (New York: Bantam, 1971), 32–33.

68. Wagar, *Next Three Futures*, 61; Commoner, *Closing Circle*, 26–27.

69. McKibben, *End of Nature*, 132–34; Chandler, *Doomsday*, 166–67.

70. Begley, "Is It Apocalypse Now?" 42; Lowther, "Threat to Human Life," 43; "Evidence Points to Regeneration of Ozone Layer," *Wichita Eagle*, 31 May 1996, p. 5A; Chandler, *Doomsday*, 167–68.

71. Ehrlich, *Population Bomb*, prologue. See also Rubinsky and Wiseman, *End of the World*, 148; Paddock and Paddock, *Famine—1975!*

72. Paul R. Ehrlich, *The Population Explosion* (New York: Simon and Schuster, 1991). See also Chandler, *Doomsday*, 171; William F. Allman, "Fatal Attraction: Why We Love Doomsday," *U.S. News and World Report*, 30 April 1990, 12; Shaw, "Apocalypse Again," 51.

73. Taylor, *Doomsday Book*, 193–97; Colin Clark, "World Population," *Nature*, 3 May 1958, 1235–36; Kevin Kelly, "Apocalypse, Juggernaut, Goodbye," *Whole Earth Review* 65 (Winter 1989): 38–40.

74. Taylor, *Doomsday Book*, 194–209; McKibben, *End of Nature*, 144–45; Barry B. Hughes, *World Futures* (Baltimore: Johns Hopkins University Press, 1985), 58; Cohen, *Waiting for the Apocalypse*, 176; Wagar, *Next Three Futures*, 53–54; Tim Stafford, "Are People the Problem?" *Christianity Today*, 3 October 1994, 47–48; Ehrlich, *Population*

Bomb, 69–71; Donnella H. Meadows et al., *The Limits to Growth* (New York: Universe, 1974), back cover.

75. Commoner, *Closing Circle*, 131–32; Rubinsky and Wiseman, *End of the World*, 148; Brian J. L. Berry, *The Human Consequences of Urbanization* (New York: St. Martin's, 1973).

76. Hughes, *World Futures*, 55–58; Cohen, *Waiting for the Apocalypse*, 174–75 (quote); Wagar, *Next Three Futures*, 53; Meadows et al., *Limits to Growth*, 48–49; E. A. Wrigley, *Population and History* (New York: McGraw-Hill, 1969); Carlo M. Cipolla, *The Economic History of World Population* (New York: Penguin, 1972); Clark, "World Population," 1235; *The Global 2000 Report to the President of the U.S.*, ed. Gerald O. Barney (New York: Pergamon, 1980), 12.

77. Commoner, *Closing Circle*, 131–36; Cohen, *Waiting for the Apocalypse*, 175; Meadows et al., *Limits to Growth*, back cover; Paddock and Paddock, *Famine—1975!* 7–23.

78. Friedrich, *End of the World*, 116, 129–30.

79. Robert E. Lerner, "The Black Death and Western European Eschatological Mentalities," *American Historical Review* 86.3 (1981): 534; Philip Ziegler, *The Black Death* (New York: Harper and Row, 1969); Barbara W. Tuchman, *A Distant Mirror: The Calamitous 14th Century* (New York: Ballantine, 1978); Rubinsky and Wiseman, *End of the World*, 87.

80. Cohen, *Waiting for the Apocalypse*, 179; "Why Viruses Push Our Hot Buttons," *Newsweek*, 22 May 1995, 54.

81. Cohen, *Prophets of Doom*, 128–29; Matthew Naythons, "Commandos of Viral Combat," *Newsweek*, 22 May 1995, 50. See also Frederick F. Cartwright, *Disease and History* (New York: Mentor, 1972).

82. Cohen, *Prophets of Doom*, 128–29; Larry Martz, "A New Panic over AIDS," *Newsweek*, 30 March 1987, 18–19; Brian K. Murphy, "Waiting for the Apocalypse," *Canadian Forum*, October 1989, 31.

83. Quoted in Chandler, *Doomsday*, 156. See also Cohen, *Prophets of Doom*, 129.

84. Jack Van Impe, "The AIDS Cover-Up" (TV sound track) (Troy, Mich.: Jack Van Impe Ministries, 1986). See also Chandler, *Doomsday*, 157.

85. Hal Lindsey, *Planet Earth—2000 A.D.* (Palos Verdes Estates, Calif.: Western Front, 1994), 109.

86. *World Almanac: 1992*, 198; Chandler, *Doomsday*, 157; Bernard Gavzer, "What Keeps Me Alive," *Parade*, January 1993, 4; Martz, "New Panic over AIDS," 18–19.

87. Dan Wooding, "Former Football Player Aids Ugandan AIDS Victims," *Evangelical Press News Service*, 10 July 1992; Chandler, *Doomsday*, 159 (quote); "Massive AIDS Epidemic Festers in Latin America," *New York Times*, 25 January 1993, pp. A-1, A-8; Rod Nordland, "AIDS: Fear of Foreigners," *Newsweek*, 6 April 1987, 36.

88. Geoffrey Cowley, "Outbreak of Fear," *Newsweek*, 22 May 1995, 48–55; idem, "New AIDS Optimism," *Newsweek*, 22 July 1996, 68; Michael D. Lemonick, "Return to the Hot Zone," *Time*, 22 May 1995, 62–63; Mark Jaffe, "Deadly Outbreak a Mystery," *Wichita Eagle*, 15 May 1995, pp. 1A, 14A; Shannon Brownlee, "Horror in the Hot Zone," *U.S. News and World Report*, 22 May 1995, 57–61; "Drug Combinations Make Inroads on AIDS Virus," *Wichita Eagle*, 12 July 1996, p. 3A.

89. Lemonick, "Return to the Hot Zone," 63; Cowley, "Outbreak of Fear," 51–53; Brownlee, "Horror in the Hot Zone," 61. See also Richard Preston, *The Hot Zone* (New York: Random House, 1994).

90. Cohen, *Waiting for the Apocalypse*, 179, 181.

91. John R. Albright, "The End of the World," *Dialog* 30.4 (Autumn 1991): 280–81.

92. Sharon Begley, "The Science of Doom," *Newsweek*, 23 November 1992 (quote); Melinda Beck, "And If the Comet Misses," *Newsweek*, 23 November 1992, 64; Frank Close, *Apocalypse When? Cosmic Catastrophe and the Fate of the Universe* (New York: Morrow, 1988), 204–21.

93. Cohen, *Waiting for the Apocalypse*, 110–11; Chandler, *Doomsday*, 129; *Cambridge Encyclopedia*, ed. David Crystal (Cambridge: Cambridge University Press, 1992), 786.

94. Cohen, *Waiting for the Apocalypse*, 91, 113; Bradley E. Schaefer, "Comets That Changed the World," *Sky and Telescope*, May 1997, 46–51.

95. Michael Barkun, *Crucible of the Millennium* (Syracuse: Syracuse University Press, 1986), 54–56, 107–17; Cohen, *Waiting for the Apocalypse*, 85–86; idem, *Prophets of Doom*, 108; Close, *Apocalypse When?* 23, 35, 43, 59; Schaefer, "Comets That Changed the World," 49–50.

96. Begley, "Science of Doom," 56; Cohen, *Waiting for the Apocalypse*, 92; Close, *Apocalypse When?* 53–69; Adam Rogers, "Attention: Incoming Object," *Newsweek*, 24 March 1997, 64–65.

97. Chandler, *Doomsday*, 115–16; Cohen, *Waiting for the Apocalypse*, 98–106; Begley, "Science of Doom," 59; Albright, "End of the World," 280; Close, *Apocalypse When?* 9–10.

98. Begley, "Science of Doom," 58–59; Chandler, *Doomsday*, 131; Blaine P. Friedlander Jr., "Comet Could Collide with Earth in 2126," *Washington Post News Service*, 22 October 1992; Close, *Apocalypse When?* 44.

99. Begley, "Science of Doom," 58; Cohen, *Waiting for the Apocalypse*, 111–21; Close, *Apocalypse When?* 13–20.

100. Begley, "Science of Doom," 56; Chandler, *Doomsday*, 130–31; Close, *Apocalypse When?* 40; "Asteroid Making Close Pass," *Wichita Eagle*, 28 November 1996, p. 3A.

101. Beck, "And If the Comet Misses," 64; Chandler, *Doomsday*, 133; Rubinsky and Wiseman, *End of the World*, 163.

102. Beck, "And If the Comet Misses," 64; Chandler, *Doomsday*, 132–33; Close, *Apocalypse When?* 111–12.

103. Beck, "And If the Comet Misses," 64; Chandler, *Doomsday*, 133–34; Close, *Apocalypse When?* 204–9; Albright, "End of the World," 281; Morrison, "Actuary of Our Species," 249, 259.

104. D. E. Thomsen, "End of the World: You Won't Feel a Thing," *Science News*, 20 June 1987, 391.

Chapter 10. 2000 and a Few Afterthoughts

1. Charles B. Strozier, *Apocalypse* (Boston: Beacon, 1994), 249; Peter N. Stearns, *Millennium III, Century XXI* (Boulder, Colo.: Westview, 1996), 54–55. See also Ulrich H. J. Körtner, *The End of the World* (Louisville: Westminster/John Knox, 1995), 12–13; Amos Funkenstein, "A Schedule for the End of the World: The Origins and Persistence of the Apocalyptic Mentality," in *Visions of Apocalypse*, ed. Saul Friedländer et al. (New York: Holmes and Meier, 1985), 44–60.

2. Körtner, *End of the World*, 12–13. See also Robert W. Thompson, "2001: A Millen-

nial Odyssey?" *Military Chaplain's Review* 18.4 (Fall 1989): 36.

3. Körtner, *End of the World*, 13–14.

4. Ibid., 14; Stephen D. O'Leary, *Arguing the Apocalypse* (New York: Oxford University Press, 1994), 7.

5. Körtner, *End of the World*, 14–15; Stearns, *Millennium III*, 45.

6. O'Leary, *Arguing the Apocalypse*, 7.

7. Strozier, *Apocalypse*, 249, 290.

8. Bernard McGinn, *Visions of the End* (New York: Columbia University Press, 1979), 3; O'Leary, *Arguing the Apocalypse*, 10; Robert C. Fuller, *Naming the Antichrist* (New York: Oxford University Press, 1995), 8–9.

9. Hillel Schwartz, *Century's End* (New York: Doubleday, 1990), 201; Fuller, *Naming the Antichrist*, 8; Stephen J. Patterson, "The End of Apocalypse," *Theology Today* 52.1 (1995): 33.

10. Catherine Keller, "Why Apocalypse Now?" *Theology Today* 49.2 (1992): 184–85.

11. Frank Kermode, *The Sense of an Ending* (New York: Oxford University Press, 1967), 8–9; Stearns, *Millennium III*, 57.

12. Our general survey of different millennial views in various historical periods has been drawn largely from Robert G. Clouse, ed., *The Meaning of the Millennium* (Downers Grove, Ill.: InterVarsity, 1977), 9–13. For similar material see Stanley J. Grenz, *The Millennial Maze* (Downers Grove, Ill.: InterVarsity, 1992); J. C. De Smidt, "Chiliasm: An Escape from the Present into an Extra-Biblical Apocalyptic Imagination," *Scriptura* 45 (1993): 79–95.

13. See Rousas J. Rushdoony, *Thy Kingdom Come: Studies in Daniel and Revelation* (Philadelphia: Presbyterian and Reformed, 1971); idem, *God's Plan for Victory: The Meaning of Post-Millennianism* (Tyler, Tex.: Thoburn, 1977).

14. O'Leary, *Arguing the Apocalypse*, 3; Gary DeMar, *Last Days Madness* (Brentwood, Tenn.: Wolgemuth and Hyatt, 1991), 209.

15. Hillel Schwartz, "Fin-de-Siècle Fantasies," *New Republic*, 30 July and 6 August 1990, 22; Jeffery L. Sheler, "The Christmas Covenant," *U.S. News and World Report*, 19 December 1994, 62.

16. Richard Erdoes, *A.D. 1000: Living on the Brink of Apocalypse* (New York: Harper and Row, 1988), x. See also Curt Suplee, "Apocalypse Now: The Coming Doom

Boom," *Washington Post*, 17 December 1989, pp. B1–B2; Ron Rhodes, "Millennial Madness," *Christian Research Journal* 13.2 (Fall 1990): 39; Richard Kyle, *The Religious Fringe* (Downers Grove, Ill.: InterVarsity, 1993), 376.

17. Erdoes, *A D. 1000*, x; Kyle, *Religious Fringe*, 377.

18. Schwartz, "Fin-de-Siècle Fantasies," 23; Leslie Savan, "The Biggest Party Ever!" *Working Woman*, January 1991, 72; Jill Smolowe, "Tonight We're Gonna Party Like It's 1999," *Time*, Fall 1992 (special issue), 10–11; William David Spencer, "Does Anyone Really Know What Time It Is?" *Christianity Today*, 17 July 1995, 29.

19. Schwartz, "Fin-de-Siècle Fantasies," 23–24; Daniel Cohen, *Waiting for the Apocalypse* (Buffalo: Prometheus, 1983), 247; Dick Teresi and Judith Hooper, "The Last Laugh?" *Omni* 12.4 (Jan. 1990): 43.

20. Suplee, "Apocalypse Now," B1–B2. See also Kenneth A. Myers, "Fear and Frenzy on the Eve of A.D. 2000," *Genesis*, January 1990, 1, 3.

21. Daniel Cohen, *Prophets of Doom* (Brookfield, Conn.: Millbrook, 1992), 15; idem, *Waiting for the Apocalypse*, 83; Schwartz, "Fin-de-Siècle Fantasies," 25; William A. Alnor, *Soothsayers of the Second Advent* (Old Tappan, N.J.: Revell, 1989), 99–107.

22. Quoted in Teresi and Hooper, "Last Laugh?" 43.

23. Körtner, *End of the World*, 265–66.

24. See A. T. Mann, *Millennium Prophecies* (Rockport, Mass.: Element, 1992); Thompson, "2001," 42.

25. Katharine R. Firth, *The Apocalyptic Tradition in Reformation Britain, 1530–1645* (Oxford: Oxford University Press, 1979), 5, 17, 21, 113, 196, 216, 228.

26. Ibid., 195; Schwartz, "Fin-de-Siècle Fantasies," 25; idem, *Century's End*, 90; T. F. Torrance, "The Eschatology of the Reformation," *Scottish Journal of Theology*, occasional papers 2 (1953): 43–44; John M. Headley, *Luther's View of Church History* (New Haven: Yale University Press, 1963), 240–65.

27. Michael J. St. Clair, *Millenarian Movements in Historical Context* (New York: Garland, 1992), 228, 306; Clarke Garrett, *Spirit Possession and Popular Religion: From the Camisards to the Shakers* (Baltimore: Johns Hopkins University Press, 1987), 10–11.

28. C. C. Goen, "Jonathan Edwards: A New Departure in Eschatology," *Church History* 28.1 (1959): 33; St. Clair, *Millenarian Movements*, 272; Catherine Albanese, *America: Religions and Religion*, 2d ed. (Belmont, Calif.: Wadsworth, 1992), 425.

29. N. Gordon Thomas, "The Second Coming: A Major Impulse of American Protestantism," *Adventist Heritage* 3 (1976): 4; St. Clair, *Millenarian Movements*, 271; Ira V. Brown, "Watchers for the Second Coming: The Millenarian Tradition in America," *Mississippi Valley Historical Review* 39 (Dec. 1952): 449.

30. Timothy P. Weber, *Living in the Shadow of the Second Coming* (New York: Oxford University Press, 1979), 48.

31. Alnor, *Soothsayers of the Second Advent*, 30, 35–39, 99–107; Stearns, *Millennium III*, 59.

32. Lester Sumrall, *I Predict 2000 A.D.* (South Bend: LeSEA, 1987), 74; Alnor, *Soothsayers of the Second Advent*, 39.

33. *End Times News Digest*, February 1983, 5; Alnor, *Soothsayers of the Second Advent*, 102.

34. Grant R. Jeffrey, *Prince of Darkness* (Toronto: Frontier Research, 1994), 85; idem, *Armageddon: Appointment with Destiny* (Toronto: Frontier Research, 1988); Alnor, *Soothsayers of the Second Advent*, 106–7.

35. Jack Van Impe, *2001: On the Edge of Eternity* (Dallas: Word, 1996), 16.

36. Pat Robertson, *The New Millennium* (Dallas: Word, 1990); idem, *The New World Order* (Dallas: Word, 1991).

37. David B. Barrett and Todd M. Johnson, *Our Globe and How to Reach It: Seeing the World Evangelized by AD 2000 and Beyond* (Birmingham, Ala.: New Hope, 1990), 130; Robert M. Bowman Jr., "Mission for the Third Millennium," *Christian Research Journal* 14.4 (Spring 1991): 37; Russell Chandler, *Doomsday* (Ann Arbor: Servant, 1993), 279; David A. Lewis, *Prophecy 2000*, 6th ed. (Green Forest, Ark.: New Leaf, 1990), 12.

38. Steve Terrell, *The 90's: Decade of the Apocalypse* (South Plainfield, N.J.: Bridge, 1994), xv–xvi; Chandler, *Doomsday*, 280; Chuck Freadhoff, "Europeans Squabble over Unity," *Investor's Business Daily*, 9 September 1992, 1; Lewis, *Prophecy 2000*, 14.

39. Edward Bellamy, *Looking Backward: 2000–1887* (Garden City, N.Y.: Dolphin,

1951); Schwartz, *Century's End*, 269; Martin Ebon, *Prophecy in Our Time* (New York: New American Library, 1968), 181–91.

40. Francis Fukuyama, "The End of History?" *The National Interest* 16 (Summer 1989): 3–18; idem, *The End of History and the Last Man* (New York: Free, 1992), xi–xii. See also Cullen Murphy, "The Way the World Ends," *Wilson Quarterly* 14.1 (Winter 1990): 51–52; Catherine Keller, *Apocalypse Now and Then* (Boston: Beacon, 1996), 85–86.

41. Charles Berlitz, *Doomsday: 1999 A.D.* (Garden City, N.Y.: Doubleday, 1981), 1–5. See also Murphy, "Way the World Ends," 54–55.

42. Peter Jay and Michael Stewart, *Apocalypse 2000* (New York: Prentice Hall, 1987), 234–46.

43. Ravi Batra, *The Great Depression of 1990* (New York: Simon and Schuster, 1987). See also Ray Corelli, "Boom Time for Futurists," *World Press Review*, December 1989, 28; Barry Brummett, "Popular Economic Apocalyptic: The Case of Ravi Batra," *Journal of Popular Culture* 24.2 (1990): 153–63.

44. Robert L. Heilbroner, *An Inquiry into the Human Prospect*, rev. ed. (New York: Norton, 1980). See also Paul D. Hanson, "The Apocalyptic Consciousness," *Quarterly Review* 4.3 (1984): 26.

45. Jacques Attali, *Millennium: Winners and Losers in the Coming World Order* (New York: Times Books, 1991).

46. Paul Kennedy, *The Rise and Fall of the Great Powers* (New York: Random House, 1987); idem, *Preparing for the Twenty-First Century* (New York: Random House, 1993).

47. C. Owen Paepke, *The Evolution of Progress* (New York: Random House, 1993).

48. Quoted in John Hogue, *The Millennium Book of Prophecy* (San Francisco: Harper, 1994), 83. See also Leo M. Braun, *Apocalypse 1998* (New York: Vantage, 1993), 73–74.

49. Mann, *Millennium Prophecies*, 44–49; Joey R. Jochmans, *Rolling Thunder: The Coming Earth Changes* (Santa Fe: Sun, 1980), 117–19; Alnor, *Soothsayers of the Second Advent*, 174–87.

50. Quoted in Hogue, *Millennium Book of Prophecy*, 69. See also Braun, *Apocalypse 1998*, 71–90; Jochmans, *Rolling Thunder*, 135–37; Berlitz, *Doomsday*, 1–9; Moira Timms, *Prophecies and Predictions* (Santa Cruz, Calif.: Unity, 1980), 173–84; Peter Lorie,

Nostradamus: The Millennium and Beyond (New York: Simon and Schuster, 1993), 194–217.

51. Mann, *Millennium Prophecies*, 122–28; Braun, *Apocalypse 1998*, 92–111; Rhodes, "Millennial Madness," 39; *Millennial Prophecy Report*, May 1994, 12–15; John Naisbitt and Patricia Aburdene, *Megatrends 2000* (New York: Avon, 1990).

52. Jochmans, *Rolling Thunder*, 52, 107–8; Mann, *Millennium Prophecies*, 122.

53. Hogue, *Millennium Book of Prophecy*, back cover.

54. For examples see Jochmans, *Rolling Thunder*, 185–94; Hogue, *Millennium Book of Prophecy*, 45–47, 87, 99, 103, 125; Mann, *Millennium Prophecies*, 23–39.

55. Cohen, *Waiting for the Apocalypse*, 245.

56. Alnor, *Soothsayers of the Second Advent*, 151–87; Mann, *Millennium Prophecies*, 78–104; *Prophecies on World Events by Nostradamus*, ed. Stewart Robb (New York: Liveright, 1961), 137–40.

57. Bernard McGinn, *Antichrist* (San Francisco: Harper, 1994), 16; Sheler, "Christmas Covenant," 71.

58. Wendy Murray Zoba, "Future Tense," *Christianity Today*, 2 October 1995, 19–20; Alnor, *Soothsayers of the Second Advent*, 191–205.

59. C. Marvin Pate and Calvin B. Haines Jr., *Doomsday Delusions* (Downers Grove, Ill.: InterVarsity, 1995), 21.

60. Chandler, *Doomsday*, 290; Zoba, "Future Tense," 22.

61. Chandler, *Doomsday*, 290.

62. Pate and Haines, *Doomsday Delusions*, 35–36; DeMar, *Last Days Madness*, 23–25.

63. Pate and Haines, *Doomsday Delusions*, 22 (quote); David Batstone, "Jesus, Apocalyptic, and World Transformation," *Theology Today* 49.3 (1992): 38.

64. Pate and Haines, *Doomsday Delusions*, 31–32; DeMar, *Last Days Madness*, 188–206. See also Hal Lindsey, *The Late Great Planet Earth* (Grand Rapids: Zondervan, 1970); idem, *Planet Earth—2000 A.D.* (Palos

Verdes Estates, Calif.: Western Front, 1994); William R. Goetz, *Apocalypse Next and the New World Order* (Camp Hill, Pa.: Horizon House, 1991); Salem Kirban, *Guide to Survival* (Chattanooga: AMG, 1990); Dave Hunt, *Peace, Prosperity and the Coming Holocaust* (Eugene, Ore.: Harvest House, 1983); Ed Hindson, *End Times, the Middle East and the New World Order* (Wheaton, Ill.: Victor, 1991).

65. Mark A. Noll, *The Scandal of the Evangelical Mind* (Grand Rapids: Eerdmans, 1994), 14. See also Zoba, "Future Tense," 19.

66. Paul Boyer, *When Time Shall Be No More* (Cambridge, Mass.: Harvard University Press, 1992), 304–11. See also Timothy P. Weber, "Happily at the Edge of the Abyss: Popular Premillennialism in America," *Ex Auditu* 6 (1991): 96–97.

67. Mark A. Noll, *Scandal of the Evangelical Mind*, 10–15; idem, "The Scandal of the Evangelical Mind," *Christianity Today*, 25 October 1993, 28–32; Os Guinness, *Fit Bodies, Fat Minds: Why Evangelicals Don't Think and What to Do about It* (Grand Rapids: Baker, 1994). See also Diogenes Allen, "The End of the Modern World: A New Openness for Faith," *Princeton Seminary Bulletin* 11.1 (1990): 16–17; Anna Marie Aagaard, "Apocalypse Now—Spirituality in the 80s," *Studia Theologica* 35.2 (1981): 146–48.

68. Grenz, *Millennial Maze*, 198–204; Pate and Haines, *Doomsday Delusions*, 150–55; D. Brent Sandy, "Did Daniel See Mussolini?" *Christianity Today*, 8 February 1993, 35; Spencer, "Does Anyone Really Know What Time It Is?" 29.

69. Grenz, *Millennial Maze*, 198–200; D. W. Bebbington, *Patterns in History* (Downers Grove, Ill.: InterVarsity, 1979), 43–67; Ramesh P. Richard, "The Premillennial Interpretation of History," *Bibliotheca Sacra* 138, no. 551 (1981): 208–10.

70. Chandler, *Doomsday*, 291–92; Grenz, *Millennial Maze*, 202; Bebbington, *Patterns in History*, 43–67; Richard, "Premillennial Interpretation of History," 208–10; Aagaard, "Apocalypse Now," 149.

Selected Bibliography

Abanes, Richard. *American Militias*. Downers Grove, Ill.: InterVarsity, 1996.

Alnor, William A. *Soothsayers of the Second Advent*. Old Tappan, N.J.: Revell, 1989.

Anderson, Robert. *The Coming Prince*. Grand Rapids: Kregel, 1975 reprint.

Ball, Bryan W. *A Great Expectation: Eschatological Thought in English Protestantism to 1660*. Leiden: E. J. Brill, 1975.

Barkun, Michael. *Crucible of the Millennium*. Syracuse: Syracuse University Press, 1986.

———. *Disaster and the Millennium*. New Haven: Yale University Press, 1974.

———. "Divided Apocalypse: Thinking about the End in Contemporary America." *Soundings* 66.3 (Fall 1983): 257–80.

———. "Racist Apocalypse." *American Studies* 31.2 (Fall 1990): 121–40.

———. *Religion and the Racist Right*. Chapel Hill: University of North Carolina Press, 1994.

Bloch, Ruth H. *Visionary Republic*. New York: Cambridge University Press, 1985.

Boyer, Paul. *When Time Shall Be No More*. Cambridge, Mass.: Harvard University Press, 1992.

Butler, Jonathan M. "From Millerism to Seventh-day Adventism: 'Boundlessness to Consolidation.'" *Church History* 55.1 (1986): 50–64.

Chandler, Russell. *Doomsday*. Ann Arbor: Servant, 1993.

Clouse, Robert G. "The New Christian Right, America, and the Kingdom of God." *Christian Scholar's Review* 12 (1983): 3–16.

———, ed. *The Meaning of the Millennium*. Downers Grove, Ill.: InterVarsity, 1977.

Cohen, Daniel. *Waiting for the Apocalypse*. Buffalo: Prometheus, 1983.

Cohn, Norman. *The Pursuit of the Millennium*. Rev. ed. New York: Oxford University Press, 1974.

Commoner, Barry. *The Closing Circle*. New York: Bantam, 1971.

Curry, Melvin D. *Jehovah's Witnesses: The Millenarian World of the Watch Tower*. New York: Garland, 1992.

Davidson, James West. *The Logic of Millennial Thought*. New Haven: Yale University Press, 1977.

Doan, Ruth Alden. *The Miller Heresy, Millennialism, and American Culture*. Philadelphia: Temple University Press, 1987.

Ehrlich, Paul R. *The Population Bomb*. New York: Ballantine, 1968.

———, et al. *The Nuclear Winter*. London: Sidgwick, 1984.

Emmerson, Richard K. *Antichrist in the Middle Ages*. Seattle: University of Washington Press, 1981.

———, and Bernard McGinn, eds. *The Apocalypse in the Middle Ages*. Ithaca, N.Y.: Cornell University Press, 1992.

Falwell, Jerry. "The Twenty-first Century and the End of the World." *Fundamentalist Journal* 7.5 (May 1988): 10–11.

Firth, Katharine R. *The Apocalyptic Tradition in Reformation Britain, 1530–1645.* Oxford: Oxford University Press, 1979.

Friedrich, Otto. *The End of the World: A History.* New York: Fromm International, 1986.

Fuller, Robert C. *Naming the Antichrist.* New York: Oxford University Press, 1995.

Gianakos, Perry E. "The Black Muslims: An American Millennialistic Response to Racism and Cultural Deracination." *Centennial Review* 23 (Fall 1979): 430–45.

Goen, C. C. "Jonathan Edwards: A New Departure in Eschatology." *Church History* 28.1 (1959): 25–40.

Gore, Al. *Earth in the Balance: Ecology and the Human Spirit.* Boston: Houghton Mifflin, 1992.

Graham, Billy. *Approaching Hoofbeats.* New York: Avon, 1983.

Grenz, Stanley J. *The Millennial Maze.* Downers Grove, Ill.: InterVarsity, 1992.

Hagee, John. *Beginning of the End.* Nashville: Nelson, 1996.

Harrison, J. F. C. *The Second Coming: Popular Millenarianism, 1780–1850.* New Brunswick, N.J.: Rutgers University Press, 1979.

Hogue, John. *The Millennium Book of Prophecy.* San Francisco: Harper, 1994.

Jewett, Robert. "Coming to Terms with the Doom Boom." *Quarterly Review* 4.3 (Fall 1984): 9–22.

Kaplan, Jeffrey. *Radical Religion in America.* Syracuse: Syracuse University Press, 1997.

Keller, Catherine. *Apocalypse Now and Then.* Boston: Beacon, 1996.

Kermode, Frank. *The Sense of an Ending.* New York: Oxford University Press, 1967.

Kirban, Salem. *666.* Wheaton, Ill.: Tyndale, 1970.

Klaassen, Walter. *Living at the End of the Ages.* Lanham, Md.: University Press of America, 1992.

Körtner, Ulrich H. J. *The End of the World: A Theological Interpretation.* Louisville: Westminster/John Knox, 1995.

Kyle, Richard. *The New Age Movement in American Culture.* Lanham, Md.: University Press of America, 1995.

———. *The Religious Fringe: A History of Alternative Religions in America.* Downers Grove, Ill.: InterVarsity, 1993.

Lee, Martha. *The Nation of Islam: An American Millenarian Movement.* Syracuse: Syracuse University Press, 1996.

Lerner, Robert E. "The Black Death and Western European Eschatological Mentalities." *American Historical Review* 86.3 (1981): 533–52.

Lewis, Chris H. "Science, Progress, and the End of the Modern World." *Soundings* 75.2 (Summer-Fall 1992): 307–32.

Lewis, James R., ed. *The Gods Have Landed.* Albany: State University of New York Press, 1995.

Lindsey, Hal. *The Late Great Planet Earth.* Grand Rapids: Zondervan, 1970.

Lorie, Peter. *Nostradamus: The Millennium and Beyond.* New York: Simon and Schuster, 1993.

McClain, Alva. *Daniel's Prophecy of the Seventy Weeks.* Grand Rapids: Zondervan, 1940.

McGinn, Bernard. *Antichrist.* San Francisco: Harper, 1994.

———. *Visions of the End.* New York: Columbia University Press, 1979.

Mann, A. T. *Millennium Prophecies.* Rockport, Mass.: Element, 1992.

Moorhead, James H. "Between Progress and Apocalypse: A Reassessment of Millennialism in American Religious Thought, 1800–1880." *Journal of American History* 71.3 (1984): 524–42.

———. "The Erosion of Postmillennialism in American Religious Thought, 1865–1925." *Church History* 53.1 (1984): 61–77.

———. "Searching for the Millennium in America." *Princeton Seminary Bulletin* 8.2 (1987): 17–33.

Numbers, Ronald L., and Jonathan M. Butler, eds. *The Disappointed.* Knoxville: University of Tennessee Press, 1993.

O'Leary, Stephen D. *Arguing the Apocalypse.* New York: Oxford University Press, 1994.

Patterson, James Alan. "Changing Images of the Beast: Apocalyptic Conspiracy Theories in American History." *Journal of the Evangelical Theological Society* 31 (Dec. 1988): 443–52.

Penton, M. James. *Apocalypse Delayed: The Story of the Jehovah's Witnesses.* Toronto: University of Toronto Press, 1985.

Randi, James. *The Mask of Nostradamus.* Buffalo: Prometheus, 1993.

Reeves, Marjorie. *The Influence of Prophecy in the Later Middle Ages*. New York: Oxford University Press, 1969.

———. *Joachim of Fiore and the Prophetic Future*. New York: Harper and Row, 1976.

Robertson, Pat. *The New Millennium*. Dallas: Word, 1990.

Rubinsky, Yuri, and Ian Wiseman. *A History of the End of the World*. New York: Morrow, 1982.

Sagan, Carl. *Cosmos*. New York: Random House, 1980.

Samples, Kenneth R., et al. *Prophets of the Apocalypse*. Grand Rapids: Baker, 1994.

Sandeen, Ernest R. *The Roots of Fundamentalism*. Chicago: University of Chicago Press, 1970.

Schwartz, Hillel. *Century's End*. New York: Doubleday, 1990.

Scofield Reference Bible. New York: Oxford University Press, 1909.

Smith, Wilbur M. *Israeli/Arab Conflict and the Bible*. Glendale, Calif.: Regal, 1967.

St. Clair, Michael J. *Millenarian Movements in Historical Context*. New York: Garland, 1992.

Stearns, Peter N. *Millennium III, Century XXI*. Boulder, Colo.: Westview, 1996.

Strozier, Charles B. *Apocalypse: On the Psychology of Fundamentalism in America*. Boston: Beacon, 1994.

Toon, Peter, ed. *Puritans, the Millennium and the Future of Israel*. Greenwood, S.C.: Attic, 1970.

Tuveson, Ernest Lee. *Millennium and Utopia*. New York: Harper, 1964.

———. *Redeemer Nation: The Idea of America's Millennial Role*. Chicago: University of Chicago Press, 1968.

Underwood, Grant. *The Millenarian World of Early Mormonism*. Urbana: University of Illinois Press, 1993.

Van Impe, Jack. *2001: On the Edge of Eternity*. Dallas: Word, 1996.

Wagar, W. Warren. *Next Three Futures: Paradigms of Things to Come*. New York: Praeger, 1991.

———. *Terminal Visions*. Bloomington: Indiana University Press, 1982.

Walvoord, John F. *Armageddon, Oil and the Middle East Crisis*. Rev. ed. Grand Rapids: Zondervan, 1990.

Watts, Pauline Moffitt. "Prophecy and Discovery: On the Spiritual Origins of Christopher Columbus's 'Enterprise of the Indies.'" *American Historical Review* 90.1 (1985): 73–102.

Weber, Timothy P. "Happily at the Edge of the Abyss: Popular Premillennialism in America." *Ex Auditu* 6 (1991): 87.

———. *Living in the Shadow of the Second Coming*. Rev. ed. Chicago: University of Chicago Press, 1987.

Wilson, Dwight. *Armageddon Now! The Premillenarian Response to Russia and Israel since 1917*. Grand Rapids: Baker, 1977.

Wright, Stuart A., ed. *Armageddon in Waco*. Chicago: University of Chicago Press, 1995.

Zamora, Lois Parkinson, ed. *The Apocalyptic Vision in America*. Bowling Green, Ohio: Bowling Green University Popular Press, 1982.

Index

Richard Kyle is professor of history and religion at Tabor College. He is the author of *The Religious Fringe* and *The New Age Movement in American Culture*. He received his Ph.D. degree from the University of New Mexico.